Armoured Warfare in the British Army, 1939–1945

The Comet – seen here nearing completion – was the best British tank of the Second World War, but it came as the result of hard-won experience and only appeared in the last few months of the conflict.

Find, Fix and Strike

Armoured Warfare in the British Army, 1939–1945

Dick Taylor

THE **TANK** MUSEUM
Produced in collaboration
with the Tank Museum,
Bovington

Pen & Sword
MILITARY
AN IMPRINT OF PEN & SWORD BOOKS LTD.
YORKSHIRE – PHILADELPHIA

First published in Great Britain in 2022 by
PEN & SWORD MILITARY
An imprint of
Pen & Sword Books Ltd
Yorkshire – Philadelphia

ISBN 978 1 39908 103 0

A CIP catalogue record for this book is
available from the British Library

Typeset in Ehrhardt 11/13.5
by SJmagic DESIGN SERVICES, India.

Printed and bound in the UK
by CPI Group (UK) Ltd.

Pen & Sword Books Ltd incorporates the imprints of Pen & Sword
Archaeology, Atlas, Aviation, Battleground, Discovery, Family History, History,
Maritime, Military, Naval, Politics, Social History, Transport, True Crime, Claymore
Press, Frontline Books, Praetorian Press, Seaforth Publishing and White Owl

For a complete list of Pen & Sword titles please contact

PEN & SWORD BOOKS LTD
47 Church Street, Barnsley, South Yorkshire, S70 2AS, England
E-mail: enquiries@pen-and-sword.co.uk
Website: www.pen-and-sword.co.uk

Or

PEN AND SWORD BOOKS
1950 Lawrence Rd, Havertown, PA 19083, USA
E-mail: Uspen-and-sword@casematepublishers.com
Website: www.penandswordbooks.com

Contents

Acknowledgements and Thanks

The author wishes to thank the staff of the Archive and Library, Bovington Tank Museum, and in particular the Curator, David Willey, the Archive Manager, Stuart Wheeler, and Archivist, Jonathan Holt, as well as the staff of the various regimental Home Headquarters and Museums who have so generously helped with this volume. All images are reproduced by the kind permission of Bovington Tank Museum unless otherwise stated.

Abbreviations and Terminology

2Lt	Second Lieutenant
ABTU	Arms Basic Training Unit
AC	Armoured Car
ACC	Armoured Car Company
ACI	Army Council Instruction
ACV	Armoured Command Vehicle
Adjt	Adjutant
AFV	Armoured Fighting Vehicle
AG	Adjutant General
AO	Army Order
AP	Armour Piercing
APC	Armoured Personnel Carrier
APC	Armour Piercing Capped
APCBC	Armour Piercing Capped Ballistic Cap
APDS	Armour Piercing Discarding Sabot
APFSDS	Armour Piercing Fin Stabilized Discarding Sabot
ATDU	Armour Trials & Development Unit
Bde	Brigade
BEF	British Expeditionary Force
Besa	7.92mm MG
Bn	Battalion
Bren	.303in Light Machine Gun
BTA	Battalion Technical Adjutant (sometimes BTO (officer), or Regimental Technical Adjutant (RTA))
Bty	Battery
Capt	Captain
CDL	Canal Defence, Light
CID	Committee for Imperial Defence
CIGS	Chief of the Imperial General Staff
CLY	County of London Yeomanry
CO	Commanding Officer
Coax	Coaxial armament, usually MG
CoH	Corporal of Horse
Coy	Company

Cpl	Corporal
Cpl Maj	Corporal Major
CS	Close Support (and Central Schools)
D&M	Driving & Maintenance
DCM	Distinguished Conduct Medal
DD	Duplex Drive
Div	Division
DOW	Died of Wounds
DR	Despatch Rider
DRAC	Director/Directorate Royal Armoured Corps
DSO	Distinguished Service Order
DY	Derbyshire Yeomanry
EAF	Experimental Armoured Force (1928)
EMF	Experimental Mechanized Force (1927)
ERY	East Riding of Yorkshire Yeomanry
FFR	Fit For Role/Fitted For Radio
FFY	Fife & Forfar Yeomanry
FOO	Forward Observation Officer
FVPE	Fighting Vehicle Proving Establishment
GMT	General Military Training
GOC	General Officer Commanding
HCav	Household Cavalry
HCR	Household Cavalry Regiment
HCMR	Household Cavalry Mounted Regiment
HE	High Explosive
HEAT	High Explosive Anti-Tank
HESH	High Explosive Squash Head
HF	High Frequency
HQ	Headquarters
IoC	Inns of Court Yeomanry (sometimes ICR: Inns of Court Regiment)
IP	Indian Pattern
IS	Internal Security
JNCO	Junior Non-Commissioned Officer (LCpl, Cpl)
KDG	King's Dragoon Guards
KIA	Killed in Action
KRIH	King's Royal Irish Hussars
LBH	Lothian & Borders Horse
LBY	Lothian & Borders Yeomanry
LCoH	Lance Corporal of Horse
LCpl	Lance Corporal
LSgt	Lance Sergeant

LDY	Leicestershire & Derbyshire Yeomanry
LMG	Light Machine Gun
Lt	Lieutenant
Lt Col	Lieutenant Colonel
Lt Gen	General
Lt Tk	Light Tank
Maj	Major
Maj Gen	Major General
MC	Military Cross
MEE	Mechanization Experimental Establishment
MG	Machine Gun
MGC	Machine Gun Corps
MGO	Master General of the Ordnance
MM	Military Medal
MMG	Medium Machine Gun
MoM	Ministry of Munitions
MT	Motor Transport
MTO	Motor Transport Officer
MVEE	Military Vehicles Experimental Establishment
MWEE	Mechanical Warfare Experimental Establishment
NAAFI	Naval, Army and Air Forces Institute
NCO	Non-Commissioned Officer
NIH	North Irish Horse
NS	National Service/Serviceman
NWE	North-West Europe
OC	Officer Commanding
OCTU	Officer Cadet Training Unit
OR	Other Ranks
ORBAT	Order of Battle
PBI	Poor Bloody Infantry
Pdr	Pounder, a classification of a projectile by the weight of its HE shell
PO	Potential Officer
POW	Prisoner of War
PRI	President of the Regimental Institute
QF	Quick Firing
QM	Quartermaster
QM(T)	Quartermaster Technical
RA	Royal Artillery
RAC	Royal Armoured Corps
RAOC	Royal Army Ordnance Corps
RARO	Regular Army Reserve of Officers

RASC	Royal Army Service Corps
RCB	Regular Commissions Board
RE	Royal Engineers
Recce	Reconnaissance
Regt	Regiment
RE	Royal Engineers
REME	Royal Electrical and Mechanical Engineers
RGH	Royal Gloucestershire Hussars
RHQ	Regimental Headquarters
RMO	Regimental Medical Officer
ROF	Royal Ordnance Factory
RQMS	Regimental Quartermaster Sergeant
RRAC	Rolls-Royce Armoured Car
RSigs	Royal Signals
RSM	Regimental Sergeant Major
R/T	Radio Telephony
RTanks	RTC, RTR
RTC	Royal Tank Corps
RTR	Royal Tank Regiment
RTU	Returned to Unit
RUSI	Royal United Services Institute
RWY	Royal Wiltshire Yeomanry
SCpl	Staff Corporal
Sect	Section
Sgt	Sergeant
Sgt Maj	Sergeant Major
SHQ	Squadron Headquarters
SMG	Sub-Machine Gun
SNCO	Senior Non-Commissioned Officer (Sgt, SSgt)
SPG	Self-Propelled Gun
SQMS	Squadron Quartermaster Sergeant
Sqn	Squadron
SRY	Nottinghamshire Sherwood Rangers Yeomanry
SSgt	Staff Sergeant
STT	School of Tank Technology
SY	Staffordshire Yeomanry
TA	Territorial Army
TC	Tank Corps
TEWT	Tactical Exercise Without Troops
Tk	Tank
Tp	Troop
Tpr	Trooper

TTS	Tank Testing Section
UEI	Unit Equipment Inspection
VA	Vickers Armstrong
VHF	Very High Frequency
Vickers MMG	.303in Vickers Medium Machine Gun
WD, WDgns	Westminster Dragoons
WIA	Wounded in Action
WO	War Office, Warrant Officer
WOI, II, III	Warrant Officer Class 1, 2, 3
WOSB	War Office Selection Board
W/T	Wireless Telephony
WY	Warwickshire Yeomanry
YD	Yorkshire Dragoons
YH	Yorkshire Hussars

Introduction

> History has assigned to it the task of judging the past, of instructing the present for the benefit of ages to come.
>
> *Leopold von Ranke*

This history proved to be both fascinating to research and difficult to write. Kenneth Macksey's concise history of the Royal Armoured Corps ends in 1975, and I was therefore left with two options: to continue from that point, or to start from the beginning and attempt to compose a coherent history covering a busy hundred years or so. I chose the latter, in part to continue from Patrick Mileham's companion volume on the pre-mechanized cavalry, covering an even longer period. Like Macksey's earlier work, this is, in the main, a history of the Royal Armoured Corps. It is also, to a slightly lesser degree, a history of the British invention, development and evolution of the tank and its armoured fighting vehicle cousins and off-shoots, as used in other arms; I trust the reader will forgive me for the necessary brevity of the latter part, in which the infantry, Royal Artillery and Royal Engineers make up the supporting cast. The sheer range of the task, covering a century plus of complex history, meant that it could not be captured in one volume, hence the decision to break it into three parts, but it remains at heart a single work.

Why Find, Fix and Strike? This phrase, much used in modern military parlance, was taken from naval doctrine and describes the three main actions that a force must conduct in order to have a desired effect upon an enemy. Firstly, they must be found, and once found, must stay found. This implies reconnaissance. Secondly, they must have their freedom of action removed, in both time and space, in order to allow us to fight the battle on favourable terms. This can be carried out by both the reconnaissance and the main forces. And then they must be struck, with all the force necessary – plus a little more – in order to have the desired effect. (Guderian is said to have summed this up as '*Klotzen, nicht kleckern!*' – roughly translated as 'Spew, don't dribble.') This is the task of the main force. Finally, the pedants will remind me that the fourth term used is Exploit: after the main battle, exploit the victory for all it is worth, in terms of intelligence, follow-up and, in general terms, the pursuit. I would offer that this whole work is an attempt to exploit over one-hundred years of history of British armoured warfare, in order to understand the past and inform the future.

I also wanted this series to be as much a social history of the RAC as an operational one. Fascinating as they are, the campaigns and battles in which tanks and armoured vehicles have fought are only one aspect of the whole, and from the outset I wished to include also those essential but frequently unrecorded aspects of the tank crewman's life; training, recruitment, pay, equipment, both vehicle and personal, and not least, how these have evolved or remained constant through the hundred years under investigation. As Wavell once said to Liddell Hart:

> If I had time and anything like your ability to study war, I think I should concentrate almost entirely on the 'actualities of war' – the effects of tiredness, hunger, fear, lack of sleep, weather. . . . The principles of strategy and tactics, and the logistics of war are really absurdly simple: it is the actualities that make war so complicated and so difficult, and are usually so neglected by historians.

I hope that I have not completely neglected this aspect.

In terms of combat, it was never my intention to try to present a complete picture of any of the many battles or campaigns featured in this work; that would be foolhardy and would simply take up too much space as well as miss my point. Rather, I have selected those incidents and actions which can be used either to give a flavour of the use of armour and the parts they played, or to make a point about their effectiveness – or otherwise. Therefore, I hope to be excused if I devote as much time looking into the four-day Gulf War of 1991 as the whole of the Italian campaign which lasted nearly two years, or to cram the Second Battle of El Alamein into a couple of paragraphs. I have chosen, very deliberately, to devote a large proportion of the operational history to those periods that I deem to be of particular importance. These are, the First World War and the birth of the tank; the inter-war period in which the foundations for doctrine were laid; within the Second World War, the campaigns in France, 1940, North Africa and North-West Europe. In the Cold War era, I have elected to focus on Korea, Suez, Malaya and Northern Ireland, before moving into the modern era with the Balkans, Iraq and Afghanistan. That is not to say that I ignore the remainder: I would be mortified to discover that there is an armoured theatre of operations that I have missed entirely, even if it has just been condemned to an endnote.

Throughout, what I have attempted to do is to highlight those parts of campaigns and battles that are of direct interest to those interested in armoured warfare, particularly but not exclusively members, past and present, of the RAC; and also to seek to identify enduring historical lessons that explain the past and inform the future – for example, from 1917, do not throw your tanks away on clearly unsuitable ground, and if you expect infantry and tanks to co-operate effectively, you must plan and rehearse. Whether I have succeeded in getting what Monty described as the 'balance' right will remain to be seen.

I need to reiterate that this is a book about the British Royal Armoured Corps. I fully acknowledge the welcome presence of Australian and South African armoured units in the Middle East, Canadians in Italy and North-West Europe, and New Zealanders and Indians in Italy.

Chapter One

The Beginning

Now day has come, the calm and leisured tread
Of time must change abruptly. In its stead
The rush and hurry, the excited shouts
And racing engines claim the eye and ear
And night has been repulsed, with all its doubts.
Life suddenly becomes sweeter than one dared
To think it could, the issues crystal clear.
We think of all the boredom we have shared,
The waiting for this chance, our hearts are light.
And now the time, the longed-for moment nears.
The dreaded moment too, our hopes and fears
Have centred on, the chance to prove our worth
The chance to earn our right to this dear earth
Which now may see us die, which gave us birth.
At last, the moment's here, at last the chance.
'Start up!' 'Stand by!' 'Be ready to advance!'[1]

The RAC in 1939

In July 1939, the RAC and War Office confirmed their requirements for a much-expanded tank force, which comprised the following. Cruiser tanks: 2,231 (1,298 for the field force in the UK, 314 for Egypt and 619 as a training and reserve pool). Infantry tanks: 1,646 (1,356 for the UK and a pool of 290). Light tanks: 1,618 (1,325 in the field force, 144 for Egypt and 149 in the pool.) However, this impressive total of 5,495 tanks hid one important fact – the majority of them did not exist. In fact, orders had been placed for only 3,370 (61 per cent), and of those that had been made, the vast majority were the less effective Light models. In October of the same year, after a month of war, the actual tank state was only 1,275, with 1,068 of these being Lights, 117 Cruisers and 90 Infantry tanks, with only 6 of the latter being the gun-armed Matilda II model. Britain was going to war with an obsolete tank fleet mainly armed with machine guns.

In terms of armoured units in the UK, 51 regiments now belonged to the new Royal Armoured Corps. In theory 11 of these were divisional cavalry regiments, 15 (all from the RTR) were in the Army Tank Brigades, 1 was the sole UK-based

Four sergeants from the 13th/18th Hussars learn to become Light tank D&M drivers under the tutelage of the RTC in summer 1939. Within a year the regiment would have fought their first tank actions in France.

armoured car regiment and the remainder were found in the 2 armoured brigades owned by each of the 3 armoured divisions, which included the 5 regiments stationed in Egypt. But even the latter claim was partly smoke and mirrors: the planned third armoured division, the 2nd Armoured, would not come into being until January 1940.

The British Expeditionary Force

Twenty-three years after becoming the first nation to deploy tanks in battle, Britain entered a new world war with something of an apology for an armoured army. Although – certainly in comparison with any other country – the army had made great advances in becoming motorized, much more could and should have been done in producing modern tanks. But on 3 September 1939 recriminations would have to wait, and within a few days of the declaration of war, the first armoured units started to move to France, as part of a new British Expeditionary Force (BEF) under General Lord Gort VC.

The Cabinet decision that had been studiously avoided for two decades, to be prepared to deploy an expeditionary force to Europe, was only taken on

2 February 1939. This left little time to organize the force, and it was clear that, like its predecessor of 1914, the small regular army would have to bear the brunt of the initial deployment, hopefully allowing sufficient time to equip and train the territorials in the new formations that were to follow. The confusion of the period is illustrated by the war diary of the 9th Lancers, which recorded the chaos of the days leading up to embarkation for France:

> The period was spent in preparing for embarkation, the date of which was continually being changed. Frantic efforts were being made to bring the regiment to war establishment in personnel, vehicles and equipment. New vehicles and tanks kept arriving, others were withdrawn or transferred to other units. Small drafts kept arriving from various training regiments. In all about fifty men were received. It was subsequently found that they had done very little tank training few having driven a tank for more than one hour, others never at all. Stores & equipment were being issued daily, and peace equipment withdrawn from Sqns and returned to R.A.O.C. All this bustle made a tremendous amount of work for the Q.M. staff. Their difficulties were not lessened by the fact that for every single item, peace procedures of issue & receipt accountancy was supposed to be maintained. This was of course quite impossible. Moreover no G.1098 [equipment scaling] for the regiment had been issued so no one knew the correct scale of war equipment. The regiment eventually received all B vehicles, but tanks continued to arrive up to the last moment. A good proportion of the latter were transfers from other units and arrived in very bad condition. During the last two days a certain number of A9 and A10 tanks, some Close Support were received. No one in the regiment had had an opportunity of driving or maintaining the type before. It was thought that if we could get them to France, we would have opportunity then. Definite orders were eventually received that vehicles & drivers were to proceed to Southampton. Tanks, MGs, spare parts, equipment and stores of every description continued to arrive right up to the last moment. This made it impossible to sort out loads. Stores were loaded on as they arrived. Hardly one vehicle was dispatched with its correct load.

Within weeks, the four regular infantry divisions, organized in two corps, and commanded by GHQ BEF, were in France.[2] Operating as the sole General Headquarters (GHQ) armoured car regiment was the 12th Lancers. With each of the infantry divisions went their divisional reconnaissance regiments equipped with a mix of Light tanks and carriers: 4th/7th Dragoon Guards (2 Div), 5th Dragoon Guards (4 Div), 13th/18th Hussars (1 Div) and 15th/19th Hussars (3 Div).[3] By early October all were in France, along with 4RTR from the 1st Army Tank Brigade with its Matilda I tanks. Notably, despite the frequent protests

The Light Tank Mk VI was the most modern and numerous tank in Britain's inventory in September 1939. Their use by the BEF in 1940 would demonstrate that they had no place on the modern armoured battlefield.

As well as Light tanks, the divisional cavalry regiments were also mounted in scout carriers, armed with the .55in Boys anti-tank rifle.

during the 1930s that the days of the horse on the modern battlefield were not over, there were no calls for cavalry to accompany the force; the remaining horsed cavalry regiments were all earmarked for Palestine.

The heaviest British anti-tank weapons in France were in the hands of the newly created RA anti-tank regiments, with their brand-new 40mm 2-pounder guns (although some had to use the stop-gap Hotchkiss 25mm instead). The RAC units were armed mainly with machine guns, the heaviest weapons being the .55in Boys anti-tank rifles operated by the 12th Lancers in their Morris armoured cars, and in the Scout Carriers of the other cavalry units.[4] 4RTR had to rely upon the 0.50in Vickers MMGs mounted in a minority of their two-man Matildas, with 7RTR bringing some brand-new Matilda IIs mounting 2-pounder guns with them in early May. When the German invasion of the west started on 10 May, these twenty-three Matilda II tanks were the only RAC tanks in France that mounted a gun.

Fortunately for the crews, they were not involved in the tedious preparation of defensive positions on the 45-mile-long sector of the Franco–Belgian border allocated to the BEF, leaving them more scope to conduct training than the infantry. However, limits on 'track-mileage' and a complete ban on the use of radio (imposed by the French for security reasons) constrained such exercises, as did the fact that by the end of April, there were no less than eighty-seven infantry battalions in the ten 'active' divisions, meaning that the majority never saw a British tank before the Germans attacked, let alone practised co-operation with them. The particularly severe winter weather did not help; November was persistently wet and extremely muddy, followed by a very white Christmas accompanied by frost, snow and below freezing temperatures.[5] February saw a thaw followed by a lot more mud. Most of the crews were lucky enough to be housed in billets throughout the period, and some fortunates were allowed short periods of home leave. By spring 1940, following the deployment of three Yeomanry regiments in Light tanks, plus the spares held in ordnance depots, over 430 tanks were in France.[6] From April two of the Light tank regiments were taken away from their parent infantry divisions and brigaded into the two newly created Armoured Reconnaissance Brigades, each with an HQ and two regiments.[7]

As Belgium (and the Netherlands) were pinning their hopes on the Germans respecting their declarations of neutrality, the French and British generals could not deploy forward of the French border until the Germans struck. Following an appeal from the Belgians for help – which did come – the so-called Plan D allowed the armies to rapidly move forward about 70 miles to occupy defensive positions on the River Dyle, the best anti-tank obstacle in central Belgium, but of course neither the route nor the positions could be reconnoitred in advance. The possible use of the Ardennes route by German armour, well to the south of the British positions, had been looked at and discounted as unfeasible by the French.[8] Lieutenant General Dill, who spent the period from September until late April commanding I Corps, was blunt when he assessed that the German armour 'can always break through, always. The only question then is if it can be contained later on. I can't say I'm happy about it.'[9]

The War of the Cavalry

In the early hours of 10 May 1940, the Germans at last invaded, as expected violating the neutrality of the Netherlands, Belgium and Luxembourg, many regiments first hearing the news on their military radios tuned in to the BBC. The race for the Dyle was ordered to commence. The 12th Lancers – who under Lieutenant Colonel Herbert Lumsden were to use their ten years of armoured car experience to become probably the stellar RAC regiment of the campaign – were the first off, leaving their start line at Hebuterne, near Arras in mid-morning, and crossing the frontier at 1330, the three sabre squadrons each reconnoitring one of the three routes to be used. Fortunately, the Luftwaffe were occupied elsewhere and made no great attempt to interfere with the deployment, and at this stage there were no refugee problems, Brussels appearing to be functioning as normal. At 1800 the Lancers radioed through to GHQ the message that they were on the Dyle. (Colonel Lumsden had been on leave in London and, hearing the news, made his way to join his command, using a French taxi to complete the journey and arriving just before midnight.) A motorized battalion of 50th Infantry Division followed, their mobility provided by scout cars and motorcycle combinations, in order to picket the routes. Next came three of the regular RAC regiments; 4/7 DG on the 2nd Division route in the south/right, 13/18H in the centre (1st Division) and 15/19H on the left (northern) route for the 3rd Division, the 4th Division with 5DG being in reserve. With the infantry divisions starting to take up their positions just before midnight, the following day the 12th Lancers pushed further north and east as far as Diest, about 15 miles forward of the main defensive positions, in a classic light armour screen, with the three forward cavalry Light tank regiments also east of the Dyle behind them.

The following day the Lancers had their first sight of German tanks and, 'with a little brash prompting', forced them to veer north and south, away from the BEF.[10] The Lancers, who had thought ahead and arranged to have a small group of territorial sappers from the Royal Monmouthshire Engineers attached to them, proceeded to blow bridges, one of the main tasks that they excelled at throughout the withdrawal that was about to commence. At nightfall the following day, the 13th, the Lancers were forced to start to withdraw; unfortunately, the Leyland truck carrying their solitary No. 3 radio set became stuck in a bomb crater and the only means of direct communication with GHQ was lost.[11] Communication difficulties were to plague the BEF for the whole campaign, with the British command system still far too over reliant on line and cable rather than radio, and almost every decision made suffered from being made on the basis of incomplete and out-of-date information.

The 12th Lancers were the only armoured car regiment available to the BEF, and fought spectacularly well in the withdrawal to Dunkirk, despite being equipped with new but poorly designed Morris CS9 armoured cars.

The initial withdrawal brought the Lancers into conformity with the tank screen slightly forward of the Dyle, formed by (from the north) 13/18H and 15/19H, although contact with the 4/7DG in the south had been broken. This was because they had French forces on their right, and when those French troops withdrew early on the 14th behind the Dyle, the 4/7DG were forced to comply and lost their first casualty, a B Squadron carrier knocked out by a French anti-tank gun.[12] Two features of the unfolding campaign were seen in microcosm in this one incident: problems with identification leading to so-called friendly fire incidents, and the requirement for the BEF to comply with the commands and movements of its French allies. It must also be stressed that the equipment of the British cavalry regiments was not in any way designed for defensive operations against the German Medium tanks; the mobility and small size of the armoured cars, Light tanks and carriers were the greatest assets, along with the determination and initiative of the individual crews. However, they all lacked the armament required to inflict damage on heavier tanks, and were poorly armoured, the Morris cars of the 12th Lancers and the carriers being particularly vulnerable as they were open-topped. The history of the 4th/7th Dragoon Guards records incidents from their first action:

Reaching the town [Wavre, near Waterloo], the bridge had already been mined by the sappers. The mines were carefully removed to allow the squadron to cross, and then equally carefully replaced – without thought for the hazard they would present in any subsequent hasty withdrawal. … On the left 2nd Troop under TSM Emerton encountered a 37mm anti-tank gun which put an AP round through the turret of the leading tank, killing Sergeant Morgan and wounding his gunner, Tpr Smart. But the latter immediately took command and, pumping .5 in rounds from his heavy machine gun, charged the position, killing the gun crew and destroying the gun. Then the driver was hit, so, taking the controls, Trooper Smart drove the damaged tank out of action. Reaching the bridge at Wavre, they again went through the nerve-wracking performance of hurriedly removing the mines, before recrossing the Dyle and re-joining the regiment after a hectic seven hour recce.[13]

The three Light tank regiments attempted as best they could to coordinate their movements, and found that they were extremely effective when engaging the enemy armoured cars and motorcyclists being used for reconnaissance. However, two other features of the campaign were to manifest themselves around this time; increasing attention from the Luftwaffe, both bombing and strafing, and also the streams of refugees heading eastwards, clogging the roads and preventing rapid redeployment and manoeuvre. The regiments controlled the movements of the screen back over the Dyle and during the afternoon of the 14th, all six road bridges over the river were blown. The problem that the 4/7DG had encountered earlier now reappeared writ large: the BEF found itself with open flanks as the Belgians to the north and the French to the south withdrew, forcing the British troops to retire westwards despite not being threatened frontally. Unknown to GHQ at this stage, the German Army Group A had emerged from the hills and forests of the Ardennes, and was sweeping all before it 'at unheard-of speed' as it drove into the rear of the French defences – exactly the type of mission and bold handling of tanks that the RTC had been preaching for two decades.

The withdrawal in contact that started at the Dyle and ended up at Dunkirk was conducted as well as it could be in the circumstances, and in retrospect can be broadly seen as three (overlapping) phases. Firstly, the reasonably orderly westward withdrawal through Belgium from the Dyle to the Escaut (Scheldt), then the increasingly chaotic retirement through France, initially westwards but then north towards the coast, and finally the formation and defence of the Dunkirk perimeter. Amongst other things, the 12th Lancers were tasked with flank protection for the whole BEF, being frequently switched from one side to the other by GHQ as required and reacting well, despite the enormous logistic and communication challenges, erosion of combat power and, not least, lack of sleep.[14] On the 17th the Lancers blew the bridges over the River Haine in the face of the enemy, and managed to hold off further enemy advances – just – until mid-morning, buying 48th Infantry Division time to withdraw, before they too could retire. At this stage, the two Matilda-equipped RTR battalions were suddenly

Carriers of the 15th/19th Hussars withdraw through the bombed streets of Louvain, 14 May 1940. The second vehicle is a Dragon, designed to tow artillery guns, and doubtless in use with the cavalry due to a general lack of armoured vehicles.

thrown into the battle, being ordered by the over strained and confused I Corps commander to move to the town of Hal to stop a perceived penetration by Panzers. In the middle of loading onto a train when they received the order, they detrained and set off as fast as they could for Hal, a 9-mile journey. They had almost reached their destination when they learned that the local commander, Brigadier Miles Dempsey, had not asked for them and that there were no Panzers in the area. This meant that they had to retrace their steps, which added 18 useless miles to their tracks and made them miss the opportunity to use the train, committing them to a journey which then added even more miles to tanks that had never been designed for long road marches.

As the withdrawing forces approached the Franco–Belgian border, they were losing not only combat power but also overall cohesion; although individual units and formations were often successful in maintaining control internally, it was increasingly difficult for GHQ to obtain a clear picture of what was happening, especially of the overall strategic situation. The cavalry regiments continued to do their best in the main tasks of reporting enemy movements whilst acting as a covering force/rear guard, but all knew that they would struggle to contain attacks made in force, particularly if the heavier German tanks were used. On 18 May exactly this happened to the 15/19H.

The cavalry units were conducting screening operations to allow the infantry divisions to withdraw in contact. At the small town of Assche (modern Asse), north-west of Brussels, the 15/19H were protecting the left (northern) flank of the BEF, which was gaping open as the Belgian army had virtually disintegrated, meaning that the regiment was standing in the path of anything and everything that the Germans moved around the north of Brussels.[15] The speed of the German advance meant that some of their forward units were already to the west of the Hussars as they were trying to conduct the rear guard. Regimental headquarters had been told that they were not to withdraw from Assche without permission, which was finally received at 1300 – but by then it was too late. The majority of A Squadron were pinned down in the town, fighting a German attack made with tanks and supported by anti-tank guns; attempts to contact them were unsuccessful, partly because the Germans appeared to be, either accidentally or deliberately, jamming communications. Every single tank and carrier was knocked out, the OC Major Cockayne-Frith was killed and the majority of the squadron were either killed or taken prisoner, most of the latter carrying wounds. B Squadron, after successfully engaging a large patrol of German motorcyclists, attempted to withdraw into areas already occupied by the enemy, and ended up surrounded in a large, boggy wood. The already twice-wounded regimental second in command Major Robert 'Loony' Hinde took command and ordered that all vehicles should be destroyed and that personnel should attempt to evade capture in small parties, which many of them did, including by swimming the River Dendre. Meanwhile, RHQ, attempting to withdraw, found itself heavily engaged and the CO, Lieutenant Colonel Frazer, managed to escape when his tank was knocked out but was later captured when trying to evade on foot. By the evening, only C Squadron remained more or less intact.[16] This marked the end of the regiment's main contribution to the campaign. A composite squadron was formed out of the remaining troops, which was ordered to be attached to the Fifth Skins at 1900, as they had not been as roughly handled that day.

By the 24th the Skins, including the composite squadron, were involved in defending the Dunkirk perimeter, and engaged in deception as well as aggressive direct action, trying to convince the attackers that there was rather more armour opposing them than was in fact the case. On the 26th the composite squadron handed over its remaining AFVs – two Light tanks and seven carriers – to the Skins and the remaining Hussar personnel were organized to fight as infantry. On the 28th their remaining transport vehicles were ordered to be destroyed, to prevent congestion within the perimeter, and the troops made a testing 25-mile route march through the night. The remaining personnel embarked for evacuation during the morning of the 30th and the remnants of the 15/19H arrived back in Dover in the early afternoon. Their story was a microcosm for all the other Light tank-equipped regiments; unable to stand up to any form of strong attacks, and vulnerable to the German 37mm anti-tank guns, the units were depleted in action by anti-tank fire, as well as suffering breakdowns and losses from lack of petrol, they all gradually lost combat power as they approached Dunkirk, and often ended up fighting on foot as infantry.[17] It must have been terribly galling to destroy the few serviceable tanks remaining rather than allow the Germans to capture them intact, but it was necessary and allowed the crews, many proudly carrying the dismounted Brens and Boys rifles, to be repatriated back to England.

By the 25th those infantry divisions still in action were fighting desperate rear guard actions, and being asked to hold lines three times longer than those prescribed in doctrine; this meant that defence in depth was impossible and that breakthroughs were possible anywhere. The 12th Lancers were still in the thick of the action, and on 28 May Lumsden, seemingly acting on a hunch that there was a gaping hole on the left caused by the surrender of the Belgian army, sent two patrols out with his faithful Monmouthshire Engineers to destroy any intact bridges around Diksmuide and Nieuwpoort. At Diksmuide, the most vulnerable bridge, Second Lieutenant Edward Mann with two cars managed to blow it minutes before a strong German column roared into view. Mann and his men then held the site all day, preventing the Germans from crossing and gaining a very well-deserved DSO. A more substantial defence was organized later, but the initiative of the Lancers prevented a possibly catastrophic break-in to the perimeter. On 29 May:

> The remainder of the regiment concentrated at Vinckem, south of Furnes, destroyed its surplus vehicles and then marched through roads lined with ditched vehicles, to Ghyvelde to link up with the rest of B Echelon, which had shown its opinion of the situation by collecting a vast stock of Brens and shooting down two enemy planes. At 4am on the following morning the remaining vehicles were destroyed – thoroughly … then, carrying all Boyes [*sic*] and Bren guns the regiment marched to a collecting area three miles south of Le Panne and waited the order to embark for home.[18]

The Skins were the most intact of the four original divisional cavalry regiments, and each squadron, on arrival at Dunkirk, was allocated to support a different division; on 2 June, their remaining vehicles were destroyed, and what remained of the regiment returned to England.

Arras

Although the Dunkirk evacuation started on 27 May, the need for it had been identified a week previously. By 20 May GHQ – and Gort in particular – were starting to confront the possibility that evacuation from the continent might be necessary in order to save the BEF. It was not something that he could even mention to the French, of course, but early planning started to take place.

As a preliminary, and in order to attempt to stem the German advance, territorial divisions that had been engaged in lines of communication duties were brought into the fight, despite them lacking much of their support systems and equipment, and being only part-trained at best.[19] In order to assist, a small force of armour was formed known as Cooke's Light Tanks, the name coming from Major Cooke of 2nd Armoured Recce Brigade, the vehicles from spares held at RAOC depots, and the crews from the brigade HQ staff.[20] Increasingly, new ad hoc commands were formed from groups of troops, usually brigade-sized, and taking their name from the commander: Polforce, Petreforce, etc. This showed a welcome ability to react to the demands of an uncertain situation, but was not doctrinally based, and was definitely not how the British army preferred to conduct business, but the sheer operational tempo achieved by the Germans had unhinged the command structure – Fuller and Hobart would have approved.[21] A large ad hoc force known as Frankforce was formed and employed in the most dramatic use of concentrated armour force during the campaign by the RAC.

General Franklyn was the GOC of 5th Infantry Division, the fifth and last of the regular divisions and one which had been formed in France during November. Frankforce was an unusually large ad hoc formation, and was created in order to command all the forces around Arras, and to allow some form of counter-stroke to be conducted whilst not undermining the main defensive battle on the Escaut. It consisted of the two regular brigades of his division, the Territorial 50th Infantry Division (under Giffard Martel, no less), plus the two RTR units in 1st Army Tank Brigade, and also the 12th Lancers. All the RAC units were already positioned on the vulnerable right wing of the BEF, but the Matilda Infantry tanks had suffered mechanically from their 90-mile enforced – and, as noted earlier, unnecessary – road march withdrawal from Belgium, conducted at an average 3mph. Another 30 miles were now demanded simply to get them to the assembly area. Franklyn, in conjunction with Martel, decided that the most effective attack his force could put together should be conducted starting from the north, around the west and then swinging eastwards around the southern outskirts of the town of Arras, a BEF logistic hub and well known to the Tommies of the previous war. Liaison with the French secured an agreement that they would be responsible for protecting the right flank of the British attack. The plan was for two parallel columns of armour to attack in two sweeping arcs around the town, with 7RTR on the inside and 4RTR on the outside. Martel was placed in command of this small tank force, none of whom had seen any direct action at that point. Their confirmatory orders noted that the expected opposition was 'elements of armoured cars and Light tanks', even though it was known that German Medium tanks were in the area and thus likely to be encountered. This economy with the truth may have been necessary for morale purposes, as to indicate that the attack was likely to meet stronger opposition was not conducive to a successful outcome. It must also be stressed that the two infantry battalions committed to the attack (6th and 8th Battalions Durham Light Infantry) had not conducted any cooperation training with the two RTR battalions, and there may even have been some amongst them who had not even seen a British tank prior to the attack starting. And both RTR battalions would be advancing into the unknown, with no reconnaissance screen in front of them – the battle was thus going to be a meeting engagement, in which two moving forces crash into each other, a type of battle that is notoriously difficult to control.

The Arras counter-attack, as it is commonly known, was launched on Tuesday, 21 May. In order to better balance the force, 4RTR, who only had their two-man Matilda I tanks, were loaned six of the larger, gun-armed Matilda II tanks by 7RTR. 4RTR therefore had these plus thirty-five Matilda Is and a few Light tanks, whereas 7RTR retained nine Matilda IIs, twenty-three Matilda Is, and again some Light tanks, a total of eighty-eight. The crews were tired, maintenance was desperately needed, the necessary time to properly tune and net the wireless sets was not available and some tank commanders were given a simple 'follow me' order by their squadron leaders – almost none of the junior commanders had maps.[22] Cohesion started to break down from the start, as the tanks immediately moved off ahead of the already tired and footsore infantry, and some fire was exchanged between 7RTR and French units to their right; the day was hot, adding to the physical burden, and the tanks created clouds of dust which betrayed their presence and hindered visibility. 4RTR even had to avoid driving into some trenches from the First World War, but they were cheered by the sight of a destroyed German 150mm howitzer battery that had just fallen prey to the attentions of the 12th Lancers. The Fourth then encountered a long column of German lorried infantry, and tore into them to great effect. German anti-tank gunners were dismayed to find that their 37mm guns were unable to penetrate the armour of either Matilda variant. Two members of 4RTR recalled their memories of the action:

> Sergeant Major 'Muscle' or 'Jock' Armit [was] just ahead of me getting repeated hits on his tank turret ... my driver was finding me targets quicker than I could myself ... everyone was firing away briskly, and I claimed a motorcycle and sidecar machine gun outfit ... I decided to polish off two lorries parked near where an anti-tank gun was placed. Next thing, a flash and a cloud of smoke. This had been an ammo lorry and its demise also stopped the gun ... I could not see a thing as the corn was higher than the driver's visor ... suddenly the glass in my driver's visor shattered, we found afterwards that a shell had knocked a rivet clean out of the armour plating ... to our great surprise we found that we had come straight into the flank of a German mechanised column ... there was a glorious free-for-all. We knocked out quite a lot of their lorries, there were Germans running about all over the place ... some of them had a go at jumping on our tanks and

I myself had a German who climbed on the outside of my tank and looked in the periscope, then a neighbouring tank very kindly turned his machine gun on me and that removed my passenger … It is quite an experience seeing guns getting trained on your tank and wondering if the shell is going to come through … My own tank was hit twice by anti-tank gun fire which just bounced off. Another tank was hit fourteen times with no ill results.[23]

Tanks from 7RTR reached the Arras–Doullens Road, where they attacked transport and infantry of Rommel's 7th Panzer Division which they had inadvertently hit in the flank. Further on, the tanks caused something of a panic within units of the SS Totenkopf Division; German army reports later accused the SS troops of scattering, but these were likely to have been somewhat exaggerated by the army who wanted to do reputational damage to their rivals. At Achicourt, six Matilda II tanks overran a line of German anti-tank guns but, as the tanks continued towards Wancourt, the attack ran into a hastily prepared defence line with both field artillery and 88mm Flak guns used in the anti-tank role, and these could penetrate the armour and took a dreadful toll in a few minutes. Fighting was costly to both sides and by late afternoon the order was given for the British force to retire. Bombed by Stukas as they returned, only two Matilda II and twenty-six Matilda I tanks remained operational, and both RTR battalion commanders were killed in the action.[24] However, this one limited attack had a profound influence on the course of the war. During the attack, the German forces were undoubtedly completely thrown off balance, and worse: in the middle of the action a panicked radio message from the 6th Rifle Regiment cried: 'Strong enemy tank attack from Arras. Help, help!' A new generation of German infantrymen was experiencing tank terror. When reporting the action afterwards, it is Rommel who deliberately exaggerated the number of tanks he had faced – he spoke of 'hundreds' – in order to emphasize his own success. But strategically, this exaggeration misfired badly. Hitler was rattled by what he referred to 'the crisis at Arras', fearing that the Panzers might be cut off, and as a result the Panzer divisions were ordered to halt, preventing their advance to the Channel ports and reducing the pressure, thus buying critical time for the BEF to form the Dunkirk perimeter and begin evacuation.

The Arras attack was therefore a strategic – if unexpected – success for the BEF, but it left both RTR battalions shattered, hardly surprising at they had engaged elements from three German divisions, and caused Rommel's 7th Panzer Division to suffer its worst single day's losses of the whole campaign. A composite Infantry tank battalion, known as 4/7RTR, had to be formed under Major Parkes on the 23rd from the remnants of the two regiments, with only eighteen Matilda Is, two Matilda IIs and a few Light tanks by now left operational, all of them desperately in need of maintenance, with their tracks in particularly poor state and with little fuel and ammunition left. Engaging the enemy again on a rescue mission at La Bassée as it moved north towards the Channel, another eight tanks were lost. By the time it reached Dunkirk on the 27th, only two tanks remained of the force, with the others lost to breakdown, running out of fuel and, occasionally, to enemy action.

The 1st Armoured Division

The only other armoured force available to the BEF was the 1st Armoured Division, which had remained in the UK over the winter in order to receive its new Cruiser tanks straight from the production lines and train with them – if time permitted. Tank production over the winter was slow, and the division was not ready to move to France until 3 May; even then it still lacked a lot of its equipment, but the German success forced the issue. Even before it moved, 3RTR, part of 3rd Armoured Brigade, as well as the divisional infantry, had been removed from the order of battle for an independent mission at Calais. A high-level decision had been made to fortify Calais, and 3RTR were selected to be sent there not as part of any defensive force but rather with an independent, offensive mission in mind: to create routes through to Dunkirk in order to connect the two ports, and particularly to clear the routes to the south around St Omer. Arriving on the 22nd but taking nearly a day to unload due to the (not unreasonable) windiness of the civilian dockers as the port was under heavy air attack, the task proved impossible – only three Light tanks managed to force a passage through to the western side of the Dunkirk peninsula, and twelve of the precious Cruisers were knocked out in a meeting engagement when moving south of the town.[25] The remains of the regiment was then committed to the defence of Calais under the command of Brigadier Claude Nicholson, a 16th/5th Lancer, with his 30th Infantry Brigade. Calais benefited from being surrounded by dikes and water obstacles, as well as defences and forts designed by Vauban for a rather earlier era, but despite these advantages, could not be held indefinitely by such a small force. Heavy losses were inflicted on 10th Panzer Division when it attacked, and where possible 3RTR made use of such manoeuvre space as was available to conduct forays, but by the evening of the 25th such space was all but gone. Lieutenant Colonel Keller, commanding 3RTR, ordered his remaining four tanks to try to breakthrough to Dunkirk but all were lost en route, although many of the crews managed to reach the evacuation beaches on foot. The heroic last stand managed to buy the evacuation of Dunkirk three extra days, but led to the destruction of the defending forces despite Nicholson's gallant and inspired leadership.

The deployment of 3RTR to Calais left the 1st Armoured Division with only five regiments to send to France: all three in 2nd Armoured Brigade (the Bays, 9L and 10H), and the remaining two in 3rd Armoured Brigade (2 and 5RTR). These regiments began to arrive in Cherbourg on 20 May, on exactly the same day that Gort was starting to consider the necessity of an evacuation. It had

Looking impressive, an A9 Close Support tank of A Sqn 3RTR. Such tanks were modern but horribly unreliable, and as many were lost due to breakdowns or lack or spares as to enemy action.

284 tanks, but only 143 were Cruisers, the remainder being made up with Light tanks, and so each regiment was a mix of both types; the Bays, for example, possessed twenty-nine cruisers and twenty-one Mk VIc Light tanks. This was a new model mounting a 15mm Besa that the crews had not even seen before; one troop leader of the 9th Lancers had a brand-new Light tank but it came *sans* armament, the only weapons being the crew's pistols and a rifle. The two RTR units in 3rd Brigade were in an even worse state. It was a sad fact that throughout the division many of the crews had insufficient training on the tanks that they were to fight in, particularly the Cruisers which came in three different types. In deploying the force to France, it was not the intention of Ironside, the CIGS, to commit the division to the BEF and the defence of Dunkirk, but rather to support the French in resisting the Panzers further south.

Commanded by Major General Roger Evans, a cavalryman, he was forced into precipitate action, committing his units piecemeal as they arrived, rather than as a complete formation and following at least some work-up training with the new vehicles. On the 23rd he was told by GHQ that 'immediate advance of whatever elements of your division are ready is essential. Action at once may be decisive; tomorrow may be too late'. This was relayed by a liaison officer and Evans had no way of communicating with GHQ, and therefore had to obey these orders without being able to seek clarification. The Bays were the first into action the following day, followed by the other four regiments, all the

AGILITY, an A13 Cruiser of the 10th Hussars. This tank was lost in action and burned out on 27 May.

troops starting the day in a very tired state due to a series of preliminary moves. There was at least an intention to use the two brigades en masse as complete formations, although both were placed under the command of a French HQ on the 25th, which almost guaranteed problems. In particular, the French did not realize how lightly armoured the British tanks were, and intended to use them in an assault role, which they were never designed for. The attacks were ill-coordinated with confusion over the H-Hours, and the 10th Hussars were shot to pieces on the 27th as they advanced into a well-prepared defensive position near Huppy. Although some bailed-out crews continued to fight on foot with pistols (and in one case a crowbar), such gallantry was insufficient. The Bays were caught by concealed anti-tank guns advancing through open country in an attack resembling many from the previous war.[26] Richard McCreery, the brigade commander, declined to commit his reserve regiment, the 9th Lancers, to a clearly hopeless cause.

On the left, the two RTR units in 3rd Brigade made somewhat better progress, under the direction of John Crocker, an RTC veteran of the 1934 armoured exercises under Percy Hobart. Nonetheless, at the end of the day the division as a whole had lost sixty-five tanks in action, and very nearly as many – fifty-five – through breakdowns. The division remained under French command, often being asked to participate in defensive schemes that the British knew were hopeless. By the 28th, after less than a week of action, the division had lost sixty-nine Cruisers and fifty-one Light tanks. Therefore, a composite regiment was formed, made up from RHQ, A and C Squadrons 9th Lancers, plus the B Squadrons of the Bays and the 10th Hussars.

The division was finally given permission to withdraw westwards over the Seine on the 9th, Dunkirk having been captured some days previously. On the 13th, for the first time in the twenty-four days since they had landed, the crews of 2nd Armoured Brigade found some time to carry out maintenance and repairs.[27] It was clear that this one understrength division could not help to stave off the defeat of France, and that it was now more important that all the tanks and crews possible should be returned to England. On 15 June all of the remaining tanks in 2nd Brigade were loaded onto a train at Le Mans, intended for the port of Cherbourg, but for an unknown reason never reached the destination. The even more valuable crews were transported to Brest, 270 miles away by road, and were able to be evaluated on the 16th, together with Evans. On the same day Crocker managed to force a passage through to Cherbourg, arriving with his remaining twenty-six or so tanks late in the evening; these tanks were the only ones able to be rescued from France.[28]

The Aftermath

Eight regular cavalry regiments, five battalions of RTR, and three yeomanry regiments made up the RAC contingent that had fought in France. In total around 715 tanks were sent to France, but only 26 of these, all from 3rd Armoured Brigade, were recovered back to the UK, leaving the remainder either destroyed or in the hands of the Germans, who examined them with interest and even turned many of them to their own use.[29] This windfall was critical to the conduct of the armoured campaigns over the next two years; it gave the Germans a huge technical advantage, as they could evaluate examples of every type of tank in use with the RAC, whereas not one example of a captured German tank was available for examination in Britain. As a result, and because of experiences with the inability of their 37mm guns to penetrate Matilda and the heavier French tanks, the Germans immediately started to up-gun their Panzer III tanks to 50mm, as well as increasing the armour carried. This was one of the main reasons why British tanks fell behind their German opponents in both gun power and armour, and this quality gap was to remain for the rest of the war, and was most noticeable until 1944. Like the British, the Germans realized the vulnerability of Light tanks, and decided to concentrate on their Medium tank fleets.

During the BEF battles, and despite popular misconceptions, the quality of the British tanks was comparable to the Germans, and the 2-pounder gun was superior to the 37mm. What they needed more than anything else was stronger armour and better reliability on the Cruisers.[30] In operational terms, 'at the core of German success lay the simple fact that they were willing to take risks to concentrate strength against weakness … The Germans emphasized the need

Two Light tanks abandoned on a French beach. Before leaving them, crews would attempt to render them useless, by seizing the engines and destroying or removing critical components. The ability of the Wehrmacht to inspect captured British tanks gave them a huge advantage over the next two years.

to embrace the inevitable chaos of battle by decentralizing decision-making to the commander on the spot.'[31] Almost the exact opposite, the British doctrine emphasized the need to plan and control set-piece battles, and this proved to be impossible, leaving commanders and troops bewildered and unclear about what they should do.

The pre-war British conception of large tank forces, manoeuvring in close order under the direction of a single commander and then delivering a devastating attack, was not to be realized. Rather, much more emphasis had to be placed upon squadron and troop actions, partly due to losses sustained, but also because of the need to spread the available armoured jam thinly across a much longer front line than had been planned for. There were also the first, worrying indications that having three separate types of tanks was causing problems. Light tanks were simply unable to survive in the main battle area, as their armour was too thin to withstand anti-tank gunfire, and their armament was not capable of inflicting meaningful damage on Medium tanks. In future, wherever possible, their use would be limited to reconnaissance. The long-term issue that needed identifying and rectifying was the artificial division of heavier tanks into the two classes of Infantry and Cruiser, each designed for different roles. 4 and 7RTR had used their Matildas in a Cruiser tank role at Arras, and Evans' 1st Armoured Division had been asked to use his Cruisers as Infantry tanks in both the attack and in defence. This dichotomy was to plague the RAC for the remainder of the war.

Another issue was that from the technical perspective, it was not at all clear what the lessons of France were. On 26 May 1940 Major General Vyvyan Pope (in his capacity as Adviser AFV to the BEF) had sent a letter to the AFV department in the War Office summarizing the technical lessons that he had identified so far. He stated that the Light tanks were 'clearly useless'; the 2-pounder gun was 'only just good enough'; the armour on all tanks was too thin, needing to be in the region of 40–80mm; the Infantry tanks were too slow; and the Cruisers were 'horribly' unreliable. The armoured cars handled so imaginatively by the 12th Lancers were 'invaluable for recce, and 12L have done marvels, but the Morris is not tactically or technically good enough. The armour [need] not be very thick, but the car must mount a gun: the 2-Pounder will do'.

Poor quality was one thing, a lack of quantity another entirely. The scarcity of tanks in England, where a German invasion was expected as the next logical step, was a major concern. In fact, it caused what this author contends was nothing less than a great tank crisis, one which would exert negative pressure on the tank crews for the remainder of the war. With the Germans on the Channel coast, invasion was the greatest concern and would be for the remaining months of summer and autumn, until the winter weather in the Channel could be relied upon to halt any attempt before spring 1941. Merely to replace the tank losses from France took until the end of October, which was the equivalent of five months' lost production. On 1 June 1940, the total number of AFVs held by

If only? This is a trials vehicle, with a 2-pounder gun mounted on the chassis of a Light tank; it was not proceeded with. Had such weapons been available to the RAC regiments deployed to France, they could have taken a heavy toll on the German armour.

units in the UK was recorded as follows: Infantry tanks – 110; Cruisers – 103; Light tanks – 618; Obsolete Mediums – 132.[32] But of the 963 tanks in Britain at this point, only the Cruisers plus the approximately 60 Matilda IIs could be counted as modern tanks, fit for battle, meaning there were only about 160 battleworthy tanks, or enough to equip 3 regiments in a single brigade. One thing was abundantly clear: Britain needed tanks in unprecedented quantities, and under the threat of invasion any kind of tank seemed to be better than no tank at all. But, as David French has pointed out, the threat of invasion did not mean that the huge resource problems that the army had faced for over two decades could be resolved overnight:

> German national strategy, designed to afford Nazi Germany continental hegemony, placed a premium on the army at the expense of the navy and the air force. The British army never enjoyed such favourable treatment because it was never accorded the leading role in British national strategy ... The fall of France did not cause the army to be promoted as Britain's strategic mainstay. On the contrary, the demands of national survival caused Churchill's government to place even more emphasis on the Royal Navy and RAF. It continued to have to struggle with them for adequate resources.[33]

However, the central role of tanks in a modern war was finally in the spotlight, and their ability to be the weapon of decision on the land battlefield was now unquestioned; it had taken the Germans to prove what the RTC had been preaching for two decades. Unfortunately, many of the more senior tank commanders directly involved in the actual fighting had been killed or captured and were unable to contribute to the debate, and there was still a great deal of uncertainty at every level as to why things had gone so badly. Was the root of the problem technical, or was it tactical? Was it that the tank force was simply inferior in numbers to the Germans? If the latter, then it would be easy to overlook or disregard any mechanical failings, in the belief that sheer weight of numbers had prevailed. Indeed, in his May letter quoted earlier, Pope had muddied the water by suggesting that the Germans were succeeding solely because of quantity.[34] Where the RAC did benefit in the short term was in the experience gained by the officers and crews that managed to get themselves back to England. These men, battle-hardened from only a few weeks of combat, would form the backbone of the about-to-be expanded RAC.

Chapter Two

Growing

The Expansion of the RAC

In the wake of the evacuation of the BEF from France, very few tanks existed in the UK and the limited production of new types was destined to go to the existing RAC regiments, including those that had escaped from the continent.[1] The RAC records note that the only armoured formation in the UK, the 2nd Armoured Division, was only about 66 per cent complete in terms of Light tanks, with only one regiment, 8RTR, being equipped with modern tanks in the shape of its new Matilda IIs. Any desire to rapidly increase the size of the RAC beyond its existing boundaries had to be put on hold, as at this time the fears of invasion were very real and there were few weapons to go around: picture the typical early 'Dad's Army' parade with knives tied to broom handles and Napoleonic muskets pressed into service. The only weapons readily available were around 300,000 rifles, and thus it made sense to massively expand the size of the infantry, the one arm that could both use the rifles and be trained rapidly in anti-invasion duties.[2] At this time, the future expansion of the army envisaged creating a total of fifty-five infantry divisions, doubling the size of that arm. And so many RAC units found themselves in the three improvised Motor Machine Gun Brigades, armed with rifles only and equipped with an assortment of civilian vehicles and other wheeled vehicles pressed into service, on anti-invasion duties. In short order, many were issued with Beaverettes, a Standard 14hp car chassis carrying very thin armour and a machine gun or Boys rifle – in many ways these were no better than the improvised types used by the Royal Navy in 1914. It would be some time before tanks would replace them.

On 1 January 1941, on paper at least, the RAC comprised sixty field force units organized in six armoured divisions (with a seventh about to be formed), and four army tank brigades equipped with Infantry tanks. By spring 1941 the feared invasion had not materialized, and although it was both politically and military advantageous to keep the country believing that invasion remained a possibility, the real danger had passed and the time was ripe to expand the RAC, in order to provide many more armoured formations for service in the Middle East and elsewhere. Tank production was starting to accelerate, albeit slowly, and the question of how to expand the RAC revolved largely around the need for more regiment-sized units, and the manpower for them.

Having lost almost all of the available tanks in France, Britain in summer 1940 was defended by a fleet of so-called armoured cars, here manned by the 4th/7th Dragoon Guards.

In order to achieve this expansion, there were several options open to the War Office in order to create the dozens of new units required to man the tanks. These were: to reverse the amalgamations of the eight cavalry regiments created in 1922; to mechanize the few remaining horsed cavalry units; to create new cavalry regiments; to expand the RTR; to expand the yeomanry; or to create new regiments that were not cavalry, nor RTR, nor yeomanry, but which belonged solely to the RAC. With the sole exception of the first option, all the others were used over the next two years. Eventually the RAC consisted of 26 cavalry regiments, 24 battalions of the RTR, 22 yeomanry regiments and 33 RAC battalions converted from infantry, a total of 105 operational units of regimental strength. This number excludes the many other units which operated as part of the RAC, including: headquarters, centres and depots, at least eleven training regiments, and the delivery, replacement and reinforcement units.[3] There were also numerous independent squadrons and deception units operating dummy tanks and the like.[4] Also operating tanks and armoured cars at regimental strength, but outside of the RAC chain of command, were the two operational regiments of Household Cavalry (1 and 2 HCR) and the seven Foot Guards battalions converted to armour and employed solely within the Guards Armoured Division – see below.

The Regular Cavalry

Unit	Wartime Service	Remarks
1st (King's) Dragoon Guards (KDG)	UK NA ME NA IT Greece NA	Tanks initially, armoured cars from Jan. 41. To Egypt 30 Dec. 40. To Palestine Jun. 41–Dec. 42. Tunisia and Italy. Greece Dec. 44–Apr. 45, then to Egypt.
2nd Dragoon Guards (The Queen's Bays)	UK BEF UK NA IT	Tanks. To BEF 20 May 40. First action 24 May 40. Recovered to UK 17 Jun. 40. To Egypt 25 Nov. 41. El Alamein. To Italy 27 May 44. 2nd Armoured Brigade throughout.
3rd Carabiniers (Prince of Wales' Dragoon Guards)	India FE	Tanks. Sialkot, India until Nov. 41. All tanks handed over end 41, became lorried infantry. Jul. 43 Lees issued. To Assam end 43. First action Kohima 20 Mar. 44. Rangoon 26 May 44, Irrawaddy Feb. 45. Mandalay Mar. 45. To Madras 24 Apr. 45. VJ day at Ahmednagar. KIA 104.
4th/7th Royal Dragoon Guards (4/7DG)	UK BEF UK NWE	Tanks. To BEF 22 Sep. 39. First action 18 May 40. To UK (Dunkirk) 2 Jun. 40. UK Jun. 40–Jun. 44. First DD tanks issued Jun. 43 (B and C Sqns). To France 6 Jun. 44 (DD Tanks).
5th Royal Inniskilling Dragoon Guards (5DG)	UK BEF UK NWE	Tanks. To BEF 29 Sep. 39. First action 18 May 40. From BEF (Dunkirk) 2 Jun. 40. To France 18 Jul. 44, to 7 Armoured Div vice 4CLY. KIA 86. AKA the Skins.
1st Dragoons (The Royals)	ME NA IT UK NWE	Armoured cars. To Palestine Sep. 38. To Egypt Nov. 40. Hand in horses 28 Dec. 40. Mechanized early 1941. To Libya Nov. 41. El Alamein. To Sicily (A Sqn) 10 Jul. 43. To Italy 1 Oct. 43. To UK 4 Jan. 44. To France 27 Jul. 44. KIA 108.
2nd Dragoons (The Scots Greys)	ME NA IT NWE	Tanks. To Palestine Oct. 38. Mechanization announced 21 Feb. 41. Regt transferred to RAC 19 Jul. 41. To Egypt Feb. 42, first Grant received 27 Mar. 42. El Alamein. To Italy Sep. 43 (Salerno). To UK 10 Feb. 44. To France 7 Jun. 44.
3rd (King's Own) Hussars (3H)	UK NA FE (B Sqn) NA ME IT NA	Tanks. To Egypt 30 Sep. 40. C Sqn to Crete 22 Mar. 41. To Cyprus 27 Sep. 41. B Sqn to Sumatra and Java Feb. 42 (all KIA or POW). To Palestine 17 Mar. 42. To Egypt 10 May 42. El Alamein. To Syria/Palestine Jan. 43. To Italy 4 May 44. To Egypt 11 Jan. 45.
4th (Queen's Own) Hussars (4H)	UK NA Greece NA Cyprus NA IT	Tanks. To Egypt 31 Dec. 40. To Greece 11 Mar.– end Apr. 41. El Alamein. To Cyprus 18 Jan. 43. To Egypt Jun. 43. To Italy 4 May 44. Nov. 44 converted to Kangaroos.
7th (Queen's Own) Hussars (7H)	NA FE ME NA IT	Tanks. In Egypt Sep. 39. Burma, India 21 Feb.– Oct. 42. To Iraq 17 Oct. 42. To Syria May. 43. To Egypt 28 Sep. 43. To Italy 4 May 44. Sep./Oct. 44 converted to DD tanks.

Unit	Wartime Service	Remarks
8th (King's Royal Irish) Hussars (8H)	NA Cyprus NA UK NWE	Tanks, then armoured cars, then tanks. In Egypt Sep. 39. El Alamein. To Cyprus 31 Dec. 42. To Egypt 25 Jun. 43. To UK 8 Dec. 43. Converted to tanks Jan. 44. To France 9 Jun. 44.
9th (Queen's Royal) Lancers (9L)	UK BEF UK NA IT	Tanks. To BEF 21 May 40. First action 24 May 40. To UK 17 Jun. 40. To Egypt 28 Nov. 41. El Alamein. To Italy 27 May 44. 2nd Armoured Brigade throughout. KIA 131.
10th (Prince of Wales' Own Royal) Hussars (10H)	UK BEF UK NA IT	Tanks. To BEF 21 May 40. First action 27 May 40. To UK 17 Jun. 40. To NA 27 Nov. 41. First action 23 Jan. 42. El Alamein. May 43 to May 44 in Tripoli, Tunis and Algeria. To Italy 27 May 44. 2nd Armoured Brigade throughout. KIA and DOW 162; Wounded 222; POW 93.
11th (Prince Albert's Own) Hussars (11H)	NA IT UK NWE	Armoured cars. In Egypt Sep. 39. El Alamein. To Italy 23 Sep. 43. To UK 5 Jan. 44. To France 9 Jun. 44.
12th (Prince of Wales' Royal) Royal Lancers (12L)	UK BEF UK NA IT	Armoured cars. To BEF 16 Sep. 39. To UK 1 Jun. 40. To Egypt 25 Nov. 41. El Alamein. To Italy 9 Apr. 44.
13th/18th Royal Hussars (Queen Mary's Own) (13/18H)	UK BEF UK NWE	Tanks. To BEF 19 Sep. 39. First action 14 May 40. From BEF (Dunkirk) 30 May 40. UK Jun. 40–Jun. 44. DD training started 10 Apr. 43 (A and B Sqns). To France 6 Jun. 44 (DD tanks). KIA 154.
14th/20th King's Hussars (14/20H)	India ME IT	Tanks. Secunderabad Sep. 39. To Iraq 3 Jul. 41. To Egypt Oct. 43. To Syria Mar. 44. To Italy 21 Jan. 45. A Sqn converted to Kangaroos Mar. 45.
15th/19th King's Royal Hussars (15/19H)	UK BEF UK NWE	Tanks. To BEF 4 Oct. 39. First action 18 May 40. From BEF (Dunkirk) 30 May 40. UK Jun. 40–Aug. 44. To France 15 Aug. 44. To 11 Armoured Div vice 2NY 18 Aug. 44. First action 19 Aug. 44. KIA and DOW 101. POW 107.
16th/5th Queen's Royal Lancers (16/5L)	India UK NA IT	Tanks. To UK 7 Jan. 40. To Algeria 22 Nov. 42. To Italy 14 Jan. 44. KIA 101.
17th/21st Lancers (17/21L)	UK NA IT	Tanks. To Algeria 13 Nov. 42. To Italy 26 Mar. 44.

Notes: UK = United Kingdom; BEF = France 1940; NWE = Europe 1944–5; NA = North Africa; ME = wider Middle East; IT = Sicily and Italy; FE = Far East. KIA includes DOW. Primary source is the War Diaries.

The War Raised Cavalry Regiments

Rather than temporarily reverse the amalgamations of the eight regiments created in 1922 – the so-called vulgar fractions who were now well-established regiments – the somewhat questionable decision was made late in 1940 to create a number (initially three, quickly increased to six) of new cavalry regiments, bearing the numbers of regiments that had last existed in the order of battle in the nineteenth century.[5] Creating cavalry regiments from scratch was a difficult proposition, as by virtue of being cavalry the units felt the need to uphold certain traditions and ways of doing business – a sense of 'cavalry style'. The six regiments were therefore formed from cadres taken from existing regular cavalry regiments, as shown in the table below, and which must have created a great deal of disruption for those regiments who were themselves trying to settle down into new establishments with new vehicles and equipment, not to mention large numbers of part-trained officers and men. Rather than harken back to the histories and regalia of the regiments bearing the same numbers that had last existed well over one hundred years before, not surprisingly, these cadres took the opportunity to create the new regiments in a similar image to the parents. For example, the 26th Hussars adopted an eagle cap badge, reflecting the link to the 14th/20th Hussars, and the 27th Lancers' sidecap was almost the same as that of the 12th Lancers, but with silver piping instead of gold. The choice of the new regimental colours by the six often had clear links to those of their proud parents – the 22nd Dragoons combined the yellow and black from the 4th/7th Dragoon Guards with the green of the Fifth Skins.

Taking their seniority from their numerical order, the six regiments were placed into the army list immediately after the 17th/21st Lancers and before the North Irish Horse; this had the strange effect of instantly making them senior to the eight regular battalions of the RTR, which may have caused some raised eyebrows at the time but which seems to have been accepted with good grace.[6] The first three units were formally created by Army Order 213 of 10 December 1940, although the actual creation preceded the official announcement with formation beginning on 1 December 1940; presumably posting orders must have been sent to individuals during November. Similarly, the other three were created by Army Order 7 of January 1941 and began forming on 1 February.

Two of these regiments were to be disbanded during the war, one following a short but intense period of operations, with three of the remaining four surviving for the first few months of peacetime before being disbanded; the final regiment to leave the order of battle was the 25th Dragoons, who were involved in security duties in India in the run-up to partition and remained active until mid-1947.[7] Each of the regiments performed valuable and often gallant service during the war, with their members being just as proud of their regiment as those from the regular cavalry. Although by this time all six regiments had ceased to exist, the announcement of their official disbandment only took place on 26 June 1948.

The War Raised Cavalry Regiments

Regiment	Parent(s)	Formed	Service	Disbandment
22nd Dragoons	4/7DG, 5DG	1 Dec. 40, Blundellsands, Liverpool.	4/7DG supplied the CO, QM and 5 other officers. 5DG provided the 2IC and Adjt plus 134 ORs came from the two regiments with the remaining manpower coming from the training organizations. The regiment operated Sherman Crab flail tanks as part of 79th Armoured Div from D–Day and throughout the NWE campaign. KIA/DOW 61.	30 Nov. 45, Germany.
23rd Hussars	10H, 15/19H, 16/5L	1 Dec. 40, Penkridge, Staffordshire.	10H supplied the 2IC, two squadron leaders, the adjt, the QM, plus three others and 69 ORs. 15/19H provided one squadron leader, the BTA, 5 other officers, the RQMS and 51 ORs.[8] 16/5L provided the RSM. The regiment operated in 29th Armoured Brigade, 11th Armoured Div as a tank regiment throughout the NWE campaign.	21 Jan. 46, Germany.
24th Lancers	9L, 17/21L	1 Dec. 40, Cannock, Staffordshire.	9L supplied the CO, 2 squadron leaders, the QM, the adjt plus 3 other officers, and 64 ORs including the RSM. 17/21L provided the 2IC, 2 squadron leaders plus 4 other officers, and around 70 ORs. Around 250 recruits arrived during mid-December. The regiment operated as a Sherman tank regiment in Normandy as part of 8th Armoured Brigade until the end of July when it was replaced by 13/18H prior to disbandment.	10 Aug. 1944, France.
25th Dragoons	3DG	1 Feb. 41, Sialkot, India.	3DG supplied the CO, 2IC, QM and 8 other officers with Lt Massy RTR as the adjt. 3DG also supplied 102 ORs, with 91 others coming from volunteers from 4 different infantry battalions.[9] The regiment served as a Lee armoured regiment in Burma from Jan. 44. DD training in India from May 45.	31 Jul. 1947, India.
26th Hussars	14/20H	1 Feb. 41, Meerut, India.	14/20H supplied the CO plus 9 other officers, with 103 ORs; Maj Good RTR became 2IC. The main manpower came from volunteers from 12 different infantry battalions, in total 13 officers and 336 ORs. No operational service, many personnel posted to Long Range Patrol Group (Chindits) on disbandment.	Oct. 43, India.
27th Lancers	12L	6 Jan. 41, Dorking, Surrey.	12L supplied 7 officers and 112 ORs, with 5 officers from other cavalry regiments. 235 ORs arrived from the Infantry Training Centre (Welch Regiment) in Jan. 41. Served in the Middle East on deception duties from Jan. 44. From 17 Jul. 44 in Italy as 10 Corps armoured car regiment, with dismounted operations during winter 44/45, then part conversion to Buffaloes in Mar. 45.	30 Sep. 45, Austria.

The Regular RTR

The RTC (renamed RTR in April 1939) had existed for much of the inter war period with five battalions, with expansion only somewhat grudgingly authorized from mid-1933 when the 6th Battalion was formed in Egypt, although even then only on a two-company basis. The 7th Battalion started to form up in May 1937, and the 8th one year later. On the order of battle at the outbreak of war were these eight units, and it was these that would be considered as the 'regular' component of the RTR, which during the war was often mere semantics, but which would increase in importance towards the end, when the regular army needed to be reformed, as we shall see.[10]

The Regular Battalions of the RTR during the Second World War

Unit	Wartime Service	Remarks
1st Battalion Royal Tank Regiment (1RTR)	NA IT UK NWE	To Egypt 38. Siege of Tobruk. El Alamein. To Italy 22 Sep. 44. To UK 5 Jan. 44. To France 7 Jun. 44.
2RTR	UK BEF UK NA FE ME IT	To BEF 23 May 40. To UK 16 Jun. 40. To Egypt Sep. 40. Burma/India 21 Feb. 42–21 Sep. 42. To Iraq 1 Oct. 42. To Syria May 43. To Egypt Oct. 43. To Italy 4 May 44.
3RTR	UK BEF UK NA Greece NA UK NWE	To BEF (Calais) 22 May 40. To Egypt 23 Dec. 40. Greece 12 Mar.–27 Apr. 41. To Egypt 30 Apr. 41. El Alamein. To UK 10 Dec. 43. To France 13 Jun. 44.
4RTR	UK BEF UK NA NWE	To BEF 21 Sep. 39. To UK 27 May 40. To Egypt 17 Feb. 41. B Sqn to Eritrea 28 Dec. 40 until early May 41. Ceased to exist on capture of Tobruk 21 Jun. 42. Brought back into being 1 Mar. 45 by renaming 144 RAC in NWE.
5RTR	UK BEF UK NA IT UK NWE	To BEF 23 May 40. To UK 19 Jun. 40. To Egypt 23 Dec. 40. El Alamein. To Italy 15 Sep. 43. To UK Jan. 44. To France 7 Jun. 44.
6RTR	NA ME IT	Reformed in Egypt 1 Apr. 33. Third (A) company added Mar. 39. First A9 Cruiser received Oct. 39. Equipped with captured Italian tanks Mar. 41. El Alamein. To Iraq 26 Dec. 42. To Palestine 10 May 43. To Italy 4 May 44.
7RTR	UK BEF UK NA UK NWE	Reformed 24 May 37. To BEF 7 May 40. To Egypt 25 Sep. 40. Ceased to exist on capture of Tobruk 21 Jun. 42. Brought back into being 1 Apr. 43 by renaming 10RTR in UK. To France Jul. 44.
8RTR	UK NA IT	Reformed 16 May 38. To Egypt 13 Jun. 41. El Alamein. To Italy 4 May 44.

Notes: UK = United Kingdom; BEF = France 1940; NWE = Europe 1944–5; NA = North Africa; ME = wider Middle East; IT = Sicily and Italy; FE = Far East.

The Yeomanry

Not all of the Territorial Army (TA) units bearing the title Yeomanry were to be mechanized and become part of the RAC during the Second World War; between the wars many had become units of the Royal Artillery, with a few going to the infantry or Royal Signals, and they continued in these roles during the conflict. The senior yeomanry regiments who could demonstrate strong recruiting were the ones allowed to remain as horsed cavalry between the wars, and six of these were initially deployed on horseback to Palestine at the start of the Second World War, eventually becoming motorized and then mechanized as armoured regiments in about 1941. The final regiment to be listed as horsed cavalry on the British army order of battle was a regiment of yeomanry, the Yorkshire Dragoons, who eventually relinquished their horses as late as 1942.

In total, sixteen Yeomanry Cavalry units were converted into armoured or armoured car roles either immediately before, or during, the Second World War.[11] Of these units, six were subsequently ordered to generate a second line or duplicate unit, formed from the first and distinguished by (in most cases) the numeral 2.[12] (In the British army it is an unwritten law that for every rule that there must always be an exception! In this case 3rd CLY generated a mirrored unit called the 4th CLY.) This expansion came about as an immediate result of Hitler's annexation of the rump Czech territory in March 1939; the War Minister, Hore-Belisha, formulated a plan – largely without consultation with other bodies – whereby the existing TA units would be immediately brought up to their war establishment manpower strength, and then doubled to produce a force totalling 340,000 men, with instructions issued out of the blue to units on 12 April. Of course, this was fine on paper but, as well as ignoring the equipment and infrastructure needs of the existing and new units, it created huge turbulence as the existing units had to surrender a large number of (relatively) experienced officers and NCOs in order to form the duplicate. By May 1939, this process had started, and the units had been brought into existence – on paper, at least. Some of the established units used the second line regiment as a recruiting and training unit, and also held their 'immatures' – soldiers and officers under the authorized minimum overseas deployment age of 19 – within its ranks.

With war imminent, from late August 1939 the Yeomanry regiments went through a specific process to mobilize them and their personnel. On 1 September mobilization of the armed forces was announced, and on this day the remaining TA units received formal orders called Embodiments. These orders brought the unit into being as part of the wartime, rather than territorial, order of battle, and also confirmed their order of precedence in the army list. Within the territorial cavalry, the senior unit was the North Irish Horse who took precedence immediately after the 17th/21st Lancers, followed by the remainder in the order shown in the table below.[13] From that moment onwards, in most respects they were treated as if they were regular units, although they remained more vulnerable to being placed into suspended animation, converted to other roles, amalgamated or disbanded, as we shall see.

Yeomanry Cavalry Regiments (in Order of Seniority)

Unit	Details
North Irish Horse (NIH)	Officially the only Cavalry Militia – rather than Yeomanry – regiment.[14] In 1934 the NIH had only one officer on its strength leading to it being known as the 'one-man regiment'. 31 Aug. 39 reconstituted as an armoured car regt, transferred to RAC 11 Sep. 39. Converted to tanks from Apr. 41. Algeria and Tunisia from 1 Feb. 43, Italy from 18 Apr. 44. KIA 73. Disbanded at Wuppertal 7 Jul. 46.[15]
Royal Wiltshire Yeomanry (RWY)	To Palestine as horsed cavalry in 1st Cavalry Division 20 Feb. 40. B and C Sqns used as searchlight units in western desert. Regiment motorized early 41. To RAC 12 Apr. 41. May 41 relief of Habbaniya. Conversion to tanks started Dec. 41. El Alamein. Italy from 4 May–11 Oct. 44. To UK 24 Oct. 44. KIA/DOW 54. Disbanded 1947.
Warwickshire Yeomanry (WY)	To Palestine as horsed cavalry in 1st Cavalry Division 40. To RAC 12 Apr. 41. Converted to tanks autumn 41. North Africa, El Alamein, Italy from 4 May to Aug. 44, then to UK in Oct. 44.
Yorkshire Hussars (YH)	To Palestine as horsed cavalry in 1st Cavalry Division 28 Jan. 40. Last horse left 7 Mar. 42. To Cyprus 14 Mar. 42, A13 tank training commenced. To Beirut/Egypt 19 Jan. 43. To UK 11 Dec. 43. Converted to recce then used as Reinforcement Holding Unit in SE England Apr. 44–May 45. Placed in suspended animation Mar. 46.
Nottinghamshire (Sherwood Rangers) Yeomanry (SRY)	To Palestine as horsed cavalry in 1st Cavalry Division Jan. 40. Used as coastal gunners in siege of Tobruk. To RAC 12 Apr. 41, converted to tanks Jun. 41. North Africa, El Alamein, North-West Europe from 6 Jun. 44 to May 45. Placed in suspended animation 1 Mar. 46. KIA 247.
Staffordshire Yeomanry (SY)	To Palestine as horsed cavalry in 1st Cavalry Division 9 Jan. 40. Mechanization of A Sqn only commenced Oct. 40. North Africa, El Alamein. To UK late 43. North-West Europe 6 Jun. 44–May 45. Converted to DD *c*. Oct. 44. Placed in suspended animation 1 Mar. 46. KIA/DOW 132.
Cheshire Yeomanry (CY)	The regiment was transferred to the RAC 26 Sep. 41, becoming 5th LoC Signals and transferring to the Royal Signals 13 Feb. 42.
Yorkshire Dragoons (YD)	To Palestine as horsed cavalry in 1st Cavalry Division Jan. 40. Last horsed cavalry regiment on active service in British army; last horses left 1 Mar. 42. Converted to motor battalion Sep. 42 and then converted to infantry (9 KOYLI) Dec. 42. YD were placed into suspended animation Sep. 44.
North Somerset Yeomanry (NSY)	The regiment was transferred to the RAC 26 Sep. 41, becoming 4th Air Formation Signals Regt on 28 Feb. 42, and transferring to the Royal Signals 16 Mar. 43.

Unit	Details
1 Derbyshire Yeomanry (1DY)	24th AC Coy RTC between the wars. Late 38 authorized to become cavalry armoured car regiment. To Algeria 22 Nov. 42. Tunisia (armoured cars). Converted to tanks Jul. 43. To Italy 14 Mar. 44. Placed into suspended animation 14 Jun. 47. KIA/DOW 84.
2 Derbyshire Yeomanry (2DY)	Ordered to be formed 1 Jul. 39. To Egypt 5 Jul. 42. To UK 5 Jan. 42. North-West Europe 12 Jun. 44–May 45. Placed into suspended animation 3 Jan. 46, disbanded 1 Mar. 46.
1 Royal Gloucestershire Hussars (1RGH)	21st AC Coy RTC between the wars. Late 1938 authorized to become cavalry Light tank regiment. Mainly employed as a training regiment in UK, and used as garrison troops in Austria immediately post-war. Placed in suspended animation 46.
2 Royal Gloucestershire Hussars (2RGH)	Formed 24 Aug. 39. To Egypt 1 Oct. 41–Dec. 42 inc. El Alamein. Disbanded 15 Jan. 43.
1 Lothian & Borders Horse Yeomanry (1LBY)	19th AC Coy RTC between the wars. Late 38 authorized to become divisional cavalry regiment. Service: To 12 Jan. BEF 40, North-West Europe 15 Jul. 44–5. Commonly referred to as 1LBY. Suspended animation 15 Jul. 46.
2 Lothian & Borders Yeomanry/Horse (2LBY/H)	Formed 2 May 39. Service; Tunisia Dec. 42–43. Italy Mar. 44–May 45. Name officially changed to Horse in 1944. Commonly referred to as 2LBH. Suspended animation 20 Jan. 46.
1 Fife & Forfar Yeomanry (1FFY)	20th AC Coy RTC between the wars. Late 38 authorized to become divisional cavalry regiment. BEF 21 Jan.–*c.* early Jun. 40. North-West Europe 6 Jun. 44–5 (Flamethrowers from Oct. 44).
2 Fife & Forfar Yeomanry (2FFY)	Formed 26 Apr. 39. Service: North-West Europe 17 Jun. 44–May 45. Converted to infantry role early Aug. 45. Disbandment instructions received 6 Jan. 46, to be complete by 9 Jan. 46.
Westminster Dragoons (2nd County of London Yeomanry) (WD)	22nd AC Coy RTC between the wars. 37: change of role to 102 OCTU at Blackdown camp until 22 Nov. 40 when regiment became armoured. Flail unit from Dec. 43. To North-West Europe 6 Jun. 44–May 45. Placed in suspended animation early 46.
3rd County of London Yeomanry (3CLY)	23rd AC Coy RTC between the wars. Late 38 authorized to become cavalry Light tank regiment. From 24 Aug. 39 retitled 3CLY. To Egypt Oct. 41. North Africa, Tunisia. To Sicily 10 Jul. 43. To Italy 22 Sep. 43. To UK 10 Feb. 44. To North-West Europe 7 Jun. 44. Combined with 4CLY 1 Aug 44 to form 3/4CLY.
3rd/4th County of London Yeomanry (3/4CLY)	Formed 1 Aug. 44 at Carpiquet by combining 3 and 4CLY with same seniority as 3CLY.[16] North-West Europe. Placed in suspended animation Sep. 46.
1 Northamptonshire Yeomanry (1NY)	25th AC Coy RTC between the wars. Late 38 authorized to become cavalry Light tank regiment. To North-West Europe 13 Jun. 44. Conversion to Buffaloes 30 Jan. 1945. KIA/DOW 87. Armoured cars from Mar. 46. Placed in suspended animation 28 Sep. 46. Reinstated 3 Nov. 47.

Unit	Details
2 Northamptonshire Yeomanry (2NY)	Formed May 39. To North-West Europe 19 Jun. 44. 18 Aug. 44 replaced by 15/19H and personnel dispersed to other units and disbandment complete 15 Sep. 44. KIA/DOW 75.
1 East Riding of Yorkshire Yeomanry (1ERY)	26th AC Coy RTC between the wars. Late 38 authorized to become divisional cavalry regiment. To BEF 29 Feb. 40–30 May 40. Commonly referred to as ERY post-Jun. 40. Apr. 43 to 79th Armoured Div as DD regt. To North-West Europe 6 Jun. 44–May 45. Converted to Buffalo 31 Jan. 45. Re-equipped with tanks 4 Apr. 45. KIA 106. Disbanded 7 Mar. 46. Reformed as TA unit Mar. 47.
2 East Riding of Yorkshire Yeomanry (2ERY)	Embodied 24 Aug. 39. Service: Home only. Note: most trained personnel were absorbed into 1ERY during Jun. 40, the unit was then converted to infantry as 10th Bn Green Howards 25 Jun. 40.
4th County of London Yeomanry (4CLY)	4th CLY was disbanded in 24. The title was resurrected as the duplicate unit of 3CLY 24 Aug. 39. To North Africa Oct. 41. El Alamein, Tunisia. To Italy 22 Sep. 43. To UK 6 Jan. 44. to North-West Europe. Combined with 3CLY 1 Aug. 44 to form 3/4CLY.
Inns of Court (IOC/ICR)	2 squadrons converted to Light tanks in April 1937, one squadron remaining horsed. Initially served as the RAC OCTU at Sandhurst producing RAC officer cadets. The regiment became part of the RAC on 1 Dec. 40, and became an operational armoured car unit in Jan. 41. To North-West Europe 6 Jun. 44–May 45. Remained in-being in British Army of the Rhine until TA reorganization of early 1947.

The War Raised RTR Battalions

At about the same time that the creation of the six war raised cavalry regiments were being considered, it was decided to raise another four battalions of the Royal Tank Regiment, numbered 9th to 12th. It might reasonably be asked why do both and not just one or the other? The answer was probably rooted in a desire to maintain some sort of balance within the overall RAC – fears of an RTR takeover still resonated in some senior minds, but increasing the size of the RTR was beneficial as, unlike the individual cavalry or yeomanry regiments, the regiment was more easily able to dip into its larger pool of talent (and generally greater individual experience) in order to create additional units. For these reasons the 9th, 10th, 11th and 12th Battalions RTR were formed between the end of 1940 and early 1941.

The Ninth were raised from cadres sent by 3RTR in November 1940, in Gateshead. The battalion landed in Normandy on 21 June 1944, and saw a lot of action as a Churchill regiment throughout the North-West Europe campaign, having the distinction of being under command, at various times, both armies, and also under every single infantry division bar one. The unit was disbanded on 13 December 1945.

10RTR were formed from a cadre of personnel from 5RTR on 4 November 1940. However, in February 1943 the battalion was redesignated as 7RTR. This was to reconstitute that regular battalion that had ceased to exist with the fall of Tobruk in June of the previous year, and as such saw action in Europe from 1944 (see 7RTR).

Formed on 1 January 1941, in June the Eleventh was converted into one of the top-secret Canal Defence Light (CDL) units, but did not see any action despite being deployed to Egypt between September 1942 and April 1944. They were sent to North-West Europe in mid-August 1944 but were subsequently re-equipped as a Buffalo amphibious vehicle regiment in early October, taking part in the winter campaigning in the Netherlands and then the Rhine Crossing of March 1945 and having the honour of taking Winston Churchill across the great river. The battalion dwindled in strength due to its no-longer required specialist role, and was placed in suspended animation on 13 January 1946.

12RTR was raised on 18 December 1940 from cadres from 4RTR, in Gateshead. Moving to Algeria on 25 March 1943, it then fought as a Churchill regiment in Tunisia before being sent to Italy on 3 May 1944 where C Squadron were converted to Crocodiles. Disbandment was announced on 4 July 1945 and was completed on 1 September.

The Territorial RTR Battalions

Six additional battalions of the RTR were formed by converting Territorial Army infantry battalions, and then each regiment created a duplicate in the same manner, and with all the attendant problems, as the yeomanry. All served as Infantry tank units, although some took on additional roles with specialized armour.

Territorial RTR Battalions

Regiment	Original Unit	Formed	Service	Disbandment
40 RTR	7th King's Regt	Oct. 38, Bootle	To NA 5 Jul. 42. First action 22 Jul. 42. El Alamein. Given unofficial title of 'Monty's Foxhounds'. Tunisia. To IT (Salerno) 9 Sep. 43. To Egypt 1 Jun. 44. To Greece 16 Oct. 44.	Into suspended animation 9 May 46. Reformed as TA unit 17 Mar. 47.
41RTR	10th Manchesters	Oct. 38, Manchester	To Egypt 9 Jul. 42. El Alamein. Converted following dispersal order to become 1st Scorpion Regt RAC (flail tanks) 15 Feb. 1943, serving in Tunisia until May 43. Became the basis of the 1st Assault Regiment RE in Italy.	Ordered to be 'dispersed' 7 Dec. 42. Into suspended animation 1 Jan. 44.

Regiment	Original Unit	Formed	Service	Disbandment
42RTR	23rd London Regt	1938 St John's Hill	To NA 14 Jun. 41. Converted to CDL role Aug. 42. To UK 22 Apr. 44. To Normandy 12 Aug. 44.	Suspended animation 30 Oct. 44. Reformed as TA unit 1 Jan. 47.
43RTR	6th Royal Northumberland Fusiliers	1 Nov. 38, Newcastle	The only RTR battalion not to be used on active service. Motorized until first tanks received 5 Dec. 40. Equipped with Matildas then Churchills, the Bn remained in UK, used as a training, development, and demonstration unit. Trained as CDL unit in Feb. 45, it arrived in India 2 Aug. 45 and was stationed in Secunderabad. The battalion left India on 11 Sep. 47, and was disbanded on arrival in UK.	43RTR was still serving in India when 43RTR was reformed as part of the TA revival in early 47. The new unit therefore became known as 2/43RTR until the original battalion was disbanded in late 47.
44RTR	6th Gloucesters	Nov. 38, Bristol	NA from 13 Jun. 41. Sicily 10 Jul. 43, Italy 23 Sep. 43. To UK Jan. 44, NWE from 7 Jun. 44 to VE day.	Ordered to disband 5 Feb. 46. Reformed as 44/50RTR (TA) in 1947.
45RTR	7th Leeds Rifles	1 Nov. 38, Leeds	Embodied 1 Sep. 39, Carlton Barracks. Arrived in Egypt 4 Jul. 42. Only action El Alamein. KIA 6, DOW 3, WIA 35, Missing 10.	Ordered to be 'dispersed' 7 Dec. 42. Disbanded 8 Mar. 43. Reformed as 45/51RTR (TA) 1 Jan. 47.
46RTR	Duplicate from 40 RTR	May 39, Liverpool	To Egypt 5 Jul. 42. El Alamein. To Sicily (B Sqn) 10 Jul. 43. To IT 23 Sep. 43. To Greece 16 Oct. 44.	Disbanded 14 Feb. 46. Reformed post war as 653 Heavy AA Regt RA (TA).

Regiment	Original Unit	Formed	Service	Disbandment
47RTR	Duplicate from 41RTR	May 39, Oldham	To Egypt 9 Jul. 42. El Alamein.	Ordered to be 'dispersed' 7 Dec. 42. Disbanded 15 Jan. 43.
48RTR	Duplicate from 42RTR	26 Apr. 39, Clapham Junction.	Tunisia from 25 Mar. 43. To Italy 3 May 44– May 45. KIA 83.	Disbanded Aug. 45.
49RTR	Duplicate from 43RTR	May 39, Newcastle	Mobilized 25 Aug. 39, Fenham Barracks. Conversion to CDL role Mar. 42. To France 12 Aug. 44. 25 Oct. 44 reorganized as 49 APC Regt with Ram Kangaroo. (B Sqn remain as independent CDL sqn on Grant CDL, used on Rhine Crossing). 22 Sep. 45 designated as an occupation unit.	Ordered 26 Nov. 45, complete 13 Dec. 45.
50 RTR	Duplicate from 44RTR	May 39, Bristol	To Egypt 6 Jul. 42. El Alamein. To Sicily 10 Jul. 43. To Italy 26 Sep. 43. To Egypt, Palestine 1 Jun. 44. To Greece 16 Oct. 44.	Disbanded summer 46. Reformed as 44/50 RTR (TA) in 1947.
51RTR	Duplicate from 45RTR	May 39, Leeds	Formed in Morley, Leeds from A Sqn 45RTR. Algeria 2 Feb. 43. Tunisia from 28 Feb. 43. Italy 18 Apr. 44– May 45. Flail (B Sqn) and Crocodile tanks (A, C sqns) from Jan. 45. KIA 91.	Disbandment notified 8 Sep., completed 22 Oct. 45. Reformed as 45/51RTR (TA) 1 Jan. 47.

The RAC Regiments

In July 1940, an additional sixty infantry battalions were raised in UK, partly as a response to the threat of invasion, and partly due to the needs of an army that was expanding rapidly. But with a larger army came the need for more armoured units, and so it was decided that a number of the battalions should be converted from infantry into armour, with thirty-three eventually being transferred between November 1941 and July 1942. These were then given a three-digit number as a regiment of the Royal Armoured Corps, for example, 107 Regiment RAC – the numbering sequences, from 107 to 116 and 141 to 163 probably being chosen as part of a larger deception plan. In many cases, the regiments, semi-officially at best but often with the tacit approval of the authorities, managed to incorporate their old battalion title into the new one, for example, 149 Regiment RAC (King's Own Yorkshire Light Infantry); many retained their old cap badge on the RAC black beret rather than using the RAC cap badge, and 116 RAC, out of the public eye in Burma, even managed to keep wearing the tam-o'-shanter of the Gordon Highlanders! Regular officers were not transferred to the RAC but were 'posted for duty'; the remainder, being called up for the duration, were transferred.

The majority of these battalions saw no action, and some were reconverted back to infantry or into other roles within a matter of months, but twelve saw extensive service; those that remained were disbanded soon after the end of hostilities.[17] Some units stationed in the UK after D-Day found that they were constantly being drained of their fit, trained personnel who were posted to units on operations, receiving instead many wounded soldiers in the process of recuperation.

The RAC Regiments

Regiment	Original Unit	To RAC	Service	Disbandment
107th Regt Royal Armoured Corps (107 RAC)	5th Bn KO Lancaster Regt	1 Nov. 41	UK. 11 Tk Brigade Nov. 41 to Nov. 43. 34 Tk Brigade Jan. 44 to May 45. To NWE Jul. 44. See also 147, 151, 153 RAC.	Summer 45
108 RAC	1/5th Bn Lancs Fusiliers	1 Nov. 41	UK	31 Dec. 43
109 RAC	1/6th Bn Lancs Fusiliers	1 Nov. 41	UK	30 Dec. 43
110 RAC	5th Bn Border Regt	1 Nov. 41	UK	Dec. 43
111 RAC	5th Bn Manchesters	1 Nov. 41	UK	Dec. 43
112 RAC	9th Bn Sherwood Foresters	1 Nov. 41	UK	Nov. 44
113 RAC	2/5th West Yorks Regt	Jul. 42	UK	Sep. 43
114 RAC	2/6th Bn Duke of Wellington's	Jul. 42	UK	Feb. 44

Regiment	Original Unit	To RAC	Service	Disbandment
115 RAC	2/7th Bn Duke of Wellington's	Jul. 42	UK	Feb. 44
116 RAC	9th Bn Gordon Highlanders	Jul. 42	India, Burma	Post-war
141 RAC	7th Bn The Buffs	8 Nov. 41	UK, 31 Tk Brigade Nov. 41 to May 45. Converted to Crocodile Feb. 44. 2 troops to NWE 6 Jun. 44.	Post-war
142 RAC	7th Bn Suffolk Regt	8 Nov. 41	UK, 25 Tk Brigade Feb. 42 to Nov. 44. To NA Feb. 43. To Italy 18 Apr. 44.	Effectively disbanded end Dec. 44, officially 22 Jan. 45
143 RAC	9th Bn Lancs Fusiliers	Nov. 41	UK. 10 Tk Brigade Nov. 41 to Nov. 43.	11 Dec. 43
144 RAC	8th Bn East Lancs Regt	22 Nov. 41	UK. NWE 16 Jan. 45 converted to Buffalo. The Bn was used to reform 4RTR 1 Mar. 45.	1 Mar. 45
145 RAC	8th Bn Duke of Wellington's	15 Nov. 41	UK. NA, IT 21st Armoured Brigade. To North Africa 4 Apr. 43. 'Ineffective' Nov. 44.	17 Jan. 45
146 RAC	9th Bn Duke of Wellington's	15 Nov. 41	To India (Initially to 50th Indian Army Tank Brigade) 25 Oct. 41.	Feb. 47
147 RAC	10th Bn Hampshire Regt	1 Dec. 41	UK. 34 Tk Brigade Dec. 41 to May 45. To NWE 2 Jul. 44. 23, 25 Jun. 45 personnel posted to 107 RAC as B (Hampshire) Sqn.	31 Oct. 45
148 RAC	9th Bn Loyal Regt	22 Nov. 41	UK. To NWE 14 Jun. 44.	27 Aug. 44

Regiment	Original Unit	To RAC	Service	Disbandment
149 RAC	7th Bn KOYLI	Oct. 41	Poona, India. To 50th Indian Army Tank Brigade 31 Dec. 41. Kohima. Last AFV (Churchill) handed over 8 Dec. 45.	28 Feb. 46
150 RAC	10th Bn Yorks & Lancs	Oct. 41	Poona, India. All ranks 'compulsorily transferred' to RAC 26 Oct. 41. To 50th Indian Army Tank Brigade 31 Dec. 41. Imphal. Last tank handed over 10 Jan. 46.	28 Feb. 46
151 RAC	10th Bn King's Own Lancaster Regt	Jan. 42	UK, 35 Tk Brigade Jan. 42 to Jul. 42. All personnel transferred to RAC 1 Jul. 42. 11 Dec. 43 disbanded and immediately reformed as 107 RAC.	11 Dec. 43
152 RAC	11th Bn Kings Regt	Jan. 42	UK	Dec. 45
153 RAC	8th Bn Essex Regt	1 Dec. 41	UK. 34 Tk Brigade Dec. 41 to Aug. 44. NWE from 3 Jul. 44. On 19 Aug. 44, one complete sqn transferred to 107 RAC as C (Essex) Sqn. KIA 108.	Disbanded 28 Aug. 44
154 RAC	9th Bn North Staffs	Jan. 42	UK	Reverted to infantry 30 Jul. 43
155 RAC	15th Bn DLI	Jan. 42	UK. 35 Tk Brigade Jan. 42 to May 45.	13 Jul. 45
156 RAC	11th Bn HLI	1 Dec. 41	UK. 36 Tk Brigade Jan. 42 to Jul. 43.	Reverted to infantry 31 Jul. 43

Regiment	Original Unit	To RAC	Service	Disbandment
157 RAC	9th Bn Hampshires	Jan. 42	UK. 36 Tk Brigade Jan. 42 to Jul. 43.	Reverted to infantry 30 Jul. 43
158 RAC	6th Bn South Wales Borderers	Jul. 42	India	Reverted to infantry 1 Apr. 43
159 RAC	10th Bn Gloucesters	Jul. 42	India	Reverted to infantry 1 Apr. 43
160 RAC	9th Bn Royal Sussex Regt	Jul. 42	India	Reverted to infantry 1 Apr. 43
161 RAC	12th Bn Green Howards	Jul. 42	UK. Initially tanks, then armoured cars from Jul. 42.	Became 161st Regt Recce Corps 12 Oct. 43
162 RAC	9th Bn Royal West Kents	Jul. 42	UK. Armoured cars.	Reverted to infantry 20 Jul. 43
163 RAC	13th Bn Sherwood Foresters	Jul. 42	India	Reverted to infantry 1 Dec. 43

Notes: UK = United Kingdom; NWE = Europe 1944–5; NA = North Africa; IT = Sicily and Italy.

As soon as new tanks came off the production lines they were issued to units. These A13s of the Bays are committing a common yet fundamental error that would take years of operational experience to iron out – bunching.

Also belonging to the Bays, a squadron leader giving orders over the No. 11 radio set on an exercise in the UK. The cloth bands around his side cap and the turret denote that they are playing enemy.

The Household Cavalry

On the outbreak of war, the Life Guards were stationed at Hyde Park Barracks in London, with the Royal Horse Guards (The Blues) at the Cavalry Barracks, Windsor. Both units immediately came together to create one operational horsed regiment, the Household Cavalry Composite Regiment, formed on 10 September. Additionally, a ceremonial mounted element was retained in the form of the Household Cavalry Reserve Regiment although, for obvious reasons, most ceremonial duties were suspended. In order to conduct their own training, the Household Cavalry Training Regiment was also stood up, also at Windsor. Because there was insufficient manpower in the two original regiments to form these three units, roughly a hundred line cavalry reservists were called up, and the majority were posted to the Composite Regiment.

On 13 January 1940, the Composite Regiment – never a popular title – was renamed as the Household Cavalry Regiment (HCR), and early the following month was sent to Palestine. In June of the same year the Training Regiment became an operational unit known as the Household Cavalry Motor Regiment. In October 1941 both operational regiments were again renamed, the HCR becoming 1 HCR and the Motor Regiment 2 HCR; these designations were to be retained until just after the end of the war.

The HCR had already said farewell to most of their horses in Palestine in December 1940 and became a 'Motorized Cavalry regiment' in March 1941, shortly before being deployed to Iraq as part of the Habforce (Habbaniya relief force) that broke the siege of RAF Habbaniya in mid–May and then occupied Baghdad on the 31st.[18] The regiment was then involved in the occupation of Syria, assisting the Free French to wrest control of the strategically important country from their Vichy brethren.[19] Another strategic deployment to northern Persia (Iran) then followed, before the unit returned to Palestine, where it was notified that it was to become an armoured car unit on 6 February 1942. Its armoured car conversion training, for a regiment that although officially motorized was still very horse-minded and lacking mechanical experience, was assisted by the experienced 11th Hussars. Due to the reorganization, the regiment reduced from four to three sabre squadrons, and the excess manpower was posted to become 101RTR, a dummy tank unit operating in the Western Desert. Internally, the unit referred to itself as 'Smithforce' after the squadron commander, and most of the personnel seem to have managed to return to 2HCR later.

The new unit was sent to Cyprus in March 1942, remaining there until late August when it returned to Egypt. The regiment served at El Alamein in October 1942, after which it returned to northern Syria in order to patrol the Turkish border area, a thankless task in poor conditions. On 12 April 1944 it was sent to Italy, before being returned to England in mid–October 1944 in order to retrain and re-equip, prior to joining the final six weeks of the North-West Europe campaign from 16 March 1945 working within I Corps. It ended the war at Stade, on the Elbe estuary west of Hamburg.

Back in the UK, and just before being renamed 2 HCR, conversion of the Motor Regiment to become an armoured car regiment was started in September 1941. Based at Bulford, 2 HCR trained mostly with the Guards Armoured Division until deploying to France as the VIII Corps armoured car regiment on 13 July 1944, fighting with considerable distinction throughout the remainder of the campaign. For a short time in August it was converted to an infantry role, and whilst there it was visited by General Montgomery, who asked Lieutenant Peake what he thought of his new job, and probably expected a textbook answer. Instead, the doughty lieutenant replied, 'I hate it sir, and the sooner I am allowed to get back to my armoured cars, for which we have been trained, the better!' Peake was thereafter nicknamed 'The Field Marshal', and the unit did indeed return to its beloved armoured cars shortly afterwards. 2 HCR ended the war at Cuxhaven, just to the north-west of 1 HCR. Throughout the campaign, the regiment took great pride in the fact that it worked on verbal and radio orders, and issued very little in the way of written instructions, something some of the formation headquarters in the army could have learned from.

As officers and soldiers from both the Life Guards and the Royal Horse Guards were to be found mixed within both of the wartime units, it was necessary at the end of the war to reinstate the two regiments and return the personnel to their rightful regiments – even though the majority had never served in them. This happened in mid-July, when all Life Guard personnel in 2 HCR were posted to 1 HCR, now in the Goslar area, which then became the Life Guards once more at the end of August, and at the same time all RHG personnel in 1 HCR were sent to 2 HCR in Brühl, where the pre-war title was adopted, again in August.

The Armoured Foot Guards

Between September 1941 and January 1943, seven infantry battalions of the Brigade of Guards were converted to become tank regiments, for service within the Guards Armoured Division. The rationale was that as the Guards were reckoned to be the finest and most disciplined infantry, they should also show the same qualities as armoured units. During consultations in spring 1941, many Guards officers were (perhaps surprisingly) enthusiastic about the proposal, so it was definitely seen as a positive move rather than an enforced one; the divisional HQ was formed on 19 June 1941. The divisional units started to form up on 15 September in the Salisbury Plain area; the HQ was at Redlynch House near Wincanton, the 5th Guards Armoured Brigade around Warminster and Shaftesbury, the 6th Guards Tank Brigade at Codford, and the support elements around Castle Cary and Frome, with 2 HCR located in Bulford. Once in their stride, a divisional training wing was formed at Pirbright, starting instruction on 29 November 1941. After completing the process of converting and training in the UK, the division joined the North-West Europe campaign in July 1944 and fought there for the rest of the war.[20]

In mid-1943, the 2nd Bn Welsh Guards became the armoured (tank) divisional reconnaissance regiment and thus was not brigaded. Within the Division in North-West Europe was one armoured brigade in the order of battle. The 5th Guards Armoured Brigade had been converted from the 20th Infantry Brigade on 15 September 1941, and consisted of the 2nd (Armoured) Bn Grenadier Guards, the 1st (Armoured) Bn Coldstream Guards, and the 2nd (Armoured) Bn Irish Guards. The brigade was equipped with Sherman tanks in North-West Europe. Separately, the 6th Guards Tank Brigade had been formed from the 30th Infantry Brigade and was employed in an independent role equipped with Churchill tanks for the North-West Europe campaign, consisting of the 4th Bn Grenadier Guards, 4th Bn Coldstream Guards and the 3rd Bn Scots Guards.[21] On 9 June 1945 the division and its constituent parts reverted to the infantry role, holding a splendid final 'Farewell to Armour' parade at Rotenburg airfield.

The Reconnaissance Corps

Officially raised on 14 January 1941, the Recce Corps was formed to provide vehicle-mounted reconnaissance forces for infantry divisions, and the role was seen to be sufficiently different to armoured car reconnaissance to warrant the formation of a separate corps. Over twenty regiments were formed, either from a complete infantry battalion, or from the three anti-tank companies within an infantry brigade brought together as a regiment. The regiments mostly bore the number of the infantry division that they supported: 1st, 2nd, 3rd, 4th, 5th, 15th, 18th, 38th, 43rd, 44th, 45th, 46th, 49th, 50th, 51st, 52nd, 53rd, 54th, 56th, 59th, 61st, 80th and 161st. The 38th and 80th were both holding regiments rather than operational units. Corps training was conducted separately to the RAC, initially at No. 1 Reconnaissance Training Centre at Winchester and later at Loch Maben in Scotland. A second training centre was then formed at Scarborough as 63rd Reconnaissance Training Regiment, but in August 1943 both centres closed and relocated as a single entity in Catterick. Although it ran its own Officer Cadet Training Unit (102 OCTU), from 1942 all potential officers for the corps went via the RAC OCTU, and from this point the writing was on the wall. By October 1943 questions were being raised about the future of the corps as an independent organization. Two options were presented: absorbing the corps into the RAC, or allowing it to continue as a part of the RAC, in the manner of the RTR (in which case it may have become the Reconnaissance Regiment). On 1 January 1944, the Recce Corps was formally absorbed into the RAC (AO277/43), although this was frequently as much de jure as de facto, and many units managed to retain their dress distinctions, including wearing a khaki (occasionally green) beret and corps cap badge, for many months. Despite the incorporation, the corps did manage to retain its existence as 'a corps within a corps' to some degree until it was finally disbanded as part of the reduction of the wartime RAC back to its peacetime size. The corps was given notification of the decision that it was to 'waste' down on 21 September 1945, finally disbanding on 1 August 1946.

Training the Armoured Soldier

Until 1938, the demanding basic training syllabus for a new RTC tank crewman lasted between twenty-four and twenty-seven weeks; this training took place at the RTC Depot in Bovington, and also at the nearby Gunnery Wing at Lulworth, and gave every recruit a really solid grounding in the basic tank skills. This included eight weeks of general military training; three weeks of basic driving and maintenance; and then six weeks in their specialized trade skill of either gunnery or driving.[22] The course finished with four weeks of collective training, which, despite their recruit status, covered tactics and the handling of armour. During 1938, as the prospect of war increased, so did the pressure on an expanding training base: in the training year 1938/39 1,450 recruits passed through Bovington and Lulworth to go to field force units, representing a huge increase over the peacetime steady-state.

On 1 April 1937, the British army had established a new Armoured Fighting Vehicle School, located at Bovington (the Wireless and Driving & Maintenance wings) and at Lulworth (the Gunnery wing). In April 1939, following the formation of the corps, the RTC Depot at Bovington was renamed the RAC

Depot. On 11 September 1939 it was again renamed, to become the 52nd Training Regiment RAC; around this time many more RAC Training Regiments were formed to cope with the sheer numbers needing to be trained. Eventually eleven training regiments were in operation:

- 51st (Infantry tanks, Catterick). On 1 January 1944 it became a combined RAC/Recce Corps training unit[23]
- 52nd (US tanks and from March 1942 the Middle East preparation and holding unit). Originally formed 11 September 1939 at Bovington
- 53rd (Cruiser tanks, Tidworth, later Catterick). Disbanded in December 1943
- 54th (Cruiser tanks, Perham Down, then Deerbolt Camp, Barnard Castle)
- 55th (Cruiser tanks, Farnborough)
- 56th (Infantry tanks, Catterick). Disbanded mid-July 1943
- 57th (Infantry tanks, Tidworth/Warminster, later Waitwith Camp, Catterick). Disbanded July 1943
- 58th (All tank types, Young Soldiers and Potential Officer Selection, from November 1941 at Stanley Barracks Bovington, later moved to Farnborough)
- 59th (Armoured Cars from November 1942, Barford Camp, Barnard Castle)
- 60th (Pre-OCTU. Valentine Tanks, Tidworth, later Shaiba Camp, Catterick). Disbanded July 1943
- 61st (Cruiser tanks, Tidworth, later Streatlam Camp, Barnard Castle)[24]

The reason for the move of some of the regiments to the north of England during July and August 1942 was to allow space for Operation Bolero, the movement of US army personnel into the west and south of England. By 1941, the training of RAC crewmen had been reduced in both length and complexity: at the height of the war, about 2,000 recruits arrived at Bovington every month to commence training, with around 300 of these going on to pre-Officer Cadet Training Unit (pre-OCTU) and about 250 to the OCTUs themselves.[25] The demand at this stage of the war was huge: the RAC expansion had resulted in there being over a hundred major units within the RAC, with an authorized holding of 6,707 AFVs.

From 1941 until mid-1942, primary training took place at one of the many RAC Training Regiments.[26] This usually lasted for between six and twelve weeks. For example, at the 30th Primary Training Wing (PTW) at Bovington, the training was mainly run by RAC instructors with some infantry assistance, and the main elements in the syllabus were: kit issue, drill, weapon training (both .303 rifle and the Bren LMG), drill, anti-gas precautions, physical training (PT) including gym, forced marches and sports (but not much running), basic map reading, more drill and of course kit inspections, with a lot of emphasis still placed on turnout and what the army calls bearing – producing a soldier who took pride in their appearance, sometimes to a ridiculous degree. At the Bovington PTW in January 1943, Norman Smith recorded his disgust at having to wear 'a badge of ignominy', the General Service cap badge in brown plastic, rather than the 'shining silver metal of the RAC', which he only got to wear once he completed PTW and moved to the 58th Training Regiment RAC.[27] After successfully completing PMT, the recruits then spent a further three weeks undergoing General Military Training, or GMT. In 1942 the syllabus for this included more drill, more PT, camouflage, further map reading, basic wireless, wheeled vehicle driving and sometimes motorcycle riding, and various medical inspections and inoculations. The weapons covered varied with time, but could include the Boys A/T rifle, revision on the Bren LMG, hand grenades (sometimes including throwing these from the turrets of AFVs), the Sten and Thompson sub-machine guns, and the personal weapon, the .38in pistol. After completing GMT recruits could then finally start training to become tank or armoured car crew members.

In many cases, it was discovered that recruits could progress to this point and then be found to be unsuitable for the increasingly technical training they were faced with, which was clearly a waste of time and resources. Therefore, from July 1942, all new army recruits first attended an Elementary Selection Unit which

Physical training was a large element of all types of basic training, and in the era before gymnasiums became common, most PT took the form of outdoor exercise.

decided on their aptitude and placed them into a corps that they were deemed to be suitable for; they then underwent a centralized basic recruit course (aka Primary Training) regardless of which arm they were intended for, before being posted to a Training Regiment and beginning their specialized training.[28] There is no doubt that many recruits opted for the RAC as it was seen to be new, dynamic and reasonably technical. The allure of certain famous cavalry regiments also came into it, although soldiers were not always guaranteed the regiment of their choice. From 1941 some of the regiments in UK were able to send their vehicle fitters, motor mechanics and electricians (this was a year before the formation of REME, and these trades were found within regimental personnel as well as the RAOC) to receive vehicle-specific training with civilian firms for up to six weeks, prior to continuation training at the AFV School or the RAC Specialist Training Unit. Tactical training was usually only conducted for personnel selected to be tank commanders, and then frequently of a rudimentary variety, concentrating on drills and minor tactics but leaving little scope for initiative, which was to prove to be a major failing, of which more later.

Basic principles of how engines worked formed a large part of D&M instruction.

An RTR instructor with a crew of trainees learning about the Vickers medium machine gun on the Matilda II tank.

By mid-war, the output required from the training regiments was huge, with well over 20,000 recruits per year being needed for the RAC. In the second half of 1942 the RAC Training Regiments trained personnel in the following trades:

Driver Mechanics	1,883
Driver Operators	2,171
Gunner Mechanics	711
Gunner Operators	1,352
Drivers	2,906
Gunners	672
Electricians, Fitters and Motor Mechanics	375
Technical Storemen	74
Motorcyclists	61
Other trades	116
TOTAL	10,321

In order to efficiently train soldiers in all these trades, the RAC Training Regiments were divided into different wings, one each for the three main tank trades – gunnery; signals/wireless; and driving and maintenance. Each of these wings taught the two main elements of each trade: the servicing and maintenance of the equipment, including how to make repairs, and the use of the equipment for the purpose for which it was designed, i.e. shooting the guns, driving the tank and using the wireless to communicate. Norman Smith recorded that, in early 1943, all three trades were taught simultaneously, which he agreed with, as it allowed the recruit 'to evolve as a tankie equally and at the same rate in each of the main disciplines'.[29] It may come as a surprise, but it appears that for the first half of the war, many recruits were not formally tested in the trades they had learned before being posted to units; it seems that the criteria was simply to complete the training course. It was not until late 1943 or early 1944 that formal trade tests were introduced with a pass/fail criteria. The results from this change were worrying; of Driver Operators, only 59 per cent passed the final test, and only 53 per cent of Gunner Operators. Things were even worse with the mechanic trades: only 36 per cent of Driver Mechanics and 26 per cent of Gunner Mechanics were able to pass the test. This could of course reflect an over strict testing criteria, but it did help to highlight a problem of competence and allowed training to be modified to improve standards – and pass rates.[30]

Once training was completed, most recruits were posted, usually after a short period of leave, straight to their regiments – there was an element of choice in the selection, but it was never guaranteed.[31] The unfortunate surplus personnel were sent to 'the infamous and enormous' RAC Holding Unit in Catterick, where they remained in limbo until they were posted to a unit. It was the task of the field force units to integrate these newly trained and inexperienced soldiers into effective crews, the regiments had to provide such continuation training as they felt necessary; it was very much up to the unit to decide exactly how this should be done, and there is no doubt that this varied enormously between units. Once

Wireless training was possibly the most complicated of the three trades, with the brainier trainees selected to specialize in the subject. This student is working on the excellent No. 19 wireless set, which equipped most British AFVs from 1942 onwards.

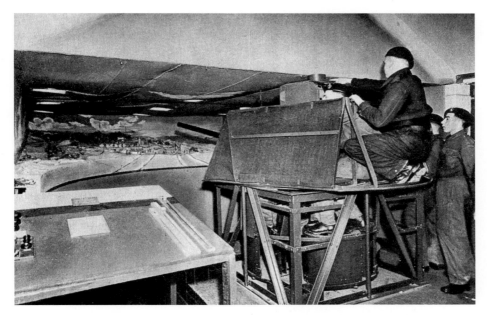

The field miniature range or FMR was the only real simulator used in training, and fired an air rifle onto targets on a sand table.

in a unit, other, strange and esoteric training sometimes took place, for example, 150 RAC received 'an interesting, exciting and amusing lecture given to Officers and N.C.O.s by Captain Instone, M.M. Intelligence Corps, on his experiences on his escape from France'. Even more arcane instruction was noted in the war diary of the Airborne Light Tank Squadron RAC, which recorded that on 11 May 1943, 'sewing instruction given to all troops by the manageress of the YWCA'.

It should be noted that in the dark days of the second half of 1940, such a sophisticated and centralized system of selection and training was not possible. Peter Beale remembered the formation of 9RTR in the immediate aftermath of Dunkirk:

> Later in the war most civilians who joined a tank unit went first to a training regiment, where they learnt the basic military skills and the technical tank skills … life in late 1940 was more urgent, and 9RTR had to do all this training itself … after basic training, technical wings were formed to teach the three basic tank skills.[32]

Instructor qualification courses in the three trades were also run at Bovington and at the Gunnery Wing at Lulworth for both officers and NCOs, thereby allowing training courses to be run within regiments; these lasted about seven weeks and produced many extremely competent instructors.[33] Edward Wilson described a break from active operations in Libya during January 1943, 'There was an intensive training programme, coupled with shoots for all tanks on the range, lectures for all tank commanders on mines and gunnery, [and] sand-table exercises …'.[34] The 5RTR War Diary for 7 July 1944 during a break from active fighting in Normandy recorded, 'Regimental courses: wireless, D&M and gunnery commenced in tank area.'[35] A similar entry for 17–19 November of the same year read, 'This period was utilised for re-organization and training, including courses in wireless, driving and maintenance, and gunnery.'

In Egypt, an RAC School was set up at the pre-war tank barracks in Abbassia, Cairo, to avoid the ridiculous situation of having to send soldiers to the UK for instruction; it was responsible for providing individual courses and to control conversion training to new AFVs as they entered service; many of the conversion courses for the new American tanks were organized there.[36] Other schools were established as required; for example, in 1944 an RAC School was established in Rieti, north-east of Rome, and a Far East RAC School was also set up in Ghorpuri near Poona, India. This last establishment had a reputation for unnecessary 'bullshit' and in late September 1943 was commanded by 'a cavalryman, [who] hated tanks'. Fred Thompson recorded that:

> I watched one old soldier carefully run a cigarette packet over his hose tops to make sure they were turned over at the same length. We all wore Khaki Drill, boots were polished, and webbing was scrubbed and bleached in the sun and virgin white. Brasses were polished to maximum brightness. All of this for men who were going up to the Burmese jungle to fight the Japanese. They were ready made targets for snipers … Topees were worn all day, our cherished berets were forbidden … [we were] introduced to the Grant, the Lee and the Honey … the extinguishers were often removed as the crews had found that the CTC extinguishant was ideal for removing the stains from coveralls and KD … I was posted away after about three months at Poona … KD had gone, jungle green replaced it.[37]

In the field, replacements for casualties could be brought into a unit as an individual or as part of a complete crew, with tank or armoured car as well if necessary. In North-West Europe, for example, the 2nd Armoured Replacement Unit was responsible for channelling forward RAC reinforcements through the Army, Corps and Forward Delivery Squadrons. 2ARU consisted of 99 personnel on its permanent staff and was capable of administering and holding up to 1,500 personnel at a time, ready for rapid postings to wherever the need lay.

Officer Selection

Because almost everyone joined the army as a conscript private soldier during the Second World War, the 'system' was very aware that the officers for a much-enlarged army would have to be found from within the ranks. As the pamphlet dealing with the selection of potential officers (POs) stated in late 1941:

> The importance of finding suitable personnel serving in the ranks for training as officers has been constantly stressed since the outbreak of war … Where men who are fitted to hold commissions have not been earmarked as potential officers, and the necessary procedures carried out, then it shows both a failure of duty and a failure to appreciate one of the essential needs towards the complete war effort. In no circumstances will a potential officer be held back on the grounds that he cannot be spared from a unit … The duty of finding suitable men rests with the CO and subordinate commanders … The lives of men and the efficiency of the army depends on a high standard of leadership, and only those individuals with personality, power of command, intelligence, and ability must be selected. The qualities of leadership are made up of character, knowledge, and confidence.[38]

In broad terms, once a unit commanding officer identified a PO, they were placed on a conveyor belt system designed to train them as an officer, or to deliver them back into the Field Army as an other rank, as effectively as possible. A PO were only meant to be selected from corporals and above, as NCOs could be expected to have had opportunities to demonstrate leadership, although it seems that this rule was not always obeyed, particularly when a PO was identified very early in their basic training. There were certain preconceived ideas of what a PO should look like; as Todman noted, 'Officer selection was a matter of meeting upper-middle-class social mores as well as displaying military aptitude'.[39] As soon as each PO was identified, regardless of cap badge, he was to be given 'a course of instruction in motorcycle riding and MT maintenance', and the candidate also had to be at fully trained soldier status. In the RAC, specific requirements were made; the soldier should not be over 30 years of age, unless he possessed 'exceptional qualifications', and he had to be in medical categories A1 or A2, because of 'the strain which training and operation in AFV involves, outstanding physical fitness [is] essential'. Ideally, technical knowledge of 'motor vehicles and/ or wireless or mechanical ability is desirable, owing to the amount of mechanical knowledge which has to be assimilated in a short space of time'.[40]

Before being sent to one of the RAC Officer Cadet Training Units (OCTU), the candidate had to pass the massive hurdle of the War Office Selection Board or WOSB. This was an interview panel headed by an RAC officer of at least the rank of lieutenant colonel, and many fell at this hurdle. Within the RAC, the 58th Training Regiment at Stanley Barracks, Bovington, conducted pre-selection for volunteer Potential Officers, with an intense six-month course in which not only the main tank trades were taught, but also a four-week period was spent dealing with minor tactics and AFV commanding. WOSB was undertaken

For reasons best known to the War Office, all Potential Officers were required to be able to ride a motorbike – it is not clear whether it was compulsory to smoke whilst doing so.

towards the end of this period. On successful completion the candidates moved to the pre-OCTU at Blackdown (later Bulford, and from late 1942 located in Brasenose College, Oxford, before moving once again to Oriel College in December 1943).[41] This lasted another twelve weeks, and only then the candidates moved on to Sandhurst to the Officer Cadet Training Unit (OCTU), for officer training proper – which all too often turned out to be just more of the same.

With war looming, in early July 1939 both the senior and intermediate terms at RMC Sandhurst received immediate commissions, and on 26 August 1939 the junior term returned to the college for a final six weeks of accelerated training after which they too were commissioned. This was the last regular pass-out held until after 1945. On 4 September 1939 the RMC became OCTU Sandhurst, with two wings: 101 OCTU for the RAC, and 161 for the infantry (with two companies allocated to the Brigade of Guards, which included the Household Cavalry).[42] On the same day the Inns of Court Yeomanry arrived to take on the responsibility of running 101 OCTU, with two squadrons; at this point, the cadets only did their wireless training at Sandhurst, and had to go to Bovington for both D&M and gunnery training.[43] Once posted to the OCTU, all candidates became Cadets, with their previous rank removed so that all were equal; white side cap and shoulder bands designated their status; from 1941 RAC black berets with white diamond cap-badge backings were worn.

HM King George VI takes a ride in a Universal Carrier; these vehicles were frequently used in training establishments to teach the rudiments of tracked vehicle driving.

By 1941 three RAC OCTUs were operating; in addition to 101 at Sandhurst, 102 was at Blackdown Camp, Camberley, and 103 was at Perham Down, near Tidworth. In July 1942, a review of the capacity needed by the RAC OCTUs calculated that to match the expansion of the RAC, the output would need to nearly double, with 1,750 new officers required. This led to the relocation of the infantry 161 OCTU to Mons Barracks, Aldershot, and, one week later, on 27 July, the closure of both 102 and 103 which moved their resources to Sandhurst. The new larger unit, now called the RAC OCTU (Sandhurst), quickly revised the accommodation to make it more suitable for AFV training.[44] At this point the OCTU only held 23 Light tanks and a few carriers; soon it would hold over 200 vehicles. The armoured wing delivered tank training and comprised three squadrons. Another squadron produced officers for armoured car units, and from October 1942, 162 OCTU (HAC) joined the set-up as a fifth squadron, responsible for the Recce Corps cadets.

From mid-war the RAC OCTU course ran like this: the first five weeks were GMT – the even shinier and more-blancoed Sandhurst version. The final week of GMT culminated in a week-long infantry live-firing battle exercise at Capel Curig in North Wales, and all the cadets climbed Mount Snowdon. This was followed by four weeks of D&M, and then another four weeks of wireless. After a much-needed week's leave (recognized as necessary to prevent complete

RAC Potential Officers studying signals at an OCTU. Understanding radio was a key part of an officer's training, although far too much time was spent on learning Morse code.

overload and burn-out), four weeks of gunnery training followed, with the fifth week spent live firing on the ranges at Warcop. The final seven weeks at OCTU were spent on collective training, allowing the cadets to bring all aspects of the course together, along with subjects such as administration in camp and in the field, tactics, three Tactical Exercises Without Troops (TEWT) and a visit to the School of Tank Technology to view captured enemy equipment. Every two weeks there was a formal pass-out parade for the successful ones – the course could still be failed in the final week. Cadets had to continue to show officer qualities throughout, and those failing to come up to the right standard could find themselves 'relegated' (usually known as back-squadding) for additional training, returned to their unit with a recommendation to try again after not less than three months or be failed outright, known as RTU – returned to unit. Successful candidates – the majority – received Emergency Commissions and were posted to a unit; it seems that unlike ORs, most newly commissioned RAC officers were not allowed to specify a preferred regiment and were instead sent to where the need was, unless there was a definite family link.[45] The best student on each course received a Sam Browne belt signed by the inspecting general, and then after a short leave, the newly minted second lieutenant was sent to his unit. Between 27 July 1942 and 15 August 1945 (VJ Day), the unit produced 4,412 commissioned officers, with another 320 failing the 6-month long course and being RTU, a 7 per cent failure rate.[46] Naturally, the Household Cavalry (and Foot Guards) were an exception to this system. Rather than be recommended by their CO and then go through WOSB, POs were interviewed by the major general commanding the Brigade of Guards, and successful applicants were then posted directly to the Guards OCTU.[47]

The top student on each PO course was awarded a Sam Browne belt, signed by the inspecting officer.

A different route applied to those 'commissioned in the field', the appellation generally used for those receiving an immediate Emergency Commission from the ranks of non-commissioned and warrant officers. This allowed COs to fill gaps in their ranks by commissioning suitable NCOs and WOs without having to pass WOSB or be trained at an OCTU. Such soldiers could be commissioned, usually up to the age of 40; for example, 27-year-old WO2 (RQMS) Bill Close of 3RTR, a pre-war regular, recorded his experience:

> We also received several replacement troop officers [after the Battle of Sidi Rezegh in November 1941] though more were needed. I and another Sergeant [*sic*], Bud Harned, who had won the DCM, were recommended for immediate commissions by our squadron commanders ... We were interviewed by our CO, seen by the Divisional Commander, Major Gen Jock Campbell VC, and approved. ... The paperwork was completed on the spot and we merely went from the sergeants' mess into the officers' mess. I drew my special kit allowance of £48, had two day's leave in Cairo, got myself re-kitted and reported back to my new squadron commander, Major Jim Hutton, sporting two shiny new pips on each shoulder. As I had been commissioned from the rank of WOII I automatically became the senior subaltern in the battalion with the rank of full lieutenant.

Bill Close was a typical example of an experienced and proven soldier correctly being identified for a commission; he had already fought in France in 1940, in

North Africa since 1941 and in the debacle in Greece in the same year. He went on to become an extremely able squadron commander in his old regiment right up until the end of the war in Europe, winning two Military Crosses in the process. As a temporary major and having been commissioned in the field, he knew that he was very unlikely to be granted a regular commission despite his outstanding record, but could not return to the ranks, and so left the army at the age of 30, becoming a captain in the TA.

Even fairly late in the war, the training given, both initial and continuation, was not always the most appropriate for either officer or soldier. William Brownlie, a subaltern with 2FFY serving on Shermans in North-West Europe, recalled:

> … being told that I was going to Lulworth for a gunnery course on a new British tank. Reveille was at 6, and at 9.30 I was in a jeep heading for Ostend. All the others on the draft were from units equipped with Cromwells, and I was doubtful that we would switch from American to British tanks at that stage in the war. I therefore concluded that I was there by mistake, but naturally said nothing, with the prospect of a cushy course followed by leave at home. While at Lulworth, I spent as much time on a course dealing with the new Sherman 76mm gun as on that of the Comet 77mm, reasoning that this would be more likely to be of use. I was wrong and was slightly taken aback on returning to my regiment to find myself addressing the senior officers of the brigade as a kind of technical adviser on the new Comet, as well as being Regimental Gunnery Officer for the re-equipping, which was to take place back in Belgium.

A major failing of the training system throughout the war – and for tank and armoured car commanders in particular – seems to have been the lack of realistic vehicle-based exercises in which low-level fire and movement could be demonstrated and then practised. Rather, there was a great deal of reliance on lectures, sand-table exercises and TEWTs, which were necessary, but which lacked realism. An RAC Officer's Tactical School was eventually founded, located firstly in Bulford, and then relocating to Brasenose College, Oxford, in November 1942, before moving once more in July 1943 to Oriel College; it eventually ended up at Lulworth in late June 1944. However, it could only deal with about 500 students a year, so the majority of RAC officers never attended such formal armoured tactical training. Thus, the burden for producing competent troop and tank commanders was devolved to the operational regiments themselves, with all the obvious pitfalls that this method involved, particularly for a unit which received replacements whilst actively engaged in operations.

Chapter Three

Up the Blue

The North African Campaign, 1940–3

At the outbreak of war in September 1939, British Troops Egypt included the newly created Egypt Mobile Division Egypt, renamed the 7th Armoured Division on 16 February 1940, and better known from their formation sign as the Desert Rats. The Mobile Division had been created by Percy Hobart and consisted of the Cavalry Brigade (7th Hussars, 8th Hussars and 11th Hussars, which became the Light Armoured Brigade in February 1940, and two months later, the 7th Armoured Brigade) and the Tank Group (1RTR and 6RTR, which was renamed the Heavy Armoured Brigade in February 1940, and became the 4th Armoured Brigade in April).[1] This small formation, experienced in desert conditions, was to change its order of battle frequently over the coming months, but was to provide the nucleus around which a whole desert army was to grow, eventually to become the famous Eighth Army – but that was in the future.

The conditions in the North African desert were, according to Field Marshal Sir Michael Carver RTR, 'unlike any other in which they had previously been engaged … Nobody, senior or junior, had any experience of highly mobile operations, ranging over wide areas, in which tanks fought each other.'[2] The distances were huge; from the vast British camps in the Nile delta to the Libya/Tunisia frontier is around 1,500 miles; the desert area in between was referred to by the old hands as 'the blue'.[3] The most

The 8th King's Royal Irish Hussars were old desert hands by the outbreak of war. Here is a squadron officers' mess in the desert, the wearing of the distinctive Tent Hat being de rigeur. In the original it is possible to pick out the swarms of flies captured by the camera.

notable feature of much of this area was the coastal escarpment, a rocky cliff that in places was up to 450ft high and impassable to vehicles other than where passes had been created to allow the passage of a coastal road, such as at Sidi Rezegh and Halfaya Pass – 'Hellfire' to the troops. Ancient tracks and caravan routes criss-crossed the area, and modern man had improved those by placing occasional signposts or lines of oil drums to mark the way, but the majority of the area remained devoid of features. It is also surprisingly rocky, the sweeping sand dunes of Lawrence of Arabia can sometimes be encountered but mainly in the great sand sea to the southern flank, impassable to all but the best-prepared traveller.

Fortunately, the pre-war experience gained by the troops stationed in Egypt gave the British a head start in working in the extreme conditions, and the long-range patrols and expeditions organized by the 12th Lancers, 11th Hussars and the RTC units all helped to better understand desert navigation, logistic requirements and equipment challenges.[4] General Hobart's training of the Mobile Division in Egypt was critical to its future, and when he was unfairly replaced in late 1939 he left behind a new formation, poorly equipped with mostly obsolete vehicles and equipment, but which nonetheless could still be described by an admirer as 'the best trained formation I had ever seen'.[5] For the next three years the deserts, hills and wastes of western Egypt, Libya and finally Tunisia would become a battleground that was viewed as vitally important by Churchill and was the scene of fierce combat.[6] The RAC was to be front and centre in these battles, and if there was ever a predominantly armoured campaign fought by the British, this was to be it.

Italy declared war on Britain on 10 June 1940, which immediately threated Egypt, the Suez Canal and the whole Middle East area under British control, as very large Italian forces were stationed in Libya. The moment war was declared the 11th Hussars in their ancient Rolls-Royce armoured cars crossed 'the wire', the boundary between Egypt and Libya, and began aggressive patrolling and raiding; the 7th Armoured Division had already moved up to the area around Mersa Matruh in order to conduct more intensive training in preparation for hostilities. On the 14th the 7th Hussars captured Fort Capuzzo, taking over 200 prisoners, and during which attack 'those cruiser tanks lucky enough to have guns bombarded the walls of the fortress with 2-Pounders', which tells us that some of their new cruisers must have been supplied without main armament, and probably deployed armed with MGs only. They did not always have it their way, as the armoured car equipped 11th Hussars recorded when investigating Fort Maddalena:

On June 13th when TSM Clarke and his troop had driven up almost to the front door – within 500 yards of the main gate – they had been met by concentrated fire from what turned out to be a dozen machine guns;

then they had been chased back across the wire by six Caproni bombers and nine Fiat fighters. At this time, the *Regia Aeronautica* had complete air superiority.[7]

But mere pin-prick attacks and short-duration raids were not going to be the solution. Partly as the result of an extremely timid (and mainly symbolic) Italian excursion into western Egypt in September, General Richard O'Connor launched an offensive with his Western Desert Force.[8] This was called Operation Compass, and began against the Italians at Sidi Barrani on 8 December 1940, taking advantage of the Italian reluctance to engage in mobile warfare, as well as their weakness in tanks, most of which were light two-man tankettes, and all of which were unfit for modern war. Designed initially as a large scale five-day raid to reduce the threat to Egypt from General Berti's Tenth Army in western Egypt and eastern Libya, O'Connor reinforced his early success by pushing ever westward, and the operation culminated in the stunning success at Beda Fomm on 7 February 1941, in which 25,000 prisoners were captured, despite the British only having 1 regiment of Infantry tanks, 7RTR, and as few as 22 cruisers, 45 Light tanks and the single armoured car regiment.[9] The wide-ranging armoured car patrols, adept at avoiding contact with the Italians, became expert at reporting useful intelligence – they 'became a force-multiplier of considerable magnitude'.[10] At the end of Beda Fomm, the troops were exhausted, vehicle availability precarious, and as strategic priorities had changed because of the need to assist Greece, it was

The 1924 Pattern Rolls-Royce armoured cars formed the mainstay of armoured car operations in North Africa for the first year or so.

decided not to try to exploit the success any further. However, an unfortunate side-effect of Compass came about because of the ease with which the much larger Italian forces had been defeated by a small but aggressive force. The Italians had made life easy for O'Connor: aside from their artillery which was well managed and frequently deadly, the other components of the Italian army were of a very low standard, with an over reliance on fortified, static positions that were able to be isolated and then defeated in detail, as well as a lack of fighting spirit. The big problem was that the short campaign seemed to reinforce the notion that war in the desert could best be conducted with tanks exclusively, and that operating as a balanced, all-arms formation was not necessary. This was soon to prove a fallacy both in attack and defence, and the next two years were spent in trying to determine the best structure for the brigades and divisions, to meet the challenges not just from the enemy but also from the conditions and logistic issues.[11] This problem persisted and was much magnified when the Germans arrived, and according to Carver, when discussing the Cauldron battles of summer 1942:

> Time and again our attacks on the enemy, even against the Italian Ariete division, proved completely ineffective and resulted only in heavy casualties. It has been generally assumed that our failure was due to the enemy's great superiority in tank and anti-tank guns. That the Germans were at an advantage in the case of anti-tank guns, with their 88mm and 50mm guns, is true, but the number of each was not very great and they were not invulnerable. The total number of 88mm guns in the whole Panzer Army was probably never more than forty, and not all of these were used in an anti-tank role. ...[The 88mm was] a high, conspicuous and comparatively immobile anti-aircraft gun, particularly vulnerable to HE fire. Our real weakness was the failure to develop tactics for a concentrated attack, employing tanks, artillery and infantry in depth on a narrow front. Time and again tanks motored or charged at the enemy on a broad front, until the leading troops were knocked out by enemy tanks or anti-tank guns; the momentum of attack immediately failed ... Artillery indulged in some ineffective spattering of the enemy, after which the tanks motored about or charged again with the same results as before, the infantry taking no part, their task being to follow up and occupy the objective after it had been captured by the tanks. It is little wonder that the tank crews became demoralized at being sent over to charge against enemy guns ... If the attacks had been carried out by successive brigades which had stayed grouped together throughout, supported by a concentrated artillery plan, is there any doubt but that it could have succeeded in completely defeating the Afrika Korps? But instead, only a small proportion of the strength available was used, the tanks and the infantry operated completely independently, and nothing but disaster resulted.[12]

Strategically, the biggest problem with Compass was that it was too successful. The decision by Hitler to deploy armoured forces to Libya was taken in response to the transparent success of the offensive, for which planning had started much earlier; as early as autumn 1940 the Germans were conducting contingency planning in case of the need to send forces to Libya to support their Italian ally; they clearly had a low opinion of Italian fighting power even before Compass was launched. On 9 January 1941 Hitler stated that he intended to send armour to 'block' the British. He was not so much interested in the Italians being militarily defeated as he was in the political ramifications of such a defeat, fearing that it could topple Mussolini and hand the Mediterranean theatre to Britain on a plate. Two days later he issued Directive No. 22, ordering the preparation of a *Sperrverband* (blocking detachment) for movement to Tripoli. On 3 February, just before the culmination of the campaign at Beda Fomm, he directed the Wehrmacht to deploy the formation to Libya, and, without consulting the army high command, decided that Rommel was to command the force. *Unternehmen Sonnenblume* (Operation Sunflower) was the codename allocated for the operation. On 19 February the force was given the name *Deutsches Afrika Korps* (DAK), a title which would go down in history, not least because of Rommel's aggressive, often foolhardy, handling of it. The deployment was meant to be defensive: Rommel was ordered to block further British advances westward, and to be prepared to assume offensive operations to recapture Cyrenaica – but only in due course and, although not made implicit, following orders from Berlin. As is well known, he disregarded his orders and immediately went on the offensive. The British view of what he was likely to do was actually much more realistic than Berlin's orders; in a 5 March intelligence report issued just after the arrival of the first German troops, the three likely tasks identified for the DAK were to ensure the safety of Tripolitania, to recapture Cyrenaica and to invade Egypt.

The first batch of tanks belonging to the two battalions of Panzer Regiment 5 had arrived in Tripoli on 11 March, mainly up-armoured Panzer III Medium tanks but with many light Panzer II models as well, and also heavy armoured cars. A second Panzer regiment was transferred from Italy but was not complete in Libya until 6 May 1941 with a total of 132 Medium tanks; this was part of the 5th Light Division (renamed 21st Panzer Division on 1 August).[13] The appearance of these larger German tanks mounting the short 50mm gun came as a rude shock to the British, who were dismissive of the capabilities of the 37mm tank gun following their experiences in France, but who were nowhere near getting their own 57mm 6-pounder into service. As well as the version mounted on tanks, the standard German towed anti-tank gun was now the 50mm, introduced as a result of the Battle of France, and capable of penetrating the until-now virtually impregnable Matilda frontally and the thinly armoured Cruisers and Light tanks at almost any range. This gun, small and both easily moved and concealed, was to become the scourge of the British armoured forces, much more so than the fearsome 88mm which was much larger, harder to move and conceal, and available in only limited quantities. Following Compass, the entry of the Germans into the theatre changed the situation completely, and for the next eighteen months the outcome was in the balance, and more often than not it felt like a defeat was in the offing. But even before the Germans made their presence felt, another theatre of war was to have a huge impact on the desert campaign: Greece.

Greece and Crete, 1941

Two RAC regiments from the 1st Armoured Brigade, the 4th Hussars and 3RTR, were deployed to Greece in early March 1941, the former on Light tanks and the latter on Cruisers. Neither type was suitable for the terrain or the opposition. Bob Crisp, who went on to earn a rare DSO as a lieutenant with 3RTR during the campaign, described his A9 tanks as 'impressive-looking [but] near obsolete cruisers' – despite them being no more than two years old.[14] During the brief campaign he was to witness at first-hand some of the problems that made the tanks so unreliable:

> [After their first move] five tanks were left lying out in the vineyards with hopelessly broken tracks … My right-hand tank edged slowly forward [and I heard a voice] in the ear-phones: 'Hullo *Cool*, this is *Collected* calling, I have broken a track' … I told the driver to start up. The starter whirred and stopped. There was no answering roar from the engine. 'We've had it sir, ruddy petrol pump's unserviceable …'. We were about to destroy the tank for want of a flipping petrol pump.

The decision to deploy the tanks to Greece, as part of a nearly 60,000-strong British Expeditionary Force, was a purely political one, and it seems incredible with hindsight to imagine that anyone believed that military success was achievable. Once the German invasion commenced on 6 April, the two RAC units lost at least as many tanks to breakdown or through running out of fuel as from direct enemy action, and for those who had fought in France less than a year previously, the experience brought back awful memories of the Luftwaffe domination of the air. Fortunately, the majority of the RAC crews were able to be evacuated back to Egypt, leaving all their tanks behind; the campaign was over in little more than two weeks.

Nine Matilda II tanks belonging to 7RTR and sixteen Light tanks of C Squadron 3rd Hussars were deployed around the same time to bolster the defences on Crete, as that island had become vulnerable to invasion, and despite fighting as

CALM was the troop sergeant's tank in C Sqn 3RTR in Greece. Like so many others, it had to be abandoned after a relatively minor mishap, in this case a broken track. Early war British tanks were notoriously unreliable, the endemic problem only being solved in late 1943.

well as they could to defend the vital aerodromes on the island, they were penny-packeted and all were lost after fierce fighting, when the Germans succeeded in capturing the island by airborne assault in late May. The loss of Greece and then Crete created difficulties in the eastern Mediterranean, where the Royal Navy based in Alexandria had until then enjoyed dominance, but now became vulnerable to air attack. Operationally – and, in hindsight, strategically too – the reduction in British tank strength to reinforce Greece and Crete could not have come at a worse moment.

The First Axis Offensive in North Africa

In order to send the 2 regiments to Greece and then the smaller detachment to Crete, totalling 129 tanks, Wavell in Cairo had to seriously deplete his armoured force in Libya, as well as diverting 8,000 vital wheeled vehicles that were intended for logistic use in the Western Desert, not to mention the majority of the RAF aircraft belonging to the desert air force. A weak covering force of inexperienced units was placed in penny-packets across the western side of the British-controlled Libyan desert. This decision involved risk, but it was necessary at the conclusion of the successful Compass offensive against the Italians, the soldiers in 7th Armoured Division were exhausted, having been in action for eight months, and having only twelve cruisers and forty Light tanks still operational. In Wavell's own words, the division:

> … was mechanically incapable of further action; only a fraction of its tanks had succeeded, thanks to the most skilful maintenance, in reaching Beda Fomm … the armoured vehicles in this division would require a complete overhaul and would be in workshops for many weeks to come. For all practical purposes, the 7th Armoured Division had ceased to be available as a fighting formation. The 2nd Armoured Division [had] arrived from the UK on 1st January 1941, consisted of two cruiser regiments and two Light tank regiments only.[15]

No one was expecting Rommel to do anything offensive, and certainly not any time soon. After he had allocated armoured forces for the defence of Crete and Greece, Wavell had a single newly arrived and inexperienced armoured brigade, the 3rd, in the field capable of action, equipped with only one Cruiser regiment (5RTR) and one two-squadron Light tank regiment (3H), plus the divisional armoured car regiment, KDG, which had arrived at the end of December and which was were starting to make a name for itself. Controlling this weak force was their parent division HQ, 2nd Armoured. In order to increase the armour available, Wavell took the unusual move of ordering 6RTR to equip itself with captured Italian Medium tanks. It was this ad hoc formation that stood between the much larger Axis forces and the road to Egypt.[16] On 31 March, less than three weeks after the first German tanks arrived in Tripoli, Rommel launched an armoured attack with three divisions, two of them Italian but with only about fifty tanks, which he concentrated together in order to give the impression of greater strength – which worked a treat.[17] Initially, the units of 2nd Armoured Division fell back slowly, not under much pressure but in order to seek an advantageous position from which to launch a decisive attack into the enemy flank. As the result of a calamitous mis-appreciation of the threat, the main British petrol dump was destroyed on 3 April, and from that point on, the ability of the armour to manoeuvre was 'almost entirely dictated by the lack of petrol'. Breakdowns, as usual, caused more problems than enemy action, and by the early morning of 4 April, the brigade could only muster about a dozen cruisers, twenty Light tanks and twenty of 6RTR's Italian fleet. HQ 2nd Armoured Division had lost touch with its component parts and was never in a position to influence the battle; on the night of 6/7 April the corps commander, O'Connor, was captured and the 3rd Armoured Brigade commander was also taken 'into the bag'. On the 7th, Gambier-Perry, the commander of the 2nd Armoured Division, surrendered at Mechili. Effective command and control had virtually ceased to exist, and individual units had to fall back as best they could. 2nd Armoured Division had to all intents and purposes ceased to exist; Wavell attributed this to 'the poor mechanical state of its vehicles, nearly half of which were in workshops while the remainder were in no condition for a prolonged retreat'.[18]

Rommel had won the first round without ever decisively engaging the British.[19] In less than a fortnight he had advanced 450 miles and swept the British out of Libya. One thing had become clear, and would remain so for the rest of the campaign. Most of the ground was of no real importance, other than for local tactical advantage. What would win the battle was the possession of the superior tank force, supported by effective logistics. The destruction of enemy armour became the main preoccupation of both sides. It was thus very clear that in order to beat the Germans, many more (and if possible, much improved) tanks were urgently needed. As a result, Operation Tiger was mounted from the UK in early May 1941 to deliver urgently needed tank and aircraft reinforcements to Egypt. Starting out with 295 tanks, only one ship was sunk en route, and the high-risk, high-reward convoy arrived in Alexandria on 12 May, delivering 238 tanks: 21 obsolete Light Mk VI, 82 cruisers (including the first batch of 50 of the latest Crusader type) and 135 Matilda II Infantry tanks. This eased the immediate problem, but thousands more new tanks would be needed over the next two years to replace losses, the majority being shipped by the longer but safer route via South Africa. A strategic problem caused by the arrival of the Tiger convoy was that Churchill immediately pressed Wavell for an offensive, using his new 'Tiger cubs', not understanding the inexperience of the crews and the need to 'desertize' all the vehicles.

The initial failure to contain Rommel and destroy his armour before his second armoured regiment arrived in May 1941 – almost concurrently with Tiger – set the conditions that led to the prolongation of the campaign for the next two years, as each side tried to find and then destroy the other's armoured forces. Had the British armour been in better mechanical condition after Beda Fomm, and had a large amount of the RAC combat power in Egypt not been directed to Greece and Crete, it is quite possible that Rommel's impetuous charge to seize the initiative might have been blunted and turned against him: had that happened, there is little doubt that Italian resistance in Tripolitania would have quickly crumbled and the campaign ended before 1942.

The Elastic Campaign, 1941–2

What followed need not be described at length; the scene has been set and many other books have described the campaign in great detail. In short, Rommel was determined to advance to the Nile and defeat the British forces in Egypt, seizing the Suez Canal and opening up the possibility of a drive to link up with German forces in southern Russia, and bringing Turkey into the war for the Axis. The British were determined to protect Egypt for the same reason, and could see the strategic advantage in not just defending the same, but in capturing Italian

Libya and taking complete control of the Mediterranean. In truth, the ambition of the ground forces was always more focused on destroying the German tank forces, which, if successful, would bring the campaign to a rapid conclusion, regardless of ground taken. The difficulty was in doing that. For a number of reasons, detailed below, the larger and better supplied British forces failed to inflict a crushing defeat on the Axis armies, and many hundreds of tanks – and crews – were fed into the theatre in an attempt to gain the numerical advantage that was seen as being needed to overcome the (perceived) German technical superiority. Over the course of the campaign, within the Eighth Army, nearly forty RAC regiments fought in the desert, and when the First Army landed in November 1942, another nine RAC units were added to the list.

To some degree, all of the ensuing battles had one binding feature; a successful advance could be made, but the limit of its success was determined by the availability of logistic support and the endurance of the crews. The further each side advanced, the longer the logistic lines of communication became, and eventually a culminating point arrived, which prevented any further movement forward. At that stage, the exhausted advancing force lost the initiative and became vulnerable. And of course, the force withdrawing – retreating if you prefer – was all the time shortening its own lines of communications as it fell back on its bases – Cairo and Alexandria for the British, Tripoli and Tunisia for the Axis. In this way the campaign resembled two armies linked to their supply bases by a short length of elastic – the winning side would be the one that could provide the longer and more robust piece of elastic.

The major offensive and tank operations during the period were as follows. Operation Brevity of May 1941 was a fairly small-scale offensive in the frontier area involving 11H, 4RTR and 7RTR, which succeeded in capturing the vital terrain of Hellfire Pass – although it was subsequently recaptured before the month was out. Overall, Brevity failed either to destroy the enemy armour or to relieve the besieged Tobruk garrison. The siege of Tobruk was to last over eight months from April 1941, when Tobruk was invested by the Axis forces advancing eastwards to the frontier wire, leaving Tobruk surrounded and eventually 80 miles inside enemy territory. The besieged harbour held out, and a small force of British tanks, lights, cruisers and most usefully, Matilda Infantry tanks, were deployed as part of the force defending a 30-mile-long perimeter. The Germans were determined to capture the port for the logistic advantage it would bring, and the British (and Commonwealth) forces equally determined to deny it. The small tank force in the garrison was often used imaginatively, the tanks being well dug-in and camouflaged, and used either as a mobile anti-tank force to blunt penetrations, or as a 'sally' force on raids, a more aggressive use of the armour.[20] Supplies, reinforcements and casualties were brought in and out by sea. In armour terms, although both sides used tanks, the whole Tobruk battle was something of a sideshow.

The Marmon Herrington armoured car was known as the Monkey Harry by its users, and this one, probably in service with the King's Dragoon Guards, can been given more punch by adding a captured Italian Breda gun.

The second British attempt to seize the initiative was Operation Battleaxe, launched on 15 June; in many ways it was an up-scaled Brevity, and was fought over much the same ground. Battleaxe was mainly intended to force Rommel's tank forces to give battle and be destroyed, as it was known that the second German Panzer regiment, with two more tank battalions, had arrived during May. The plan was to recapture Halfaya Pass, as well as the small towns of Sollum and Fort Capuzzo, using infantry assisted by the available Infantry tanks, thus allowing the 7th Armoured Division with its new Cruisers to break through and relieve Tobruk. After that, the large garrison would become part of the force to continue to push westwards. Despite Rommel being alerted by radio intercepts, the first part went well, but an attempt to hook the armoured division, led by the 7th Armoured Brigade, around the south was met by stiff resistance, with the brand-new Crusaders proving their vulnerability in terms of both thin armour and an alarming tendency to break down; the new tank was fast and sleek, but was entirely unsuited to desert warfare in 1941.

Finding himself fighting his first real defensive battle, Rommel was able to use his 88mm anti-aircraft guns in a static role, defending Halfaya from armoured attacks – it was during this operation that the Matildas lost their supposed invincibility, as they could be penetrated frontally at over a mile by the powerful anti-aircraft guns. Rommel sensibly refrained from committing his armour whilst the situation remained confused, and he found it easier than the British to reinforce, as the Battleaxe plan had one great flaw: there were no armoured reserves to allow the reinforcement of success, the application of additional pressure at the vital point, or indeed to react to an unexpected enemy move. Rommel seized the initiative by attacking at dawn on the 16th, and by the end of the day the 7th Armoured Brigade was down to the equivalent of just two squadrons, with breakdowns a major cause of the loss of combat power.[21] Rommel, intercepting panicked communications between the divisional and corps commanders, realized that an opportunity had presented itself and struck again, requiring the remaining Infantry tanks of 4RTR and 7RTR to be thrown in to attempt to stem the tide, but the pressure was too much and what had started out as a British offensive turned within two days into another retreat to avoid encirclement, leaving many of the brand-new 'Tiger cubs' abandoned behind them. Overall casualties were light, but the British had lost about twice as many tanks as the opposition, none of which could be recovered. Starting with 190 tanks, the British lost 99, whereas, after recoveries, the Afrika Korps had only suffered 12 destroyed. Despite the German strategic attention being taken

In the June 1941 attacks to capture Halfaya – Hellfire – Pass, the German use of the 88mm gun proved that the Matilda II was not totally invincible. In fact, even the 50mm anti-tank gun using the latest ammunition could penetrate it frontally.

up with the developing invasion of Russia, which would limit Rommel's requests for reinforcement, the British, even with a superior ability to reinforce, could not sustain such losses.

For the next few months there was something of a lull, with the majority of attention taken by the siege of Tobruk. Wavell was sacked and replaced by Auchinleck, and on 18 September, the Eighth Army was formed. By the end of October 1941 the British had reorganized to form two corps, XIII and XXX, with the latter being the main armoured formation and included within it the majority of the tanks.[22] The total number of tanks had greatly increased, and included 300 of the new and very welcome US Light tank, the M3 Stuart or Honey as it became known, and these were used to re-equip the 4th Armoured Brigade. The 22nd Armoured Brigade was also added to the order of battle from the UK, the three regiments of which were all yeomanry and given the by-now notorious Crusader. Against them, Rommel's command now consisted of three German and five Italian divisions.

Operation Crusader

The third British offensive, Operation Crusader, was designed not to take ground but to lure the Panzers into a tank battle where they could be destroyed. Deception was extensively used for the first time, and if anything was too effective. The offensive started well on 18 November; somewhat surprised by it, Rommel was initially confused as to what it was designed to achieve and where the British tanks were; he therefore chose not to commit his armour. The lack of German tanks on the battlefield confused the Eighth Army leadership, who had expected the Germans to present themselves as targets in accordance with the plan, and as a result made the mistake of dispersing the force in order to try to find them, in the process throwing itself open to being defeated in detail. The new 22nd Armoured Brigade, on the left flank of the advance and in its first action, dashed itself against a strong Italian defensive position, which it tried to assault using tanks alone and ended up being seriously weakened. 7th Armoured Brigade captured Sidi Rezegh airfield – it was to constantly change hands throughout the battle – and continued to move towards Tobruk, whilst 4th Armoured used their Stuarts for the first time against 21st Panzer, discovering the many pitfalls of their new tanks as they did so.[23] By the 23rd Rommel was able to bring both 15th and 21st Panzer Divisions along with the Italian Ariete armoured division together in an attempt to destroy a sizeable pocket of XXX Corps; by the end of the day's fighting British tank losses were numbered in the hundreds, and Rommel himself was down to about a battalion's worth. Rather than allowing the battle to peter out, Rommel chose the aggressive (foolhardy) and therefore unexpected option: on the 24th his remaining forces attacked eastwards towards the frontier, hoping to get into the rear echelon troops and dislocating the entire Eighth Army. By the following day he was, once again, on the Egyptian frontier, and by doing so, gave the British forces valuable breathing space. Instead of collapsing into a retreat that would turn into a rout, the armoured brigades used the time to replenish and reset themselves, including recovering and repairing many of the tanks that they had seemingly lost over the last few days, and re-establishing control – there had been precious little of this after the first day. On the 26th Rommel, low on supplies and in danger of losing the initiative, returned westwards and re-started the fight over Sidi Rezegh. By the end of the month, he realized that the fight had developed into attritional warfare masquerading as manoeuvre, and with the greater British resources, it could only have one outcome. At the point of exhaustion and with obvious reluctance, Rommel started to withdraw in good order deeper into Cyrenaica on 8 December, allowing the siege of Tobruk to be lifted, but still conducting a couple of well-timed spoiling attacks towards the end of the month which resulted in 22nd Armoured Brigade losing another fifty tanks. On Christmas Eve 1941 KDG armoured car patrols entered the abandoned and badly damaged harbour of Benghazi; the Bardia pocket of Axis troops surrendered on 2 January 1942 and the remainder, those around Sollum and Halfaya, on the 17th. By the end of the year, the battle had dwindled to exhaustion, and the Axis withdrawal allowed Crusader to be portrayed as a great victory, which it was not; much ground had been re-gained and Tobruk relieved, but the main effort, the defeat of the German and Italian armour, had not been achieved.

During the battle, the RTR gained its first Victoria Cross of the war, awarded to Captain Pip Gardner MC of 4RTR, a former TA officer in the Westminster Dragoons. The citation read:

On the morning of 23rd November 1941, Captain Gardner was ordered to take two tanks to the assistance of two armoured cars of the King's Dragoon Guards which were out of action and under fire in close proximity to the enemy, southeast of Tobruk. He found the two cars halted two hundred yards apart, being heavily fired on at close range and gradually smashed to pieces. Ordering the other tank to give him covering fire, Captain Gardner manoeuvred his own close up to the foremost car: he then dismounted in the face of intense anti-tank and machine gun fire and secured a tow rope to the car. Seeing an officer lying beside it with his legs blown off, he lifted him into the car and gave the order to tow. The tow rope, however, broke, and Captain Gardner returned to the armoured car, being immediately wounded in the arm and leg: despite his wounds he lifted the other officer out of the car and carried him back to the tank, placing him on the back engine louvres and climbing alongside to hold him on. While the tank was being driven back to safety it was subjected to heavy shellfire and the loader killed. The courage, determination and complete disregard for his own safety displayed

By the middle of 1941 the A13 Cruiser and Light Tank Mk VIb were seriously outclassed, with armour too thin to survive on the modern battlefield. But in late 1941 these vehicles still formed the armoured backbone on Operation Crusader, which turned into a gruelling slugging match.

A 2RTR A13 totally destroyed in the area of Sidi Rezegh; the tank has been holed multiple times by AP shot, and appears to have suffered from an internal ammunition explosion. Inadequately protected ammunition caused many more fires than fuel, but this was not realized at the time.

Originally a trooper in the Westminster Dragoons, Captain Pip Gardner of 4RTR won the first armoured VC of the war during Operation Crusader.

by Captain Gardner enabled him, despite his own wounds, and in the face of intense fire at close range, to save the life of his fellow officer, in circumstances fraught with great difficulty and danger.

As so often in desert warfare, for the crews Crusader was completely confusing and utterly tiring; sometimes a tank crew might go a whole day without sight of an enemy vehicle, on others a troop or squadron might stumble upon a whole enemy division. In many ways Crusader was the epitome of confusion in tank combat; this is poignantly portrayed in Bob Crisp's book *Brazen Chariots*, devoted to his impressions of the battle. At the tactical level, however, the key point was that the British armour ending up fighting small-scale, dispersed battles without the assistance of other arms, whereas the Germans made better use of their balanced all-arms battlegroups to blunt British attacks, primarily by the skilful use of anti-tank guns employed in a mobile role, and were able to retain both command and control in order to concentrate their armour to decisive effect. After the battle, Rommel commented to a captured officer: 'What difference does it make to me if you have two tanks to my one, if you send them out and let me smash them? You presented me with three brigades in succession.'

Concurrently with Crusader, the East African campaign was successfully concluded in late November 1941, which, although a minor operation in many respects, was still another drain on combat power from Middle East Command, including B Sqn 6RTR in the Sudan in autumn 1940, and B Sqn 4RTR in Eritrea in early 1941. The East African campaign of 1941 only came about because of the presence of large numbers of Italian troops in the region, who were there due to Mussolini's colonial expansion in the 1930s, and these had to be dealt with because of the potential effects on shipping along the east coast of Africa. Although generally seen as something of a sideshow, removing the Italian presence from the region had strategic implications, as it allowed President Roosevelt to declare the area a no-combat zone, and thus allowing American ships to carry much-needed supplies, including their latest tanks, directly into Egypt.

The Gazala Gallop

The first half of 1942 saw the fortunes of the Eighth Army in the doldrums, and Rommel came as close as he ever managed to winning the campaign. The events have come to be known as the Battle of Gazala, named after the small town at the north of the defensive line adopted by the British. At the end of their withdrawal of December 1941, the Axis forces were in the area of Agedabia, on the Gulf of Sirte. Despite German strategic attention being focused on the problems in Russia, Rommel acquired some of the new tanks that he desperately needed: during January 1942 he received eighty-one Panzer III, eighteen Panzer IV and twenty-one other types. Importantly, some of the Panzer IIIs were the new Ausf J model, which carried a new, longer version of the 50mm gun, and which were dubbed as Mk III Specials by the British – this was three months before the first examples of the new 57mm 6-pounder reached the Eighth Army; once again, the Germans retained the upper hand in firepower by up-gunning their tanks before they became obsolete. The entry of Japan into the war on 7 December led to Hitler declaring war on the US, and as a result Middle East Command was ordered to deploy an armoured brigade with two experienced regiments (3H and 2RTR) to Singapore, another unwelcome reduction in British tank numbers, which is discussed in more detail later.

The nearest tank forces to Rommel in January 1942 was 2nd Armoured Brigade of 1st Armoured Division, which had been brought forward from Palestine to

The Panzerkampfwagen III, or Panzer III, was the mainstay of the German tank forces in North Africa; armed here with the short 50mm gun, it was capable of being both up-armoured and up-gunned, and was more than a match for the early British Cruiser tanks.

Much hope was vested in the introduction of the A15 Crusader in late 1941, but it was still under-armoured, only equipped with the increasingly obsolescent 2-pounder gun, and was dreadfully unreliable.

relieve 7th Armoured Division. The Desert Rats were once again exhausted by the fighting, and were withdrawn to rest and refit, prior to a renewed offensive which was to be called Acrobat. However, Rommel once more took the Allies by surprise and launched his own attack on 21 January. The three widely dispersed regiments in the forward armoured brigade, the Bays, 9th Lancers and the 10th Hussars, were unable to fight as a coherent formation and consequently quickly lost over half of their tanks. The subsequent withdrawal was a confused affair, with disaster probably only averted by the sorties of the RAF. By the 28th Benghazi had been recaptured, along with huge quantities of fuel and ammunition that had been stockpiled there in preparation for Acrobat. By 4 February, the German offensive had once again petered out, and the British had withdrawn to the so-called Gazala line, only 30 miles west of Tobruk, at which point there was another operational pause.

The Gazala line was not a continuous defensive line, nor did it demonstrate the principle of defence in depth. Rather, it consisted of a number of infantry brigade 'boxes' protected by minefields, stretching across a 45-mile front from the Mediterranean to an open flank beyond the southernmost box at Bir Hacheim – this flank was thus susceptible to being turned. The majority of the British tanks were held back in their formations, with both armoured divisions under command of XXX Corps, and which now included the first examples of the American M3 Grant Medium tank with its medium velocity 75mm gun, which would come as a rude shock to the Germans because of the ability to fire high-explosive shells. The infantry corps, XIII, only had the two Tank Brigades, 1st and 32nd. Ritchie, the Eighth Army commander, intended to use the boxes and minefields as 'rocks' on which the Germans could dash themselves, and in so doing allow XXX Corps to manoeuvre its armour to destroy the remaining Panzers. The RA anti-tank regiments were by now receiving the excellent 6-pounder gun, with infantry battalions being given the redundant and near obsolete 2-pounders which, although unable to deal with the up-armoured Panzers at battle ranges, could knock them out at close range and also deal with Light tanks and armoured cars. Unfortunately, the static defensive dispositions played into the Axis hands, as the infantry and artillery units within the boxes were rendered immobile, exposed and liable to attack from any direction and, most importantly, unable to support one another.[24] Once again, the British plan was fatally flawed, and Rommel was adept at noting flaws and taking advantage of them, which he did with a renewed offensive. This was Operation Venezia, and was deployed against the British defence starting on 26 May, having received another eighty or so tank reinforcements in the meantime.[25]

Rommel intended to feint to the north to commit the British armour, and then destroy the Bir Hacheim box in the south with his three Afrika Korps divisions plus the Italian Ariete, allowing him to hook south and then north-east into the

3RTR was the first unit to receive the American Light Tank M3, officially the Stuart but universally known as the Honey. Fast, reliable and easy to drive, it nevertheless was only armed with a 37mm gun and was thinly skinned, as this crew have found out. Many tanks that received hits were nevertheless repairable and able to be put back into action.

3RTR was also the first unit to receive the American Medium M3, known as the Grant. The introduction of this tank came close to being a game-changer, as its 75mm hull gun could fire high-explosive shells. Unfortunately, poor tactical use frittered away the advantage.

British rear. Despite heroic resistance by the Free French Brigade, his armour managed to get behind the box, and threated the Allied rear and supply lines. British armour reacted piecemeal, making the same mistakes as previously, with individual regiments finding themselves up against much stronger opposition. One of the biggest tactical errors committed by the British armour time and again was to try to close with the enemy by charging at them over the open desert. The problem was that the Germans expected and encouraged the British to do this, as it was the only way they could seek to get their tanks in range of the Germans with their superior guns, and who used their tanks as bait, with a strong and well-concealed anti-tank-gun screen hidden and awaiting the onslaught. Almost invariably the British regiments took the bait, charging towards the Panzers, only to be decimated by the concealed guns; throughout the campaign, the RAC regiments generally thought that they were being knocked out by enemy tanks when in fact, in most cases, it was deftly handled anti-tank artillery that was causing the majority of the casualties.[26]

Such actions are often described in memoirs as 'cavalry charges' – Sir Baker Russell, a 13th Hussar in the late nineteenth century, was once said to have declared that the role of the cavalry soldier was 'to look pretty in time of peace

New units often took time to discover the best tactics to use against the wily Germans – the arrival of 23rd Armoured Brigade equipped with Valentines is a case in point. Thrown into action only a fortnight after arriving in Egypt, many of its tanks were destroyed in brave but naive attacks on the Germans in Ruweisat Ridge.

and to get killed in war'.[27] Of course, the description is flawed, as horsed cavalry would never attempt to charge over such long distances, otherwise the horses would be 'blown' long before getting close to the enemy. Bob Crisp noted the tendency when describing the desperate attempts by the Stuarts of the 8th King's Royal Irish Hussars to close the range between themselves and the Germans during the earlier Crusader battles:

> They had seen the Hussars charging into the Jerry tanks, sitting on top of their turrets more or less with their whips out … This first action was very typical of a number of those early encounters involving cavalry regiments. They had incredible enthusiasm and dash, and sheer exciting courage which was only curbed by the rapidly descending stock of dashing officers and tanks.

An officer in the 2nd Royal Gloucestershire Hussars considered that 'a frontal attack by armour on a defended position, and an attack of this kind by cavalry tanks, though even then considered part of their role, is one of the surest methods of suicide that exists'.[28] However, cavalry units were not the only ones who could be lured into such mistakes, as the need to close the range was common to all, and there is no doubt that sheer desperation at being out-ranged played its part. Lance Corporal Fred Digby of 2RTR recalled that:

> Our orders were to pursue and destroy some lorried infantry. We set off line-abreast at great speed, charging after them and firing on the move; too late it was found that we had been lured into a trap, because we ran into some dug-in artillery, and I saw several tanks hit within minutes. Then I heard and felt a thud, followed by a shout from Ginger, the driver, and the tank came to a halt.

General Brian Horrocks, a charismatic infantryman who unusually had been selected to command 9th Armoured Division in the UK and then XIII Corps in the desert, gave his considered opinion as to why such charges took place:

> During previous desert battles our tank commanders had been accused over and over again of charging recklessly onto the enemy anti-tank guns … but as long as the enemy guns out-ranged ours, the Germans could sit back out of range of our guns and destroy our tanks one by one … [When the Shermans arrived] Lumsden, the armoured corps commander, issued orders that there were to be no more Balaclava charges.[29] A brewed-up tank is not a pleasant sight. Walking over the battlefield afterwards I counted on one stretch of a few hundred yards eighty-five tanks belonging to the 9th Armoured Brigade, all burned out.[30]

The Gazala battle lasted nearly one month. Particularly intense for the armour was the fighting around what came to be known as The Cauldron, in the area east of the 150th Infantry Brigade box, where the Germans deployed their anti-tank guns and which took a heavy toll of the British armour; by 6 June, the British tank strength had fallen to less than 200. By the 13th the boxes had been individually rolled up, and another east-bound withdrawal, verging at times on a rout, took place, allowing Rommel to finally attack and capture the prize of Tobruk on 21 June, after having eluded him for nearly nine months the previous year. This uncoordinated withdrawal, the so-called 'Gazala Gallop', was a low point in British fortunes, but Rommel, just promoted to Field Marshal, had also expended much of his combat power in the attack. He only had forty-four tanks operational in the three German divisions, whilst the two Italian mechanized divisions had only fourteen tanks between them. Despite this, Rommel judged that Alexandria and the British rear bases were within his grasp, if only his exhausted troops could make one more effort; he was also no doubt aware that time was against him, and that Eighth Army would only get stronger if it was allowed time to recuperate. On 26 June he resumed the advance heading into Egypt, taking Mersa Matruh which Auchinleck had decided, wisely, not to try to hold. Carver described Rommel's continuation of the offensive as, 'Rash in the extreme … He should never have succeeded'. There was a misunderstanding within the British that a general withdrawal would take place if Rommel attacked again, and so when he did, many units started to fall back even though they were not seriously threatened. Carver commented that, 'Once more, with a greatly inferior force … operating on a logistic shoestring, Rommel had routed a force, superior in numbers of tanks, artillery and infantry. Command in the Eighth Army had been totally ineffective.'[31]

During the Gazala battle, the actions of Lieutenant Colonel H.R.B. Foote, commanding 7RTR, brought him a fine VC, made all the more exceptional as it was not for the single act of valour as most of the awards are given for, but rather for sustained valour over twenty days. The citation read:

> For outstanding gallantry during the periods 27th May to 15th June, 1942. On 6th June, Lt Col Foote led his battalion, which had been subjected to very heavy artillery fire, in pursuit of a superior force of the enemy. While changing to another tank after his own had been knocked out, Lt Col Foote was wounded in the neck. In spite of this he continued to lead his battalion

Deception was successfully used in North Africa by the British, including 'Sunshield', the ingenious idea of constructing frames over the tanks to make them look like lorries from the air. Note how the three centre wheels on this Crusader have been painted black to add to the veracity of the disguise.

from an exposed position on the outside of a tank. On June 13th, when ordered to delay the enemy's tanks so that the Guards Brigade could be withdrawn from the Knightsbridge escarpment and when the first wave of our tanks had been destroyed, Lieutenant Colonel Foote re-organized the remaining tanks, going on foot from one tank to another to encourage the crews under intense artillery and anti-tank fire. As it was of vital importance that his battalion should not give ground, Lieutenant Colonel Foote placed his tank, which he had then entered, in front of the others so that he could be plainly visible in the turret as an encouragement to the other crews, in spite of the tank being badly damaged by shell-fire and all its guns rendered useless. By his magnificent example, the corridor was kept open and the brigade was able to march through. Lieutenant Colonel Foote was always at the crucial point at the right moment, and over a period of several days gave an example of outstanding courage and leadership that it would have been difficult to surpass. His name was a byword for bravery and leadership throughout the brigade.[32]

But sheer guts from individuals would not be enough. Two factors saved the British, and the campaign. The first was the exhaustion of the Axis forces, who, despite the exhortations of their commander, could go no further without rest; he had only about fifty tanks remaining and overall was at about 30 per cent of his effective strength. The second was that a new defensive line, much stronger than

Lieutenant Colonel Foote, the Commanding Officer of 7RTR, was the second and last RAC soldier to win a VC during the Second World War; his award is unusual in that it was the only one from both world wars which recognized that it was possible to win the ultimate gallantry award whilst being inside a tank.

the poorly conceived one at Gazala, had been under construction for some time. It was only slightly shorter than Gazala at 40 miles long, but had the advantage of a secure southern flank made up of the impassable terrain of the Qattara depression. Auchinleck ordered Ritchie not to attempt to make a stand at Mersa Matruh, but to withdraw even further eastwards and base his defence on the new line. This was called the Alamein line, the name taken from the – until then – insignificant railway halt near its northernmost extremity.

On 1 July, despite the parlous state of his force, Rommel attacked once again in what is usually known as the First Battle of El Alamein, which lasted for another month. Such panic was caused by the continuing of the advance, now well inside Egypt, that staff officers in Cairo began burning secret documents on 1 July, in what became known as Ash Wednesday; plans were being made to withdraw over the Nile and into Palestine. Just before this fresh attack, Ritchie was sacked and Auchinleck took direct command. The old desert hand Strafer Gott was promoted from XIII Corps to take over Eighth Army – he was a substantive colonel but acting lieutenant general – but was killed when his aircraft was shot down on 7 August.[33]

On 12 August Lieutenant General Bernard Montgomery arrived from the UK to take command of Eighth Army, and although historians have argued endlessly about his impact, there is no doubt that his appointment marked a sea-change in the army's fortunes, not least because of his style of command. Experienced, self-confident and cautious of expending lives unnecessarily, he was a breath of fresh air and was able to build on fundamental changes in organization that were two years in the making. He was not an armoured soldier – like Rommel, he was an infantryman – but he understood the need for all-arms cooperation and, possibly more importantly, the pressing need for a simple plan that was understood by all. He insisted on what he called balance, and was meticulous in his logistic preparation. He sacked under-performers ruthlessly, and, like all successful leaders, surrounded himself with a team of officers he knew and could trust. Brigadier Kippenberger, a hard-bitten South African, noted that:

> The new army commander made himself felt at once. He talked sharply and curtly, without any soft words, asked searching questions, met the battalion commanders, and left me feeling very much stimulated. For a long time, we had heard nothing from [Eighth Army HQ] except querulous grumbles that the men should not go about without shirts on, and things of that sort. Now we were told that we were going to fight, there was no question of retirement … We were delighted, and the morale of the whole army went up incredibly.

Monty did not care for dress regulations, which suited the notoriously scruffy RAC crews perfectly. What he wanted was soldiers who would fight for him on

The arrival of Monty in August 1942 marked a decisive change in the fortunes of the Eighth Army; although there is doubt that his success was built on the foundations of previous commanders, his steely determination and unshakeable self-confidence soon transmitted itself throughout his new command.

his terms, and they did; for all his faults, it was a case of cometh the hour, cometh the man.[34] Montgomery knew that Rommel would have to attack again, probably repeating his favoured outflanking manoeuvre. Therefore, the army would need to fight a defensive battle initially, absorb the assault, and in so doing write down their fighting power, before going on the offensive. He fought a successful defensive battle at Alam el Halfa at the end of August into early September, having forbidden the armour to chase around the battlefield, but instead used it to destroy the Axis tanks from well-selected hull-down positions; this had the effect of allowing the range to be reduced without charging, and negated Rommel's use of anti-tank gun screens. Coordination of the infantry with the anti-tank guns, field and medium artillery, and armour was given new emphasis. His plans were simple, and his orders brief, unlike the over-complicated and wordy staff work used previously; his order for the opening phase of Second Alamein, a three corps operation, was only two pages long, and was phrased around what he was intending to achieve, rather than unworkably complicated phased timetables.[35] After defeating Rommel at Alam el Halfa, he chose not to exploit immediately, but preferred, in his pursuit of balance, to ensure that he had overwhelming material superiority as well as time to conduct training (and put into place an exceptionally good deception plan) before beginning his offensive. Confidence was restored within the army and the new commander had got off to a good start.

El Alamein

The turning point of the desert war was the Second Battle of El Alamein, usually simply known as Alamein. Montgomery resisted pressure, not least from the ever impatient Churchill, to attack before he was ready. The two-month interim allowed him to build up his logistics and reserves, bring in new leadership where he thought necessary, re-organize and train; he was a great trainer and knew the value of low-level skills and all-arms rehearsal and cooperation. Morale improved when he took steps to improve rations and the supply of post. By the end of October, he was ready; by this time more armoured formations were available to him: in addition to the veteran 4th, 7th, 22nd Armoured and 1st Tank Brigades, he now had the 8th, 9th, 23rd and 24th Armoured and as importantly, the older and less reliable tanks were now in the minority. Critically the first of the new American M4 Shermans arrived in early September, with 318 being enough to equip about 2 brigades; it was necessary to keep their arrival a secret and they were referred to by the codename Swallow. Those regiments unfortunate enough not to receive the new tank had to soldier on with a mixture of Grants and Crusaders, a strange combination but one intended to prevent some units being entirely equipped with the now-notorious Crusaders.[36] By the start of the battle the motorized infantry battalions had each received sixteen 6-pounder guns, making them much better able to defend themselves. Monty knew that despite these improvements, the attack would be far from easy, and confided in his diary that he expected a 'dogfight', one which could last twelve days.[37] Alamein was not really a battle of manoeuvre; it was more a set-piece battle in which manoeuvre was attempted, not always successfully, to break through a dogged defence in depth protected by deep belts of wire and mines.

The start of the battle was heralded on the evening of 23 October by an artillery barrage of First World War proportions, with over ½ million shells being fired in less than 6 hours. The attack was called Operation Lightfoot and a key component was the coordination of the artillery, engineers, infantry and armour. As ever with attacks on a well-prepared defensive position occupied by a tenacious enemy, it was critical to get the sequencing of these four arms correct; the engineers needed to be up front with the infantry to clear obstacles, especially the vast belts of minefields, but the armour also needed to be close on their heels to offer support

The latest American Medium tank, the M4 Sherman, arrived in the desert only a few weeks before Second Alamein, just in time for the crews to get used to the new tank, which was a massive fillip to those lucky enough to be so equipped. This is C Squadron of the 9th Lancers. However, over reliance on the design would handicap the development of better designs for the remainder of the war.

Dummy tank units, often labelled as fictitious battalions of the RTR, were used as part of the overall deception plan. Such devices looked totally realistic when spotted by air reconnaissance, and care was taken to add tank tracks so that the overall effect was believable.

where required and to be able to exploit as soon as the opportunity presented itself; the planners of Cambrai would have understood and approved. The battle needed to develop in the traditional three phases: break-in, break-through and break-out. Extensive use was made of deception and diversion both in the lead-up and in the evolving battle, and use was made of specialist Scorpion mine-flailing tanks, with mixed results.[38] Carver spoke of the 'real problems faced by the tanks in attempting to emerge in broad daylight, in line ahead, from narrow gaps through the minefields to which the enemy's attention had been concentrated by the artillery programme'.[39] Some of the armoured car units, including the 11th Hussars and the Derbyshire Yeomanry, unable to be used in the free-roaming manner that they preferred, had to be content with the worthy but unfamiliar role of acting as traffic policemen, trying to sort out the chaos of multiple and often mixed up units trying to use the narrow minefield lanes. A flavour of the first night and morning of the great battle comes from the Royal Wiltshire Yeomanry's history, also describing their first 24 hours in action as an armoured unit:

> The body of the Royal Wilts has been ploughing with great difficulty through our own minefields to get into position … End to end, almost touching, they crawl along the track called 'Bottle'… in a short while it becomes obvious that we are in for a most unpleasant time; even before reaching the enemy minefields, the dust begins to make itself felt. A heavy choking fog builds up as the tracks churn the desert into powder. When all the tanks are on the move the fog is blinding … visibility is only a few yards and it is all the drivers can do to keep in touch with the tank ahead of them.
>
> This is the moment for which they have been waiting for so long. They are about to take their Sherman tanks into action. What will it be like? Will their 75mm guns be a match for the Germans? But we're off now … after two or three hundred yards we shall enter the gap in the enemy's forward minefield, yes, here it comes, the green and amber lights blink at us through the murk … Let's hope the sappers have done a good job! Funny feeling this: death caged on either side of you in little round tins and ready to spring at you like a jack-in-the-box if you make the slightest mistake. The sappers however have made it and as dawn breaks the two heavy squadrons begin to trickle through to the far sides of the gap.
>
> A sort of orderly confusion reigns everywhere and the activity is intense … A Squadron has run into an uncharted minefield … the extent of this calamity becomes increasingly apparent as daylight grows. The two heavy squadrons are dotted about near the ridge in grotesque attitudes which clearly show how they have tried, but failed … in this manner starts a fantastic day. The battle develops into a long-range duel between the opposing masses of huge modern tanks. Thank heavens we are able to compete with our 'seventy-fives' on the Shermans and the Grants.

But fate still has trouble in store. At a quarter to eight Lt Col Sykes is hit in the chest by a shell splinter. Major Gibb the second in command is at the NZ brigade headquarters, so Major Lord Weymouth takes over in the meantime; for fifty hectic minutes he commands the regiment ... The regiment's initiation into armoured fighting has been a severe one. By the middle of the afternoon the Royal Wilts, having very little left with which to fight, had largely become spectators.[40]

As Monty had predicted, the battle was long and hard, and culminated in Operation Supercharge, a largely armour and infantry battle starting on 2 November. During this action armour casualties were severe, Monty revealing that although he preferred to be economical with the lives of his men, he could be ruthless when the need arose, ordering the armour to press on and if necessary, accept 100 per cent casualties.[41] On the same day Rommel had informed Hitler that his:

> ... army's strength was so exhausted after its ten days of battle that it was not now capable of offering any effective opposition to the enemy's next break-through attempt ... With our great shortage of vehicles an orderly withdrawal of the non-motorised forces appeared impossible ... In these circumstances we had to reckon, at the least, with the gradual destruction of the army.

Almost certainly the result of a catastrophic ammunition fire and explosion, this M3 has been torn apart. The understandable desire of tank crews to receive levels of protection sufficient to make them immune from enemy fire was not achievable.

It was not all one way: German losses such as the Panzer IV were harder to replace, as the Allies had massive logistic superiority, leading the Afrika Korps to rely heavily on capturing British equipment.

Hitler responded with a 'last-man last-round stand-and-fight' order, that Rommel was too canny to obey fully, being prepared to withdraw rather than lose everything, abandoning the static formations in order to preserve his mobile units as best he could.[42] On the 4th the moment arrived, and Rommel knew he had no option but to retreat; Monty's prediction of a twelve-day battle was remarkably prescient. Well over 300 British tanks had been knocked, out, but Rommel had lost grievously too, and did not have the means to replace them; when the retreat started, he was down to only forty-five Medium tanks between his two Panzer divisions.

Libya to Tunisia, 1942–3

Once the Germans and Italians started to withdraw, the opportunity presented itself for the British forces to snap at their heels, giving them no rest and looking for the chance to strike the fatal blow, probably by encirclement. For a number of reasons this did not happen. Firstly, following nearly two weeks in action, Eighth Army was tired and would benefit from some time to rest and reorganize; nearly half of the tank fleet had been lost, and most of the remainder needed maintenance and repair. Secondly, Rommel was falling back on his supply bases, and had deliberately sacrificed static troops to retain the most important manoeuvre elements of his force, the Panzer and motorized troops, which remained a threat. The distances involved remained significant; even by the most direct route, the road from Alamein to Tunis was around 1,400 miles. Thirdly, torrential rain on the 6th and

7th made the going extremely difficult, not only for the armoured vehicles but even more so for the now ever extending logistic tail, based on wheeled transport; troops recorded flash floods and 2ft of mud as well as confusion and congestion as units and formations tried to sort themselves out in limited space. Both 2nd and 22nd Armoured Brigades ran out of fuel during the 6th, rendering them extremely vulnerable had they been counter-attacked. Montgomery constantly tried to get Lumsden's 10 Corps to get a move on and race past the Germans, but failed to ginger him up despite some uncomfortable 'interviews without coffee'. Fundamentally, the Germans were prepared to move at night and if required fight by day, whereas the British armoured units, with few exceptions, used night to laager up and sleep, which lost them the initiative and they were unable to overtake the Germans in order to halt the retreat. Although Monty was understandably keen to complete the victory using his Eighth Army alone, he knew something that the German's did not, that the Allies were about to invade western North Africa.

On 8 November, under the codename Operation Torch, powerful US and British forces landed in Morocco and Algeria in order to remove the Vichy French presence there, and to threaten Tunisia from the west. As a result, the Germans immediately took steps to occupy Tunisia (as well as Vichy France), thus shortening their supply lines across the Mediterranean. The Vichy opposition in Algeria and Morocco quickly capitulated, allowing the Allies to drive on to Tunisia. Following this rapid collapse of resistance a group was put into being called 'Blade Force', based on the 17/21L and which made a dash for Tunisia, although rain and mud hindered their progress somewhat. The Axis armies were now pinched between Montgomery coming from Libya in the south-east, and the Americans and British driving from the west. Within the Torch order of battle was General Anderson's First (British) Army. His armoured forces included the 26th Armoured Brigade of 6th Armoured Division (16/5L, 17/21L, 2LBH) in Crusaders, and 25th Tank Brigade in Churchill Infantry tanks (NIH, 51RTR, 142RAC).[43] The majority of the Crusaders were now of the Mk III type with 6-pounder guns, but as these only had a two-man turret, the troop leaders were still mounted in the completely obsolete Mk II, which still only had the 2-pounder gun, but which at least had a dedicated radio operator.

The Churchill tank, having made an inauspicious debut with the Canadians at Dieppe in August 1942 and then as a trial with Kingforce at Second Alamein in November, now proved its worth; the thick frontal armour saved many crewmen's lives, and despite their weight, they proved to be extremely adept at climbing seemingly impossible slopes, allowing them to offer intimate support to the infantry in the difficult hilly terrain of Tunisia.[44] One commentator, looking at the actions of the North Irish Horse, remembered that:

I do not think that anyone can appreciate the achievements of the NIH tank crews unless they had carried out that climb themselves, preferably in

The 6-pounder gun could be squeezed – just – into the Crusader, but the larger breech and ammunition meant that the turret crew was reduced to only two men, which meant that the commander also had to act as the loader.

charge of a mule column. Nothing in Italy or elsewhere in my experience was comparable to those trackless and precipitous mountain wastes, fit only for Berber goats and shunned even by them.[45]

By the end of the campaign six Churchill regiments were active in Tunisia; fittingly perhaps, the last armoured actions of the campaign were conducted by the Churchills of 145RAC, 'squeezing' the final pocket of resistance on the Cape Bon peninsula. 48RTR operated Churchills in Tunisia and found them to be good tanks, and whilst the armour could not cope with the 88mm, it afforded them good protection at other times:

The squadron moved off at 0230 am. *Titan* led the three tanks of 7 Troop, with Bartlett's tank following only seven or eight yards behind. All at once, our craft shuddered to a violent explosion. With one hand on the tiller I seized the microphone; 'What's wrong?' 'A shell landed between us and the tank behind,' replied my commander, with remarkable composure. 'It's blown away the towing shackles, water cans and smoke generators … don't switch over to reserve fuel.' 'Why not?' 'Because you haven't got any.' The explosion had blown away the 30 gallon reserve tank at the rear. Another round bursting in front of *Titan* blew in my driver's visor.[46]

One unwelcome addition to the German armoury in Tunisia in late November 1942 was the new Tiger tank, which quickly became notorious. Although only about thirty were deployed, the combination of extremely thick armour and, for the first time, the 88mm gun mounted in a tank, made the Tiger the most powerful weapon on the armoured battlefield, reliability and mobility problems notwithstanding. The poor armour on the unreliable Crusader was no protection: the 16th/5th Lancers reported that a complete troop of three Crusaders were knocked out by a single Tiger tank at the incredible range of 2,500yd. Famously, one of the Tigers, numbered 131, was disabled and captured, more or less intact, by a 6-pounder armed Churchill of 48RTR. This allowed it to be shipped to Britain for technical examination, although one cannot help but wonder why it was not transported with more alacrity, only arriving in October 1943.

Although the Germans reinforced Tunisia with four more infantry divisions which included some of the effective, low-profile *Sturmgeschutz* assault guns used as tank-destroyers, and fought with skill and determination, once Torch was mounted there was only ever going to be one outcome. On 13 May 1943 General Alexander, the overall British commander, was able to signal the prime minister with news of the final surrender, including the famous and stirring statement that, 'We are masters of the North African shore', with nearly ¼ million Axis prisoners in the bag. Eighth Army and its predecessors and constituent formations, with the RAC units constantly in the van, had overcome many obstacles during a

Crews from the 26th Armoured Brigade carrying out maintenance in the hilly terrain of Tunisia. Tunisia would be the last campaign when the Crusader was used as a gun tank, the brigade re-equipping with Shermans before embarking for Italy.

campaign that had lasted just shy of three years. The Axis surrender ended the phase of the war that came as close as any ever fought in support of the theories of all-tank armies, and which had been found to be impractical in practice. The lesson had finally been (re)learned, that regardless of terrain, all-arms cooperation was the key to success.

Life in the Desert

Throughout the campaign, one thing that was common for all of the RAC units – and of course the remainder, including the enemy – was the environment in which they fought. Even before a shot had been fired, the desert was an inhospitable place to live, let alone fight. Searingly hot during the summer, it was often freezing cold at night; many quartermasters made the mistake of withdrawing battledress and greatcoats when the lightweight shorts and shirts of KD (Khaki Drill) were issued. The food was monotonous, the staples being corned (bully) beef and dry biscuits, supplemented by such other rations as the logistic system could supply; those who were the furthest from the logistic bases, meaning the fighting men, were usually the last to get any extras, despite the heroic efforts of their own quartermasters. Poor nutrition led to a loss of appetite and contributed to desert sores, a skin condition that could take months to heal. Tea was the universal drink, crews being adept at brewing up quickly and in the most testing of conditions, including during sudden quiet spells in the middle of battles. Water was rationed, sometimes to as little as 6 pints a day for all needs, including drinking, cooking and washing, meaning that the latter took low priority. AFV crews often used fire extinguisher chemicals or even petrol as rudimentary cleaning fluids with which to wash filthy clothes, hoping to evaporate the solvent in the hot sun so that dermatitis did not result. Swarms of flies attracted in part by unburied dead and most notably present when trying to eat were both annoying and a hygiene risk. It comes as no surprise that units lucky enough to find themselves on the coast took every opportunity to bathe in the sea.

The lack of sleep was a constant; even during a 'routine' day, as described below, the crews often existed for long periods on a few hours at best each day, supplemented by cat-naps when they could, and the long days and short nights during the summer exacerbated the issue. On the eve of big battles and offensives, the crews would be busy with conducting maintenance, replenishment, repairs, receiving orders, etc., made worse by the inevitable night moves into position and then waiting to be committed, which meant that the crews invariably went into action already tired, and this rapidly descended into exhaustion, which became a real limiting factor on how battles were exploited, or not. The high attrition rates and the need for replacement tanks meant long and uncomfortable trips by 'unhorsed' crews to collect new vehicles from depots.[47] In many cases when a completely new model of tank was issued, the unit would get only a few hours of

Uniformity of dress was never insisted upon in the desert, as these Honey crews demonstrate. Temperatures in the desert could be very hot during the day but near freezing at night.

Monty accepts a mug of tea from his 6RTR Grant crew. It was one of these soldiers who presented him with his famous black beret which he chose to wear, against all regulations, with two cap badges. The officer on the right is Captain John Poston MC of the 11th Hussars, one of Montgomery's ADCs who was killed only days before the end of the war.

Right: Keeping clean in the desert was a near impossible task, with water strictly rationed. Crews lucky enough to find themselves on the coastal strip would take the opportunity to bathe in the sea whenever possible.

Below: Crews having a lie-in; a typical day in action would see them up whilst it was still dark, and moving off as dawn broke. Crews always slept on the inside of their tank when in leaguer, to reduce the chance of being accidentally run over.

hurried instruction before going into battle in them – the lucky ones were sent back to the camps in the Delta to receive proper instruction, but this was a luxury. Heavy casualties amongst units often led to 'composite' units being formed out of the remnants of two or even three regiments, for example, 1/6RTR, 3/5RTR and 4/8H; not a guaranteed way to achieve cohesion but a necessary fact of life.

Other factors also made life difficult, at times near impossible: dust and sand were constant annoyances, made horrendous when a khamsin, or sandstorm, blew up, a frequent occurrence and which at least affected the enemy equally, often causing battles to stop whilst crews of both sides took cover as best they could from the all-pervading sand. Navigation was a constant challenge, and most RAC units appointed their best and most experienced officers as unit navigators, flying black streamers from their radio aerials to display their position, and taking the responsibility for leading columns into action; this took a great load off the shoulders of less capable, inexperienced commanders – the pre-war invention of the sun compass was a huge benefit. And it must not go unmentioned the sterling work of the unsung stalwarts of the regimental echelons, delivering logistic supplies by day and night and without which the AFVs would have been useless. These heroes roamed the desert, close behind the F Echelon (the fighting troops), in unarmoured lorries carrying petrol and ammunition, and subject to the same conditions as the tank crews but without the prospect of medals, recognition, protection or being able to fight back – including against the not-infrequent air attack.

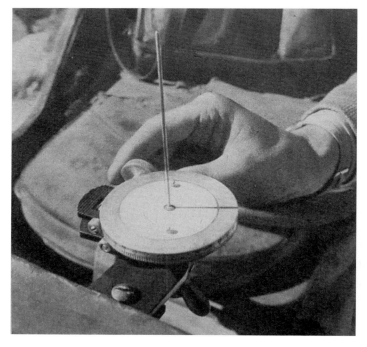

The sun compass was devised as an aid to desert navigation pre-war, and proved invaluable during the campaign. RAC regiments appointed their best navigators to move the whole unit across featureless desert when out of action.

Part of the echelon of (probably) 4th County of London Yeomanry. Frequently ignored in histories, without such men the tanks would have soon ground to a halt, devoid of fuel, ammunition and rations.

Lieutenant Bob Crisp of 3RTR painted a picture of a single, in many ways typical, day in action during Operation Crusader at the end of 1941, which was much the same for him day after day, as well as for many hundreds and thousands of other armoured crewmen throughout the whole campaign:

The daily formula was nearly always the same – up at any time between midnight and four o'clock. Movement out of the leaguer into battle positions before first light. A biscuit and a spoonful of marmalade before the flap of orders and information. The long day of movement and vigil and encounter. Death, and the fear of death, until darkness put a limit to vision and purpose on both sides. The drawing in of far-flung formations. The final endurance of the black, close-linked march to the leaguer area. The maintenance and replenishment and orders groups that lasted 'til midnight. The beginning of another twenty-four hours.

Always the last to enjoy any of the rare relaxations that came our way were the tank drivers. At night, when the tanks stood in their mute rows and the crews were silent in sleep and exhaustion, grimy drivers would be seen going over the engines and tracks. In the morning's darkness they would be the first up to get their tanks ready for the move. It was reasonable, no doubt, that they should have last access to the water and soap and towels; they were always covered in grease and oil and an abrasive amalgam of sand.

The tanks edged forward slowly. In each vehicle the scene would be the same … the driver, hands on the steering sticks and foot poised sensitively on the throttle, would be peering intently at the narrow world confined by the slit in the armour-plating in front of him. The operator would be fiddling about with the wireless set and checking the ammunition. The gunner would be settling himself, testing the traverse and the ammunition belts, squinting through his telescopic sight at the rounded O of desert beyond. Each tank commander, standing upright in the turret or perched on top with legs dangling inside, would be pushing his vision to the utmost distance to pick up shape or movement, the earphones in position and the microphone on his chest to maintain his link with the rest of the regiment and his crew below.

It was a confused day of constant skirmishing. I had several duels with enemy tanks, knocked out two and learned a great deal. I learned which of their armoured fighting vehicles I could take on and beat [with the Honey], and which I had to avoid until I could create a favourable situation for myself. We were always prepared to take on any number of Italian tanks, and any of the German Panzer IIs and armoured cars. The Panzer III and IV, however, had to be dealt with by subterfuge and the grace of God, rather than by superior fighting qualities.[48]

A Scots Greys crewman assists in replenishing his Grant with Browning machine-gun ammunition. The regiment had only just converted to tanks before being committed to the desert campaign, later fighting in Italy and then in North-West Europe.

Changing the engine on a Grant. The desert environment was terribly harsh on machinery, mainly because of dust ingress, but the often rocky ground played its part as well, shaking the tank constantly and leading to many breakdowns.

General Brian Horrocks, a thinking if not an intellectual soldier, had this to say about the campaign in North Africa:

> The desert was a desperate place for infantry because there was practically no cover from view [and even] digging was difficult. Infantry could only

attack under cover of thick smoke-screens fired by the artillery, or at night during the period of the full moon … So the tank was the queen of the battlefield. The armoured formations operated against each other by day and then withdrew … If either side suffered heavy casualties in its armoured formations, then it had lost the battle. It was as simple as that.[49]

It was simple in hindsight, but it was also complex at the time, and one of the biggest problems faced by commanders was trying to identify the exact nature of the problems that the Germans were causing, and then implement the necessary changes to prevent a recurrence. Trying to make such changes in the middle of a battle was frequently attempted and rarely successful. In terms of the performance of the RAC during the campaign, it is possible to group the main problems encountered, and the attempts to solve them, into two categories: technical and tactical.

Technical Problems

Technically, the biggest problem until summer 1942 was that most of the tanks deployed were under-gunned, under-armoured and, probably most importantly, mechanically unreliable. The reason for this was that the tank crisis of 1940

Probably belonging to 2nd Armoured Brigade, this Sherman M4A1 has been hit at least twice from the flank, the turret hit almost certainly resulting in casualties unless the crew were able to bale out first.

caused by the loss of the majority of British tanks in France had far reaching repercussions. The fear of invasion plus the lack of clarity on the shortcomings of the British tanks led to a policy of quantity over quality, and thus obsolete models were produced in large numbers long after their use-by date had passed. The need from 1941 to reinforce Egypt, both to build up strength and to replace losses, led to these unsuitable tanks being pitted against the same German types they had encountered in France, but with one major difference: the Germans had studied the captured British tanks and as a result had both up-gunned and up-armoured their own.

The mechanical unreliability of British tanks has been mentioned often, and with good reason. Poor tracks, a lack of spare parts, over complexity and poor basic design all played their part, as did their unsuitability for use in desert conditions – meaning dust ingress more than heat, although cooling remained a problem throughout. As Wavell said, 'There is no room in war for delicate machinery'. Compounding the problem was the almost complete lack of tank transporters until 1942, when more and larger types started to become available. Until then, the tanks wore themselves out by having to track hundreds of unnecessary miles under their own steam, compounding the repair and spare-part issues, and meaning that they were generally in poor condition even before combat was joined; the heroic attempts of the crews, fitters and ordnance personnel could only go so far in reducing the impact of this. Recovery of battlefield casualties was another area where the British often lagged behind, and of course the side that was advancing gained possession of the battlefield, and was thus able to recycle the many vehicles that had been abandoned but which were still usable. Rommel used some captured British tanks, but the area where he gained the greatest advantage was in wheeled logistic vehicles; precise numbers do not exist, but by the end of 1942 a large proportion of Rommel's transport was British made, often running on captured fuel.

The continued reliance on the 2-pounder gun, because of the results of the tank crisis of 1940, caused serious problems until the belated introduction of the 6-pounder from April 1942. Tragically, this excellent new gun had been designed in mid-1938, and was ready for production by September. However, production was not ordered until May 1941, as the Director General of Munitions Production had suggested that six of the smaller guns could be made for every one of the new model. This was later proved to be nonsense, but the damage was done, and the first guns designed for tank use were not available to the production lines until November 1941, by which time the Germans were about to up-gun and up-armour their tanks once more. Even fitting the new gun into the existing designs proved exceptionally difficult, as the turrets were too small to accept the bigger weapon easily. The Matilda turret could not take it at all, and although it could be squeezed into the turrets of both the Valentine and the Crusader, in both cases this meant that the third crewman – the loader – had to be removed, making the

Transporters became more available as the campaign progressed, and were mainly used for the recovery of disabled tanks. Later in the war they would become more frequently employed in carrying tanks on non-tactical operational moves, to save on track mileage.

commander responsible for loading the guns and looking after the radio, a major retrograde step.

Two other factors affected both types of gun. The first of these was to do with ammunition. The inability of either of them to fire an effective High-Explosive round was a major disadvantage, as solid shot (anti-tank) ammunition was ineffective against the small, well-concealed German anti-tank gun screens which were the predominant killers of British armour. 42RTR reported their frustration on such an occasion:

> Worse was to follow, for behind the minefield, carefully sited on rising ground with a good field of fire, well dug in so that their muzzles almost rested on the sand, was a troop of the dreaded 88mm guns. Their first shot went clean through the front of Lieutenant Hembrow's tank, set it on fire and killed the entire crew; and they followed this up by engaging all the first echelon of tanks lying crippled on the minefield. The Matilda carried no H.E. with which to reply; and though they engaged them with their Besa machine guns, they were unable to silence them.[50]

In fact, a high-explosive shell had been developed for the 2-pounder, but it was too small due to the 40mm calibre, its effect being little more than that of a hand grenade; in any case it was never issued to British tank crews. The 57mm 6-pounder had an HE shell, but it was again quite small and not available for tank crews until summer 1942, by which time a better solution was available. Additionally, the British Close Support tanks, used by SHQs and equipped with a howitzer rather than a gun, were meant, according to doctrine, to be able to provide immediate fire support when artillery was not available. This implied the delivery of both HE and smoke ammunition. However, faulty doctrine insisted that more smoke was carried than HE – in some cases *only* smoke – and so the only weapon in 1941 that was capable of producing a decent weight of direct HE fire at range was wasted by being used for creating small smoke screens. What was needed was a genuine dual-purpose gun in every tank.

The second factor was more tactical, caused by blindly following the RTC inter war policy of shooting on the move. As we have seen, this was somewhat artificial at the best of times, and in the desert simply wasted ammunition and was encouraged by the Germans. A tank moving at speed in its own dust cloud would not be a stable gun platform, as the driver jinked left and right in an effort to avoid being tracked and hit, and it was all-but impossible for the turret crew to spot targets in such conditions. Even if a target was identified, engaging it on the move was another thing entirely, not helped by the poor quality and low-magnification British optics.[51] Eventually, the tank crews realized the futility of such shooting and developed a method that came to be called the 'short halt'; the driver would brake as hard as possible, the turret crew engage with one or at most two hastily fired rounds, and then the tank would accelerate away as fast as

The introduction of the Grant in mid–1942 allowed tank crews, for the first time, to engage small dug-in anti-tank guns at range using HE fire. Over the course of the war, it has been estimated that around two-thirds of all main armament rounds fired were HE.

it could. Even then, this was made more difficult by a technical shortcoming: the free-elevation shoulder rest provided for the gunner to use when shooting on the move lacked precision when trying to correct the shot fall onto target, leading to late-war tanks being provided with geared elevation. Bob Crisp described the short-halt procedure:

> I completely discounted the possibility of shooting accurately from a moving tank. I worked out a system whereby, after the target had been indicated, a more or less automatic procedure followed … the objective was to get close enough to the enemy tank to be able to destroy it. The first order was 'Driver advance, flat out'. The gunner would do his best to keep the cross-wires of his telescopic sight on the target. The next order would be 'Driver halt!' As soon as the tank stopped and he was on target, the gunner would fire without further command from me. The sound of the shot was the signal for the driver to let in his clutch and be off again. From stop to start it took about four seconds.[52]

By the end of the campaign, another aspect of pre-war armoured doctrine was starting to come under scrutiny. This was the artificial distinction between Infantry and Cruiser tanks. There was no doubt at all that at certain times, being able to select the right type of tank for a specific job was useful – particularly when it came to questions of the amount of armour carried versus the need for speed. Infantry tanks had done well at the start, when the Matilda was all-but invulnerable and the Valentine was the most reliable British-designed tank, and at the end, when the Churchill proved its ability and protective qualities in Tunisia – but as a class it was simply too slow. Cruiser tanks, when they were on the road and not broken down, could exhibit a useful turn of speed and therefore would be the tank of choice for rapid manoeuvre and exploitation – but they were horribly unreliable and too thin-skinned. The arrival of the American tanks prompted the tank crews to ask why their own tanks were so poor in comparison. The M3 Stuart Light tank, the first to arrive in late 1941, was cramped, thinly armoured and only armed with a near obsolete 37mm gun, but it was both very fast and very reliable; the tank crews loved it and nicknamed it the Honey. The six-man M3 Grant Medium tank, from May 1942, again brought reliability plus a (admittedly hull-mounted) 75mm gun; for the first time the tank crews had a true dual-purpose gun, with adequate anti-tank performance and, more importantly, a decent HE shell.[53] The logical development of the Grant into the M4 Sherman, which became available just before the Second Battle of El Alamein, was the real turning point; Horrocks stated that 'if one item more than any other helped to win the Battle of El Alamein it was the Sherman tank'.[54] With the same 75mm gun as the Grant but now mounted in a proper all-round-traverse turret, the Sherman – despite an alarming tendency to catch fire readily – became the tank of choice for the British tank crews. Too lightly armoured to be an Infantry tank, and not sufficiently well-armed to joust directly with the newest German tanks that were now mounting a long 75mm high-velocity gun, the Sherman nevertheless offered a compromise design that, for 1942, made it extremely useful. If what was needed was a balanced, dual-purpose tank, the Sherman gave the first, if imperfect, glimpse of one.

Tactical Problems

On the tactical level, many of the problems went beyond just the RAC units, whereas others were particular to tanks and armoured cars. Dealing with the former first, a serious issue was the inability of the army's command system to deal with modern, fast-moving armoured warfare. Pre-war doctrine and practice tended to deliver long and over complicated plans that relied too heavily on all component parts being successful for the whole to work, and which became unhinged as soon as one part failed. Too many commanders were loath to issue firm orders, with many subordinates complaining that what was meant to be an Orders Group (O Group) became discussions, and sometimes not much more than just a listing of known problems. There was a need to emulate the German way of doing business – to come up with a simple plan, and then give clear orders based around the key concept of the commander's intent, allowing the man on the spot to make decisions in support of the objective. Rommel has been quoted in translations as saying, 'The Italian command was, for the most part, not equal to the task of carrying on war in the desert, where the requirement was lightning decision followed by immediate action.'[55] At times, and all too often, he might have been referring to the British. Having issued orders, there followed the requirement to insist that they were carried out to the best of the subordinate's ability, whilst allowing some, sensible, freedom of action to deal with evolving circumstances. The modern army defines 'command' as consisting of three elements: leadership, control and timely and effective decision-making. When the desert army encountered problems, very often at least one of these elements had gone AWOL. A lack of control or 'grip', particularly by certain formation commanders, was rife during the months when Rommel was in the ascendancy. Robin Neillands summed it up nicely when he said that, 'Grip is one of those military qualities that are hard to define but most noticeable when absent'. Montgomery had 'grip', and when he arrived, officers who lacked it did not last long.

It was unfortunate that many formation commanders, who often had extensive First World War experience complete with an impressive array of gallantry medals testifying to their courage, proved to be unable to cope with the demands placed upon them. As a consequence, the cohesion within brigades and divisions was often found wanting, condemning the units to fight isolated battles, which suited the Germans. Allied to this was the inability of senior officers and staff to comprehend the true nature of the problems being faced, meaning that they were unable to work out the best solution to solving them. This is a perennial problem in war, and can be, at least in part, solved by using independent operational analysts to do this important work; this was to come later in the war with the Operational Research Group, but in the desert, the commanders and staff had to try and work it out for themselves even whilst they were in action. Communication and security issues have already been noted, although in the provision of radio the RAC commanders were in the fortunate position of being able to at least attempt to control the battle that their command was involved in.

As has been commented on regularly in the last few pages, poor co-operation with other arms was rife until late in 1942, with muddled and inappropriate brigade and divisional structures exacerbating the problem, until the army was reorganized and a more balanced, all-arms organization arrived at.[56] This was difficult to change initially, as some of the pre-war proponents of mobile warfare had taken the 'all-tank' idea too far, and when it was tried on the one battlefield that seemed perfectly suited for its use, had its limitations and weaknesses ruthlessly exposed. The use of static infantry 'boxes', poorly protected and unable to defend themselves from armoured attack, led to a terrible situation in mid-1942 when trust between the infantry and the RAC completely broke down. Infantry units complained that they called for tank support when attacked, but none was forthcoming; this was exacerbated when the infantry could see tanks in the distance, but which seemed to be deliberately avoiding coming to their aid. Almost invariably, this was because the armour had either not been told of the infantry's plight, or were under orders to do something else, for example, find and attack the German tank forces.

Other problems added to the muddle. Tank units were often spaced too far apart from each other, even within brigades, preventing rapid reinforcement and mutual support. Whilst the Luftwaffe had air superiority, the need to disperse formations and individual units was clear and necessary. However, later in the campaign, when the RAF were in the ascendancy, this habit had become so ingrained that it was difficult to reverse, and as a result achieving concentration of force when required became very difficult. And of course, as has been noted, there was a tendency to commit everything up front, with no reserves to speak of. However, by the end of 1942 great strides had been made, and the Eighth Army was operating on a much higher level. However, as Niall Barr pointed out, 'The difficulty for the Eighth Army and indeed the entire British Army after Alamein was that the lessons learned in the bare deserts of Egypt were not necessarily of value elsewhere' – as the veterans were soon to find, in Sicily, Italy and in North-West Europe.[57]

Summary of Key Dates in the North African Campaign

1940

June

10: Italian declaration of war; border skirmishes begin.

17: Western Desert Force created.

September

13: Italians invade Egypt.

December

8: Operation Compass begins.

10/11: Battle of Sidi Barrani.

1941

February

5–7: Battle of Beda Fomm

March

5: First troops depart for Greece.

11: First German tanks arrive in Tripoli.

31: Rommel attacks into Cyrenaica.

April

6–30: Battle of Greece.

May

6: Second German Panzer regiment complete.

12: Tiger convoy arrives in Alexandria.

15–17: Operation Brevity.

20: Battle of Crete (to 1 June).

June

15–17: Operation Battleaxe.

September

18: Eighth Army formed.

November

Italians surrender in East Africa.

18: Operation Crusader (to late December).

1942

January

Germans deploy Mk IIIJ 'Special' tank with improved 50mm gun.

21: German counter-offensive at El Agheila.

28: Germans retake Benghazi.

February

2: British occupy Gazala line.

April

British deploy 6-pounder anti-tank gun.

May

British deploy US Grant tank with 75mm gun.

5: Operation Ironclad (invasion of Madagascar, to 6 November).

26: Battle of Gazala.

June

20: Tobruk captured by Germans.

23: Rommel crosses frontier into Egypt

24–7: Battle of Mersa Matruh.

July

1–26: First Battle of El Alamein.

August

12: Montgomery assumes command of Eighth Army.

30: Battle of Alam el Halfa (to 6 September).

October

Germans deploy Mk IVF2 'Special tank' with long 75mm gun. British deploy US Sherman tank with 75mm gun.

23: Second Battle of El Alamein (to 4 November).

November

Germans deploy Tiger tanks with 88mm gun to Tunisia.

8: Operation Torch landings in Algeria and Morocco (British First Army and American forces).

12: First Army enters Tunisia.

13: Tobruk retaken.

20: Benghazi retaken.

1943

January
23: Tripoli captured.

February
14: German forces withdraw from Libya into Tunisia.

March
British deploy 17-pounder anti-tank gun.
20–7: Eighth Army breaks the Mareth defensive line.

May
13: Final surrender of Axis forces in Tunisia.

Chapter Four

Doctrine and Design

The Early Development of British Tanks during the War

Between the wars, a number of factors had conspired that robbed Britain of its lead in tank technology. These included: financial parsimony and the effects of the Treasury's Ten-Year Rule; a genuine desire for disarmament; confusion within the army as to the future and role(s) of the tank; reticence by the CIGS and the Army Council to whole-heartedly support mechanization; very limited funds for experimentation and trials; a lack of industrial capacity able to design and build tanks; and the place of the army as the 'Cinderella service' once disarmament funds did start to become available. The only two areas where Britain still had a lead was in the intellectual sphere, with the imaginative development of doctrine being developed by some of the best brains in the army; and in tank-crew training, which was exceptional. The mechanization of the cavalry from 1928 had allowed expansion of the number of units operating AFVs, but a lack of training capacity and, most of all, lack of funds to build a new generation of tanks for both the RTC and the cavalry meant that the force looked better on paper than it did in the field. The formation of the Royal Armoured Corps in April 1939 was an attempt to homogenize the units which it did to some degree, but it also created other problems, such as the beginning of the attempts by some – not all – senior cavalry officers and supporters to side-line the RTR using the frankly ridiculous argument of regimental seniority.

The start of the war in September 1939 found Britain with a fleet of many different tank types. Within the three main classifications of tanks as Light, Cruiser and Infantry, as well as the obsolete (but still referred to) Medium category, at the outbreak of war and over the next three years or so the tank state looked as follows.

Light Tanks

Something of a hodgepodge of small numbers of earlier models existed, from the 1928 Mk I to the Mk V. Of these, many were in India or Egypt, and all of them up to and including the Mk IV were of the two-man type, armed only with a single machine gun and therefore of no operational and only very limited training value. All were simple machines, but repair was often handicapped by a lack of spare parts. The latest Mk VI and VIA versions were more usable, and the definitive Mk VIB was the 'modern' Light tank, and one which saw much operational service during the first two years of the war, by which time it was

The line of development that led to the Carrier series – with around 112,000 made during the war – also led to the development of the discredited Light tanks. The use of the carrier as shown here to carry fire support weapons and their ammunition around the battlefield was a great bonus for the infantry.

The final development of British Light tanks was the Light Tank MK VII, or Tetrarch, which was employed not only in support of airborne operations, but also in the invasion of Madagascar.

Disembarking a Tetrarch from a Hamilcar heavy glider on an exercise – note the sandbags supporting the ramp to prevent damage. Light tanks were used in small numbers in support of the airborne landings made as part of the assault over the Rhine in March 1945.

obsolete; just under a thousand were built. A Mk VIC version with a 15mm Besa cannon gave it more punch, but was only available in limited numbers as only 168 were produced. The later development of Light tanks concentrated on producing AFVs that could support airborne forces by being landed in gliders, which led to the Tetrarch tank.

Medium Tanks

Between the wars just under 200 Medium Tanks Mk I and II were built for the RTC, being introduced in 1923. These were the mainstay of the corps in the period and were used as a general purpose tank, but by the mid-1930s were tired and obsolescent. Some of the ones stationed in Egypt remained in front-line service at the start of the war and were dug-in as part of the fixed defences around Mersa Matruh, where it is not clear if they ever fired a shot in anger; it would have been a fitting end to their career if they had done so. The remainder in the UK continued to be used mainly in training regiments until replaced by more modern types, although had the Germans managed to invade in late 1940 or early 1941, there is no doubt that they would have been used to counter the German Panzer IIIs, with predictable results.

Cruiser Tanks

At the start of the war there were three Cruiser models in production: the A9, or Cruiser Mk I, the A10, or Cruiser Mk II and the A13, or Cruiser Mk III. In the period before names were allocated, the system of identifying different tank models and types was somewhat confusing; the A designation represented the project number allocated by the General Staff. The A9 was a six-man 13-ton fast but under-armoured tank that was beset by unreliability, narrow tracks that shed easily and a suspension that was unsuitable for its speed making it an unstable gun platform for shooting on the move. It was however the first tank armed with the 40mm 2-pounder gun, at the time the best anti-tank gun anywhere in the world; only 125 were built. The A10 was a development of the A9 with increased armour (up to 25mm) meant to allow it to operate as an Infantry tank. However, it could not carry sufficient armour to keep out modern anti-tank guns and was reclassified as a Heavy Cruiser, an unnecessary complication of nomenclature and one that did nothing to improve its performance; 255 were made. Both tanks saw service in France, in North Africa and in Greece, but by 1941 were at the end of their useful life. The third Cruiser was the A13, which used a simplified version of the revolutionary Christie-designed suspension which was eminently suitable for its role. Built by an industrial company set up for the purpose, Nuffield Mechanisation & Aero (NMA), the A13 was powered by the First World War vintage Liberty engine which could move the tank at 30mph but which was horribly unreliable, particularly in desert conditions; 345 were built, including some up-armoured with spaced armour panels on the turret, a world first. Despite its shortcomings, the A13 was a useful tank for 1940, and the suspension and basic design would be the basis for the remaining Cruiser tanks developed over the course of the war.

Two more of the early Cruisers need to be mentioned at this point. The first was the A13 Mk III, better known as the Covenanter and which holds the record as, without doubt, the most useless British tank of the war – and possibly of all time. This low, sleek tank looked the part but was utterly hopeless. Designed to be an updated version of the A13, the Covenanter design came about in the period of the war when both design and production were being rushed, in order to produce the maximum number of tanks in case the Germans should invade, as well as to equip the rapidly expanding RAC. In order to keep it low and light, the hull was designed with insufficient space for all the engine components and thus its cooling system had to be mounted outside the hull, with the radiator's underarmoured louvres on the front of the tank. By 1941 it was clear that the tank was badly flawed, and a lot of effort was expended on trying to get it right. Although 1,768 were built, none saw action and the best thing that can be said about them was that they helped to improve the standards of preventative maintenance and repair abilities of the crews unfortunate enough to be given them.

The A15 Crusader was another product of NMA, and despite a more than passing similarity to the Covenanter – the turret was the same basic design – the tank was designed concurrently with but separately from the Covenanter. Again, by using the tired Liberty engine to make it fast, something of an obsession, it

There is more to combat than just looking the part. Although the A13 Covenanter looked sleek and fast, it was beset by reliability problems and not one of the over 1,700 Covenanters made saw service as a gun tank.

The Crusader promised much but delivered little. It was too thinly skinned to survive on an armoured battlefield where the German tanks were armed with 50mm guns. This is an early model complete with a front-hull MG turret, an un-ergonomic design that was quickly dispensed with.

was terribly unreliable. The Crusader saw a lot of active service in the North Africa campaign where its many problems soon became apparent, including major issues with cooling, air filtration, build standards (quality control), as well as a tendency for the bolted engine cylinders to shake themselves apart over rough terrain. Over 4,200 were built, and in 1942 it was able to be up-gunned with the new 6-pounder, which extended its service life slightly at the price of reducing the space inside the turret so that the commander also had to load the gun. The new US tanks which started to be received in 1941 were better in every way compared with the British-designed Cruisers: even the small M3 Stuart which was meant as a Light tank was at least the equal of the Crusader, and the Grants and Shermans were clearly superior in every respect. In any case, the next generation of cruisers were starting to be produced in Britain, meaning that the Crusader ended its service life as a gun tank in Tunisia in May 1943.

Infantry Tanks

Entering service with 4RTR in 1937, the A11 – subsequently nicknamed Matilda which then became its official name – was Britain's first attempt to design a tank to meet the new doctrine of infantry support as a specialized role for the tank. This demanded heavy armour but there was no requirement for speed, and the MG-armed A11 suffered from being built down to a price in order to make it affordable. A two-man tank built around existing components, it was nevertheless remarkably well-armoured; it only had once chance to show its worth, at the Arras counter-attack of 1940, where the German 37mm guns could not penetrate it. Despite this success, it was clearly obsolete on a modern battlefield. Only 139 service tanks were built, with the majority being lost in France in 1940. The remainder were mainly used as training machines for a year or so before being scrapped. The second purpose-built Infantry tank was the A12, later called Matilda II. This was a 2-pounder armed four-man tank, which had up to 78mm of frontal armour making it all-but impenetrable by anything smaller than the 88mm. The tank was designed and built by a failing railway company called Vulcan Foundry, and was thus the first tank to be built in the period by a company other than Vickers-Armstrongs. Due to slow production (in large part caused by the complexity of the design), only six were in service at the outbreak of war, but a couple of dozen were employed in France by 7RTR where they performed well. Until 1941 it was the best British tank in service, despite its slow speed and mechanical complexity, but could not carry a larger gun annd was replaced by the Churchill. Many were exported to the USSR and to Australia; about 2,800 were built.

The Infantry tank Mk III was always known as the Valentine, as this was the project name given to it at Vickers, who designed it as a pre-war private venture (which is why it had no A designation) and offered it to the War Office in 1938. Initially reluctant, the WO quickly changed its mind when war was imminent, and the Valentine gave excellent service from the middle of 1940 onwards, although not in time to be used in France. Armed with the 2-pounder, the tank was later able to be up-gunned with the 6-pounder and then its larger derivative the 75mm, and was also the tank first used for series production as a DD (amphibious) tank. Well armoured, it was both faster and could climb slopes much better than the

The A11 undergoing trials. Despite being built down to a price, the armour on the two-man tank gave the Germans a nasty surprise at Arras in May 1940, but its design was archaic and it never saw action again after Dunkirk.

A Valentine crew from 46RTR wrestle with track maintenance in October 1941. The Valentine, despite being a private venture tank that was initially rejected by the War Office, was well-armoured and reliable, and was even able to be used as a makeshift Cruiser tank on occasions.

Matilda, and was for a time used as a makeshift Cruiser when production was lagging behind. Giving good if unspectacular service during the North African campaign, it was liked by its crews for its rugged design and – almost unheard of – reliability; it was obsolete by 1943 but was adapted in a number of specialist roles, most notably as a bridge-layer as well as being used by the Royal Artillery as a 'charger'. Nearly 5,900 Valentines were built in the UK, and another 1,420 in Canada, which were exported to the USSR, with some being used in the Pacific campaign by New Zealand.

Finally, the last Infantry tank was the famous Churchill. Initially known as Infantry Tank Mk IV, the slow-moving but extremely well-armoured Churchill came close to being cancelled on a number of occasions between December 1941 and October 1942 due to its chronic unreliability – itself caused by it being rushed into production without adequate trials and development.[1] Its first showing in the hands of the Canadians at Dunkirk in August 1942 was something of a debacle, but that was not the fault of the tank nor the crews. By 1943 the reliability problems had been solved by redesign and a huge re-work programme, and the tank was able to be-upgunned to carry the 6-pounder and later the British 75mm gun. In Tunisia, its hill-climbing ability proved to be astounding, and this, along with its high levels of protection, cemented its place in the order of battle. Even elements of its somewhat archaic design came to be a blessing: the track horns that projected forward of the hull and restricted visibility provided additional protection for the driver and hull machine-gunner, and reduced casualties. The rest of the Churchill story will be explored in due course.

The Valentine chassis was used as the basis for a Scissors bridge layer, the Archer self-propelled gun and here the British army's first service SPG of the war, the 25-pounder armed Bishop.

The Churchill was rushed into production with a host of attendant problems, and made an inauspicious debut at Dieppe in August 1942. Fortunately, the problems in the design were ironed out and later marks became the standard Infantry tank, proving itself in Tunisia, Italy and in North-West Europe.

Scout and Armoured Car Development

British doctrine specified two distinct varieties of these lightly armoured wheeled vehicles: the scout car and the armoured car. The former was a small, thin-skinned and lightly armed vehicle, with a crew of two or three, and which was used for liaison activities in forward areas. It was not, despite the name, meant for reconnaissance duties, but it sometimes – often – was, as the small size and low noise meant that it could be used in those circumstances where stealth was important. Scout cars were also used by liaison officers to visit nearby units and higher formations, and as run-around vehicles for squadron leaders and commanding officers.

Two main scout cars were used for the majority of the war. The first of these was the Daimler Dingo, the smaller of the two, which was introduced into service in early 1940 and became a roaring success, with over 6,000 being built. Armed with either a Bren .303in MG or a .55in Boys rifle, the two-man Dingo carried a respectable amount of armour, could achieve 60mph on the road and ran to five marks. Its larger cousin, although unrelated in terms of design, was the Humber Scout Car, or HSC. Entering service in 1942, it was bigger than the Dingo and could carry 3 men; over 4,000 were made before the end of the war. At the end of the war the HSC was quickly phased out in favour of the Dingo, which was not replaced until the late 1950s when the Ferret Scout Car (FSC) was introduced as a direct substitute.[2] Also used during the second half of the war and classed in Britain as a scout car was the American M3 series, a four-wheeled armoured box that was also the basis for the well-known American series of half-tracks. The vehicle, generally in its M3A1 configuration, was used in a variety of roles that required more room in the hull than the Dingo or HSC could provide, typically as a formation commander's command vehicle and, very commonly, as the Regimental Medical Officer's battlefield run-around.

Armoured cars on the other hand were larger and generally carried more armament, and were used by the armoured car regiments of both the RAC and the Reconnaissance Corps for the traditional cavalry scouting roles: finding out where the enemy was and where it was not, proving routes and covering flanks. The role required cunning, nerve and a degree of derring-do with a dash of the piratical that seemed to suit the British character, and there were very many examples of units that lived up to that role throughout the war – indeed, it is difficult to think of any armoured car unit that did not perform well. In terms of armoured cars, Britain entered the war with a mixed fleet, from the old Rolls-Royces of First World War vintage still in use in India, Iraq and Egypt, to 1930s-vintage Lanchesters and newer Morris CS9s, as used by the 12th Lancers in France and the 11th Hussars in Egypt.

Following the withdrawal from Dunkirk, a number of extemporized armoured cars on commercial car chassis were hurriedly brought into service; quaintly called Light Reconnaissance Cars (LRC), they boasted unusual names such as the Humberette, the Ironside and the Beaverette. Although cheap and cheerful, they performed a useful function when invasion was thought to be imminent, and many were later used in theatres such as Tunisia, Italy and in North-West

The Daimler Scout Car, or Dingo, was a nippy battlefield run-around that was also used in the reconnaissance role. It remained in service well into the 1950s.

A 3RTR-operated Humber Scout Car in action in Germany 1945. Although extensively used by RAC units, the three-man HSC was quickly phased out at the end of the war, the smaller Dingo being preferred.

The venerable Rolls-Royce armoured car was a 1914 design that remained in service well into 1941, doing valuable service in the Western Desert and in several other peripheral theatres.

Europe by the Reconnaissance Corps and RAF Regiment. Whilst these were being built, more careful attention was given to designing better armoured cars to replace the ageing 'Rollers' and the discredited Morris CS9, in order to equip the RAC armoured car regiments. As a result, such designs as the 5-ton Guy Armoured Car (originally referred to as the Guy Wheeled Tank), the Humber Armoured Car, the AEC and the Daimler Armoured Car were all produced. The Humber was a large but lightly armoured (15mm) vehicle that ran to four marks, and carried either a two- or three-man turret armed with a 15mm BESA cannon or an American 37mm gun. Entering service at the end of 1941, the Humber saw action in North Africa as well as in Europe; anti-aircraft versions carrying four 7.92mm Besa MGs were also designed. The AEC was a very large (nearly 13 tons and 9ft tall) vehicle, designed to meet a requirement for a heavy armoured car carrying a bigger gun; the Mk I version used the same turret as an early model Valentine tank, and the Mk II an even larger turret with a 6-pounder gun; the final version carried the British 75mm gun, an outrageously powerful armament for an armoured car. The AEC was used in the heavy troops of armoured car regiments, not aggressively as tank destroyers but in order to provide sufficient punch to help extract the smaller armoured and scout cars when they got into trouble. The best British armoured car of the period was undoubtedly the Daimler (DAC); armed with a 2-pounder gun, the three-man Daimler was fast (50mph), simple and reliable, with a decent cross-country capability, and was small and quiet enough to be stealthy. It entered service in mid-1941 and remained in the RAC until the late 1950s with regular regiments, when it was replaced by the Saladin, and it then soldiered on well into the 1960s with the Yeomanry recce regiments.

Other designs used during the war were the South African Marmon-Herrington, always referred to as a Monkey-Harry, extensively used in the Western Desert, as well as the large 37mm-armed American Staghound, which despite its many virtues was so big that it was unpopular for actual recce work, and tended to be used only in armoured car squadron headquarters where its roomy interior made it ideal for the role. Towards the very end of the war some American M8 Greyhounds were also supplied under Lend-Lease, the system that allowed the US to supply necessary military equipment to Britain.

US Tanks and the Effect Upon Doctrine

Approved by the US Congress in March 1941, the Lend-Lease Act allowed the previously isolationist US to supply military equipment to Britain without violating American neutrality. At this time, of course, one of the most pressing needs was for tanks, and a British military mission in Washington engaged with the US army and industry to expedite the supply of American tanks and other AFVs. One problem was that the US army had, like its British counterpart, struggled for funding during the inter war period, and had fallen behind in development; its few tanks were generally in the Light–tank class and referred to as Combat Cars to avoid offending the disarmers. This line of development led to the first American tank that the RAC units received in autumn 1941, a few models of the M2A4 Light tank followed by many more of its improved M3 and M3A1 development, this tank was officially named the Stuart in British service (American tanks being named after prominent US generals, including from both sides in the Civil War), and almost universally referred to as a Honey.[3] By 30 June 1941 the US army had agreed to 'release' 350 of its latest Light tanks (36 M2A4 and 314 M3), with 4 and 138 respectively sent directly out to the Middle East. At this point, M3 Medium Tank (Lee) production had only just started.

The Stuart/Honey was fast, reliable and, by late 1941, relatively thin–skinned, its maximum armour being 51mm. The 37mm gun was not quite as effective as the British 2-pounder and there were some issues with ergonomics, the first models lacked a turret floor, for example, but overall it was welcomed by the crews pending the issue of larger, better armed and armoured types. In North Africa the British used it as a Cruiser rather than as a Light tank. Even after it passed out of front–line service as a battle tank in late 1942, later versions (M3A3 and M5 series) were extensively used as a recce vehicle in Italy and North-West Europe, where the turret was often removed to make it smaller and faster.[4]

The next American tank to enter British service, again in North Africa in early 1942, was the M3 Grant, a British development of the M3 Lee Medium Tank.[5] The Grant/Lee – the two types were distinctive but often confused or just lumped together under the M3 designation – differed in that the Grant featured a 37mm gun turret of British design, in order to allow the radio set to be carried in the turret in accordance with doctrine; US tanks had theirs mounted in the hull and the more cramped Lee turret had a pretty useless vision cupola dominated by the breech of an equally useless .30in Browning MG.[6] The main gun was a 75mm medium velocity type mounted in a limited traverse sponson in the right front of the hull. Despite the awkwardness of the mounting, the gun brought something that the RAC had lacked up to this point: the ability to fire a high-explosive shell from a reasonable distance in order to engage anti-tank guns (rather than having to charge them firing only solid shot AP). This was a huge benefit and influenced tactics immediately. Although not used in Italy as a gun tank, it also saw extensive and valuable service in the Burma campaign, where its role and employment were not handicapped by its somewhat archaic design.

The next tank to enter service, a logical development of the M3 series, was the game-changer: the M4 Sherman. The first examples arrived just in time to take part in Second Alamein, and used the same 75mm gun mounted in an all–round traverse turret. Although not without its faults, including a high silhouette and an alarming tendency to catch fire when hit, it was reasonably well-armoured by 1942 standards, roomy, easy to maintain and reliable.[7] The Sherman remained in service with the RAC throughout the war, on all fronts, and appeared to give the crews all that they desired, although this was not so, as will be explained shortly. The popularity of the Sherman in many circles, plus the seemingly endless supply of them, led at one point in 1943 to the suggestion that the British should stop trying to build their own Cruisers and rely on American production of the Sherman; fortunately, this did not happen. In fact, by mid-1943 the Sherman was already obsolescent and needed serious development work to modernize it. In part this was due to the lack of armour, in part due to the increasingly mediocre 75mm gun. Unfortunately, General Montgomery, a man of strong ideas but no armour expert, managed to muddy the waters by insisting that the pre-war distinction between Cruiser and Infantry tanks was incorrect, and that what was needed were tanks, tank units and tank formations that could be used interchangeably in both roles. Although he was correct in this, the mistake that he made was to try to fill this new doctrine of a 'universal' or 'capital' tank with an existing design: the Sherman. The Sherman was simply not up to the task, as its armour was far too thin to be used in the close-range engagements required of an Infantry tank, and its gun was incapable of duelling with Tigers, Panthers and the long 75mm-armed Mk IVs at typical engagement ranges needed in the Cruiser role. Montgomery was no fan of the Churchill as he considered the top speed of 15mph to be too slow for exploitation, whereas in fact there were few occasions when such speed was required, and it possessed other qualities that he seemed unaware of. Montgomery's doctrine could only be fulfilled once a genuine universal tank had been produced, and this could not be done overnight: in fact, it was not fulfilled until after the war with the advent of the Centurion, although the Comet would have made a reasonable stand-in. The effects of this policy on the Normandy campaign will be discussed later. Another issue that came to light during autumn 1944 was the reliability of the Sherman when compared with the Cromwell; during the high-speed advance on Antwerp in early September 1944, only five of the Shermans in A Sqn 3RTR made it to the city, all the others falling by the wayside with various mechanical problems. The Cromwells in 7th Armoured Division had no such problems.[8]

Therefore, the RAC was stuck with the Sherman and its drawbacks until the end of the war. The tank was improved, including the placing of 1in appliqué armoured panels on the most vulnerable parts of the hull and turret fronts, and ammunition was placed in armoured stowage bins (although crews often then reduced the overall level of protection by stowing extra unprotected ammunition inside the tank). The biggest improvement was a British initiative: the fitting of the excellent 17-pounder high-velocity gun into the Sherman during 1943 to produce the Firefly. Like the flail tank and the AVRE, this came about in the face of official opposition to an initiative from a junior officer. Major George Brighty RTR was serving in the Gunnery Wing at Lulworth and believed that the Sherman would be able to mount the new 17-pounder gun, although fitting it into the space available, and accounting for the extra recoil length, larger

The very first Sherman received by Britain was named MICHAEL and is seen here with some of the staff at the Gunnery Wing Lulworth, responsible for carrying out gunnery trials; it is notable that the majority are from the RTR. The tank is now on display at the Bovington Tank Museum.

Crews of the 9th Lancers practise a staged 'crews mount' drill for the benefit of the camera. Although an important addition to the RAC arsenal, the tank would be teetering on the brink of obsolescence by 1944, not really able to compete with the better gunned German tanks.

breech and recoil system, and much longer ammunition, made it a real challenge. Separately, in Egypt, Major George Witheridge, a 3RTR gunnery officer who was recovering from wounds, was sent to the American tank centre at Fort Knox for six months where he became an expert on Sherman gunnery, and was then posted to Lulworth as a lieutenant colonel. Brighty meanwhile had been carrying out semi-official experiments, and was working on the issue of how to absorb the much larger recoil forces when Witheridge arrived and immediately became involved. Despite being told officially by the Department of Tank Design (DSD) to stop work, Witheridge used his contacts in the shape of the Director Royal Armoured Corps, Major General Raymond Briggs, another RTR officer, to get the project sanctioned, and the allocation of Mr Kilbourn from DTD to the project was the key to solving the design problems, by developing a more efficient recoil system, fitting a second hatch in the turret roof for the now–isolated loader, adding an additional armoured box behind the turret bustle for the radios and to counter-balance the longer barrel and, not least, rotating the whole gun through 90° anti-clockwise to allow easier and faster loading. Unlike many British tanks, the gunner's telescope had good magnification, x 3, allowing the gun to be fired accurately at ranges of up to 2,000yd.[9] Once approved, a conversion programme for 2,100 tanks was authorized in early January 1944, using Sherman I (M4) and Sherman V tanks (M4A4). Although – as always – the programme did not run as fast as was desired, just enough Fireflies had been converted by D-Day to allow twelve tanks to be issued to each tank regiment in the armoured divisions; the impact of the Firefly in Normandy will be examined in due course.

The Americans continued to develop the Sherman and, recognizing that the 75mm was inadequate, fitted a new 76mm gun into later model Shermans from the middle of 1944.[10] The additional penetrative performance was nowhere near as good as the 17-pounder or even the 6-pounder firing APDS, but it was still better than the 75mm, and British and Commonwealth units in Italy received some of these models pending the issue of Fireflies, which did not start to reach Italy until October 1944. Another Sherman derivative mounting a 3in gun was the M10 tank destroyer; this was developed because of an American doctrine that saw the need to provide a lightly armoured tracked anti-tank gun. Although it looked like a tank, with the same suspension as a Sherman, the turret walls were paper thin and there was no roof, making the turret crew extremely vulnerable to small arms and artillery/mortar fire. Despite this, some of the Royal Artillery anti-tank regiments in North-West Europe were issued with the M10, and towards the end of the war these were modified to accept the 17-pounder gun.[11] Finally, in 1945 the British were seriously considering bringing the new American heavy tank, the T26 (later the M26 Pershing), into service, but the end of the war stopped the project.

Chapter Five

The Mediterranean Campaign

Sicily, 1943

Following the surrender in Tunisia, the Axis forces realized that Sicily was likely to be next, and garrisoned the island with two German divisions, one of which was 15th Panzergrenadier (a reformed version of the one destroyed in Africa) and the other the Hermann Goering Panzer Division, plus ten Italian formations – four infantry and six low-grade coastal divisions. It was fortunate that the Germans were unable to evacuate the large numbers of troops captured in Tunisia, as these could have hugely strengthened the garrison. The invasion of the island, codenamed Operation Husky and starting on 10 July 1943, involved US Seventh Army landings in the west under Patton, with the British Eighth Army responsible for the landings in the east. The RAC units involved were on the east coast under XIII Corps, with two of 4th Armoured Brigade's regiments, 44RTR and 3CLY, landing in the area around Avola. Assaulting the southern tip of the island around Pachino was XXX Corps, which included 23rd Armoured Brigade with 50 RTR and B Sqn 46RTR.[1] All the tank units involved were mounted in Shermans, and although both brigades were independent armoured brigades, as there were no Infantry tank units deployed both would be tasked with assisting the infantry when required, each regiment nominally attached to support an infantry division.[2] A Squadron The Royal Dragoons provided the sole armoured car squadron for the operation. The landings were all but unopposed, with enemy air attacks more of a nuisance than a serious threat; despite the danger the troops were glad to be ashore – the previous day had been one of gales, and the Royals squadron had already spent ten days on board their landing craft.

Unbeknown to the soldiers on landing, the five-week-long campaign to subdue the defences on Sicily was to be a preview of the Italian campaign, albeit in miniature. Painting their vehicles in colours more suitable for Europe might have given the crews an idea of what was to come, as the lessons of desert fighting had little relevance on the close, often mountainous terrain of the largest island of the Mediterranean. Gone were the wide sweeps where the possession of terrain was often of little tactical value; here, every ridge, hill and olive grove was a potential ambush site. According to the history of the Royals, the troop leaders were 'learning the technique of fighting in close country, and instead of waiting

The OC of C Sqn 3CLY comes ashore on Sicily in July 1943. The campaign on the island would be short but vicious, giving the crews a taste of what to expect when the mainland of Italy was invaded later in the year.

for the hidden enemy to open fire, they used their machine guns on any cover which might serve the enemy's purpose'. The tank crews also found that they could be usefully employed as fire-bases for the infantry, sometimes firing HE and their MGs for an hour to soften up a position before the infantry started to advance.

With a lot of the countryside unsuitable for deploying tanks that now weighed in the region of 30 tons, the RAC crews found that wherever possible they had to stick to roads, if the narrow, winding and often precarious tracks could be called that. When they had to move cross-country, the rock-strewn terrain led to many tanks shedding tracks and stripping the rubber tyres from roadwheels, and as this was summer, the levels of dust were often comparable to North Africa, with the attendant maintenance problems. Another feature of the forthcoming Italian campaign also came to light, the dependence on the Royal Engineers being up with the front-line troops – often leading the advance – in order to clear obstacles and booby traps left by the retreating Germans; in time this would lead to the requirement to put the engineers into their own armoured vehicles. The Germans were starting to be equipped with new weapons, including the *PanzerSchreck* (tank terror) recoilless anti-tank launcher, the principle of which was copied from American bazookas captured during the Tunisia campaign, and the throwaway *PanzerFaust* (tank fist) anti-tank projector.[3] Almost all of the German tanks were now of newer, uprated models with more armour and better guns; self-propelled guns became more numerous, and the Tiger with its 88mm, which had put in its first appearance against the Allies in Tunisia, was also used, where it proved to be a fearsome defensive weapon. Tank crews also came under attack from other methods that had not troubled them so much in the desert, especially the threat of mortar fire and, most lethally for tank commanders, snipers. The terrain meant that commanders often needed to dismount, again leading to casualties; both 3CLY and 44RTR had their COs killed during the campaign whilst they were dismounted. Being used in an infantry support rather than exploitation role meant that new lessons of tank-infantry cooperation had to be assimilated, including working out who should lead; in general terms tanks led in open country, and infantry took the lead in close-country including in another area that was new to the desert veterans, fighting in villages and towns.

Not all movement was by roads. In an unusual small-scale action on 16 August, a small force including C Sqn 3CLY was re-waterproofed – a laborious and thankless task – in order to be landed from the sea south of Ali Marina, in an attempt to outflank stubborn resistance. The landing went well despite the tanks being put down on the wrong beach, and the move allowed the troops to link up with the Americans advancing from the west, meaning that the end of the campaign was in sight, with many of the remaining Germans abandoning Messina in order to join the evacuation to the mainland, which had started at the beginning of August. Eventually over 60,000 Germans and 75,000 Italian troops escaped, the former to fight again in Italy and thus the failure to prevent the evacuation was a major operational mistake.

Contrary to some ill-informed opinion, Sicily was no walkover; looking back on it at the end of the war, 23rd Armoured Brigade reckoned it to be the hardest campaign it had fought in. Tank actions were often fierce. In an extraordinarily productive morning's work on 13 July, a single troop of C Squadron 44RTR knocked out 8 (ex-Italian ex-French) R–35 tanks, 6 105mm guns, 29 trucks and also captured a divisional commander, 3 brigadiers, 4 staff officers and 50 other ranks. This was unusual, and many crews remember the campaign as day after day of hard slog against a well-emplaced and determined enemy. Exhaustion in the short campaign became a real problem, and some tank crews found themselves in action for literally three days solid. Men in such a condition tottered and reeled as if they were drunk; when they were at last allowed to rest, they slept where they fell, one crewman being found unconscious draped over a bush. Malaria resulted in many casualties, and the close-range nature of engagements was particularly unwelcome; one troop of 44RTR managed to get over a (rare) intact bridge, but all three tanks were knocked out in quick succession by a well-concealed anti-tank gun. Lieutenant Hale, a troop leader of the same regiment, had two tanks knocked out from under him on the same day; each time he quickly took over another tank from his troop and continued the action. One welcome change during the campaign was the introduction of the new composite (Compo) rations, a huge improvement over the monotonous bully beef and biscuit diet that the many desert rats had become used to.

Italy, 1943–5

The decision to invade Italy was a strategic one, designed to knock out Hitler's major ally of the war, as well as to draw German divisions into a new theatre of war, which would become particularly important when the invasion of North-West Europe was attempted. It was also a logical move following the capture of Sicily. Under the overall command of Alexander's 15th Army Group, the US Fifth Army and Montgomery's Eighth Army would provide the land forces; the latter now included substantial Canadian forces, and General Mark Clark's Fifth Army was in fact half British, as it included X Corps, and which contained the 7th Armoured Division.[4] Eighth Army would be responsible for the eastern side, and Clark for the west, with the Apennines mountain range an obvious but inconvenient divider. Commonwealth troops were to assume a substantial part of the armour support in Italy. By the end of 1943 two British armoured brigades (the 4th, comprising 3CLY, 44RTR, 50 RTR, and the 23rd, with the Greys, 40 RTR and 46RTR) plus KDG, the Royals and 1st Scorpion Regiment had all served in Italy. In the same period, the Canadians had committed one armoured division and two armoured brigades, and the Kiwis an armoured brigade.

The campaign to liberate Italy lasted over one-and-a-half years, due mainly to two factors. The first was that in the lead-up to, and following, the Normandy invasion of June 1944, the majority of Allied resources, including shipping and critically assault landing craft, were used in support of the main effort. This meant that Italy was regarded as an important but secondary campaign, and to a large degree was starved of the necessary resources to succeed quickly. The second factor was to do with the topography of Italy, something the Allies had an early taste of in Sicily. Italy is a long, narrow country. Over 1,000 miles from south to north, it is only about 100 miles across at its widest point. Running more or less up the centre of the country is the dominating feature of the Apennine Mountains, giving the country a definite 'spine', and from which numerous rocky ridges run east and west to the sea – the Tyrrhenian Sea to the west and the Adriatic to the east, both arms of the Mediterranean.[5] Between these ridges run deep river valleys. In addition to natural geography, in 1943 Italy was a poor and underdeveloped country, with few good roads but a profusion of mountain tracks, poorly maintained and running through numerous defiles and over bridges. As has been pointed out many times, this made Italy a defender's paradise, as an attack to gain possession of one valley and its dominating ridge would invariably have to be followed by the repeat process, up and down, over and over again.

Adding to the misery was the weather; extremely hot and sunny in the summer – with the associated dust and clouds of malarial mosquitos – in the winter rain and snow made the life of the soldier utterly miserable; one officer wryly called the Italian winter 'a feature that the Italian Tourist Board tends to be reticent about'.

Facing the Allies was a variable number of enemy divisions, but in broad terms the number of Allied divisions was roughly the same as that opposing them. On 8 September, following Mussolini's deposition Italy switched from being an Axis to an Allied power, leading the Germans to immediately take control of the country. The defensive potential of the geography was well understood by Rommel who was now the commander in northern Italy, and by Kesselring in the south. At this point there were seven German divisions in Italy, including two Panzer (16th and 26th), as well as three Panzer Grenadier and two parachute divisions; elite troops who were in Italy in order to rest and recuperate, although that quickly changed with a series of Allied amphibious landings made in early September 1943. The Germans reacted with their customary speed and aggression, seizing control of the country from the new Italian regime, and initially at least, using most of the German troops available to disarm the Italian army. In short order there were sixteen divisions in Italy, eight under Rommel in the north and the other eight under 'Smiling Albert' Kesselring, the very capable German commander in the south.

Operation Baytown on 3 September, coincidentally the fourth anniversary of the start of the war, landed two infantry divisions (supported by the Shermans of 1st Canadian Armoured Brigade) of the Eighth Army on the toe of Italy. After a preparatory naval and artillery barrage, the landing was unopposed; Kesselring had correctly assessed that this was not the main landing and decided not to contest it, preferring to hold his troops back and wait for the main assault. As they cautiously advanced, the main problems for the Eighth Army were demolitions and mines and, more perniciously, booby traps, which were to remain a problem for the rest of the campaign. As in Sicily, snipers also caused many casualties amongst tank commanders, and 1st Derbyshire Yeomanry lost Major Brundell, a squadron leader, when he stuck his head out of the hatch to get a better view of the situation: 'A sniper shot him through the head, and he fell back into the turret, spouting blood and dying.'[6]

Another unopposed British landing called Operation Slapstick was made – without armoured support – at Taranto, which was the same day that the main landing, carried out by Mark Clark's Fifth US Army, took place at Salerno. This was on the 9th, the day after the Italians switched sides. Kesselring very definitely did oppose this landing, and moved one of his Panzer divisions to interdict the Salerno beachhead. For a number of days, it was touch and go, with plans for evacuation being made, and although Monty was urged to rush his forces to Clark's rescue, his landing sites were 200 miles away and he was denied the resources to get there quicker. However, by the 15th the imminent arrival of the leading formations of Eighth Army in their rear made the German defensive position at Salerno untenable, and caused the first of a series of well-ordered withdrawals to the next defensive position, on the Volturno River, and which was a foretaste of the next eighteen months. It was also becoming clear that the Royal Engineers would be the critical component of the force, as they were needed in numbers to clear mines and booby traps, repair tracks and roads, and not least to repair or lay bridges: by spring 1945 Italy was the site of dozens of Bailey bridges replacing those blown by the Germans, some of which would remain there for many years to come. Tank crews discovered that the new German portable anti-tank weapons were deadly, often employed in 'shoot and scoot' tactics that made them difficult to counter. A favourite trick was to use the many vineyards for cover; from high up in the turret the commander would see only the canopy created by vines in full leaf, and could not spot the anti-tank teams at ground level.

By early October, the sunny weather that Italy is famed for was replaced by torrential rain, turning the fields and rural tracks into seas of mud, worsened by attempts to use them for vehicle traffic, and then made even more miserable by the December snows; many of the soldiers of all arms and services spent a wretched winter fighting both the enemy and the conditions, often soaked to the skin and plastered in the ubiquitous mud. Air support, something the Allies outnumbered the Germans in by a factor of around 10 to 1, was severely limited.

Another bloody river ... the topography of Italy made river crossings a monotonous regularity, with many conducted under fire as part of a tenacious German defence. This Sherman is being ferried using a Bailey pontoon bridge.

Even the tanks and other tracked vehicles often found the terrain impassable, and it is no exaggeration to say that for the next six months, the weather effects on the rugged and underdeveloped road system made manoeuvre warfare if not impossible, then extremely slow and inefficient; Neillands called it 'tactically ugly country', with steep hills and peaks, and large areas of marshland.[7] This meant that there was a lack of manoeuvre space and many of the armoured formations and units earmarked for service in Italy had to be held back elsewhere in the Middle East, and were not deployed until April 1944 or even later, as they would have been unable to influence the battle. Over the winter months, not only was Montgomery recalled back to the UK in order to prepare for the invasion as the commander of the 21st Army Group, but seasoned formations, units and officers went with him. In part, this was because of a desire to 'stiffen' the invasion forces with some experienced units – a policy that would have major repercussions, as will be discussed later – but also because Monty took key members of the Eighth Army with him, senior staff and commanders that he trusted and could rely on. This certainly had a negative impact on the remainder of the campaign in Italy, as the new team had to find their feet and, not least, earn the trust of the soldiers who remained in the Eighth Army. On 1 January 1944 General Sir Oliver Leese, one of Montgomery's corps commanders from the desert, took command of Eighth Army; a common feeling seems to have been that, 'He was alright, but he wasn't Monty.'

Two operations dominated the first half of 1944: the attempts to take the town and monastery at Cassino, and the Anzio landing. The Germans had once again prepared and occupied a series of defensive lines, making best use of the terrain and fortifying villages and buildings as strongpoints, and laying thousands of mines and barbed wire; one of these was known as the Winter Line, with parts of it called the Gustav and Helene lines. In the east it defended the Sangro River, whilst on the other side of the Apennines it made use of the high ground around the town of Cassino, preventing access to the Liri valley, an area which would have allowed the employment of armoured formations by the Allies. It can be argued that this was the strongest defensive line laid anywhere during the war because of the skilful use made of the rocky terrain. Although the line was eventually broken, it slowed the Allied advance for the first six months of the year, and included the assault crossing of the Sangro in the east, the four battles to take the town and monastery of Cassino, which eventually fell on 18 May, as well as the battle to capture Ortona on the Adriatic coast by the Canadians, known as the 'Italian Stalingrad'. As a sapper remarked, this was not the end, as 'behind the Sangro was the Moro, and behind the Moro was the Foro, and behind the Foro was the Pescara …'.[8] It is therefore understandable that many commentators have noted that of all the campaigns and battles fought by the British army during the Second World War, the Italian campaign was the one that most resembled the conditions of the First World War.[9] And even when the weather conditions favoured the use of concentrated armour, there was still a lack of space, particularly when compared with the campaign in northern Europe: in the Liri valley, four infantry divisions plus armour attempted to move through a narrow gap, creating great congestion. It was as well that the Allies possessed air superiority. As had happened in Sicily, the armour and the infantry needed to devise drills to get the best out of each other. The 9th Lancers realized that:

> There was no hard or fast rule as to who should lead. It might change as much as three or four times in a mile, depending on the terrain and on whether opposition was more likely to be anti-tank or anti-infantry. Each partner was aware of the difficulties and limitations of the other. If in the event tanks suffered heavy casualties, they saved the lives of many infantrymen and their sacrifice was worthwhile. All this sounds easy … it was the mass of small details that had to be solved correctly which made the complications.[10]

Getting out of synch during an attack could lead to co-operation breaking down, with fatal consequences, as 48RTR found out:

> Although the tanks managed to get into the village there was not enough infantry to clear it; as a result, Lt David Thomas was killed by sniper fire and his tank put out of action by a *FaustPatrone* [i.e. *PanzerSchreck*], and Lt Hunter's steel helmet was pierced by a sniper's bullet, which luckily only creased his forehead. Captain Ian More, commander of Recce Tp, was severely wounded in the shoulder by a mortar bomb while taking cover under his Honey, and his gunner, Tpr Wilkinson, was killed … One Churchill and three Shermans had been destroyed.[11]

In an attempt to outflank the succession of defensive lines, an amphibious landing known as Operation Shingle was planned to land forces at the seaside town of Anzio, south of Rome and 60 miles north of Cassino. This was intended to allow a rapid attack to take the operationally important terrain of the Alban hills, which would open up an advance north. Lacking enough landing craft and other naval assets to make the Anzio landing sufficiently strong, and although the landings achieved surprise, contingency plans were in place should landings be attempted and Kesselring was thus able to react quickly, with the first *Kampfgruppe* given its orders to deploy only 2 hours after the first reports. The assault force included substantial British elements, with 46RTR as the sole RAC representative. The initial landing was made on 22 January, six days after the first attempt to capture Cassino had failed. The seriousness of the situation at Anzio led to more German divisions being sent to Italy, and by the 25th, the Germans had three experienced divisions containing the landing zone and threatening the beachhead. Confusion and lack of aggression within the US chain of command led to the forces concentrating on build-up and defence rather than manoeuvre and attack, and despite extremely aggressive German counter-attacks, the subsequent impasse meant that there would be no victory for either side before spring; the intention to outflank in order to continue the advance north had failed. Conditions within the bridgehead at times resembled a siege.[12] Break-out was only achieved in late May, and the egocentric and publicity seeking Clark then dumbfounded his superiors by electing to drive for Rome rather than trying to cut off the substantial German forces attempting to retreat. Rome was symbolic but unimportant for the war effort and had, in any case, been declared an open city, meaning that it would not be defended in order to prevent destruction of its world-famous sites of antiquity. Clark got his headlines when the city was secured on 4 June, and announced to the world the following day. But the whole Italian campaign was about to become much less important when, on 6 June, the Allies landed in Normandy.[13]

Extremely useful in the conditions of Italy was the well-armoured Churchill tank. Made reliable since its first appearance, the protection afforded to the crew was well liked, as was its incredible hill-climbing ability, allowing it to conquer slopes that no other Allied vehicle could attempt. A local conversion removed the 6-pounder gun in 200 of them and replaced it with a surplus US 75mm, to produce the so-called Churchill NA75.[14] Despite the 4in of frontal armour on the Churchill, they were not invulnerable. Donald Featherstone of 51RTR, a

The American M7 Priest was a 105mm-armed SPG, used by the Royal Artillery, until replaced by the similar Sexton armed with the standard 25-pounder field gun.

Churchill unit, recorded an attempt to 'rush' a supposedly lightly held German position, supporting Canadian infantry:

> The country was very thick and wooded, and we had a number of tanks knocked out by anti-tank guns and *PanzerFausts* ... Coming into sight of the Adolf Hitler line, major losses were sustained here ... The final attack went in on 23rd May ... the German defences included dug-in Panther tank turrets, and these were intact and caused many losses. During this time, the tanks of A and C Squadrons were playing hide-and-seek in the woods with German self-propelled guns and tanks, and more losses were sustained. After this action, the Canadians asked us to wear their maple-leaf emblems on our tanks and tunics, which we did with considerable pride.[15]

Although the RAC was now much better organized in all respects than only two years previously, including access to tank transporters and the setting up of 'RAC

Senior officers from 44RTR conducting an O Group in Italy. The standard of orders groups varied enormously, with some described as being more like meetings to discuss a raft of known problems, rather than a clear set of instructions on how to make progress.

Schools' behind the lines in operational theatres, not everyone benefitted from them. Ken Riley MM, a loader/operator in 48RTR, described going into action in Shermans for the assault on the Gothic line in September 1944: 'I had only served in Churchills, and was unfamiliar with the 75mm gun on the Sherman. Many of my comrades had done conversion courses, but we went back into action before my time came. I would be alright [as long as] the gun did not jam.'[16]

During March, the 6th Armoured Division had arrived in Italy, bringing with it the 26th Armoured Brigade, containing the 16th/5th Lancers, the 17th/21st Lancers and the 2nd Lothian and Border Horse. Now equipped with Shermans, the crews found that their new mount was a huge improvement on the Valentines and Crusaders they had been used to. Although no match for the latest German Panzer IV, let alone the Panther or Tiger, the medium velocity 75mm gun had a useful HE capacity and was much used in squadron shoots, in which fifteen to eighteen tanks were lined up 'shoulder to shoulder' with piles of ammunition stowed on the engine decks and used in an artillery role. Although the M48 HE shell was nowhere near as effective as the artillery shells from the 25-pounder or the American 105mm, the speed of loading of the 75mm meant that such a squadron could deliver around 200 rounds on to an area target in a minute.[17]

Crossing rivers became a major preoccupation for the RAC units, who sometimes found themselves in front of the Royal Engineers and which could bring problems of its own. SSM Salt of the Derbyshire Yeomanry recorded a day in action thus:

At last, we were over the Rapido to stay. The Boche was withdrawing slowly and fighting desperately for every yard of ground he was losing … Around mid-day [B] squadron was ordered to recce a stretch of the river Melfa to find, and if possible to hold, a crossing. The Melfa was a very difficult river to approach, being heavily wooded on our side and to find a crossing meant going right up to the river bank. The river itself was typical of the Italian rivers. … torrents resulting from the snow thawing had, over many years, worn a deep gorge and so there were many steep banks on both sides. It was under very heavy concentrated MG fire and the use of open-topped Honeys to make the crossing was impracticable. It was decided to send the Shermans of two troops over, supported by a troop of M10s which was attached to the squadron. The four Shermans got over safely but the first of the M10s was hit by an A/T shell whilst actually on the bridge, and as the M10 brewed-up, the result was the complete destruction of both the M10 and the bridge … the three remaining Shermans, after hanging onto their hard-won bridgehead for over seven hours, were ordered to withdraw to as near the river bank as possible, to concentrate there and destroy the tanks, after which they were to try to get back on foot.[18]

A Sharpshooters' Sherman crossing the Volturno. Both 3 and 4 CLY were chosen to be returned to UK to take part in the North-West European campaign, where losses led to the two regiments being amalgamated.

After the capture of Rome, the next major German line was the Gothic line to the north, running from La Spezia on the west coast to Pesaro on the Adriatic and which had been under preparation for six months. But there were many other intermediate but still strong positions to be overcome before then, including the Albert line running west and east from Lake Trasimeno near Perugia, which was broken in late June, followed by the Arezzo line, taken in July, and then the Arno line the following month. By then the attackers, particularly the infantry and engineers, were exhausted and the decision was made to create a tactical pause. Unfortunately, although necessary, this lost around four weeks of summer campaigning weather, which took the pressure off the defenders. This allowed them to anticipate the next Italian winter with a degree of relish, with all of its attendant problems for the attackers, and meaning that the attack on the Gothic line did not start until late August, with a 15-mile-wide gap being created on the Adriatic coast after six days of very heavy fighting. By mid-September, the 1st Armoured Division was in such bad shape that by late October it was no longer effective, and was officially disbanded in early January, its regiments and brigades being dispersed, with some being converted into other roles, including the 3rd and 7th Hussars being trained to use DD amphibious tanks, and the 4th Hussars mounted on Kangaroos, tanks converted as APCs. On 1 October, a distinguished 12th Lancer and GOC X Corps, Richard McCreery, took over command of Eighth Army from Leese who was sent to the Far East.

As had happened in the previous winter, the appalling conditions prevented major advances, with a key element of Allied strategy being to remain just active enough to tie down the German divisions, to prevent them being used elsewhere. The Germans had destroyed much of the agricultural draining system and this turned a lot of the land into a quagmire, resembling Passchendaele at times. One commentator stated that the two most useful weapons were the bulldozer and the mine detector. Tanks were increasingly unable to be used, although the 10th Hussars noted that they used their 'Runnies', their nickname for the turretless Stuart tanks of Recce Troop, to evacuate wounded infantrymen.[19] The British infantry battalions in Italy had suffered badly throughout the summer, most of them being reduced from four to three rifle companies as the vast majority of infantry reinforcements were needed in North-West Europe where the manpower situation was critical. Because of this McCreery ordered that RAC units were to take their place in the line as infantrymen over the winter, to give the hard-pressed PBI a rest, and to make use of the crews even if the tanks

Although the terrain and conditions in Italy sometimes meant that armoured cars could not be used, in general they were employed with the same dash and panache that characterized their use elsewhere. In the foreground is the ubiquitous Daimler Armoured Car, with the larger American built Staghound behind.

and armoured cars were largely redundant. In yet another example of armoured crewmen being used as makeshift infantry, large numbers of tank soldiers spend long periods of the winter manning outposts, conducting patrols and fighting both the enemy and the conditions. Although they were not used in set-piece attacks, they certainly came to appreciate the lot of the infantry soldier, without access to the small but important comforts that came with being a 'tankie'. The 9th Lancers immediately christened themselves the 86th of Foot, 86 being their tactical identification number. In the same brigade, the 10th Hussars recorded their experience thus:

> On 23rd January we were warned to put our tanks into 'cold storage' and prepare ourselves to hold the line as infantry ... The regiment set about to organize itself and formed three dismounted squadrons and a machine gun troop. [This] consisted of the Reconnaissance Troop armed with .5 inch Browning AA MGs removed from the Sherman tanks, while the dismounted squadrons were organized into troops armed with personal weapons and .3 inch Browning MGs, also removed from the tanks. In addition, the 105mm Sherman tanks were formed into a regimental battery. We had a little over a week and then, on 1st February 1945, we left our billets for the frontline. Each squadron retained one of its own tanks for close support and a number of 'Runnies' ... Now we performed the unfamiliar work of filling sandbags, erecting wire and putting up trip-wires and flares. Foot patrolling was an onerous task by day and night ... On 2nd February Tpr Clarke of B Squadron failed to answer the challenge of one of our own forward sentries and was killed, and [on the 24th] Tpr Standen trod on an S-mine and subsequently died of wounds ... Nevertheless, we did our best to be good infantrymen. On 2nd March, the Argyll and Sutherland Highlanders arrived to take over our positions, the 2nd Armoured Brigade reformed and remounted its tanks.[20]

Many units recorded not only the miserable aspects of the campaign, but also the occasional delights; the 7th Hussars, occupying Giulianova, noted that:

> The inhabitants turned out to greet the leading troops. They cheered and clapped and showered the tanks with flowers ... They were greeted everywhere by thousands of cheering Italians, some with bottles of wine and some with colourful information on a wide variety of subjects – the names of the local patriots and the best restaurants, the whereabouts of escaped British prisoners, a German baroness, prominent fascists, other Italians of doubtful reputation, and even a beautiful Jewess whose reputation was not in doubt at all.[21]

The need to send troops to Greece in December had removed even more combat power from Italy, with 23rd Armoured Brigade being despatched.[22] Although the Germans had withdrawn from the country in October and November, a brutal civil war had erupted shortly afterwards, and Churchill was keen to support the Royalist side against the Communists. Two infantry divisions were sent, as well as a number of RAC units: 23rd Armoured Brigade, consisting of 40 RTR, 46RTR and 50 RTR, and the King's Dragoon Guards. All the units were involved in fierce and confusing combat, including in the centre of Athens, where the RTR units found themselves operating as much on foot as in their Shermans. In one of those bizarre decisions that only the British seem capable of making, the King's Dragoon Guards were later awarded the battle honour ATHENS, whereas the three RTR units were not, despite the armoured brigade suffering twenty-six killed in action and about one-hundred other casualties.

Once the winter weather had abated, a major spring offensive was planned for early April 1945, with Eighth Army striking towards Argenta on the 9th. Once again, Eighth Army faced more difficult terrain than the US Fifth Army in the west, particularly because of the twin obstacles of the River Reno and the area around Lake Commachio; the key would be to force armour through the gap between the two. Additionally, the majority of the German armour was now positioned in the east in order to protect the southern border of Austria. Specialist tracked amphibious carriers known as Buffaloes (sometimes referred to as Fantails) were used to transport infantry, and much use was made of the other newly reorganized specialist armour, including Churchill Crocodile flamethrowers for the first time in Italy, under the recently renamed 25th Armoured Engineer Brigade RE. The 4th Hussars found themselves converted into an APC regiment, scarcely a dashing cavalry role, but a critical one nevertheless; it was notable how in wartime most units just 'rolled their sleeves up and got on with it', whatever it was; it would not be until peacetime that the cavalry sought to reassert what it saw as its traditional – and limited – roles.

By mid–April both the Senio and the Santerno rivers had been crossed, the latest but not last in a seemingly interminable list of Italian rivers that had become indelibly printed on the memories of the British army in Italy. When the Germans attempted a withdrawal on the 19th, the 6th Armoured Division, in a rare moment of opportunity for a whole armoured formation, managed to wheel across the rear of the German retreat, helping to encircle and trap the majority of the German Army Group C. By the 25th both Allied armies were in full manoeuvre mode in northern Italy, crossing the River Po, and the Germans found themselves experiencing the same horror that had only too often befallen the British during the early years of the war, by destroying serviceable equipment that could not be evacuated; the German 65th Infantry Division was forced to destroy thirty-one Tiger tanks and eleven SPGs. On 2 May 1945, the German forces in Italy surrendered.

Summary of Key Dates in the Italian Campaign

1943

July
10–17: Invasion of Sicily (Operation Husky).

September
3: Operation Baytown landings across the straits of Messina.
8: Italy surrenders.
9: Operation Avalanche landings at Salerno. Operation Slapstick landings at Taranto.

October
1: Naples liberated.
13: Italy declares war on Germany.

November
22: Assault on Sangro River (to 1 December).

November–December
Handpicked formations and officers returned to UK.

1944

January
16: First Battle of Cassino.
22: Anzio landing.

February
15–18: Bombing of Cassino monastery.

May
18: Fall of Cassino following Fourth Battle.
23: Start of break-out from Anzio.

June
4: Rome liberated (open city).

July
16: Arezzo liberated.

August
4: Florence liberated (open city).
15: Gothic line reached.

September
2: Gothic line broken.
21: Rimini liberated.

November–December
Forces diverted to Greece.

December
4: Ravenna liberated.

1945

April
1: Allied spring offensive.
17: Argenta liberated.
28: Mussolini executed.

May
2: German forces in Italy surrender.

Chapter Six

More Design and Doctrine

The Later Development of British Tanks during the War

By late 1943 the Churchill had been improved dramatically; although the basic hull design was retained, the problems with reliability and poor maintainability had been largely solved, and a new cast turret with the 6-pounder gun gave it respectable firepower. In Tunisia it had impressed, and its showing in Italy had likewise done its reputation no harm. With its unusual design of extended side sponsons (allowing a roomy hull and, importantly, the inclusion of a side escape hatch on each side), as well as thick frontal armour (102mm), the tank was well-suited to withstanding close-range attack, particularly from the new threat of disposable infantry anti-tank weapons. In comparison with the Sherman, about 50 per cent of AP shots hitting the Churchill failed to penetrate; with the Sherman, it was only 30 per cent. It was also much less likely to catch fire, giving the crew more chance of a successful bail-out.

A re-worked Churchill Mk III, armed with the 6-pounder gun and one of six employed during El Alamein as part of 'Kingforce', where their unheralded appearance led to them being mistakenly identified as German and fired upon. The Churchill, despite some anachronistic features, proved to be a versatile and well-armoured tank.

Despite over 5,500 Churchills being produced during the war, there were not enough of them to go around in 1944, and this had implications in Normandy, as will be explained. In 1944 an improved model called the A22F (or Heavy Churchill) was introduced as the Mk VII. This had even thicker frontal armour of 152mm, meaning that only the relatively scarce King Tiger carried more. The tank was also welded, and the savings made in weight were allowed to be put back in terms of extra armour. A new turret was used, carrying the 75mm gun; unfortunately, the basic engine design was not upgraded, so the tank became even slower, with a maximum road speed of only about 12mph, one of the main reasons that Montgomery disliked the design and preferred Shermans. Overall, the Churchill was a successful design, representing the culmination of the British Infantry tank doctrine, and attracted the additional plaudits that came with being used as the basis for many of the most successful 'Funnies'.

In terms of Cruiser tanks, the period from 1943 to 1944 was dominated by the development of the Cromwell series. With the failure of the Covenanter and Crusader tanks, there was a pressing need to come up with an improved design that solved the shortcomings of poor reliability and fightability and carried more armour. The first attempt was the A24 Cavalier, which introduced a new basic hull and turret design, but which inherited many of the vices of its predecessors; only 500 were made, and the majority were used for training, a few only saw front-line service as OP tanks for the RA. Looking externally similar but very much better were the A27L Centaur and the A27M Cromwell. The Cromwell had a very low profile and featured a new six-sided turret that was designed to eliminate the shot-traps that had plagued the Crusader design, but crucially was powered by the Rolls-Royce Meteor, a 600hp modified version of the celebrated Merlin aero-engine. This made it extremely fast and very reliable, powering the Cromwell along at 37mph on roads and making, for the first time, best use of the Christie suspension. As a back-up in case the complicated Meteor project failed, a version powered by the old 340hp Liberty engine was built in parallel, called the A27L Centaur. This was designed in such a way that when sufficient Meteors became available, a Centaur could be re-engined and modified to turn it into a Cromwell, an imaginative approach. As well as serving as useful training tanks in the UK, replacing the awful Covenanters, Centaurs saw some service in North-West Europe as OP vehicles and also as the basis for AA tanks and other specialist roles.

But it was the introduction of the Cromwell that, whilst not perfect, marked a breakthrough moment in British tank design following four years of failure. At last, a reliable tank had been designed and built in Britain. In September 1944 General Verney, the commander of the 7th Armoured Division, the sole British armoured formation fighting in Cromwells, wrote to the War Office:

I feel that I must write you a short note to tell you how superb the Cromwell tank has been during our recent activities, and I hope that you will pass on the gist of this letter to the various people responsible for the production of the magnificent machine ... At dawn on August 31st we started our advance [and] it has carried us 250 miles in six days. We have lost practically no tanks through mechanical failure (I would guess four or five per regiment). Anyhow, so few that the matter has been no anxiety whatsoever. We have had actions every day [and] there has been no maintenance whatever ... The tremendous speed [has] alone made this great advance possible.

What let the Cromwell down was the gun. A lack of forethought when it was first specified meant that it was built with a turret ring that was too small to accept anything bigger than the British version of the 75mm, which was not a true dual-purpose gun.[1] The need to up-gun the tank led British designers down another rabbit hole, in which a Cromwell hull was lengthened by one additional roadwheel, and the superstructure modified to allow a 70in turret ring to be used to accept a turret capable of mounting the 17-pounder gun. This was the A30 Challenger. In all fairness, it was a good attempt at solving a specific problem in a short timeframe, but at heart it was a lash-up and only 200 were built, mainly because, fortunately, the Sherman Firefly had eclipsed the need for it. Used in

Desert Rats in the snow. The Rolls-Royce Meteor-engined A27M Cromwell was the first British Cruiser tank to be reliable. It was used solely in North-West Europe, and here crews from 7th Armoured Division are seen operating the tank during the winter of 1944–5. The 75mm gun was no improvement on the one carried on the Sherman.

Normandy within some of the armoured reconnaissance regiments until Fireflies became available, it was notable only for the first use of the name Challenger, which was conveniently ignored (or forgotten) when, in the early 1980s, the same name was given to a new Main Battle Tank.

The A34 Comet was the culmination of British tank design in the war, and was in effect a perfected Cromwell hull fitted with a new turret capable of carrying a 77mm gun and fitted with an all-round vision cupola. Unable to squeeze the large 17-pounder gun into the design, a Vickers high-velocity gun was used as the basis for development of the 77mm. Using the same projectiles as the 17-pounder but fitted to a slightly shorter cartridge case, the 77mm was given the name as a means of distinguishing it from its slightly larger cousin. Only used on the Comet, it did not have quite the armour penetration of the 17-pounder, but made up for it by being almost unbelievably accurate and consistent. The Comet was the best all-round Medium tank of the war, outperforming the Panther, the T34–85 and the later model Shermans. It only saw service with 29th Armoured Brigade (23rd Hussars, 3RTR and 2nd Fife and Forfar Yeomanry) and with the 11th Armoured Division armoured recce regiment (15th/19th Hussars) during the last three months of the war. The

In a near desperate attempt to shoehorn the excellent 17-pounder gun onto the chassis of the Cromwell, the A30 Challenger was created. It saw service in the Cromwell-equipped units in 7th Armoured Division.

The A34 Comet was the final development of the Cromwell series. Armed with the outstanding 77mm gun, the type only equipped four regiments in 11th Armoured Division before the end of the European war. These users are the 23rd Hussars.

15/19H history noted that: 'The Comet, unlike many previous British Cruiser tanks, was reliable and battleworthy from the first – a statement that bodes well for the future but provides a sorry epitaph on British tank production before and during the war'. Finally, the A41 Centurion deserves a brief mention, as it was designed during the war as a heavy Cruiser, but the first six examples arrived in Germany for combat trials just too late to see action; it then went on to be improved until it became the best battle tank anywhere in the world for the next two decades.

The Development of Specialized Armour

Without fear of contradiction, one of the great success stories of the RAC during the Second World War was the development of specialized armour. The basis of this can be traced back to 1917, the first full year that tanks were available on the Western Front. Almost as soon as tanks had been used operationally, it was realized that they had the potential to be used as the basis for specialized variants to deal with particular battlefield obstacles and conditions. Before the Armistice, these included the creation of tanks carrying wireless and telephone cables, the barbed wire-pulling tanks used at Cambrai, the re-invention of fascines, designs for self-propelled guns and armoured personnel carriers, and, not least, the modified tanks intended for Operation Hush, the planned assault on the sea wall at Ostend and which became the precursor of the tanks used in the amphibious operations of the Second World War. The inability of tanks at Cambrai to cross the canal obstacles led to urgent interest in the development of bridge-laying tanks, and which in turn led to Martel's appointment to command the Experimental Bridging Establishment at Christchurch, only 30 miles from Bovington. Before the end of the war, the most visionary of the Tank Corps officers were suggesting that every tank should be developed with an amphibious capability, and successful flotation trials were carried out on the Mk IX APC and Medium D tanks.

Between the wars, the lack of money for any concerted attempt to develop modern tanks meant that ambitions for developing specialized armour had to be placed on the back-burner, but some ground-breaking work was still done at the TTS, then at MWEE and its successor, MEE. Work was conducted on command, anti-aircraft, amphibious and bridge-laying tanks, as well as early experiments into night fighting using searchlights. Although most of these remained experimental, the grounding was created that would pay dividends when the need for such specialized types became apparent during the Second World War. The story of each type is lengthy and often technically complicated, each deserving of a book in their own right, but the development and use of each will be looked at briefly in turn, as well as the formation employed to develop their use in training and in battle, the 79th Armoured Division. As well as the types listed here, there were also literally dozens of experimental or minor types used or trialled, including bulldozers, 'Bobbin' carpet and trackway layers, mine-plough and mine-roller vehicles, and demolition charge tanks.

Amphibious Tanks

In about 1930 the Hungarian-born engineer Nicholas Straussler adapted a 4½-ton Light tank Mk II for flotation, using collapsible wooden floats either side of the hull, with the hull sealed to become waterproof and an outboard motor used to give propulsion and steering. Vickers-Carden-Loyd then developed a bespoke version, a true amphibious Light tank with a boat-shaped hull, the D12, which was demonstrated on the Thames in 1931, with two trials tanks being ordered as a result. Various technical problems dogged the project, and of course the lack of money meant that it was not adopted for service (although the USSR and Japan developed the idea and put similar Light tanks into service). Although there was general agreement that possessing amphibious tanks – at this stage for crossing rivers rather than seas – was useful, the concept was put on hold until the need for the capability was more pressing, and money available.

Once the next conflict started, both requirements were met. During June 1941 Straussler conducted trials on a different form of swimming tank, using a Tetrarch Light tank for early trials. Straussler realized that the weight of the tank was not the problem – otherwise how would a 70,000-ton battleship float? Rather it was the need to allow the object to displace a greater equivalent weight of water than the object itself weighed. He devised a scheme whereby a tank, with a carefully waterproofed hull, could carry a collapsible canvas screen all around the hull to create sufficient displacement and therefore allow the tank to float.[2] To propel the tank in the water, a power take-off from the engine would drive one or two propellors, and steering could be achieved by a rudder. This resulted in the system being known as Duplex Drive, or DD.

The first trials on a larger Valentine tank began in May 1942, and after the usual problems and empirical developments, 450 Valentine DDs were ordered to allow large-scale training to commence in mid-1943. The problem was that the Valentine, even when armed with the new 6-pounder, was approaching obsolescence as a gun tank, and a larger, more modern design was needed for the invasion of Europe. Fortunately, it proved practical to create a Sherman DD, and luckily for the units involved, they received their final quotas of Sherman DDs only a few days before the invasion of Normandy.[3] The use of DD tanks on D-Day came as a huge surprise to the Germans, as a swimming DD tank when viewed from the coast looked like a small and insignificant boat amongst a vast flotilla of landing craft and warships that all seemed to be juicier targets. Launched a few thousand yards from shore from a landing craft, it was only when

A Duplex Drive Valentine gingerly enters the water from the shore of a lake. The use of DD tanks on D-Day came as a huge surprise to the Germans, and allowed tank support to the infantry to be provided from the outset.

Once the basic techniques of using a DD tank on lakes had been mastered, the seamanship of the crews had to be tested – in conditions of great security – on open water. Entering the sea from a ship took the greatest care, as there was very little margin for error.

they reached land and dropped the screens that they revealed their true colours, and thus provided the assaulting infantry with the vital fire support needed for the first few hours, until more conventional armour could be landed from the large tank-landing ships. As well as the three RAC regiments operating DDs on D-Day, 4/7DG, 13/18H and SRY, other regiments were later converted to use the type. These included the Staffs Yeomanry, East Riding Yeomanry and 44RTR in North-West Europe, 3H and 7H in Italy, and 25D and 43RTR in the Far East. Operating the DD called for a certain amount of bravery even before engaging the enemy, as the freeboard – the distance between the top of the screen and the waves – was only 2ft or even less in a choppy sea, and despite the crews being equipped with a modified submarine escape apparatus, some crews drowned during their training. As part of Exercise Smash, 4/7DG were training in Studland Bay outside Poole harbour on 4 April 1944, when the weather suddenly deteriorated just as the tanks were launching from their landing craft, and six men drowned when their tanks were swamped and quickly sank. A different category of amphibians used by the RAC during the war in Italy as well as during the campaign in the Scheldt estuary and on the crossing of the Rhine were the so-called Landing Vehicles Tracked, or Buffaloes; these were an American design, not armoured but armed with machine guns or, in some cases, with a 20mm Polsten cannon. 4RTR, 11RTR, 1NY and ERY all operated the type. Post-war, the DD concept was retained in principle, and specifications for new vehicles generally included the requirement for them to be able to swim; this resulted in such vehicles as the FV432 and CVR series being built with flotation screens as standard, but which by the mid–1980s had gone out of fashion and the screens were seen as an embuggerance and generally removed by the crews.

Command Vehicles

The need for commanders to be able to operate just behind the front line in order to observe the battlefield and make instant decisions was fully recognized during the First World War, but the technology of the day did not allow this to happen. It was only when wireless and radio was developed during the 1920s and 1930s that the concept became practical, resulting in the need for specialized command vehicles. These came in two types: a modified Command Tank, equipped with additional radios to allow communication both upwards and downwards (for example, 'down' to the unit and 'up' to the higher formation HQ), and which gave the commander the same protection and mobility as the gun tanks around him; and the bespoke Armoured Command Vehicle (ACV), lightly armoured on either a wheeled or a tracked chassis, with more space to allow staff officers to communicate, plan and control. Both types were developed during the Second World War, including the Dorchester ACV, an armoured lorry, and command variants of all the main tank types.[4]

As well as tanks converted to become command vehicles by the addition of extra radio sets, armoured formation headquarters also used Dorchester wheeled ACVs, which were in effect mobile offices, with space for mapboards and several staff officers to work together.

Bridge-layers

Had bridge-layers been available at Cambrai in 1917, exploitation by the cavalry may have been made possible. Thereafter, the development of bridging tanks remained of great interest, and experiments between the wars initially focused on bridge-carrying tanks, meaning that the bridge, often an Inglis type, would still need to be man-handled over an obstacle, which in war would almost invariably mean under fire. In 1935 the Superintendent at the RE EBE in Christchurch developed the concept of a bridge-laying tank, whereby a hinged 'scissors' bridge could be launched over an obstacle from within the hull of a Light tank. From 1940 larger versions were developed and eventually the Valentine hull was selected for conversion, with enough being made to provide a troop of three tanks for each armoured division and independent armoured brigade; training on them started at Bovington in 1942. The bridge could be laid in about 2½ minutes and cross a 30ft gap, and despite the Valentine being obsolete as a gun tank, the Valentine Scissors remained in service until the end of the conflict, providing valuable service. Other types of bridge-layers were developed on the Churchill chassis including the armoured ramp carrier, or ARK, in which the whole vehicle was driven into a gap allowing use of the bridge structure and ramps mounted above it, and, post-war, the Centurion bridge-layer was developed (1960), followed by the Chieftain (1968). These were known as AVLB, or Armoured Vehicle Launched Bridge; during the 1960s

The invention of the Scissors bridge-layer tank was another notable invention, with three of these Valentine varieties allocated to each armoured divisional and brigade HQ from 1944 on.

The versatility of the Churchill design is illustrated by the number of different specialist roles it was used for; this is a ramp carrier, used to allow vehicles to scale otherwise impassable sea walls.

each armoured regiment was allocated their own Centurion AVLB, but they were later removed from the RAC establishment and placed under RE control, within the armoured engineer squadrons.

Armoured Vehicle Royal Engineers

It will come as no surprise to learn that thought had been given during the First World War as to how engineering tasks might be carried out using tanks; the use of fascines at Cambrai and later was in some ways such a task, as was the clearing of barbed wire obstacles using grapnels in the same battle. Had the war continued, the RE might well have found themselves crewing their own tanks, including bridge-carrying or bridge-laying variants, but the Armistice put a stop to that. It was not until the middle of the Second World War that the Royal Engineers were provided with their own task-specific armoured vehicle, the imaginatively named Armoured Vehicle Royal Engineers, or AVRE.[5] In large part this was developed following the failed raid on Dieppe in August 1942, and during which the sappers found themselves exposed and suffered high casualty rates as they attempted to clear obstacles. A suggestion after the raid led to a number of different tanks being examined for conversion potential, and the choice fell, as it so often did, on the Churchill. The tank was well-armoured, roomy inside and was available in large numbers for conversion. Its relatively slow speed was not an issue, as it would generally be used in deliberate rather than hasty operations.

The AVRE was the specialized Churchill par excellence. Armed with a 290mm demolition weapon, it could also carry fascines as well as a huge amount of specialist stores.

The main armament was replaced with a 290mm spigot mortar known as the Petard, used to 'chuck' a 40lb demolition charge up to 100yd; it was commonly nicknamed the Flying Dustbin. Although it was accurate and effective against concrete or similar targets, the downfall of the system was that it had to be reloaded from outside the turret, the 35 or so seconds it took representing an eternity when under fire. As well as the Petard, the spacious interior of the Churchill AVRE meant that a multitude of demolition and engineering stores and tools could be carried, as well as a fascine. The AVRE more than proved its worth on D-Day, being used by 1st Assault Brigade RE, with mixed crews containing both RAC and RE soldiers, the RAC members generally being the drivers. Subsequently, AVREs remained in great demand throughout the rest of the North-West Europe campaign where their contribution was significant. After the war different versions of Centurion AVREs were designed both with a 165mm demolition gun and with a 105mm gun plus mine–plough blade, and these saw active service in the 1991 Gulf War as well as, remarkably, in Northern Ireland. Later, surplus Chieftain tanks were modified as CHAVREs. The modern version is the Trojan AVRE.

Anti-Aircraft Tanks

A Light tank Mk I was modified in late 1929 as an experimental AA vehicle, mounting a pair of .50in MGs. Although such AA tanks, able to accompany a fast-moving armoured force and protect it from the increasing threat of ground-attack

A Crusader AA tank, armed with twin 20mm Oerlikon cannon; a similar turret mounted on a Centaur hull would later become the standard AA tank within armoured regiments, although some Crusaders were also used.

aircraft, were clearly a necessary part of modern mobile warfare, a lack of funds meant that the project was not developed into a service tank. The dominance of the Luftwaffe during the campaign in Belgium and France of 1940 underlined the need for such protection, and by mid-war Crusader and Centaur tanks had been modified to mount either a single Bofors 37mm or twin Oerlikon 20mm cannons, the latter model being preferred and becoming part of the establishment of the armoured regiment, as an AA troop of six tanks. Deployed during the Normandy campaign, the almost total Allied air supremacy meant that they were little used, although Lieutenant General Miles Dempsey commanding Second Army had an unfortunate incident when he was very nearly shot down by an over enthusiastic crew, which left him somewhat agitated. Some were used to great effect against ground targets, to plaster areas where snipers were thought to be taking cover, and even occasionally to deliver lines of tracer at night to mark the left and right flanks of an advance, but when the manpower crisis started to bite the troops were disbanded and the crewmen used as tank reinforcements.

Night fighting

Between the wars experiments were carried out into the use of tanks at night, which led to an appreciation that lights could be used not only as an aid to driving, navigation and gunnery, but also to disorientate the enemy. This was nothing new: Captain Douglas Browne MC Tank Corps, a First World War tank officer with G Battalion, wondered why the Germans had never thought of bringing strong searchlights up to their forward positions, in order to light up the British forward areas if they thought that an attack was imminent; this would have exposed every single tank attack as they had to approach the trenches at night before launching attacks at first light. After the war, in 1927 a series of night exercises conducted by 2 Bn RTC against infantry in Oxfordshire showed that the blinding effects of white light upon infantry were both disorientating and potentially terror inducing, and so a seed of thought was sown. Percy Hobart came to the same conclusion seven years later. His report on the tank exercises of 1934 included a comment that:

> … a strong headlight … should be provided on a sufficient number of tanks to enable an experiment to be carried out next year. If such a headlight not only dazzled the enemy but enabled tank gunners to shoot more accurately it might be possible to reduce or even abolish the star shells which are at present our only means of lighting an attack at night.

In fact, an invention called the De Thoren Dazzle Device had been submitted to the War Office for consideration as early as 1920 and was meant to be mounted on what was described as a Light tank, and despite the rights to it being obtained by the War Office, its potential was initially dismissed by many and ignored by most, leading to yet another good idea being placed into the 'too difficult or too expensive' tray.

In a separate experiment, in 1936 the RTC had begun to conduct night firing from tanks using MGs aided by spotlights. It was found that when firing at an 8ft^2 white target from a range of 300yd, nearly half of the bullets hit the target. Dark targets representing men could be picked out at about the same

A Grant CDL. The secrecy attached to the project meant that although a huge amount of resources was spent on perfecting the system and training a number of regiments in their use, the CDL was not much used and post-war was allowed to sink quietly into obscurity. It did however indirectly lead to the provision of a night-fighting searchlight on Centurion.

range. It was realized that the more powerful the searchlight, the greater the range and accuracy. The use of very powerful tank-mounted spotlights (aka searchlights or light projectors) as a means of firing accurately at battle ranges at night was not finally realized until the late 1950s on Centurion, and later on Chieftain, but before this happened the idea of using the dazzle effects of light proposed by De Thoren was to be resurrected during the Second World War. The De Thoren device was dusted off in early 1940 and it was placed in a specially designed turret on a Matilda tank. The coded title of Canal Defence, Lights (CDL) was used for the project. Tactically it was found that a line of CDL tanks could advance together about 40yd apart, with their flickering pools of light not only distracting the enemy, but also creating what amounted to black holes between the brightly lit areas, allowing advancing infantry to shelter within them, all-but invisible to the enemy until they were only 50yd away, at which point an assault could be made. It was never intended to be used as an aid to allow night combat by lighting up enemy tanks – that would only come post-war. The CDL device was extensively trialled but remained classified as Top Secret, as it had the potential to be launched in complete surprise against an unsuspecting enemy. In March 1941 a top-secret CDL training school was formed at Penrith in northern England, and two complete brigades (1st and 35th Tank Brigades) with five regiments (11, 42 and 49RTR, 152 and 155 RAC) trained in its use. After 1943 the CDL device was mounted onto Churchill and Grant hulls, but it was probably the difficulties of deciding when to spring the surprise on the enemy that led to it never being seriously used in action, and after the war the concept was quietly sidelined in favour of searchlights mounted on gun tanks.[6]

Flamethrowers

German storm troops had used portable flamethrowers in 1918, and the British thus became very aware of their potential in subduing fortified positions, particularly well-protected bunker systems that were all but impervious to conventional attack. During the Second World War, experiments with 'Ronson' flamethrowers mounted in carriers and on Valentine tanks had been carried out in 1941. Three Churchill Oke (named after its designer) flamethrower tanks were landed by the Canadians at Dieppe in August 1942, although none used their flamethrowers during the attack – probably luckily for the crews, as they were all captured. Percy Hobart, commanding the 79th Armoured Division, required the use of flamethrowers as part of his formation, and the Churchill Crocodile was developed, based on the Mk VII model.[7] This still mounted a 75mm gun, with a flame projector taking the place of the hull MG, and 400 gallons of special fuel was carried in a two-wheeled trailer towed behind the tank. With a range of about 100m, the weapon was extremely effective, and was successful in forcing the surrender of the fortified port of Le Havre in September 1944.[8] Many crews preferred to demonstrate the flame first by firing short ranging shots, with the

The fearsome Churchill Crocodile flamethrower. British crews sometimes preferred to induce the enemy to surrender by demonstrating a few warning shots. The potential of the weapon was obvious, and a squadron of Crocodiles was sent to Korea in 1950.

intention of inviting the defenders to surrender without the need to attack them directly. Units using the Crocodile in North-West Europe included 7RTR, 1FFY and 141 RAC, and in Italy they were operated by A and C Sqns 51RTR in 25th Armoured Engineer Brigade RE.

Flail Tanks

Anti-tank mines were only developed in the period between the two world wars, as an easy and cheap means of denying ground to enemy tanks, and it was found that the mere threat of a minefield could be enough to deter tanks from moving forward. If a tank did come into contact with an AT mine, there would be sufficient damage to at least disable the tank, and as the underbelly or floor was invariably the thinnest armoured part of any tank, casualties were also likely to result, the crew in the front hull being the most vulnerable. Up-armouring the floor of a tank beyond that initially specified was technically difficult and, in any case, in the era when small anti-tank guns were making their presence felt, there were more important places to add additional armour.

The original idea for what was to become the flail tank is usually accredited to Abraham Du Toit. He was a captain in the South African Defence Force serving in North Africa, and had the idea for a method to cause the mines to explode harmlessly, by beating the ground in front of the tank with something that exerted enough pressure to cause the mine to detonate. After experiments with heavy rollers and ploughs, the best method found for doing this was to use rotating chains, known as flails. The requirement to be able to clear minefields was clear and urgent, and Du Toit was sent to the UK in late 1941 with orders to develop his ideas there with the AEC company working for the Fighting Vehicles Division of the Ministry of Supply. This led to two parallel lines of development. Back in North Africa, enough was known of his ideas for experiments to begin in his absence, eventually (in August 1942) modifying a Matilda tank as the test-bed vehicle; the RE, the RAOC and the REME were all heavily involved in the design and trials, with Captain Norman Berry RAOC leading the work. The modified tank was allocated the code name Scorpion, in trials the concept was proved and destroyed up to 100 per cent of the mines in its path, although the success rate was very much less when operating over broken ground, as mines in furrows could be missed. The flails also proved to be useful at beating a path through barbed wire; they could even be used to dig away raised defensive earthworks. The rotor for the chains was projected forward of the tank on rigid latticework arms, and the drive came from a Bedford engine located in a lightly armoured box on the right side of the hull; inside the box next to the engine was the unfortunate operator, who worked from inside there during flailing operations, a most unpleasant job. The engine tended to overheat and the same must have happened to the crewman sitting alongside it.

Around thirty Matildas were converted for use in the El Alamein battle of October 1942, being operated by crews from 42RTR and 44RTR, and one tank

A Sherman Crab flail tank. Initially experimented with in the Western Desert using Matildas, the later Crab retained its 75mm gun, which was to prove very useful on D-Day when many of the Crabs found themselves being used as gun tanks during the initial assaults.

used in the battle was credited as having destroyed forty-seven mines. In early 1943 41RTR was re-titled to become the 1st Scorpion Regt, and became responsible for operating flail tanks in North Africa, as well as during the invasion of Sicily. A much-improved version based on the Sherman tank and called the Crab was developed in the UK during 1943 and was ready for the Normandy invasion. Units using Crabs throughout the North-West Europe campaign included 22D, 1 LBY and WD, all in 30th Armoured Brigade. Crabs were also deployed to Italy in the last months of the war, being operated by B Sqn 51RTR. After the war development work on flails continued, including on the so-called Churchill Toad, but by the late 1950s interest – and funding – had abated and the flails passed into history.

Armoured Recovery Vehicles

Towards the end of the First World War and in the early post-war period, some British heavy tanks were fitted with crane booms (or jibs) to the front of the hull to allow them to be used in the essential salvage/recovery operations. Between the wars tank recovery relied upon either wheeled vehicles or self-recovery using another tank. During the Second World War, as tanks became ever larger

A number of different Armoured Recovery Vehicles, or ARVs, were built during the second half of the war using the main tank types as the basis. This is the Churchill variant, complete with dummy gun. ARVs were an invaluable tool in salvaging damaged vehicles from an active battlefield, and thus helped commanders to retain high levels of combat power.

and heavier, the concept of a specialized Armoured Recovery Vehicle or ARV was developed, generally using redundant or obsolescent tank hulls; examples included the Crusader, Churchill, Cromwell and the American M32, based upon the Sherman. For use on beaches, a specialist Beach Armoured Recovery Vehicle, or BARV, was also developed, which allowed recovery to take place in deep water. By the last year of the war various types of ARVs were widespread in tank units, crewed by unit personnel, although in time the recovery function passed to the REME. Post-war, both Centurion and Chieftain ARVs were used, as well as the vehicle currently used, the Challenger based Challenger Armoured Repair and Recovery Vehicle, or CRARRV.

The Funnies: 79th Armoured Division

Formed on 14 August 1942, less than a week before the Dieppe raid, the division was originally intended to be another conventional armoured division. The requirement to categorize all the strange and experimental vehicles that were in the process of being developed led to the need to place them all under a headquarters that could organize trails, develop doctrine and offer advice on their best use, and so 79AD became such a (unique) division in April 1943. Fortunately, the divisional commander was the hugely experienced, energetic and intellectual Major Gen Percy Hobart, he of the Egypt Mobile Division, who had been rescued by Winston Churchill from an obscure and premature retirement. The division's scope and span of command was huge, with many more responsibilities than a normal armoured division would have. Quickly the nickname for the division became 'The Funnies' or 'Hobart's Funnies', and whilst this might have originally been meant to deride, its combat record would later speak for itself, the name being used with pride both inside and outside the formation. At the end of 1943 it consisted of:

- 27th Armoured Brigade
- 4/7DG, 13/18H, ERY – DD tanks
- 30th Armoured Brigade
- 22D, 1LBY, WD – Flail tanks
- 35th Tank Brigade
- 49RTR, 152RAC, 155RAC – CDL
- 1st Assault Brigade RE
- 5 Assault Regt, 6 Assault Regt, 42 Assault Regt

The formations and regiments within it changed over the course of the next two years, but one thing never altered: the sheer size and scope of the Funnies. The difference in tasks and the training locations required, including the all-important need for secrecy, meant that in an average week 'Hobo' travelled about a thousand miles, often to remote locations where the training was conducted behind very closed doors. Never one to avoid detail, he took an active part in every aspect of the division, and was critical in spotting and then developing the potentially battle-winning capabilities that would be needed to support the invasion of Europe. One key part was the experimental wings. A to E Wings were formed in the UK to oversee trials on certain specific problem areas, and F to J Wings were formed on the continent whilst in action, to do the same with new problems and ideas, such as anti-personnel mines, multi-barrelled smoke dischargers, crossing the Rhine and navigation. Every rank was encouraged to put forward bright ideas, from whole systems to improvements on existing ones, and this paid dividends time and again.

As well as the Normandy landing on D-Day itself, in which Sherman DD tanks, Churchill AVREs, bulldozers and Sherman Crab flail tanks took a leading part, the units continued to be involved in many of the set-piece attacks over the next eleven months, notably in the capture of the intricately defended port of Le Havre. New equipment was brought in as required, including the fearsome

'Hobo', Major General Sir Percy Hobart, was the energetic and highly imaginative commander of the 79th Armoured Division, the Funnies, for most of the war.

Churchill Crocodile flamethrower and the Landing Vehicle Tracked Buffalo, used both in the miserable Scheldt campaign over the winter and on the Rhine Crossing of March 1945. No other nation came anywhere close to emulating the success of the division; American generals were often sceptical of the capabilities, but their soldiers tended to appreciate them on the occasions when they were loaned to support them. The Germans and the Russians did not have anything like the appetite for specialist vehicles, with the Russians relying on mass. It is somewhat surprising that the Germans in particular did not do more in the field, but by the time they came to realize their utility, it was probably too late.[9]

Although it was by now the largest division in the army, 79th Armoured Division was overstretched in North-West Europe and could not be spared for work in any other campaign.[10] However, its utility had been proved, and in Italy in October 1944 the 8th Army's Chief Engineer proposed expanding the existing 1st Assault Regiment RE into a full assault brigade, to be ready for service by 1 February 1945; the peculiar conditions in Italy demanded this, and it was a pity that the initiative to do this had not come earlier. The 25th Tank Brigade was converted to become known as B Assault Brigade RAC/RE on 5 January 1945, to fulfil the same type of roles as the Funnies, albeit on a smaller scale and with less access to specialized vehicles. On 6 April it was designated as the 25th Armoured Engineer Brigade RE. Within the new brigade, 51RTR was equipped with Crab flail tanks and Crocodile flamethrowers, and the 'A' and 'B' Assault Regiments RE (later numbered as 1 and 2 Assault Regiments) manned Churchill ARKs, AVREs and Sherman dozers. This filled the pressing need for specialized assault engineer functions in Italy, where the terrain suited the defence and the specialized vehicles saved lives.

Individual and Collective Training in the UK

Once a soldier completed his basic and trade training at one of the RAC Training Regiments, he was usually posted to a regiment. Some would be sent overseas as 'drafts', to the Middle or Far East, and would join a regiment there, in a lot of cases being allocated to the regiment only on arrival and, for an unfortunate minority, to a different regiment to that which they thought they were going to. The majority were posted to a regiment stationed in the UK, and in the period following the invasion scare of 1940–1, settled into a routine of training, in preparation for either a posting overseas as a complete unit, or as part of the home forces, with an eye on a return to Europe at some unspecified future time.

One of the problems faced by all the RAC units stationed in the UK was that they were very vulnerable to sudden demands to send trained manpower to another unit at extremely short notice, often in order to fill gaps in that unit's establishment – usually because it had been warned off for duty overseas. Receiving a warning order for overseas service was often greeted with considerable relief by a regiment, as it meant that they were no longer liable for such demands, and instead, would be the one demanding immediate reinforcement. Allied to this constant chopping and changing, the officers (and more frequently) soldiers posted in such a way had to be integrated into the new ways, traditions and personalities within their new unit, and this often proved most difficult for three groups of personnel; members of the regular cavalry, the regular RTR and the pre-war yeomanry, all of whom had very strong loyalty to their original, parent regiment. Legally they could be compelled to move, as they were enlisted into the RAC rather than a specific regiment, and whilst such transfers never came close to mutiny, they were an unwelcome feature of life in a corps and caused much resentment. To be fair, the vast majority of unwilling transferees quickly settled down, particularly in those regiments that recognized the issue and went out of their way to incorporate the new arrivals in a sensitive manner.

Regimental training was often at the whim of the Commanding Officer who, unless directed otherwise by his formation commander, could largely do as he saw fit. This led to a large variety in what training was conducted, how well it was done, and what areas were emphasized – or ignored. The training regime could change completely, for better or for worse, on the change of the CO. For example, one CO might believe that the most important things were vehicle maintenance, physical fitness, shooting on the move and manoeuvring as a regiment: his training programme would thus concentrate on these areas. A new CO might come in and throw all this out, insisting instead on troop and squadron training, anti-gas precautions, pistol shooting and wireless procedures. It all depended on the experience, energy and intelligence of the officer concerned. It would be a rare regiment that managed to put together a balanced programme that covered all eventualities, and of course the efficacy of any training would also depend upon the professionalism of the officers conducting the training, as well as the training areas and facilities available. To be fair, the War Office and RAC were not idle in trying to assist regiments; a plethora of publications, pamphlets, aides-memoires and the like were constantly being issued, including lessons from recent operations, that needed to be assimilated and acted on. In retrospect, it is clear that there was simply too much information being sent out, some of it contradictory, to be useful at unit level; all it did was overload the officers who quite literally could not see the wood for the trees.

This did not, of course, apply to trade training. Following on from the policy set in place by the RTC pre-war, it was always the intention to have every tank crewman proficient in all three trades – gunnery, D&M and wireless – so that there was the maximum flexibility in moving crewmen around when required. As the majority arrived from the training regiments qualified in only one main trade, considerable effort was required by each regiment to constantly run internal courses, taught mainly by NCO instructors, in order to have them qualified and at a minimum level of proficiency in all three areas. Such courses were run to an approved syllabus, which made life easier for the units in terms of planning, but which still took a lot of time and resources. Not helping was the constant turnover of personnel, postings and promotions, meaning that if there was one word that could not be applied to the armoured regiments, it was stability.

Another aspect of regimental life for units in the UK was the frequency of moves of location around the country. Due to the sheer size of the army, and the need to use pre-war barracks as training centres, most regiments found themselves sent to villages and small towns to be billeted as best as could be arranged, the officers invariably doing better than the ORs; relatively obscure names such as Inverary, Castle Toward, Ogbourne St Andrew, Parnham House, Coleman's Hatch, Wickham Market and Colne Park became familiar to a generation of RAC soldiers. Where billets could not be found, tented camps were used, which would be miserable in winter. Tanks were parked in open fields, and the units were often split into squadron locations a few miles apart. The soldiers seem to have quite liked such arrangements once they became settled, as long as they were within striking distance of a decent town; the biggest complaint was being stuck in the 'arse-end of nowhere'. Unsurprisingly, many wartime relationships began as a consequence of such proximity, frequently resulting in marriages and something of a baby boom. Local agricultural areas were used

One of the most successful aspects of RAC doctrine was the use of wireless for the rapid transmission of information and orders. The No. 19 radio set was the cornerstone of this, with some experienced regiments choosing to place all the vehicles on one common radio net, to produce what later become known as an 'all-informed net'. This required great levels of discipline.

for tactical training – often with quite severe restrictions to prevent damage to crops – but units would have to travel to properly set-up ranges to carry out firing practices (and which became more difficult to manage as firepower increased and larger safety templates were required). These included Lulworth, plus the ranges on Salisbury Plain, Linney Head (now known as Castlemartin) in Pembrokeshire, Barnard Castle, Aldborough, Otterburn, Warcop/Brough, Midhope, Boyton, Titchwell, Hornsea, Seaford and Kirkcudbright.[11] As an indication of such frequent movements around the country, one regiment will suffice as an example, the Fifth Skins. After evacuation from Dunkirk in June 1940 they spent the next four years training in England and Wales, moving, according to the regimental history, on average once every three months. Places they inhabited included well-known towns such as Northampton and Whitby, and also less-familiar places including Keele Hall, Builth Wells, West Tofts, Ashington and Rowlands Castle.

The selection and training of tank – and armoured car – commanders in particular requires close examination. During the First World War, all tanks were commanded by junior officers, some lieutenants but mostly second lieutenants. The section leaders (captains), company commanders (majors) and battalion commanding officers (lieutenant colonels) were not allocated tanks, the latter two ranks being entitled to a horse instead for use out of action (and which is why RTR field officers wear spurs in mess kit).[12] However, the experiments between the wars and particularly the introduction of radio allowed control to be exercised as the battle developed rather than to some prescribed and artificial timetable, and it became doctrine for all officers in command positions to be mounted in

In a pose familiar to generations of RAC soldiers, a gunnery instructor oversees a Valentine crew going through their paces on a range. As the size of guns increased, the need for ranges firing out to sea also increased, and demand always outstripped supply.

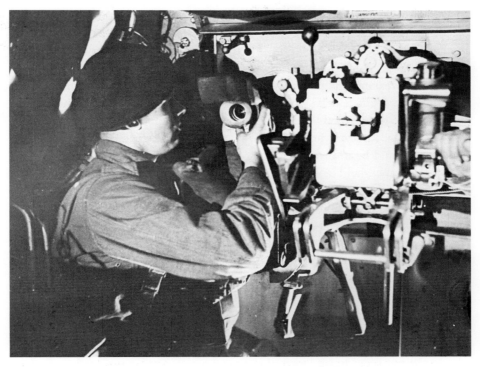

A 2-pounder gunner adjusting the sights – this was a necessary operation to give the crew the best possible chance of a first-round hit, but the quality of optics often reduced the chances. Crews were amazed by the quality and magnification of the systems used on German tanks.

tanks. At around the same time, the establishment of the RTC battalions was changed to include NCO tank commanders, generally sergeants and corporals.[13] By the start of the Second World War it was standard for a three-tank troop to have a lieutenant as troop leader, plus a troop sergeant and a troop corporal.[14] Where the troop had four tanks, the extra tank was commanded by a second corporal or, not uncommonly, by a lance corporal. In action, commanding a tank was not universally popular; it was thought that it was the most dangerous of all the crew positions – which operational research later proved to be true – and many experienced soldiers, including pre-war regulars, did their level best to avoid becoming a tank commander.[15] But for the more ambitious, it was seen as the role to aspire to. This naturally led to the requirement for some form of tank commander's course. Unlike the post-war period where tank commander became a recognized trade (with pay) in its own right, during the war the training of non-commissioned commanders was generally the responsibility of the regiments themselves, with predictable variations in quality.[16] In some units – and this applied most often during active service – a gap was filled simply by promoting a seemingly suitable soldier into the role; volunteers were preferred, and many turned down the 'opportunity', but for those who accepted the offer, it was a case of using one's previous observations and experience, and learning on the job. For many their advancement took place in the dead of night within a leaguer or harbour, being summoned to the OC's tank to hear the news, and their first experience of commanding was in a battle. Despite this, there are countless examples of exceptionally gifted tank commanders coming from the ranks, including Sergeant 'Buck' Kite of 3RTR, the only serviceman in the Second World War to be awarded three Military Medals.[17]

Large-scale force-on-force exercises were not common, but when they happened, could be impressive events, at divisional, corps or even larger levels. Exercise Bumper, held in central England during October 1941, involved twelve divisions – including three armoured – and three independent armoured brigades, totalling more than ¼ million participants. Designed to test not only anti-invasion measures but, more importantly, expeditionary warfare and the large-scale command of troops, important lessons were identified, including: commanders who remained too far to the rear to influence the battle; a reluctance to issue verbal orders; poor wireless discipline; and a general lack of understanding of the speed of modern mobile warfare. General Sir Alan Brooke, the experienced and deep-thinking CIGS, was able to identify senior officers who could not 'cut the mustard', including Carr of Eastern Command who dispersed his armoured divisions into penny-packets, and Burrows of 9th Armoured Div, a cavalryman who could not seem to understand the need for all-arms co-operation. Brooke,

During the war, sergeant majors were mounted in tanks; here the RSM (third from right) of one of the Guards battalions in the newly created Guards Armoured Division parades in front of his Covenanter.

always honest, commented in his diary: 'Sad mishandling of armoured forces by higher commanders ... I am delighted the way armoured divisions have come on, but disappointed at the way higher commanders are handling them ... Again, heart-breaking to see armoured forces wrongly handled.'[18]

Other large-scale manoeuvres included exercises like Victor in early 1942 and Spartan in March 1943, which became the largest field exercise ever held in Britain. Although some progress had been made, there were still significant concerns over the same big issues; higher command and control, slow, muddled or over complicated orders and communications remained poor, hindering the passage of information. At the lower tactical level during these immense affairs, the tank crews got less out of it than they might. Handicapped by limited track mileage, as well as orders not to damage crops needed to feed the nation, and to use roads wherever possible, they could become stifled affairs with little training values for the regiments, squadrons and crews. They were also largely unrealistic, and the crews could sometimes spend hours involved in frantic rushing to and fro, followed by days of static inactivity with no idea what was meant to be happening; junior – and even quite senior – officers were in many cases equally baffled, as their learning was purely theoretical and such information as they received from active theatres of war, meaning mainly North Africa, could be difficult to contextualize for European conditions. By late 1943, however, with plans starting to crystallize for the invasion of northern Europe, the armoured formations and regiments realized that in fairly short order they were going to form part of the invasion force, even if their exact role was not clear. The exception to this, of course, was Hobart's Funnies, who were going full-steam ahead in developing their specialist techniques in readiness for the big day.

By spring 1944 the formations and the units that had been sent to the UK from Italy to 'stiffen' the huge but inexperienced army in Britain had arrived, complete with the selected officers that Monty had chosen to bring along on his coat-tails; not all would live up to his expectations and some would face the chop in due course. It must be understood that the policy of including at least one veteran regiment in each of the armoured brigades, as well as the complete 7th Armoured Division, was not universally popular, not least amongst the units involved. There was undoubtedly a feeling that they had done their bit, and it was time for the hundreds of thousands who had not yet been sent abroad or seen action to pull their weight; in April 1944 there were about 1½ million army personnel in the UK. They had a point; many of the veteran units selected for the role had been in action for much of the war. 1RTR had been in Egypt throughout the whole campaign in the desert, as had the 11th Hussars who had also served in Italy. 5RTR had fought in France with the BEF before being sent to the desert and then Italy. 3RTR had been sent to the defence of Calais in 1940, before spending nearly two-and-half years in the desert, not to mention their contribution to the abortive campaign in Greece. Both 3rd and 4th CLY

The track maintenance being carried out on this Valentine 'somewhere in the UK' could be on an exercise, or it could equally be in one of the many muddy fields used as improvised tank parks for the expanding RAC.

had fought in some of the fiercest battles in Libya and Tunisia, as well as service in Sicily for the 3rd and Italy for both. And it was not only the unfairness that irked them; 7th Armoured Division found that it was to be re-equipped with the new Cromwell tank for the invasion, a type they were unfamiliar with and which was tainted by the reputation of the earlier British Cruisers. They would have preferred to stay on the Sherman, a type they knew well, and the conversion courses required ate into leave and pre-invasion training time.[19] And then there was the accommodation and living conditions. In the role of 'Johnny come lately' when they arrived back in the UK in early 1944, they found themselves shoehorned into wherever they could be fitted, which usually meant the worst places. In the case of the Desert Rats, the division was spread out in north Norfolk. The divisional infantry brigade was at least able to be billeted in and around the large town of King's Lynn, but the 22nd Armoured Brigade was sent to the less salubrious area around Brandon, a few scant miles from Elveden of First World War fame. The divisional history complained that:

> The area was not an attractive one, a low-lying, sandy waste with groups of decaying Nissen huts clustered beneath tall pines. There were many administrative matters to be dealt with such as the home system of documentation, less generous rations, small fuel allowances, exact accounting

for stores and barrack damages, leave and travel problems … Once again the tricky business of waterproofing the vehicles had to be undertaken, this time for wading in a depth of at least four feet. Ranges on which to fire weapons were few and hard to come by and training areas were restricted, a very different state of affairs to the old desert days and the wide-open spaces.[20]

The bronzed veterans found the leave entitlement on arrival less than generous. A soldier with up to two years overseas service received only two weeks, there was a whole extra week as reward for another two years in foreign climes, and those with more than four years would get a total of one month. 1RTR was based under canvas in the tiny hamlet of Didlington, where the CO 'encountered several problems of morale':

> Quite a few NCOs with seniority and good records applied to transfer to other units less likely to be in the front line. A few went but most stayed. Monty visited 1RTR on 17th February … [Before he] arrived we daubed slogans in large letters on our tanks 'No leave, no second front!'

Monty, to his great credit, preferred to deal with problems head-on. He jumped up onto the bonnet of a jeep and said: '"There is one thing I am going to tell you right now – you are *not* getting any leave, and you *are* getting a second front!" We all cheered.'[21] The policy was hardest on those in the units who had served the longest and seen the most action.

On arrival back in the UK units swapped around in order to have at least one experienced regiment in each brigade; for 3RTR who were sent to Bridlington, this meant replacing the 24th Lancers as part of 29th Armoured Brigade in 11th Armoured Division, under their old CO Pip Roberts, now a major general, whilst the Lancers took their place in 8th Armoured Brigade, one of the Sherman-equipped independent armoured brigades. All was not well with some of the veterans. In 3RTR, Sergeant Geordie Reay DCM suddenly asked for an interview with his squadron leader, ex-ranker Bill Close:

> 'Well Geordie?' 'I want to get out of the army sir.' It was the last thing Close had been expecting but his reply was quick enough: 'So do I. Now tell me if you've got better reasons.' 'I don't think I'm fit to command men in battle sir. I've lost my nerve.' 'Well, that's not going to help your case', said Close, pointing at the DCM ribbon. The case was referred to Lt Col David Silvertop, the Commanding Officer. Silvertop simply said 'I'm afraid you're just going to have to carry on like the rest of us Reay,' And so he carried on.[22]

Another problem faced by the AFV crews earmarked for the invasion was that, in almost all cases, they received new and often unfamiliar equipment; this meant

The 13th/18th Hussars, a DD regiment in 27th Armoured Brigade, received the last of their Shermans only days before the invasion, including their first batch of the new Sherman Fireflies, mounting the 17-pounder gun.

that a lot of the time available had to be spent on individual trade, rather than collective, training. But there was little doubt that as the units drew new tanks, including brand-new Sherman Fireflies, waterproofed their vehicles and were loaded up with ammunition, rations, gas masks, steel helmets and the like, that the second front that Monty had promised was imminent. Each of the units began a slow move towards the south coast, ending up in closed-off transit camps near the embarkation ports, where the tedious task of waterproofing the tanks took place and the final kit was issued, ready for the off. For some of them, it came in early June 1944; D-Day.

Chapter Seven

The Decisive Campaign

North-West Europe, 1944–5

Montgomery arrived back in the UK from Italy on 1 January 1944, as the new commander of the 21st Army Group. He was a very busy man, amending and enlarging the scope of the draft invasion plan presented to him, but he found the time to take a great interest in the affairs of his armoured arm. He remained convinced that the Infantry/Cruiser doctrine was flawed, and that all he required was a single type of tank, crewed by men who had been trained in both roles. Unfortunately, his tank of choice was the Sherman, based on his experience in North Africa and Sicily/Italy, and no doubt influenced by his knowledge of the unreliability of British Cruisers. He also thought that the Churchill was too slow for the type of rapid break-out and exploitation campaigns he expected to fight. Riding the crest of a wave, Monty was able to get his way, and had he been able to, the whole of his British – and Commonwealth – armoured forces could have been mounted in Shermans. As it was, supply issues forced his hand, and he had to make do with two of his three British armoured divisions mounted in Shermans (11th, Guards), one equipped with Cromwells (7th), plus four of the independent tank/armoured brigades operating Shermans (4th, 8th, 27, 33rd), the remainder operating as Infantry tank units on Churchills.[1]

The first three RAC regiments ashore were three amphibious tank regiments, each operating with two squadrons of Sherman DD tanks, plus a 'normal' third sabre squadron (including all the regiment's Fireflies) and RHQ.[2] In order to achieve the required surprise in their first ever use, the plan was for two of the squadrons to swim ashore, followed by the remainder of the regiment about 90 minutes later, once the initial beach defences had been subdued, allowing the regiment to then drive inland as a body. Approaching Sword Queen White and Queen Red beaches as part of convoy S-3, A and B Squadrons 13th/18th Hussars launched from their Landing Craft Tank (LCT) on the order 'Floater 5000' at that distance rather than at 7,000yd as had been planned, due to the 5ft swell. Intended to land at 0630, the shorter journey meant that they arrived even before the assaulting infantry.[3] Of the forty DDs launched, six were sunk during the run-in, including two which had the misfortune to be rammed by landing craft. The 2IC of A Squadron, Captain Denny, was the only survivor when his tank was hit by its own LCT immediately after launching; the LCTs were flat-bottomed and difficult to steer, particularly in rough weather. Firing from behind the DDs during the run-in were the 25-pounder Sexton SPGs from the RA regiment of each of the infantry divisions, although with what effect from a pitching platform can only be speculated – it can be said that they hit France, if nothing else. Also forming part of the invasion force were some Centaur CS tanks with 95mm howitzers plus a few Shermans, part of the only tank force ever operated by the Royal Marines, the Armoured Support Group. The force was disbanded two weeks after D-Day.

At about the same time that the first DDs reached the beaches, the Funnies of the 1st Assault Brigade RE were also coming ashore, primarily AVREs, bulldozers and Crabs, and these managed to open up the exits from Sword beach faster than on any of the other beaches. The Sherman Crab flails found themselves using their 75mm guns in fire-support tasks much more than they had envisaged; it was a fortunate design decision that, unlike the earlier flails used in North Africa, the Crabs retained the normal gun turret. By the end of the 'longest day', the Hussars had lost thirty-one out of their complement of sixty-three Shermans, the majority from the two DD squadrons. However, plans were afoot to replace them, as such losses had been predicted. On D+1 the 266th Field Delivery Squadron RAC was due to land with thirty-one replacement tanks; the AFV replacement system

DD tanks, with their canvas screens collapsed, make their way through the streets of a town. As well as their use on D-Day, these swimming tanks were employed later in the war to cross major rivers such as the Rhine.

A Royal Marines Armoured Support Group Centaur Close Support tank, armed with a stubby 95mm gun, makes its way through the Normandy rain.

throughout the campaign was extremely efficient, and able to replace losses – both tanks and crews – at a pace the Germans could only dream of. At 1030, another tank regiment was put ashore on Sword, the Staffordshire Yeomanry. Five Shermans belonging to B Squadron and the RE were knocked out along with the medical officer's half-track by a well-sited 88mm before it was itself destroyed. Later, the SY were instrumental in beating off a strong counter-attack by Mk IVs of 21st Panzer Division, knocking out about twenty of them and using the long-range gunnery of the new Fireflies to good effect, thereby preventing interference with the beach operations at a critical stage. In the early afternoon the third regiment of 27th Armoured Brigade, the East Riding Yeomanry, also landed on Sword.

On Gold Beach, 50th Infantry Division were supported by the two DD squadrons (B and C) of the 4th/7th Dragoon Guards (Gold King Red and Gold King Green), and the crews must have been grateful to be back on land, having been afloat in the poor weather since 2 and 3 June. Slightly further west on Gold were the two squadrons from the Sherwood Rangers Yeomanry, also B and C, assaulting Jig Green and Jig Red.[4] As this was the most westerly of the 21st Army Group beaches, the combat there helped to relieve at least some of the pressure on nearby Omaha, where the American forces were struggling to make headway.

AVREs proved their worth many times during the seaborne landings, with some inevitably coming to grief in the process. It is probable that this tank was rapidly recovered and repaired.

A Crusader AA Mk III of HQ 22nd Armoured Brigade makes it way ashore onto a Normandy beach. Within a few weeks the lack of a credible Luftwaffe threat led to most of these troops being broken up, and their crews used on gun tanks.

The weather at Gold was notably worse than further east, and because of this the 4/7DG DD tanks were not swum ashore but were launched onto the beach, a riskier choice for the LCT crews but one more guaranteed to at least get the tanks ashore in one piece; as the decision of when to launch lay with the LCT commander, there was a 'heated discussion' before the RN could be persuaded to comply.[5] The SRY had a similar discussion, but with them a half-way house was the result, the tanks launching at about 800yd, losing eight on the way in. Some of the tanks had the misfortune to near dry land only to drive into submerged craters caused by the large-calibre naval gunfire earlier, which were large enough to swallow a Sherman whole.

One problem that was becoming difficult to manage was the congestion on the beaches. The choice had been made to land near to high tide, as this would mean less exposed beach to cover for the attacking infantry. The downside was that the many submerged obstacles remained underwater, and once the beach was captured, there was much less sand on which to manoeuvre the ever increasing numbers of vehicles being landed. But the majority of the tanks were active on the beach, and particularly welcome was the presence of the Fireflies. Lieutenant Hoban of the Crab-equipped Westminster Dragoons remembered:

We saw three tanks of the 4th/7th Dragoon Guards hit and starting to burn some 800 yards ahead. We quickly got our tanks behind cover in fire positions ... a 4/7DG subaltern came running up to ask if we had any Fireflies with us; apparently, they were fed up of [*sic*] seeing their 75mm AP shot bouncing off the German tank.

For these units it must have been galling to realize for the first time that the 75mm gun on the Sherman was going to struggle to defeat German armour at combat ranges. At least some of the senior generals knew that this was a likelihood, but there was nothing to be gained from making this known; what was required was better tanks guns, in particular the 17-pounder in much greater quantities than the one per troop. Muddying the waters was the fact that the 17-pounder HE shell was considered to be greatly inferior to the 75mm HE, and thus the brakes were put on the issuing of Sherman Fireflies – to a maximum of two per troop – until the HE shell was improved. The experience of 1941 in the desert had been learned, in that HE fire was a necessary attribute of the tank – but perhaps it had now been over learned, and the desire for a good HE shell hindered the provision of effective anti-tank weapons.

The 4/7DG were particularly unfortunate late in the evening of D-Day when a spotter plane mis-identified them as German, and called down accurate naval gunfire from HMS *Orion*; ten men were killed and sixteen wounded, and by the end of the day, they had lost nineteen of their tanks from various causes. But it was notable that, at the very start of the invasion, two of the first three RAC regiments to land were those that had fought so gallantly in the withdrawal with the BEF, and which had been evacuated from Dunkirk. The irony could not have been lost upon them.[6] The key now for Montgomery was to push forward to create space, which would not only increase the length of front-line terrain that the Germans would have to defend, but would give him more space for his own manoeuvre and, critically, allow much more combat power and the supporting logistics to back it up to be landed behind. This lack of space was a constant headache, as everyone needed it – the formation headquarters, the combat units and their echelons, as well as the logistic support, in terms of workshops, ordnance depots, fuel and ammunition units, hospitals and the other medical units, signals, engineers, mobile laundry and bath units, temporary POW cages – in short, the whole army.

Two of the biggest users of space were the Royal Artillery, for their guns and ammunition requirements, and the RAF, who needed to establish tactical air strips as soon as possible. Therefore, the RAC units were only one moving part in this huge enterprise, and the armoured divisions, brigades and regiments were only sent across the Channel when shipping was available and there was space within the bridgehead in which to place them.[7] This meant that the third of the British armoured divisions, the Guards, had to wait until the very end of June before making the crossing, and the independent 6th Guards Tank Brigade

Camouflaged Priest SPGs of the Royal Artillery in Normandy; the need to standardize field gun ammunition swiftly led to their replacement with the 25-pounder Sexton, allowing the surplus vehicles to be returned to the US army or converted to become armoured personnel carriers.

did not arrive until 20 July. With the pre-invasion creation of the armoured reconnaissance regiments in the divisions, mounted in tanks and most often being used as a fourth tank unit, the armoured car regiments were on the strength of the different corps, and so moved with them, quickly finding themselves in action.[8] The campaign in Normandy lasted from D-Day until the closure of the Falaise gap on 19 August, signalling the defeat of the German forces there and the commencement of the fast armour led drive east towards the Seine and beyond.[9] Aside from the assault landings, the campaign was punctuated by large, planned operations designed with specific operational aims, and conducted at corps level or above.

Operation Perch and Villers-Bocage

The first of these major operations was Operation Perch. The necessity for such an operation had been considered back in the UK, with the intent being a powerful drive to the west of Caen, towards the high feature of Mont Pinçon. Miles Dempsey, the Second Army commander, was concerned that the front line might already be 'congealing', and he wanted to maintain momentum by using his armour aggressively. In essence, Perch tried to take advantage of a perceived gap between two divisions in the German defences, and required 7th Armoured Division's armoured brigade (22nd) to drive into the gap, seize the town of Villers-Bocage and the high ground (Point 213) 1 mile to the east, and thereby threaten the flank and rear of the *Panzer Lehr* division. After some unnecessarily tardy planning by XXX Corps which probably lost 24 hours – never a good idea when trying to take advantage of a fluid opportunity and particularly when it allows the enemy to stiffen a defence – the advance began late in the afternoon of 12 June, but there was not enough daylight to make much headway and the movement halted overnight. On the morning of the 13th it continued, with 4th County of London Yeomanry (The Sharpshooters) spearheading the narrow thrust. The regiment had landed on Gold Beach on the 7th, and were one of the regiments returned to the UK for Overlord, having fought in Libya, Tunisia and Italy, so although it was nominally a territorial regiment, it was in fact battle-hardened and experienced, although not used to the type of terrain and warfare that it found in Normandy.[10] Lieutenant Colonel Lord Cranley, the CO of 4CLY, had requested to be allowed to send out reconnaissance in advance of his lead squadron but this was refused by Brigadier 'Loony' Hinde, the (ex-15/19H) brigade commander, on the basis this was unnecessarily cautious and would slow the whole proceeding up; in fairness, Hinde was almost certainly being pressurized from division, corps and even army to 'get cracking'. What happened next was in hindsight avoidable, and has become probably the most famous British tank engagement of the war: the action at Villers-Bocage.

At about 0800 on 13 June 4CLY arrived in the undefended town from the west. A Sqn reached Point 213, the divisional objective, and halted in a defensive position with the infantry vehicles of A Company 1st Rifle Brigade. Unbeknown to them, the 101 *Schwere* SS Panzer Battalion, equipped with Tigers, had made an overnight march and by early morning the five Tigers of 2nd Company, commanded by *Obersturmführer* (roughly senior lieutenant) Michael Wittmann, were only a few hundred yards away at Montbrocq, undoubtedly well camouflaged to avoid the attention of the Allied air forces. The remainder of the Sharpshooters group (mainly infantry, the recce troop and the RHQ vehicles) behind A Sqn made the unforgiveable error of bunching and failing to adopt an all-round defensive posture, probably assuming that ground, once taken, was theirs, and the Germans would not contest it. Instead, the remainder of the regiment formed a nose-to-tail column stretching back into the town, although B Sqn remained outside – fortunately. Despite the presence of artillery FOOs in OP tanks, as well as anti-tank guns and infantry, when a regimental O Group was held at Point 213, the remaining crews took the opportunity to make tea and relax, and were thus ripe for slaughter when Wittmann charged at them with his solitary Tiger – having already changed tanks as his first vehicle had broken down with engine trouble. As soon as Wittman saw the Sharpshooters' tanks, he assumed that he had been spotted and reacted instantly, without informing the rest of his company who may only have known of the combat when the first noise of gunfire reached them. In effect, Wittmann conducted a reverse ambush, in which the aggressor was mobile and the victims were static.

The only tank capable of penetrating a Tiger or Panther at normal battle ranges in Normandy was the Sherman Firefly. Each troop of three-gun tanks was allocated a single Firefly, which was generally kept slightly to the rear, only called forward when necessary. The distinctive long barrel made it stand out, and German gunners would try to knock out the Fireflies first.

Wittmann quickly knocked out a Cromwell and a Firefly at the rear of the A Sqn column, blocking the exit and fortunately destroying the only tank capable of inflicting serious damage on him, and then drove along the column, destroying the Stuarts of Recce Tp and the carriers and half-tracks of the infantry. At about this time the remaining 2nd Company Tigers also began engaging the A Sqn tanks leading up to Point 213; the confusion was increased by the fact that many of the British commanders had dismounted to attend the O Group. Wittman then engaged the CLY RHQ vehicles, which were unable to reverse fast enough to get out of his sights; three of the four Cromwells were destroyed, with the Adjutant, Captain Pat Dyas, managing to escape by rapid manoeuvring and taking cover in a garden. Next to go were the two OP tanks of 5RHA, both mounting dummy guns and unable to defend themselves.[11] A scout car managed to escape and alerted B Sqn 4CLY, and a Firefly commanded by Sergeant Lockwood of 2 Troop charged up, at which point Wittmann decided that he had had his fun and tried to withdraw, during which time Dyas reappeared and managed to hit the Tiger with two 75mm rounds, but these failed to penetrate and he was then knocked out himself, to become Wittman's final victim of the morning. Wittmann's Tiger was then disabled, and after remaining mounted for a while and carrying on fighting, he and his crew made their escape on foot, walking 10 miles back to the *Panzer Lehr* divisional HQ to report the success.[12] Meanwhile, the Tigers of 1st Company of the 101 Battalion with some Panzer IVs of the *Lehr* attempted to enter Villers-Bocage but were successfully beaten off by B and C Sqns 4CLY assisted by the 6-pounder guns of 1/7 Queens, destroying about half a dozen Tigers and Panzer IVs, although the isolated remnants of A Sqn around Point 213 were gradually reduced during the morning and many were captured in the early afternoon, including Cranley, the CO. That night a German attempt at a counter-attack with around thirty tanks was halted to the north-west of the town, once again making it clear that in the terrain, regardless of the relative merits of the tanks involved, the defender had a clear advantage. Sergeant Pumphrey 4CLY was a crewman on the tank of the 2IC, Major Arthur Carr, and recorded his memories of Villers-Bocage:

It was deserted and quiet … There were none of the usual signs of devastation … Eeriness shattered into grim reality by that crack-brrrmmmph-bang than can come only from an eighty-eight. A Honey tank ahead was transfigured into a mass of roaring red and crimson flame … Wireless silence was broken by the Colonel [who had gone up to Point 213 in a scout car, along with Carr] with urgent orders to deploy for battle … I saw the second Honey immediately ahead of us share the same fate as its leader. One moment a tank, the next something without shape or form, belching flame and smoke from its turret, the ammunition inside exploding and red and yellow tracers weaving fantastic patterns around it, intermingled with vivid red and green glows of Verey cartridges.[13]

As Dyas had found out, the 75mm was no match for the Tiger, unless a weak spot could be found: Pumphrey's crew fired four rounds with no effect before being destroyed, with Pumphrey himself being badly burned and taken prisoner of war.[14]

The action at Villers-Bocage has gone down in history as exceptional, which of course it was, even though it lasted for less than half an hour. But in truth, 4CLY suffered no more casualties in those few minutes than any regiment might expect to suffer in a single day of intense combat elsewhere in Normandy. (The losses are disputed, but seem to be: 18 Cromwells, 4 Fireflies, 3 Stuarts (Honeys), 14 half-tracks, 16 carriers and the 2 5RHA OP tanks.) What made it different was that the action was concentrated in both time and space; that the attempts by the Cromwell crews to defend themselves proved how ineffective the 75mm was, even at close range; that the majority of the damage was done by a single Tiger, aggressively – even foolishly – handled; and that the whole thing was avoidable, had elementary precautions (dispersion, concealment, all-round defence, remaining mounted) been taken. Longer term, the action at the higher tactical level had clearly been mismanaged, and Dempsey and Montgomery both started to form the opinion that Bucknall (the XXX Corps commander), Erskine (7th Armoured Division) and Hinde (22nd Armoured Brigade) all lacked drive and tactical nous. In the short term, Bucknall called Operation Perch to a halt during the 14th, and overnight XXX Corps withdrew to defensive positions. Hinde, in a report to Erskine, his immediate boss, complained that the whole rationale behind a thrust such as Perch in close country was unsound:

> The idea of a massed weight of armour punching a hole in blind [unreconnoitered] country in face of anti-tank guns and tanks of superior quality is not practical … we are at a grave disadvantage having to attack Panthers and Tigers with Cromwells and Shermans. This disadvantage largely disappears when the enemy attacks us …[15]

His last comment was bang on the money: although 21st Army Group had to remain on the offensive and where possible wrest the initiative from an aggressive and experienced enemy, the German habit of throwing in an immediate counter-attack whenever a position was lost was both predictable and costly. Despite the overriding operational need to preserve their tank forces, the Germans may well have lost more tanks and men in Normandy in conducting such attacks than they lost whilst defending.

Operation Epsom

The next big attempt was code-named Operation Epsom, and followed the arrival of more British armoured units and the expansion of the bridgehead. Unloading using the two Mulberry harbours had been proceeding apace until, on the 19th, a violent 'great storm' – reputed to be the severest Channel weather for forty years – blew up and lasted three days. By the end of it the American Mulberry harbour 'A' was out of action and would remain so, with supplies having to be landed directly onto the beach. The British 'B' Mulberry was damaged but remained usable, and the Allies knew that it was going to be essential to capture a large, usable port. Until then their strategic ambitions would be constrained by logistics. Operationally, both sides knew that Caen was the key to unlocking the campaign, with Montgomery frequently referring to is as the 'pivot' about which the Allies could swing eastwards, towards Germany.

Epsom was a three corps operation, as VIII Corps had arrived to supplement I Corps and XXX Corps. The main offensive role went to O'Connor's VIII Corps, who would attack using two infantry divisions (15th Scottish, 43rd Wessex) supported by 11th Armoured Division, 4th Armoured Brigade and 31st Tank Brigade; about 600 tanks in total.[16] The Churchill-equipped 31st Brigade would support the Scots, and the Shermans of the 4th would be paired with the Wessex. 11th Armoured Division, and in particular its armoured brigade, the 29th, would be used to exploit any breakthrough made by the infantry. The terrain was tricky, with fields of high corn and bocage country, and the valley of the River Odon, an objective, was heavily wooded. The stormy weather of 19–22 June had prevented the Allies from flying over the battlefield, and the time was used by the Germans to move forces around without fear of interference from the air, and to improve their defensive positions. Attempts to secure the flanks by I Corps in the east and XXX Corps in the west largely failed, and therefore the VIII Corps thrust would have exposed flanks as it progressed south, something that British commanders were never comfortable with.

Moving off on the morning of 26 June, with the weather still poor and in heavy rain, the initial progress made by the newly landed Scots soon ran out of steam, with problems of Infantry tank cooperation once again coming to the fore. The 31st Tank Brigade had never worked with the 15th Division before, and this was where doctrine was meant to come in, by having a common understanding of procedures that all formations and units could use. But doctrine had been confusingly tinkered with in the months leading up to D-Day, and in any case had never been strictly enforced during training. This was to prove to be both a curse and a blessing, a topic that will be returned to in due course. 7RTR ran into a minefield within half an hour of starting out, as a result losing not only nine Churchills but also contact with the infantry that they were meant to support.

Due to the stalling of the infantry attack, O'Connor unwisely decided at about midday to try to push General Pip Roberts' 11th Armoured through in an attempt to regain momentum, but the point that Hinde had made after Villers-Bocage was still valid – armour, even if used in large numbers, could not hope to punch through a strongly prepared defence in depth, held by experienced infantrymen who were well supported by anti-tank weapons. *Sturmgeschutz* assault guns were starting to be encountered in numbers. These were low and well-armoured SPGs built on the Panzer III chassis, and mounting a 75mm HV gun in a limited traverse mount. Although nowhere near as flexible as tanks due to the lack of a turret, the 'Stugs' were nevertheless formidable defensive weapons, their low height and good frontal armour making them perfect for 'shoot and scoot' tactics. Following the then-received wisdom of leading an attack with the Division's armoured reconnaissance regiment, the inexperienced Cromwell-equipped 2nd Northants Yeomanry were ordered to 'dash' forward to seize bridges over the Odon; the Germans had deliberately not destroyed them as they needed them for their own movement, the perennial problem with bridge demolitions. However, only two squadrons of 2NY had arrived in Normandy thus far, and of these only one squadron, A, was used in the operation. Getting close enough to see the river but unable to penetrate further, the attempt failed and was called off in the late afternoon, and the day closed in drenching rain with the British still a mile short of the Odon. The village of Cheux, captured earlier in the day, now became a choke-point, with the narrowness of the 'Scottish corridor', as the salient was referred to, meaning that German forces only a mile or so away could bring indirect fire down onto the area, and columns of tanks returning to leaguer impeded an attempt to push the Shermans of 2nd Fife and Forfar Yeomanry (29th Armoured Brigade) through to continue the attack. Even when they got through the congestion it quickly became clear that tanks operating at night were easy prey to *PanzerFaust* teams, and after several losses, 2FFY were recalled.

The following day the attack was resumed in the continuing rain, and another enduring truth was discovered: attempts to push tanks over ridgelines covered by anti-tank guns was suicidal. Trying to use armoured division tactics in the close countryside would not work, and the small fields and sunken lanes simply caused cohesion to break down, and regimental and even squadron actions degenerated into a series of independent engagements. On 28 June the 11th Armoured finally got over the Odon and seized the high ground of Point 112 in the afternoon, the southernmost point in the advance and extremely exposed to German defenders on three sides. Initially held by the 23rd Hussars, who were then relieved by 3RTR when their ammunition was running low, both regiments who fought there found that the bare hill had very little cover and this made the tanks vulnerable to long-range fire from Tigers, 88mm guns and Panthers, as well as artillery and mortars, that could not be easily answered.

On the 29th the weather improved allowing the Allied tactical air forces to dominate the skies once more, but Ultra decrypts were indicating that a strong German counter-attack was being prepared, and the salient caused by the penetration seemed very vulnerable, particularly as the choke-point at Cheux continued to restrict logistics and resupply. Late in the evening, Roberts was ordered to withdraw all his units that were south of the Odon, thereby surrendering possession of Point 112; 3RTR had lost twelve tanks in

Major General Pip Roberts, the highly successful commander of the 11th Armoured Division, started the war as a captain in 6RTR. He is seen here in Normandy in his White Scout Car command vehicle-cum-runaround.

defending the location. Both 4th and 29th Armoured Brigades were withdrawn to the rear, to replenish and be prepared to react to any German attack that might develop.

On the morning of 30 June it was decided by Montgomery – who was much better informed because of Ultra than his subordinate commanders – that no more progress could be reasonably expected with the resources available – the so-called culminating point – and the operation was halted. About 5 miles of territory across a fairly narrow front had been captured and held. The Germans reoccupied the two dominating high points of 112 and 113, but remained south of the Odon. VIII Corps moved into a defensive posture, expecting a strong attack to try to pinch out the salient. Overall, the five days or so cost the British about 120 tanks, although these could be fairly easily replaced, and many of the knocked-out tanks could be recovered and put back into service. The Germans were grateful that they had managed to hold off what was clearly a major attack, but it came at great cost: they lost an estimated 100 tanks and nearly 20 Stugs, which they could not so easily replace. In accordance with their doctrine of immediate counter-attacks, 10th and 11th SS Panzer Divisions tried to attack northwards on 1 July, but the tables were now turned, and the British defences held, making use of the terrain in a similar way to the Germans, and in which the short-range PIAT infantry anti-tank weapon proved to be almost as good as the *PanzerFaust*.

Epsom therefore failed to make the progress hoped for, but it did succeed in the largely unintended way that all the British offensives did: by coming close enough to achieving a breakthrough to force the Germans to throw in their reserves simply to hold the line, which operationally would eventually lead to success.[17] But it was not a war of attrition that was desired, but one of manoeuvre; the Germans simply refused to play ball. Twice in succession the British had tried and failed to use an armoured division as a battering ram to create a break-in and breakthrough, whereas those tasks should have been achieved by the infantry supported by the armoured and tank brigades; the armoured division was organized and trained for break-out and exploitation, not for a set-piece assault battle.

Deployments and Replacements

By the end of June 1944, the following British armoured units were operational in Normandy:

7th Armoured Division: 8H. 22nd Armoured Brigade: 1RTR, 5RTR, 4CLY. 263 Forward Delivery Sqn

11th Armoured Division: 2NY. 29th Armoured Brigade: 23H, 3RTR, 2FFY. 270 Forward Delivery Sqn

79th Armoured Division: 30th Armoured Brigade: 22D, 1LBY, WD. 1 Asslt Brigade RE: 5 Asslt Regt, 6 Asslt Regt, 42 Asslt Regt

Guards Armoured Division: 2 Welsh Guards. 5th Guards Armoured Brigade: 2 Grenadier Guards, 1 Coldstream Guards, 2 Irish Guards. 268 Forward Delivery Sqn

4th Armoured Brigade: Greys, 3CLY, 44RTR

8th Armoured Brigade: 4/7DG, 24L, SRY

27th Armoured Brigade: 13/18H, SY, ERY

31st Tank Brigade: 7RTR, 9RTR, 141RAC (Crocodile)

33rd Armoured Brigade: 1NY, 144RAC, 148RAC

Corps Troops: 2HCR, 11H, 2DY, ICY

Recce Corps: One Recce Regt attached to each Infantry Division

The East Riding Yeomanry in Normandy; fighting initially in Shermans, the unit was one of the many that was re-rolled in the middle of the campaign, in their case onto the Buffalo amphibious tractor.

Other armoured formations and units remained in UK in their embarkation camps and were ready to go, but the lack of space in the bridgehead as well as the backlog created by the great storm and the damage to the Mulberries meant that the deployment schedule was thrown out of kilter.[18] Another factor was also about to come into play; the necessity to include regular cavalry regiments in the 21st Army Group order of battle. There was no way that famous cavalry regiments would be allowed to remain in reserve in the UK when war raised cavalry, yeomanry and RAC regiments converted from territorial infantry battalions were fighting in Normandy. In particular, this applied to two units: the 5th Royal Inniskilling Dragoon Guards, and the 15th/19th King's Royal Hussars. Both regiments had seen a lot of action in a few short weeks with the BEF in 1940, but since then had remained in the UK on anti-invasion duties and training, and it was galling to see other regiments being sent overseas. There is little doubt that the senior generals realized that opportunities had to be created to deploy the two regiments to Normandy, and the losses within deployed regiments provided the chance. At the end of May, the Skins had been issued new tanks and kit and put on standby to deploy. Eventually the regiment crossed the Channel without its vehicles in mid-July, and were disappointed to find that the unit they had expected to relieve, 3rd County of London Yeomanry, was still in action (in Operation Goodwood), and the regiment then became employed for a couple of weeks helping out with the AFV replacement organization. It was only then that they were ordered to take over Cromwells and replace the 4th CLY in 22nd Armoured Brigade on the 29th, where they remained for the rest of the campaign.[19] The 15/19H had to wait a little longer; the unit took over from the 2nd Northants Yeomanry as the Cromwell-equipped divisional recce regiment in 11th Armoured Div on 18 August. It should be noted that however glorious a regiment's previous history might be, it counted for little in combat. When the Skins arrived in Normandy, they found that hundreds of years of cavalry service was no guarantee of acceptance within 7th Armoured Division:

> These regiments and battalions had seen as much or more fighting in the war than any others in the British army, and they conveyed a strong impression to the regiment that in their eyes we were new boys whose spurs had yet to be won. The first indication occurred as the squadrons moved forward to join the brigade [consisting of the highly experienced 1 and 5RTR]. At one point the column halted beside a broken-down tank of another regiment, a member of whose crew enquired 'What mob are you?' On being given the answer he replied 'Never 'eard of yer!' and with a contemptuous shake of the head his grimy face disappeared once more into the engine compartment.[20]

By this stage of the war the description of regiments as regular, territorial, yeomanry and war raised had to a large degree lost their relevance. All units had few pre-war regular soldiers left in their ranks, as the good soldiers had been rapidly promoted to become senior NCOs and warrant officers, and often commissioned, and such experience needed to be spread around the hugely expanded corps. With the officers, this meant that good-quality captains and majors would find themselves promoted and posted into commands where, if they succeeded, would lead to further promotion. Lieutenant Colonel Herbert Lumsden commanding the 12th Lancers in 1939 was by 1942 a temporary lieutenant general commanding a corps in North Africa. Pip Roberts RTR started the war as a captain and adjutant of 6RTR; by mid-1942, having already commanded 3RTR, he was a temporary brigadier commanding two different armoured brigades in action during the year, and in December 1943 was promoted at the age of 37 to command 11th Armoured Division, becoming the youngest general in the army.

As well as the regimental perspective noted above, there was also a pressing need to give the regular officers their chance at command. Although unsaid, the phrase 'before the war finishes' was in some people's minds, and in particular regular majors with an eye on their post-war careers jostled for squadron and regimental commands in Europe, with varying degrees of success. A regular commission did not guarantee that an officer would be able to outperform a 'hostilities only' colleague, and many soldiers resented the sudden appearance of a pre-war regular major who had enjoyed what was perceived as a cushy war on the staff or in a training unit, and who now appeared to want to make his name at their expense in the time remaining.

Operations Charnwood and Jupiter

Montgomery reminisced after the war that using the River Orne as the eastern (left) flank of the British beachhead had been a mistake, as it did not give him enough room for manoeuvre to the east of Caen, and that he should have used the Dives instead. That was probably correct, as the attempts to capture or envelop Caen were always limited to the east, hence the number of operations that had to be conducted in the bocage countryside to the west. However, as both Operations Perch and Epsom had failed to endanger Caen, the next approach was more direct – an assault on the city.

Bomber Command was persuaded, not without difficulty, to use part of the RAF heavy bomber force in a tactical role, in order to carpet bomb an area covering the northern suburbs of the city, 4km wide by about 1km deep, intending to destroy and disorientate the German defensive positions therein, allowing the Allies to move into the city centre. The bombing attack began at 2150 on 7 July, the evening before the ground troops crossed the start line; over 450 bombers flying at only 3,000ft (just above the effective range of German light flak), dropped over 2,500 tons of high-explosive bombs into the area, but – because they were conscious of the proximity of the Allied front line, missed the main defensive areas intended to be targeted and instead reduced much of northern and central Caen to rubble, which, as had been shown at Cassino earlier in the year, merely aided the defenders. As Caen was within range of the Royal Navy ships in the Channel, HMS *Rodney* and other large warships also assisted, firing salvoes of large-calibre shells into the northern area, followed immediately by strikes from rocket-firing ground-attack Typhoons from the tactical air force, and then the traditional artillery strikes prior to the ground assault.[21]

Charnwood was launched at 0420 on 8 July 1944, with three divisions from John Crocker's I Corps attacking from the north towards the centre of Caen, with the Canadians coming in from the north-west. The intention was to attempt a broad-front attack which would prevent the defenders from being strong everywhere, as the narrow-thrust attacks previously used had the disadvantage of allowing the Germans to deploy their precious reserves to plug gaps as they appeared; they could not do this if multiple gaps appeared simultaneously. 27th Armoured Brigade was in support, with 33rd Armoured Brigade in reserve. Attached were specialist units from the Funnies: 22nd Dragoons in their Crab flails, 141 RAC in Crocodile flamethrowers and 5th Assault Regiment RE with AVREs and Bulldozers. After some vicious hand-to-hand fighting, by nightfall the Germans started to withdraw south through the remains of the city, and by later afternoon on the 9th Caen had been liberated as far south and east as the rivers Orne and Odon, but no further, as the rivers and the canal in the city made further progress impossible, and, in any case, the streets needed clearing of rubble before vehicles could transit through the city. In this respect, Charnwood achieved its aim, but it did not unlock the door to the better tank country to the south and east.

Even as Charnwood was drawing to a close, Operation Jupiter began at dawn on 10 July, with another attempt to wrest control of Hills 112 and 113 from 2nd SS Panzer Corps, and which was finally achieved the following day. The infantry division tasked with the thrust was 43rd Infantry, commanded by the obnoxious and overbearing Major General Ivor Thomas. Providing armoured support was 31st Tank Brigade, including the flamethrowing Crocodiles of 141RAC, which had become a much-feared weapon. 4th Armoured Brigade (Greys, 3CLY, 44RTR) were in reserve ready to conduct exploitation, living up to Monty's insistence that the independent armoured brigades must be capable of all roles. Brigadier Michael Carver had only just been promoted to command the brigade on 27 June when the previous commander was killed, and although he was newly in post, he was also an extremely experienced officer at both staff and command, and was not afraid to clash with authority if the situation demanded it – the fact that he later rose to Field Marshal gives an indication of his quality. Carver described Thomas thus: 'A small, fiery, very determined and

Crabs carrying infantry forward – this would not have been attempted in action. Mine-clearing tanks were required throughout the campaign, as mines became an increasing menace once the Normandy break-out was in progress.

grim gunner, without a spark of humour, he would bite the head off anyone who attempted to disagree with him or question his orders.' When Thomas attempted to order 4th Armoured Brigade to drive unsupported deep into enemy territory to try to capture a bridge, Carver, who had seen too many reckless charges in the desert, thought that it looked like 'Balaclava all over again', and refused to comply unless changes were made to the plan. After 'further heated argument' – Carver's way of saying a blazing row in which Thomas tried to browbeat him and in which he refused to budge – the plan was amended. However, when it came to execute the plan, Thomas once again tried to force Carver to move the brigade before the agreed preconditions had been met, and Carver once again refused, saying that the leading regiment would take 75 per cent casualties. When told that the leading regiment was to be the Greys (as they had the easiest time of it on the brigade's previous operation), Thomas, unbelievably, replied, 'Couldn't you send a less well-known regiment?' Carver, RTR and RAC to the core, was not prepared to sacrifice any of his regiments to an unsound plan, and 'blew up'. He won the argument that day but 'relations between us, poor to start with, were permanently soured'.

Carver had the courage of his convictions, and refused to sacrifice any of his troops to a poorly conceived operation planned by a general with no understanding of the capabilities and limitations of armour, and who had failed to learn from the experience of others.[22] Jupiter only lasted for two days, with the Greys and 3CLY 'spending the [second] day repelling counter-attacks'. The defending SS troops obligingly dashed themselves against the Allied tanks and anti-tank fire, and as a result sustained even more losses that they could not afford. Despite the favourable attrition rate, these 'bite and hold' successes still fell well short of the breakthrough desired by the Allies, and therefore another major operation was being planned, this time to the east of Caen.

Operation Goodwood

Even considering the action at Villers-Bocage, Operation Goodwood remains the most important and controversial armoured operation attempted during the Normandy campaign. In some ways this is unfair, as the focus should really be on the extraordinary achievements in developing and deploying the specialist armour that made not only the initial assault possible, but also greatly assisted in subsequent operations. However, Goodwood in both conception and delivery must be examined in detail, as in many ways it became the point at which armoured doctrine crystallized and allowed much better use to be made of the RAC formations and units for the remainder of the war. It was also large scale, with about a thousand tanks contesting the field, along with many hundreds of other types of tracked AFVs; it was probably the largest tank battle ever fought by Britain.

Following the – at best – partial successes of the previous operations, by mid-July most of Caen was in Allied hands but the German defences, although creaking, were still holding. There was a genuine concern that an operational stalemate might be developing that would pen the Allies in the bridgehead and prevent the necessary break-out. It was therefore proposed that both 21st Army Group in the east and 1st US Army Group in the west should conduct concurrent break-out operations in order to force the Germans to deploy all their reserves and which would cause a rupture of their line somewhere, which could then be exploited; in some ways this mirrored the contemporary Soviet doctrine of attacking on a broad front, and then shifting all available resources to exploit success wherever it occurred. Unfortunately, though, the whole principle of the mass attack foundered when the proposed American attack, codenamed Cobra, could not be launched at the same time as the British one, codenamed Goodwood. This was because the efforts by the Americans to capture Saint-Lô had taken longer than expected and a tactical pause was required to reset before resuming their offensive. Goodwood would be launched alone.

The intention of Goodwood was to once again use strategic bombing to reduce the effectiveness of the German defences south and east of Caen, and thus allow the armour to break through the German lines and exploit over much better tank country towards the town of Falaise. In the original plan, this would have been matched by an American thrust from the west, encircling the German forces in a classic pincer movement. Of course, this would not now happen, but it was still hoped that the attack would capture the dominating terrain feature, the 60–80m high Bourguebus Ridge (known as Bugger's Bus ridge to the British troops), write-down even further the German reserves, particularly their armoured forces, and if conditions remained favourable, allow a drive towards Falaise.

The ridge was key – it allowed observation into Caen and to the north, almost as far as the eastern beaches of Sword. The problem was that the Germans were well aware of the importance of it; in the many anti-invasion wargames they had conducted before D-Day, the ridge had been identified time and again as pivotal, and when the centre of Caen fell as a result of Charnwood, the Germans immediately created four lines of defence in order to retain possession of the ridge. After a loosely held and expendable outpost line of infantry, a second line used a series of close and thus mutually supporting villages to create strongpoints: Grentheville, Soliers, Four, Bras, Hubert-Folie, Frenouville, Le Poirier and Bourguebus itself. In each village was approximately one company of infantry, albeit reduced in strength to about fifty men, and about four 75mm or 88mm anti-tank guns. As the VIII Corps history noted, 'it was almost impossible for armour to move through this area without coming under anti-tank fire from two or three quarters'. Additionally, the crops were shoulder high affording good cover to the enemy, and two railway lines traversed across the line of the attack creating both obstacles and choke points through which the tanks would have to pass. South of this and along the crest of the ridge was the next defensive line, where no less than 78 88mm guns were emplaced, along with about 70 field guns and 270 of the hated Nebelwerfer multi-barrelled mortars emplaced behind. Also holding the ridge were 6 battalions of SS infantry, and further to the south was the German mobile reserve of a Panther tank battalion and 2 companies of Mk IV tanks. In all, the Germans could muster about 210 tanks – Mk IV, Panther, Tiger and, for the first time, some of the brand-new Tiger II (King Tiger) – as well as 35 Stugs and 30 75mm anti-tank SPGs.[23] Many weapon pits and dug-in fire positions were created for the vehicles to move between, and the crews had ample time to reconnoitre these, clear the fields of fire, and note engagement ranges to the meter. The only thing they lacked in a strong position that was up to 10 miles deep was minefields; all the mines in Normandy had been used in the defence of the beaches, and Allied air supremacy prevented the Germans being able to move mines up to improve the Bourguebus position.[24]

As well as the German defences, there were significant challenges on the British side, mostly due to a lack of space. If the attack was to have any chance of success, security was paramount, and to try to move three complete armoured divisions across the front into a very small concentration area would be exceptionally difficult even out of contact, but trying to do it in conditions of absolute secrecy was nigh-on impossible. Because the bridgehead area east of the River Orne was so small, it was decided to move the three armoured divisions allocated to VIII Corps – 11th, Guards and 7th – up to the west of the dual water obstacle of the Orne and the Caen canal and only cross, using the existing three bridge pairs plus two additional Bailey bridges constructed during the night before the attack, in the morning.[25] It was hoped that detailed scheduling and rigorous traffic control would allow the divisions to cross, shake-out ('debouch') and advance, but as it turned out huge congestion was the result, and it was indeed fortunate that the Luftwaffe was ineffective, as the target created was possibly the most vulnerable of the whole war.[26] Another complication was that the British defensive minefields previously laid to protect their gains from German counter-attacks had to be lifted, again in conditions of secrecy, at night, to create seventeen lanes for the armour to move through. The Germans realized that the ridge must be subject to attack at some point, and for once British security precautions were inadequate and the Germans knew an attack was forthcoming – if for no other reason than the immense clouds of dust created and the low rumble as hundreds of tanks and thousands of other vehicles started to move forward.[27]

Dempsey's plan was to use strategic bombers to blast the flanks of the attack route with HE to lessen the possibility of an armoured counter-attack, as well as to use medium bombers to carpet the area in front of the assault force with fragmentation bombs, so as not to crater the ground, and also to attack depth targets beyond the range of the British artillery, which, until and unless it could move forward, could only cover as far as the foot of the ridge. The use of strategic airpower in a tactical role was fundamental to the plan; if it could not be provided or had to be cancelled, the whole operation would be called off. Once the bombers had done their stuff and after a very large artillery bombardment, Dempsey would then push 11th Armoured Division's armoured brigade (29 Armoured Brigade: 23H, 3RTR, 2FFY) in their Shermans on a narrow axis with a frontage of only some 2,000yd to advance rapidly uphill to take the ridge and the fortified villages on it: Vimont in the east and Hubert-Folie and Verierre to the west.[28] Roberts questioned this use of his armoured brigade, largely without accompanying infantry and, once past the railway lines, beyond the range of most artillery support. In particular, he was unhappy that the divisional lorried infantry brigade was to be used to capture two villages shortly after the start line, rather than being kept behind 29thArmoured Brigade for their immediate use when – inevitably – the fortified villages had to be cleared later in the day. Roberts was told by O'Connor that if he didn't like it, another armoured division (probably the Guards) would lead the advance instead, and, somewhat uncharacteristically, Roberts bit his lip despite deep reservations that were about to be proved right.[29] All that his tank regiments would have with them in terms of immediate support was one infantry company each (from 8th Rifle Brigade) in half-tracks and an SPG battery per regiment from 13 RHA.[30]

One of the reasons for Dempsey and O'Connor taking this approach was the now worrying lack of infantry in Normandy: 'Second Army had plenty of tanks; what it lacked was a sufficiency of infantry. Dempsey therefore persuaded Montgomery to allow him to mount an all-armoured attack.'[31] It was well known at the time that the attrition of infantry soldiers in the rifle companies could not continue at the current rate, and soon the situation would arise when there would be no more reinforcements and some of the infantry divisions and other units would have to be broken up, which in fact did happen slightly later.[32] What Dempsey did not realize was that although there were plenty of spare tanks, a similar situation was starting to develop regarding trained tank crewman, and that he should have preserved the manpower in both of his front-line arms.[33] In numerical terms the operation looked certain to succeed: the British had total air superiority and could muster over 750 Medium and Cruiser tanks in the three divisions against the (accurate) estimate of 250 German, and thus achieving the doctrinal 3:1 ratio required. The trouble was of course that numbers counted for nothing if the tanks were fed into battle piecemeal, and the congestion behind the front line prevented successive waves of armour being echeloned through to keep up the momentum of the attack, or to deal with hot-spots of resistance. With all of these factors considered, it must be said that the plan behind Goodwood, for all its detail and complexity, was deeply flawed, and came down to launching thinly armoured Medium tanks in a hopefully fast attack up rising ground over a narrow frontage that was, at its heart, that most discredited of operations – the cavalry charge against a prepared position held by a determined and well-armed enemy.[34]

H-Hour for the ground attack was confirmed as 0745 on 18 July. The units lined up in the order 11th Armoured Division, Guards Armoured Division, 7th Armoured Division; the Shermans of Brigadier Roscoe Harvey's 29th Armoured Brigade were the spearpoint, with 3RTR and then 2FFY leading, then 23rd Hussars in immediate reserve, followed by the divisional armoured recce regt, 2NY, in their Cromwells. The air attacks had gone in as scheduled, starting with the heavies at 0545 and then the mediums at 0700. It was during this second attack, lasting 45 minutes, that 29th Brigade moved forward from the concentration area, through the gaps in the minefields, and onto the start line. For 3RTR the attack started badly when, having negotiated the bridges in the dark, it found itself crammed into too small an area. Consequently, the regiment was ordered to move 100yd forward of the start line to try to create more space behind, with the result that part of the opening artillery barrage fell on them, killing several tank commanders including the OC of C Sqn, Major Peter Burr, and two troop leaders.

By 0830 all three regiments from 29th Armoured Brigade were clear of the minefield gaps and making good progress, with little resistance from the German outpost line that seemed suitably stunned by the heavy bombing they had endured. At that point 2FFY came up and moved to the left of 3RTR, allowing the advance to continue with two regiments up. By 0935 the leading squadrons from both regiments had crossed the second railway line, but then 2FFY came under 'considerable anti-tank fire' from the village of Cagny. Although hit hard from the air, the Germans had had time to recover from the shock and moved a number of Tigers of 503 Heavy Tank Battalion, some of which had needed to be dug out from the effects of the bombing, to the south of the village to replace those of the 3rd Company that had been knocked out by the bombing.[35] In the village and unharmed by the bombing (which had devastated half the buildings, leaving the remainder untouched) was an 88mm Flak battery of four guns, now being used in the anti-tank role from an orchard to the north of the buildings. The failure to secure Cagny, rather than just 'mask it', was one of the major reasons why the attack started to stall from this point. Panthers and SPGs started to be spotted on the ridgeline, and progress started to be measured by the ever increasing tank casualties. As 3RTR tried to make progress in the open country between the villages, they discovered that there was no cover, and adopting a hull-down position was very difficult if not impossible in the open countryside – 'bare arsed' in the parlance. Johnny Langdon, troop leader of 1 Troop A Squadron, was hit mid-morning between Hubert-Folie and Bras:

The tank lurched as though it had been struck by a giant's hammer, in fact we had been hit by an AP shell which penetrated near the bottom of the turret on the right side. All was noise and confusion, I shouted to bail out; it was apparent that Hume was badly wounded … we somehow managed to get Hume out and onto the ground. The tank was by now on fire. Millington and Pickering were both slightly wounded. Hume had both legs shattered above the ankles; he must have been in great agony. As an officer I carried morphine capsules in my field dressing pocket, I injected him in the arm with one of these ... We contacted Doc MacMillan who came forward in his half-track. Mac took over Hume, but I could tell from the look on his face that he didn't expect him to live long. Hume died after a short while ... It was now after 1100. I went over to Cpl Killen's tank and took over command.[36]

An infantry carrier had earlier reported that Hubert-Folie appeared to be unoccupied, but it seems that the German defenders simply laid low whilst it conducted a high-speed drive through the village. Some of the fire was coming from the village of Ifs to the west, nearly 2km distant, and was probably 88mm. 23rd Hussars and its company of 8th Rifle Brigade attacked Grentheville, and 2FFY even got a few tanks across the open fields and on the road running along the ridge (the D89 road), but were then forced to retire. Behind the 11th Division, by 0945 the armoured brigade of the Guards had moved south and was halted about 500yd behind the tail of 29th Armoured Brigade at Demouville – the congestion, despite efforts to avoid it, was starting to cause real problems, and the timetable was now seriously out of synch with events. Once the Guards were able to shake out, they also advanced two-up, with 2 Grenadier Guards right and 2 Coldstream Guards left, each battalion also having one motorized company of infantry. The attempt to use the Guards to secure the left flank of the main advance failed in the face of continuing heavy anti-tank fire from the Cagny area, including the first encounter with the huge Tiger II tank, and this delay in turn prevented 7th Armoured Division from moving forward to where it could be deployed.[37] At the leading edge of the advance the Germans had recovered from the initial shock of the bombing and began to throw counter-attacks in to restore the situation which still remained in their favour, as the Bourguebus ridge had not been seriously threated. The fortified villages around Bourguebus, Hubert-Folie and Soliers had been bypassed by the British armour but the garrisons remained largely intact, as there were no infantry available to take them. Groups of Panthers and SPGs started to appear, using good concealment and taking advantage of their superior range. Sherman Fireflies, the only tanks that could hope to duel with the German 75mm guns, became prime targets.[38] Far from just fighting a static defensive battle, the Germans were making use of manoeuvre in order to inflict maximum damage on the British armour.

By noon 29th Armoured Brigade had advanced nearly 7 miles. This was not only because the ridge was still strongly held and pouring fire onto them, and also of course directing the German artillery, but also because throughout the afternoon more and more German counter-attacks had to be dealt with.

Insufficient infantry up front with the tanks was one of the reasons for the failure of Operation Goodwood. British doctrine was firmly against the carriage of infantry on tanks, although as the war progressed it became more common, as illustrated here by the 1st Northants Yeomanry. The Germans and especially the Russians could not see a problem with the practice.

There was also the issue of areas which had been bypassed – once again, due to the lack of accompanying infantry – and which now sprang back to life, either because the defenders had recovered from the shock of the bombing or because they were re-occupied by fresh troops. The three forward armoured regiments were at the extreme range of supporting artillery, and, not least, had been on the move all through the previous night and having been in action all morning were now desperately tired. The British were thus enmeshed in the German second line, with little prospect of breaking out in order to move up to the objective: the ridge. 22nd Armoured Brigade of 7th Armoured Division was ordered to come up on the right of the 29th, which would have added fresh impetus to the advance, but was still snarled up in the bridgehead congestion. (It was not until about 1800 that 22nd Armoured Brigade, with 5RTR leading, managed to get through and appeared between the Guards and the 11th Armoured.) 5RTR was the only unit of 22nd Armoured Brigade to see action on the first day; the tail of the division did not get across the Orne until 0430 on the following day. The armoured regiments at the front were now seriously engaged in beating off the persistent counter-attacks, with both 2FFY and 23H thus engaged.

Nor was 3RTR in any better situation, for in its uncomfortable position overlooked from both the south and west it was now subjected to a sharp counter-attack from both Hubert-Folie and Bourguebus, lost several more tanks, and by 1530 had been forced to withdraw some 500 yards to a position west of Soliers, where it was told to 'hang on as long as possible'.[39]

In fact, all three regiments found themselves having to stop counter-attacks throughout the late afternoon and into the evening, and C Sqn 23H lost nine tanks stopping one conducted with Panthers that they nevertheless (just) managed to repel. The last attack was made just as night was falling, at 2240. During the evening, in the fading light 2NY were attached to the brigade and tried to push forward, but failed to meet up with the forward troops of 3RTR and were withdrawn, having only encountered 'a few burning tanks abandoned by their crews'. By 2300 the fighting had petered out, with the British occupying a narrow and very exposed salient 7 miles long at its furthest point. 11th Armoured had lost 126 tanks out of 244 – the exact figures for losses on both sides are still hotly disputed – which represented about half of its fighting strength; both 3RTR and 2FFY lost about two-thirds of their tanks, and by the end of the first day 2FFY had been reduced to only eighteen tanks.[40] The Guards had lost about sixty. The congestion over the bridges, as well as the risks involved to unarmoured wheeled vehicles, prevented the echelon vehicles from moving forward to bomb up and refuel, and many tanks were now seriously low on ammunition. During the night, the Germans managed to reinforce the garrisons in Bras, Huber-Folie, Bourguebus, Soliers, Four and La Hogue with fresh SS troops, ready for the following day, the 19th, with some of the infantry reinforcements making their way to the front on bicycles.

The problem that VIII Corps faced was that the salient was not, in itself, tenable; as all salients are, it was overlooked by the enemy from at least two sides, and just as had happened during Epsom, the narrowness of the penetration allowed the Germans to fire artillery and mortars into the tenuously held terrain. At 0600 the next day 2NY were pushed forwards in their normal role as a reconnaissance force, but unsurprisingly the guns on the ridge spotted them and forced them to retire. Shortly afterwards the first of the day's counter-attacks began, against the 3RTR position, and the regiment, severely depleted, once again had to cede some ground. Until the network of fortified villages had been captured there was no chance of getting forces up onto the ridge, and so a new tactical plan was formulated for the late afternoon to use small set-piece attacks involving infantry as well as the corps artillery, which had by now been able to be moved forward. 11th Armoured Div would be responsible for capturing Bras (2NY) and then Hubert-Folie (3RTR), starting at 1600; the Guards would wait an hour and then subdue Le Poirier; and concurrently with this the freshest formation 7th Armoured would take Soliers and Four, followed by Bourguebus. These attacks were all completed, but the latter was 'the toughest nut to crack' and although surrounded during the evening, was not finally subdued until early the following morning, the 20th. Key to achieving results proved to be a rapid aggressive drive into each village by both tanks and armour, and good cooperation thereafter; the SS troops fought bravely but not quite to the last man, and an attempt to escape en masse from Bras by up to a hundred defenders 'provided a good shoot both to the troops [in] the village and to 3RTR on the outskirts'. By the end of the second day 29th Armoured Brigade had lost another sixty-five tanks, thirty-seven of them belonging to 2NY.[41] 22nd Armoured Brigade was able to get its leading regiment, 5RTR, within 200yd of the Bourguebus–La Hogue road, but no closer, whilst 1RTR with a company of 1st Rifle Brigade captured Four in the late evening. It was estimated that the Germans had lost about sixty tanks.

The final day of the operation, the 20th, coincided with the attempt on Hitler's life, which of course was not known at the time. The Germans elected not to defend the increasingly isolated Frenouville and pulled all their troops out overnight. Although the village of Bourguebus was secured, the majority of the ridge remained in German hands and air reconnaissance showed that the Germans were constructing more positions behind it, in effect reinstating their defence in depth. Although the area was often referred to as 'good tank country', its very nature meant that the Germans would, once again, be able to take advantage of the much greater range and hitting power of their anti-tank guns. Meanwhile the final German counter-attacks were repulsed, and about another twenty enemy tanks destroyed, and the Inns of Court, in armoured cars, managed to get beyond the ridge and 'explored for several miles southward' down the road to Falaise. Dempsey sensibly decided to consolidate the ground gained by replacing the tired armoured units with infantry formations, and from about 1600 the heavens opened, quickly turning the fields into a muddy morass and restricting most vehicles to the roads. Some tanks became completely bogged and Erskine, commanding 7th Armoured Division, ordered that their crews were to remain mounted and be prepared to fight as 'pill-boxes'. Goodwood was at an end. Buckley summed it up thus:

> Attempting to push three armoured divisions across six bridges in the space of a few hours, partly in darkness, was ambitious enough, but the frontage of the assault was to be just 2000 yards, initially along narrow lanes cleared through minefields and then across mine-cratered terrain. Whatever the advantages of a narrow-front assault, the problems it created for armour were nowhere better exposed than Operation Goodwood.[42]

Although the planned breakthrough had not happened, and tank losses on the Allied side had been very heavy, the Germans had lost proportionally more, and had expended resources that they could ill-afford to lose.[43] Another positive effect was that the Germans remained convinced that the Caen sector was the *schwerpunkt* (main focus) and sent the majority of their armoured reinforcements there, so that by 20 July, seven Panzer divisions faced the British and Canadians but only two were deployed against the Americans. Field Marshal von Kluge, commanding the German forces, believed that the battle represented a catastrophic loss for the Germans, and felt compelled to write to Hitler warning him that the situation was extremely precarious, and that the remaining defenders were facing 'slow but sure annihilation'. He continued with a prescient warning, that when the line was – inevitably – broken, 'once the enemy is in open country, an orderly command will hardly be practicable in view of the insufficient mobility of our own troops'. Despite the apparent failure of Goodwood to break through into open country south of the ridge, the conditions for the 'breakout from Normandy were now in place. Ironically, an operation which had been designed largely around the need to preserve infantry strength by relying on armour alone had largely failed because there were insufficient infantry in the right place at the right time to co-operate with the tanks.'[44]

Operations Cobra and Spring

Whilst Goodwood was ongoing, the Americans were preparing for their big offensive, Cobra. Delayed for a second time, caused by the bad weather that started on the 20th as well as the requirement for heavy bomber support, the attack was shifted back to the 24th but then had to be postponed shortly before it started due to more inclement weather in Normandy. Tragically, not all the bomber units already in the air received the recall signal, leading to American casualties. The weather improved the following day allowing the thrice-delayed offensive to begin on the 25th and, once again, American bombers contrived to accidentally bomb their own troops, with even more casualties. In order to keep the Germans guessing as to where the main offensive was, and to continue the policy of trying to draw the Panzers eastwards towards Caen, a concurrent British offensive, Spring, was also launched. Spring was conducted by II Canadian Corps, to which was attached the 7th and the Guards Armoured Divisions, and was intended to capture the Verrières ridge, extending westward from Bourguebus and commanding the ground to its north. The attack was thrown up against the strongest-held part of the whole German line, and both armoured divisions – having learned from their experiences during Goodwood – were careful to minimize risks and not charge unsupported at the defences. However, the over cautious performance of 7th Armoured Division in particular gave Dempsey more concerns that the division had, to a degree, lost its nerve.[45] Although the attack was largely over by the end of the first day, for two days the Germans concluded that Spring was the main offensive, taking pressure off the American forces as intended and allowing them to break out to the south and west and get out of the bocage.

Op Bluecoat

In late July Operation Bluecoat was planned. Again preceded by the use of heavy bombers, Bluecoat was a deliberate two corps offensive, involving VIII Corps and XXX Corps with all three British armoured divisions once again required, along with two of the independent armoured brigades. The attack was in the direction of another prominent piece of high ground, Mont Pinçon, and beyond it towards Vire, an important road junction and supply depot for the Germans. The attack plan was put together quickly in order to protect the flank of the American forces as the Cobra break-out continued to make progress. Originally scheduled for 2 August, events on the ground meant that it had to be advanced by three days.

The three British armoured divisions had all suffered during Goodwood and Spring, with the four regiments in 11th Armoured the hardest hit.[46] The extremely efficient armour replacement organization had made up the losses in tanks, and additional Fireflies were now slowly starting to appear, allowing the wish to have two per troop to start to become reality. Crews could also be replaced from the holding units, although naturally these were all inexperienced, including the new 'batch' of troop leaders required by each regiment. More difficult to replace were NCO tank commanders, as this required the elevation and often promotion of junior NCOs into the role, with no formal crew commander course to give them the basis of the job; instead, they had to rely on their own experience and whatever advice they could get from their peers and superiors. Even when experience was available and disseminated, it was not always acted on appropriately. Lieutenant Bishop of the 24th Lancers remembered that:

> In the afternoon, all officers are summoned to a lecture in a nearby field, given by Major Bourne, 2IC of the 3rd RTR, who has apparently had quite a lot of experience of fighting in this class of country. It is a warm day, and a lot of drowsy officers pay scant attention to this important advice ...[47]

The area chosen for Bluecoat was thought to be largely free of Panzers and was on the extreme west of the British sector, the area adjoining the Americans; in fact, for the operation the American V Corps handed over part of their sector, near Caumont sur Aure to the south-west of Caen, necessitating long road moves for the armoured divisions to the assembly areas.[48] One commentator described the area over which the attack would take place as 'the worst Bocage countryside in Normandy. To the usual small fields, high hedgerows, and sunken lanes of the Bocage were added heavily wooded areas and many steep hills, ridges and valleys – the southern part of it was so hilly that it was referred to as '*la Suisse Normande*'.[49] This made navigation particularly difficult, and during the operation many units and individuals got lost, hindering both the advance and attempts at co-operation. Additionally, the Germans had plenty of time to prepare their defences, which now included substantial minefields and roadblocks, as well as the usual well-sited MG and anti-tank positions, not to mention the menace – particularly for tank commanders – of snipers.[50] Assisting the provision of reinforcements was the fact that, finally and belatedly, the Germans accepted that an attack using the shorter Channel crossing to the Pas de Calais area was not going to happen, and that Normandy was indeed the main effort.

Just before the start of Bluecoat O'Connor ordered the Guards Armoured Division to reorganize into battlegroups so that, instead of the official one armoured and one infantry brigade organization within the division, each of the armoured battalions was paired with an infantry battalion, with whom they would work. The regrouping, done in haste, led to two Grenadier battalions working together, so that the 2nd (Armoured) worked with the 1st (Motor) Battalion. However, the other two consisted of the 1st (Armoured) Coldstream paired with the 3rd Irish, and the 2nd (Armoured) Irish grouped with the 5th Coldstream.

Before the welcome introduction of the All-Round Vision Cupola, the prudent tank commander would be very aware of the need to keep low in the turret to avoid the attention of snipers. The RAC steel helmet, although not bulletproof, was worn by the majority of units in action, and certainly prevented some head wounds from shell and mortar fire.

This illogical arrangement came about solely because the regrouping was based upon where the various battalions were camped at that time, the pairings being of those units closest to each other. It also meant that the Grenadier battlegroup had the great advantage of the infantry being mounted in half-tracks, whereas the other two infantry battalions were lorried infantry, and moved into battle on foot. The 2nd (Armoured Reconnaissance) Bn Welsh Guards remained as divisional troops. The performance of the newly arrived 6th Guards Tank Brigade in its first battle would lead to its commander, Verney, being promoted to take over 7th Armoured Division when Erskine was removed after Bluecoat, although, in the event, he only lasted for four months himself. If the war was demonstrating anything, it was that commanding armoured regiments, brigades and divisions was far from easy, requiring both technical and tactical ability, and those who were found wanting were (mostly) quickly 'given the bowler hat'.[51] Within 11th Armoured, Roberts, the GOC, also realized that a reorganization was required to facilitate better cooperation, but did it differently. One of his three tank regiments, 2FFY, was attached to the infantry brigade, and 29th Armoured Brigade received, in their place, one infantry battalion, the 3rd Monmouth. Although the two brigades were now 'unbalanced', becoming what would later be known as a 1:2 brigade (159th Infantry Brigade) and a 2:1 brigade (29th Armoured Brigade), Roberts hoped that this would give him added flexibility, as one was infantry heavy with an armoured component, the other the reverse.

New tactics were also being developed and varied between units. Lieutenant Brownlie of 2FFY referred to one that the unit called 'baffing'. This meant charging down the lanes flat out, at top speed wherever possible, on the assumption that the faster you moved, the more difficult you were to hit. Brownlie reported that this scattered 'Germans all over the place, running and scampering. We fired wildly at them, overtook them and left them far behind. There were targets at every turn of the road. It was exhilarating.'[52] The trouble with this approach was that although when first used it came as a surprise, and prevented the effective use of *PanzerFauste*, it didn't allow the crews to fire accurately on the move. More importantly, it couldn't be used all the time as the narrow and twisty lanes tended to slow the Shermans down, and speed counted for little when the German sited their anti-tank guns to fire down straight sections of road. Another more considered tactic developed and used widely both during and after Normandy was the 'snake patrol'. This had the lead tank moving to a bend in a road where it would halt and cover forward as far as observation allowed. The next tank would move up alongside the first and take over the responsibility for observation and covering fire, allowing the first tank to move forward to the next bend (or the limit of covering fire, and known as a 'bound'), where the whole procedure would be repeated. This was clearly much slower than baffing but – almost for the first time as a recognized tactic – took advantage of that fundamental principle of fire and movement: never move unless you are being covered by someone else's fire.[53]

For Bluecoat 7th Armoured were now in XXX Corps, whose task was to drive southwards towards Mont Pinçon, whilst the 11th and Guards Armoured Divisions (plus the newly arrived 6th Guards Tank Brigade) in VIII Corps were to advance towards Vire via La Beny-Bocage. When the attack started on 30 July, VIII Corps made more significant progress, and their advance had to be reined in because of slower progress from XXX Corps; the reason for this was the fear of the 'exposed flank', which was a hardy perennial in British tactical handling, but which should only have come into play if the enemy retained sufficient forces to make an exploitation of the open flank a reality, which was debatable.[54] Some innovation was tried: the 2nd Armoured Grenadier Guards used their 20mm AA tanks to support an infantry assault on the village of Sept Vents.

After two days 7th Armoured was still 5 miles away from its objective of Aunay-sur-Odon, and it was this perceived over caution that finally led to the sacking of Bucknall, the corps commander (replaced by Horrocks), as well as Erskine, the GOC, and Hinde, the 22nd Armoured Brigade commander. The VIII Corps included the 6th Guards Tank Brigade, mounted in Churchills, and despite only having been in Normandy for ten days, demonstrated a better level of Infantry tank cooperation (with the 15th (Scottish) Division) than had previously been seen; in part this was due to the fact that despite conversion to armour they remained, at heart, infantry soldiers, but also and more importantly because the two formations had trained together in England. Doctrine was meant to standardize procedures but the confusion over its application, as well as the usual reticence to enforce it during training, meant that there was a real advantage when troops who had trained together fought together. If anyone had bothered to ask either the infantry or RAC commanders, they would have doubtless all agreed, and they preferred operating with units that they knew. Fortunately, if belatedly, the point was sinking in, and it started to become standard to group the same tank and infantry units together and, wherever possible, fight in these groupings.

Some noteworthy armoured actions occurred during Bluecoat, which demonstrated that there was still dash and initiative aplenty – as well as a real threat from Germans who had the same qualities. On the first day, S Squadron of the 3rd Scots Guards in Churchills was supporting the 15th (Scottish) and found themselves in a somewhat exposed forward position near Les Loges. Without warning, following an artillery barrage that knocked out one tank with a lucky direct hit, three more tanks were knocked out in quick succession from direct fire from their supposed rear. The fire came from three Jagdpanther SPGs; these fearsome new weapons mounted 88mm guns on the Panther chassis, in a low, well-armoured and well-sloped hull. The three Germans then moved out of their position about 500m away and advanced towards the Guards, shooting up anything they saw. This was an unusual tactic for such weapons, as they were handicapped by the gun mounting which only had 12° traverse either side of

Churchills of 7RTR make their way forward, with the accompanying infantry alongside. One of the biggest problems during the Normandy campaign was the poor co-ordination of infantry with armour, with more examples of failure than success, but by the end of August the situation had improved somewhat through hard-won experience.

centre, making them well fitted for defence but less so for attack. Nonetheless, the German commander seized the opportunity aggressively and as well as knocking out the Battalion 2IC, which was unlucky enough to show up at that exact moment, ten other Churchills were destroyed in a very brief action which although smaller in scale, bore striking similarities to Villers-Bocage. And in another parallel, the 75mm guns of the Guards were unable to penetrate the enemy SPGs which disappeared to the north.[55] (In order to bolster the tank-killing ability of Churchill tank units, which were not allocated Fireflies, RA-operated M10 tank destroyers from the divisional RA anti-tank regiment were often allocated to support Churchill regiments.)

An armoured car regiment, 2 HCR, was attached to the 159th Brigade group in 11th Armoured, and on the second day of Bluecoat, a patrol of two of their cars – one armoured, one scout – from 1 Troop C Sqn under Lieutenant Dickie Powle entered the heavily wooded Forêt l'Évque where they cheekily followed a German armoured car patrol moving south past the village of La Ferrire-Harang, until around midday they came upon a small bridge over the River Souleuvre guarded by a single sentry who was 'ruthlessly dealt with'. The patrol camouflaged itself up nearby, and reported back to their RHQ who passed the information up to HQ 11th Armoured. Roberts immediately ordered 2NY to reinforce the bridge and they managed to get two troops of Cromwells forward to join the HCR. VIII Corps, 'elated' at this success, issued instructions to use the new route that the seizure of the bridge, subsequently called 'Dickie's Bridge', had allowed, and attempts to get 23H forward (carrying the Monmouth infantry on their tanks) were frustrated by US army columns using the same route, despite assurances that the route belonged exclusively to VIII Corps. Four cars from D Sqn 2HCR tried to find another route but as was typical of such aggressive use of recce, went off the air, the four cars being found burned out the following day. After about 3 irritating hours B Sqn 23H finally reached the bridge, and by 2100 the whole regiment was there. Better still, it was then discovered (from a radio intercept) that the bridge was on the boundary between the German II Parachute and LXXIV Corps, each formation assuming that the other was responsible for guarding it. The HCR were then ordered to carry on patrolling south, towards Vire, which they reached on 1 August and reported that it was virtually undefended. It was the opening up of this opportunity that led to Dempsey, hugely frustrated by the pedestrian progress of XXX Corps and 7th Armoured, ordering VIII Corps to take over as the main effort.[56]

During the afternoon of 1 August both 9th and 10th SS Panzer Divisions had been ordered to move from the Caen area, still perceived by the Germans to be the *schwerpunkt*, to the Caumont area to reinforce the German defences which were showing signs of breaking. By the morning of the third they were in position, unbeknown to the British. A Sqn 3RTR had spent the night in a close

The excellent Daimler Armoured Car, mainstay of the armoured car regiments. Fast and quiet, the DAC suited the British doctrine of 'recce by stealth', using the cars to find where the enemy was, and, more often, trying to find where the enemy was not.

defensive harbour in an orchard near Le Grand Bonfait when they were suddenly hit by enemy indirect fire with most of the tank crews dismounted; to make things worse, seven German tanks and infantry were seen advancing towards them. Sergeant Frederick 'Buck' Kite, already the holder of two Military Medals, saw two of the tanks, Panzer IVs, only 200yd away, leading to 'pandemonium in the orchard'. Most of the crews were taking cover under their tanks because of the incoming fire, but Kite mounted his tank:

> I got my crew back in the tank and traversed and fired as I had a clear view. I managed to halt the two tanks I'd first seen … In any case, by this time three more had appeared and were having a go. If they'd started to come forward, the Shropshires in the cornfield would have had it, so I engaged them … We fired so many shots at these three Jerries that I ran out of armour-piercing and started to use HE, which wasn't a great deal of use against armour but was better than nothing. [Kite then remembered he had a Firefly nearby.] I had no idea where the crew was, but the tank seemed to be in one piece, so I said to my gunner, Herbie Barlow, 'Come on Herbie, let's go and have a look at it' … when we reached it Herbie got into the gunner's seat, but I decided to stand on the back with the turret between me and the enemy tanks which were only 300 hundred yards away. We fired a few shots when [we were hit] … an AP shell had gone straight through into the engine … after a minute or so it caught fire. I went back into my own tank with Herbie and Shaw [the loader] and started using up what was left of my HE … There was a whole lot of AP ammunition in the OP Sherman that was immobilized about 50 yards away … I told the boys to go and get me some. Some of the infantry left their trenches and helped form a chain passing the shells from hand to hand and up into the tank. There was no shortage of targets … We were concentrating on one Panther [when] I saw the flash of the Jerry's gun … I must have blacked out because when I came to, I was on the back of the tank.

During the action Kite was wounded in three places and had to be evacuated back to England. He only received another Military Medal, his third, for this astonishing piece of leadership and bravery, which surely warranted at least a DCM if not higher.[57]

In another little-known but deadly encounter on 3 August 2nd Northants Yeomanry were operating close to Vire when B Squadron was counter-attacked by a force of Tigers; nine Cromwells were knocked out in a matter of minutes, and as always, their 75mm shells had no effect on the German tanks. Attempts to call an artillery strike on the Panzers was unsuccessful, partly due to the lack of an artillery forward observation officer, and partly because of the difficulties associated with trying to drop artillery onto a moving target. That evening,

2NY's A Squadron lost another eight tanks to German tank-killing patrols armed with *PanzerFauste*; in one 24-hour period, the regiment lost eighteen tanks, the equivalent of an entire squadron.

The ruined remnants of Villers-Bocage were finally captured by an infantry division on 4 August, and Mont Pinçon, one of the main objectives of Bluecoat, was taken by the 13th/18th Hussars (8th Armoured Brigade) on the 6th. In this action, following two unsuccessful days of assaults, the Shermans of the Hussars broke through a German line and discovered a 'perilous, narrow track' that led up the side of the plateau to the summit. The CO, Lieutenant Colonel Dunkerly, ordered that the track was to be used to get tanks to the top, with the infantry to follow on as quickly as they could. On the way, one tank slipped off the track and overturned, and another was hit by an anti-tank gun, but as soon as the first tank reached the top, two more troops reinforced it and held it until the early evening when they were joined by infantry who quickly dug-in.[58] Fortunately, a sudden fog made the situation somewhat easier for the new defenders, as the Germans could not see the tanks on the summit and use long-range gunfire to engage them.

Bluecoat had taken eight days of hard fighting, and was often seen from the combatant's perspective as yet another Normandy set-piece slogging match. Despite the slow progress of XXX Corps being criticized, many of the RAC units had used skill and demonstrated initiative, and the new tactics and groupings were starting to improve cooperation with the infantry. The operation forced the Germans to once again redeploy their precious Panzer reserves and, in so doing, rendered them vulnerable to being written down. By the 7 August, after five days of combat, 10th SS Panzer Division only had five tanks and five SPGs still operational, and 9th SS was scarcely much better off with only twenty-three fit AFVs.

One of the reasons for the lack of exploitation when favourable situations seemed to present themselves was that Bluecoat also suffered from the same lack of space that had bedevilled Goodwood: at one point XXX Corps was allocated one single track unsuitable for tanks as its main axis of advance, plus a single road it shared with VIII Corps – small wonder that the formations could not 'shake out' and deploy their combat power effectively.[59] The CO of the 2nd Armoured Irish Guards referred to the traffic chaos as 'grotesque'.[60] Another reason for halting the advance on the 7th was that the British commanders were fearful of outrunning the range of their supporting medium and heavy artillery, and which meant that Vire, although reported by 2HCR as being undefended, was not captured; had it been seized, the possibility of a complete encirclement of the Germans was a real possibility. And it must not be forgotten that opportunities that are obvious now, particularly through access to German archives, were not as clear cut at the time, and on many occasions the British released the pressure just at the point that the Germans thought that they were about to crack – the benefits of historical hindsight.

Even before the battle had ended Montgomery and Dempsey had made the decision to sack Bucknall, Erskine and Hinde, because of the perceived poor showing within 7th Armoured Division and 22nd Armoured Brigade; in what amounted to a cull, about a hundred other officers and men were also effectively sacked, by being posted out – undoubtedly in many cases to their great relief.[61] When Verney, after his good showing during Bluecoat, was promoted to become the new GOC he was not impressed by what he saw in 7th Armoured:

> There is no doubt that familiarity with war does not make one more courageous. One becomes cunning, and from cunning to cowardice is but one short step … the tank man can easily find a fault in his engine or wireless and thus miss taking part in the battle … if he happens to also have done a lot of fighting and especially if he has been brewed-up in his tank once or twice, he gets slow and deliberate and is quite unable to take advantage of a situation that required dash and enterprise … The 7th Armoured (and 51st Highland) were extremely swollen-headed. They were a law unto themselves, they thought they need only obey orders that suited them.[62]

Verney had a point, although there is a suspicion that his Guards upbringing and inexperience of combat meant that he could not understand the casual approach to dress and military discipline exhibited by the desert warriors.[63] What the system – and Monty in particular – had got wrong was in assuming that battle-experienced units from the Mediterranean would continue to perform well in the unfamiliar terrain of northern France, month after month and year after year. Better use could have been made of many of the veterans as trainers and instructors, as fresh and unbloodied units almost always performed more aggressively, at least at first. Every man had his breaking point, and collectively the same could be said of whole units. Too much had been expected of the veterans. What was needed to get the best out of them was a degree of understanding, allied with compassionate leadership.

Operations Totalize and Tractable

The launching of Cobra in late July and its success in striking out to the south and west of the American positions placed the German defence in an impossible position. As long as they could restrain the size of the Allied perimeter, they could – just about – maintain a credible defence, even if it required the mobile reserves to be frequently moved around to the place of greatest need as attacks developed. As soon as genuine mobile warfare commenced at the end of July, the resources available were insufficient and avoiding an encirclement between the twin pincers of the Americans and the British/Canadians became the operational imperative. However, Hitler interfered, and insisted that the Germans threw all their available armour into an ill-conceived attack. The so-called 'Mortain counter-attack' was launched on 7 August, initially with three Panzer divisions. After a short period of initial success, the Germans were quickly halted and much of the armour involved was destroyed.

Operation Totalize was a largely Canadian operation that included British armoured forces, and began late on 7 August, the same day that the German counter-offensive had started.[64] By driving south from Caen, it was hoped to capture the high ground north of Falaise, and although the attack had been in planning for some time, it was hoped to profit from the sudden German concentration on Mortain. As most of the experienced British units were still involved in Bluecoat, Totalize was assigned to the newly created Canadian First Army, which was allocated XII Corps including the Churchill-equipped 34th Tank Brigade (107RAC, 147RAC, 153RAC) in its first action as a brigade.[65] A key element of Totalize was the first use of converted tanks known as Kangaroos in the APC role. Guy Simonds, the Canadian II Corps commander and the lead planner for the operation, had recognized the pressing need to give the infantry better mobility and protection to allow them to keep up with the tanks; only by doing this could there be genuine tank/infantry cooperation. The new ability to keep the infantry up with the tanks immediately paid dividends, although the design was not perfect: the design meant that the infantry section was very vulnerable to airburst artillery and mortar fire, and mounting and dismounting had to be done over the sides of the hull.

'Defrocked Priests', with their guns removed, the SPGs have now become APCs and known as Kangaroos.

The RAM Kangaroo gave more protection to the sides than the Priest version, and had the benefit of a small MG-armed turret for the commander.

As before, strategic bombing was used as a preliminary, and the initial advance was impeded both by the dust and the darkness, and several vehicles drove into large craters caused by the bombing. To try to keep direction, some of the AA vehicles fired streams of tracer along fixed lines. The frontage was once again too narrow to allow the armour to be used effectively, and adherence to the timings in a too-rigid plan created a 6-hour pause, giving the Germans time to recover and react. Nonetheless, break-ins were achieved at a number of places, and by taking the infantry forward in the Kangaroos to around 200yd from the enemy, some of the defended villages were quickly subdued with less casualties than usual. By midday on the 8th the Verrières Ridge had been captured. The expected counter-attacks began shortly thereafter, and the movement of the German armour also took them out of the target area for the next round of aerial bombing, allowing them to blunt the next attacks. Simonds believed that a lack of boldness was responsible for the slowing of the advance, and consequently momentum, that much-prized but often elusive quality, was lost.[66] In another minor but costly action that could have been avoided, fifty or so tanks in the so-called Worthington

A problem with both types was mounting and dismounting, which had to be done over the sides. Another negative was the lack of overhead cover, but the use of the Kangaroos was a huge step forward in improving Infantry tank co-operation.

Force were lost during the 9th in an attempt to keep the pressure on the defenders and, the force becoming isolated, had to withdraw.[67] Further attacks eventually gained more ground, but the Germans used the time they had bought to establish yet another line of defences, this time on the Laison River. By the morning of the 11th Totalize had come to its end. Once again, a breakthrough but not a break-out had been achieved, and Falaise remained in German hands.

Operation Tractable was, to all intents and purposes, an extension of Totalize. Again a Canadian affair, it began on 14 August and was the last major 21st Army Group operation in Normandy leading to the closing of the Falaise Gap, encircling large numbers of the German defenders, particularly those unable to move rapidly enough to escape. Following the by-now standard pummelling of the German defences by heavy bombers, including the almost typical infliction of friendly casualties when some bombs fell short, the Canadians moved forward under the cover of smoke rather than darkness, but still became disorientated and lost their way. Despite the bombing the Germans resisted fiercely, and even killed the commander of the 4th Canadian Armoured Brigade, Eric 'Leslie' Booth. Between the 16th and the 18th Falaise itself was captured and subdued, allowing a drive towards Trun. Using the battlegroup organization adopted by the British, the Polish Armoured Division split into four, capturing the town and the dominating high feature known to the Poles as the Mace; despite all efforts to dislodge them, the Poles tenaciously held the feature with its exceptional views over the valley floor. The advancing American forces were very close, and the scene was now set to conclude the encirclement, which was completed on the 21st. The Battle of Normandy was over, and the next stage of the advance towards the Seine River and beyond could begin, which would be a totally different type of warfare akin to a hot pursuit and which came to be known as The Great Swan. But before examining that, it would be beneficial to look in some more detail at the conditions that the British armoured troops had encountered in Normandy.[68]

The Life of a Tank Crewman in Normandy

Whichever regiment he belonged to, life on a tank – or indeed on an armoured car – in Normandy was remarkably similar. All the petty differences – between cavalry and RTR, yeomanry and converted infantry battalion, cruiser and infantry – were very much in the background as each crewmen fought the enemy and learned to exist in the particular circumstances that he found himself in. The training regime in the UK could only go so far, and the soldiers and officers had to quickly adapt to the environment, learning new skills, devising methods of coping and living with the constant reminders of death and injury in all their horrible forms, as well as dealing with the terrain and the climate.

The weather conditions during the three months of the Normandy campaign varied greatly. Most histories and accounts take pains to detail the difficulties encountered during the heat of the Normandy summer. Although the blazing sun was never quite as trying as in North Africa or even Italy, the dry conditions created clouds of dust whenever vehicles moved, which was very unpleasant for the crews and also raised the possibility of German shelling; many road signs were made reminding vehicle crews that 'dust brings shells'. But it was not all glorious sunshine: it will be recalled that D-Day was launched between two periods of Channel storms, and the great storm in mid–June not only wrecked one and badly damaged the other Mulberry harbour, but also brought torrential rain that made life difficult for the soldiers. As a result, swarms of mosquitoes were another unpleasant effect of the combination of heat and rain, particularly when operating close to the many rivers and streams.

Unlike the Infantry, tank crews were able to carry additional items on their vehicles, and the engine decks of all types soon accumulated a pile of such kit. Crewmen took their luxuries where they could, and in many respects had things much better than the PBI:

> Commanders did not care to get wet when it rained, of course, and some
> had large black umbrellas which were raised at such times … From a purely
> practical point of view it made sense, for the umbrella was large enough to
> cover the hatch opening and so the occupants of the turret were able to keep

Tank crews became adept at quickly cooking up a meal when the opportunity presented itself, and the provision of the new Composite (Compo) rations made the experience more palatable, as well as nutritious.

dry. One luxury peculiar to our tank was a supply of hot water for washing at the end of the day. The bottom half of the waterproofing exhaust chute had been left in place, and a jerrican of water placed in this was heated by the exhaust gases during the day. Bed-rolls were always warm and dry as they rested on the engine covers.[69]

All crews managed to carry a huge amount of additional items on the engine decks, in addition to the issued bed-rolls; some tanks even carried mattresses and items of furniture. A couple of crews 'liberated' bicycles, although Johnny Langdon quickly ditched his when he realized that carrying it was more trouble than it was worth. Other more prosaic items frequently carried were extra jerricans of fuel and water, a soot-blackened biscuit tin used as a field cooker and empty ammunition boxes, sometimes spot-welded into place to become permanent stowage bins. (The other item often found on the engine decks – during non-tactical route marches only – was the gunner, who, almost to a man, preferred to travel outside whenever possible.) Although the practice was officially discouraged, it became commonplace in some units, particularly on Shermans and Churchills, to carry spare lengths of track on the glacis plate and elsewhere, ostensibly to give additional protection. This was sometimes tolerated for morale reasons, although in fact this added nothing in the way of extra armour against AP shot and could, if overdone, reduce mobility by adding a lot of extra weight. (It was later realized that the additional 1in appliqué armour plates officially welded onto Shermans had done little to make them better protected, but again, the morale effects for the crews were positive.)

Another constant problem in Normandy was dead animals, killed mainly by artillery and mortar fire. As the region was largely agricultural, farm animals were extremely vulnerable, and hundreds and thousands were killed, rotting where they lay: 'There was the unforgettable stench of Normandy in one's nostrils ... Here in Normandy lay bloated corpses of the cattle, the finest breeds in the world, rotting. There were horses too ... the ditches and cross-roads were littered with them, and their bodies had become the breeding ground for flies.'[70] The various weapons that killed the animals were a constant reminder of the Germans' determination to inflict casualties. Although the Allied artillery, particularly the British, was a fine-tuned instrument of war that could outperform the German in both control and effect, enemy shelling became a constant ordeal. 'We rapidly became accustomed to the whine of an approaching shell and judging where it would fall. There was perhaps a three second warning.'[71] Major How of 3RTR described the suddenness of such an attack:

> The attack burst with an unnerving shriek of falling missiles. The flash of exploding shells and mortar bombs darted erratically about the branches of the trees. Denotations shattered the air. Earth and stones fountained up; showers of leaves floated down ... Then the din stopped as suddenly as it started.[72]

One of the most insidious aspects of coming under artillery fire was the randomness of the casualties. It was quite possible for a shell to land between two soldiers, tearing one to pieces and leaving the other completely unscathed. Edward Wilson of 5RTR recorded one such incident: 'I was sitting on the cupola to get a better view through my binoculars, an airburst overhead caused a shell fragment to pass between my legs and into the back of my gunner, Trooper Baldrey, severely wounding him.'[73] Mortars seem to have particularly intimidated the soldiers, due to the reduced warning. 'Unlike a shell, there is no warning whistle from a mortar fired at close range; it is only the firing of the bomb which is heard, and one is not aware of its direction until it arrives.'[74] One particular weapon that was universally loathed was the Moaning Minnie, or *Nebelwerfer*, which was a multi-barrelled mortar that could deliver six bombs onto a position more or less simultaneously, accompanied by a whistling shriek that gave them their nickname. One RAMC officer in Normandy estimated that up to 70 per cent of the casualties he treated came from mortars.[75] When coming under any form of indirect fire there was a fine line to be chosen between taking the sensible course of going to ground, which would be accompanied by ribald derision if the shells landed elsewhere, and affecting a studied nonchalance that could prove fatal if overdone.

At the end of the long summer day, as darkness closed in for a few all-too-short hours, the tanks would pull back into leaguer; Johnny Langdon described the procedure:

As soon as the tanks settled in leaguer everyone had their set tasks which were tackled without delay or supervision, the drivers and co-drivers checked their tanks thoroughly on the mechanical side and if there were any problems got word to the squadron mechanist sergeant, who would arrive as soon as possible from A1 Echelon in his half-track with the squadron fitters.[76] Petrol and ammunition replenishment was top priority, the 3-ton lorries coming up to the tanks from A1 Echelon. Petrol was supplied in four and a half gallon jerricans. While the drivers and co-drivers got on with topping up with petrol, the gunners and wireless operators stowed any replacement ammunition. Amidst all this a brew and a quick meal was prepared. Troop commanders had to receive orders for the following day which in turn had to be passed on to tank commanders and, if possible, the whole troop ... By the time refuelling and replenishment was completed, and orders received and issued it was well past midnight and only two or three hours remained of the night before stand-to at first light. I decided to put my bedroll on the engine covers which were still warm from the day's running.[77]

A crew from the 7th Armoured Division clean the barrel of their 75mm gun – a lack of time meant that such deep maintenance could only be attempted when out of action.

Leaguer activity was thus both routine and urgent: everything had to be completed correctly in the fading light, as no lights would be permitted after dark – orders groups were often conducted by dim torchlight under canvas, and heavy maintenance, such as changing a track or engine, would take twice as long as it would do in daylight. Any faults found during the 'last parade' check would result in at least some of the crew staying up, working with the fitters to rectify them before the following day. Simply filling up with petrol took a long time, as replenishment was done by cans, with no bowser lorries available to pump fuel.

Although wherever possible the tank leaguers were protected by the infantry from the motor battalion, this was not always possible, and so the sleep that was available was then interrupted by guard duties, usually called 'stag', short for standing guard. Corporal Ken Wheeldon 5DG related an unusual incident during one of his stags:

> We had drawn the midnight to 2 am turn. I slung my Sten over my shoulder … when our two hour stint was up, I roused Spinky and told him to wake up the two who were to relieve us. 'Tell them not to bother looking for their Stens,' I said, 'they can use ours', hoping to speed up the handover … I saw a figure moving away from the tanks and towards the gap. I unslung my Sten and stepped forward … I must have moved very quietly because the leading figure stood on my foot. I was about to swear when he turned his head

Well, someone had to do it. Members of the Pioneer Corps re-filling jerricans with petrol, far enough behind the lines that steel helmets are not necessary. It was then the job of the RAC units' echelons to take the cans forward to the AFV crews, often into the battle zone itself.

sideways and he was wearing one of those helmets which dipped very low at the back of the neck. 'It's a bloody German' I thought, jumping backwards. I collided with Spinky who was sleepily about to hand over his gun. I said the first thing that came into my head: 'Hands up!' A split second passed before the Jerry at the rear of the party raised his hands – to convince me of his friendship he repeated my words in his best English. Spinky dropped his gun and started to raise his hands. 'Not you, you silly b ... d' I yelled. The others were disarmed, and marched across the field to SHQ. I roused the first person I found, which happened to be the squadron leader. 'It's Wheeldon sir,' I beamed 'I've got five prisoners.' My dreams of mitigation were shattered. 'What the hell do you expect me to do with them? Take them to RHQ – and close the flaps as you go out!'[78]

The lack of sleep was a real and persistent problem. For the majority of the campaign, and this applies to all campaigns, not just Normandy, troops spent most of the time desperately tired, and the long summer days and short nights added to the problem. When set-piece actions took place, it was common for the tank crews to spend the afternoon, evening and night before the battle moving into their start positions, thus all-but guaranteeing that they would start the battle already tired, and the intensity of the combat that followed, with nerves a-jangle for hours on end, simply added to the problem. Sympathetic tank commanders allowed their crews to cat-nap in position when they could, although the need to remain vigilant often over-rode this. The longer the battle continued, the worse the cumulative effects of lack of sleep became. One memoir thought that:

> Five hours was a good night's rest. As soon as the tank was safely in the leaguer, the men realised how hungry they were but seeing to the tanks' needs took precedence over the crews. One culinary short-cut was to put tins of whatever the compo pack provided on the tanks' exhausts: either the crew got a nice hot meal, or the tank got a nasty mess in the engine compartment when the tins overheated and exploded.[79]

Many days could be tiring and wearing without the enemy ever being sighted. During others, the whole day seemed to be one engagement after another. Although the majority – about two-thirds – of all main armament rounds fired were HE, the main purpose of the tanks was to destroy the enemy armour, and most of these AP engagements were against static vehicles, often well camouflaged and dug-in as part of a prepared defensive position. Occasionally, however, an engagement against a moving target might occur:

> I suddenly saw on my right at about eight hundred yards an enemy tank, a Mk IV, travelling fast across my flank. 'Gunner traverse right,' I yelled, 'AP,

eight hundred yards, enemy tank moving left to right'. The turret swung round, Hume found the target and fired, the tank was still moving fast, I heard the breech close and Millington's shout of 'Loaded!' 'Same target, lay off a bit right, fire.' I shouted; a direct hit, the tank had stopped, and I could see some of the crew bailing out. I made my report on the air but in the general excitement I doubt if it was noticed.[80]

The only time that the crews might get more than a few snatched hours – often interrupted with a sentry duty – is when the unit was pulled back out of the front line for a few days. Even then sleep was not guaranteed. Johnny Langdon recorded a period of so-called rest in which his regiment were out of 'the line', but as they were surrounded by field, medium and heavy artillery positions, they found the location 'very noisy'.[81]

Crews had different views of where they should sleep. If out of contact, the favourite method was to rig up a canvas shelter on the side of the hull – always the side on the inside of the leaguer, for safety reasons – or, if the weather was kind, to simply sleep along the side of the tank – boots off, but generally still wearing their clothes. Sleeping bags were for the future, and the standard method involved wrapping oneself up in blankets and gas capes. Keeping one's bedding dry was a major preoccupation but well worth the effort. John Fisher noted that, 'There was a tarpaulin on the back of the tank and the bed-rolls were laid on this. The tarpaulin was then folded over them, to make a waterproof parcel. The whole thing was tied down by an empty [webbing] ammunition belt from the Browning.'[82] If within German mortar or artillery range, extra precautions had to be taken. In extremis, crews would sleep inside the tank, but this was uncomfortable and after a day cooped-up inside, they desperately needed to stretch themselves out, even if this increased the risk. Shell scrapes could be dug but after a long day of fighting followed by maintenance and replenishment, few had the energy to do this, and in any case, scrapes did not give any protection from airburst shells.[83] If the ground was firm, some crews would elect to sleep under the tank, and whilst stories abounded of crews being crushed when their tank sank into soft mud, in reality this was all-but unheard of.

Night administrative moves – as opposed to tactical moves made during combat which were much rarer – were a frequent task and one more thing that conspired to deprive crews of much-needed sleep. Of course, during the hot summer days the dust was still prevalent, even at night, and Bill Close described one such move in the lead up to Goodwood:

The night moves proved to be horrendous, moving nose to tail along dusty winding tracks, tank commanders peering with bleary eyes out of their turrets trying to maintain station with the tank in front. The first move on the night of the 16th/17th July was accomplished without undue incident and we arrived in an area west of the Orne about 0100. Our orders were to lie-up for the day, camouflage our tanks and get as much rest as possible. However the guns and instruments in the tanks had to be cleaned of the appalling dust which covered everything after the night march. We were able to cook meals on our small tank stoves although no fires were allowed, and all movement was kept to a minimum ...[84]

Lieutenant Johnny Langdon, 1 Troop leader in Major Close's A Squadron, described the same night march:

It was soon apparent that this move wasn't to be a piece of cake. The only light we had to follow was the rear light of the preceding tank, a minute red dot, but the most trouble was caused by the clouds of dust which completely enveloped everything. The dust got everywhere, inside our goggles and clothing, cutting visibility to practically zero.[85]

Bill Bellamy, a troop leader with A Squadron 8th King's Royal Irish Hussars, recorded similar memories:

Dust thrown up by the tracks presented us with an additional problem as our front mudguards had been ripped away by the dense hedgerows, and the dust and grit always seemed to blow in our eyes. This was especially bad for the driver and co-driver, as they were actually sitting between the tracks ... By the end of the day we were all filthy, mouths full of grit and eyes raw. Conjunctivitis was prevalent. Despite that, the problem was mild at this time [June], compared to the dust which we experienced later in the July battles. I was unable to wear goggles, as that prevented me from using my field glasses.[86]

Brewing up and bailing out were two terms that formed a large part of the tank crewman's vocabulary. Crews knew that they could be hit in any number of ways, not only by direct fire from a tank or anti-tank gun, but also from a *PanzerFaust* or *PanzerSchreck*, by striking a mine, from directed or just random small arms fire, as well as by shelling and mortaring. Much thought was given on how best to bail out, and some units and crews preferred to keep their hatches open, despite the increased threat from shell or mortar splinters, in order to buy a few precious seconds, as there would be no notice given when the time came:

There was a terrific explosion, and I was flung high into the air. I hit the ground with a bump. I was momentarily winded, but one thought possessed me as I struggled to my feet: Dick and Smudger were still inside the tank, which was burning fiercely. Dick was struggling to pull himself out, his face blackened and cracked, and his hair scorched. I managed to get an arm under his shoulder and haul him out, together, we fell off the tank. The flames were now belching from the engine compartment and the turret, and I hoped desperately that they had not reached the driver's compartment. I was also fearful that the gun barrel would be over the driver's hatch … dashed back. As I did so, Smudger appeared through the smoke, staggering as though blind … I took a look at Dick. He was in a bad way, his boyish face blackened and burned. But he was conscious and managed to tell me he had a pain in his chest. I injected him with morphine and smothered his burns with burn cream…I began to drag Dick along the ditch to the safety of the trees … I began to feel pain in my left leg and for the first time realised that I too was wounded … We learned that the medical half-track was on its way…I realised that we were about to make our last journey together as a crew … I never saw Dick again. He died in hospital.[87]

I was suddenly aware that we were on fire. Smoke billowed from the engine covers. Fire is the fear of all tank crews, with perhaps 150 gallons of fuel and a number of sensitive grenades and shells stowed below, the machine is a fire bomb itself. 'Bail out' I ordered. We seemed to hit the ground together and ran for cover. The commander in the following tank sized up our plight and fired his smoke canisters over our heads … We gazed at our beloved tank, now engulfed in flame. The blankets and rubber tracks burned fiercely and flames from the turret and engine were reaching heights of thirty feet. We had been the victim of a German SP. All we owned was what we stood up in.[88]

Bailing out became the norm when hit; most crews were not prepared to spend time in an AFV that had been hit to work out just how bad things were, preferring to get out first and take things from there. Early AFV designs often had flaws in the design of hatches, making it very difficult if not impossible for some crew members to escape if the turret was in a particular position. As the war progressed, this improved and, for instance, the initial design of the hull hatches on the Cromwell was modified so that both driver and hull machine-gunner were equipped with side opening doors that greatly improved the chances of a rapid egress, and the large hull side escape hatches on the Churchill undoubtedly saved many lives. But other, less obvious areas also affected the chances of survival following a bail-out. The issue of the RAC steel helmet before the Normandy campaign was seen as a good thing; it replaced the Mk II Brodie 'Tommy' helmet that was useless inside a tank, with a design based upon the Paratrooper/Despatch Rider stell helmet shell. It was made in such a way that the crew members could wear headsets underneath it, and the lack of a protruding rime meant that they could use the sights and periscopes; many units insisted that it always be worn in combat, and many soldiers took no persuading. However, when worn outside the tank it looked more like a German 'coalscuttle' helmet than the British infantry models, and caused problems. John Fisher of 4CLY was told by a more experienced soldier to 'take that helmet off, it looks like a Jerry!' Fisher complied and put on his beret, as 'Helmets, obviously, were not *de rigeur* in the CLY'.[89] Lieutenant Johnny Langdon of 3RTR nearly learned the same lesson the hard way after bailing out:

> I thought it best because of the enemy infantry positions we had passed to use the corn as cover as much as possible … Every now and again I took a quick look above the corn, on the last occasion saw our infantry advancing with Bren carriers one hundred yards away. At first, I felt sure they thought that we were Germans trying to surrender as two of the crew were wearing the new type of tank helmet … They trained their rifles and Brens on us but luckily a few quick shouts, including the usual soldier's swear words, convinced them that we were a bailed-out tank crew.[90]

In some cases, bailing out led to an immediate problem, if the enemy were in the vicinity, as some members of the Skins discovered in one notable incident:

> Corporal Carr's tank was brewed up. The crew bailed out successfully but were attacked by German infantry as they dismounted. Corporal Carr was able to get hold of his Sten gun which was kept on the outside of the tank for such a purpose. He shot three enemy at close range, enabling the rest of his crew to get back safely. [91]

Another new item issued to tank crews just before Normandy was the lightweight denim tank suit, the first time that a genuine tank coverall had been produced and it proved popular. In late 1944 a heavier tank suit with a blanket lining and an ingenious system of full-length zips that allowed the legs to be zipped together to convert the bottom into a sleeping bag was issued; it was immensely warm and practical, but had one great flaw. Unlike the denim tank suit, which was a camouflage green, the winter 'Pixie' suit was a pale sand colour, and this rendered bailing out crews terribly conspicuous to the enemy. Bill Bellamy recorded seeing:

> Mike's body lying by the side of the road … It was a lesson to me, as he was wearing one of the new tank-suits with which we had been issued. They were made out of semi-waterproof material but were a yellowish creamy colour and there was no way that the wearer could have taken cover without being easily visible … I resolved not to wear mine in the future.[92]

Casualty reporting was always important, and most officers believed that it was their solemn and painful duty to write to a deceased soldier's next of kin personally. Although meant with the best of intentions, the interplay between this private correspondence and official channels could, occasionally, go badly wrong. Major Gibson of A Squadron the Skins wrote to the parents of Trooper

Makepiece, three days after he was killed in action when his tank was hit twice, probably by *PanzerFaust* fire. The letter deliberately tried to conceal the fact that he had died in a burning tank; indeed, it was not clear whether he had been killed outright when his tank was initially hit, or whether the fire had claimed him (and two others), and so the gentler option was understandably taken, implying that he had been killed instantly. Gibson received a thankful letter from the mother, saying that 'your letter has consoled me, and I feel comforted'. However, the War Office then informed Mrs Makepiece in somewhat different terms, and once again she wrote to Major Gibson:

> I received a letter from the War Office telling me that my son lost his life when his tank was set on fire and it stated that his body was never found. You gave me the impression that my son was killed instantly and did not suffer … [I] made continuous enquiries until information has reached me that my son was seen hanging out of the tank but could not be saved … Surely, sir, as my son was only half in the tank, there must have been some remains? Is it possible that he is still living somewhere? Will you please write and tell me the full facts, no matter how painful they may seem?

Gibson then had to write to explain that when a tank carrying ammunition and fuel caught fire, nothing in the way of human remains might be left to identify. (The whole situation was made much worse by the desperate mother, who employed a medium (spiritualist) who told her that her son was still alive.) Such tragedies simply added to the burden of command, carried by relatively young men who were as desperately tired as their subordinates.[93]

One of the unexpected results of taking casualties, and the attrition of tank commanders in particular, was that sergeants often found themselves thrust into the role of troop leader. Generally speaking this was as the result of an agreement rather than an order, and a sensible squadron leader would think long and hard as to which troop sergeant might be able to make the step up – it was not simply a question of seniority. Indeed, many of the most experienced and often decorated sergeants were not at all interested in leading troops, preferring to take tactical orders rather than give them. In the majority of cases such an appointment was temporary, and lasted only until an officer replacement could be pushed forward through the system. However, there are occasional instances of sergeants remaining in posts for many months, although if they were successful, they would generally come under pressure to take an immediate battlefield commission. The Skins recorded an instance of an NCO commanding a troop who happened to be in the right place at the right time, making a considered tactical decision:

> A troop of A Squadron tanks, commanded by Sergeant Archie Carr, moved along the eastern bank of the Risle, to seek a crossing point and came to a

mill with a wooden bridge. It spanned the river over a width of some twenty yards and though supported in the centre by wooden pillars was clearly not intended for anything heavier than a horse and cart. Realising that he would never know the strength of the bridge unless he tried it, Archie cautiously edged his tank forward to the centre and over to the other bank. It had not budged an inch. The remainder of the troop moved over and headed down the road ... That bridge was to carry all the tanks and echelon of the regiment and the whole of the 7th Armoured Division.[94]

Another NCO troop leader in the same regiment, Sergeant Bob Price, was later awarded a Military Medal and the citation, in part, read:

During the action [at Borken on 28 March 1945], his troop leader had to be evacuated and from that time to the present he has been commanding the troop. As a troop leader he has been outstanding ... He showed the same qualities of coolness when under fire, skill in manoeuvre, leadership and determination to close with and destroy the enemy ... Sergeant Price has proved himself unquestionably the best troop leader in my squadron ... his personal courage, coolness and judgement, and his technical and tactical efficiency have been an inspiration ... No other troop leader in my squadron has made a greater single contribution to its successful operations.[95]

Casualties could come from accidents as well as from enemy action. Traffic accidents were all too frequent in all theatres, and there was a suspicion that men who were dealing with death on a daily basis might be inclined to take risks when out of direct action, somehow considering themselves to be immortal in normal life, and speeding was a common cause. Weapon and ammunition accidents were another source of death and injury: 'A tragic accident in Tac HQ caused the death of our adjutant, Captain Maurice Williams. Tiredness and fatigue was affecting efficiency, and the gunner of the tank following Maurice's accidentally put his foot on the firing switch, firing a burst into the forward vehicle killing Maurice instantly.'[96] Such incidents were unfortunately not uncommon. In the same unit Sergeant 'Darky' Bowley, a particularly popular NCO, was killed on 22 September 1944:

Tiredness, fatigue, familiarity with dangerous weapons, all played some part in a freak accident. Darky was standing on the engine cover of his tank whilst other crew members were checking their areas of responsibility – drivers looking at tracks, operators netting their areas radios, and gunners making last-minute adjustments and oiling guns. Suddenly, from one of the tanks came a loud explosion as the 75mm was fired accidentally. The shell struck poor Sergeant Bowley and he died almost instantly ... How does the gunner and commander of the tank who had failed to ensure that the safety catch was applied live with that responsibility?[97]

All the factors described thus far – tiredness, fear, taking casualties, even the weather – would affect the morale and nerves of individuals, and it was starting to be recognized that each man had a personal bank of courage and endurance, that varied between individuals but which, if completely drained, would lead to breakdown. It could affect the hero as well as the craven, and the effects on a close-knit crew could be sudden and dramatic:

> My driver started to query every order I gave. Later that day, when leading over a crest and in full view of the opposite ridge, he stopped. We were a sitting target, but he refused to move another inch. I told him to get out of the tank and threatened to shoot him if he refused but he was incapable of even understanding our situation. The gunner kicked him. Eventually he was pulled out of the driver's seat and the operator took over. I left him sitting by the side of the road, a broken, weeping wreck. I never knew what happened to him.[98]

The Echelon

It is only too easy to neglect all the other members of an armoured or armoured car regiment in favour of the more glamorous parts played by the tank crews. This would be unfair, as the whole enterprise depended on sound and often courageous logistics. Lieutenant Langdon of 3RTR described the echelon system as seen through his eyes in mid-June 1944:

> By 18th June, all A and B vehicles of the battalion arrived in the divisional concentration area. A1 Echelon was situated approximately four hundred yards away with A Echelon a further six hundred … Each squadron had its quota of wheeled vehicles known as B vehicles or soft-skins. Under operational conditions these joined one of the three echelons, which came under the HQ squadron commander. The echelons, known as B, A, and A1, were responsible for supplying everything needed by the ranks. B Echelon was furthest to the rear and collected and received supplies direct from the RASC. A was intermediate, and A1, normally commanded by the 2IC HQ Squadron, delivered straight to the tanks. The [mostly wheeled] vehicles in each of the fighting squadrons consisted of three 15–cwt trucks for squadron office, officer's mess, and personnel; thirteen 3–ton lorries: one for the fitters, one for the SQMS and baggage, three for petrol, seven for ammunition, and a mobile kitchen; a 5–cwt car, normally a jeep; [and] a carrier containing a slave battery for helping to start tanks with battery problems.[99]

The 3CLY served in 4th Armoured Brigade in Normandy. One of their Humber Scout Cars is alongside a half-track, probably belonging to one of the squadron fitters' sections or the LAD. During this time, fitters could come from either the unit itself or from the newly formed REME.

If the unit had suffered casualties during the day, vehicles or men, these would also have to be replaced and integrated before dawn. During the night after the first day of Operation Goodwood, 3RTR 'had a very disturbed night with little chance of sleep. We were reinforced with ten tanks and crews from the Forward Delivery Squadron. This brought the strength of the regiment to twenty-two.'[100] Although the tank crews had the means to cook for themselves, wherever possible the evening meal would be prepared for them in the leaguer by the cooks' truck, which also made hot soup and tea by the gallon during night work. A member of 9RTR recalled that 'the arrival of the cooks' 3-tonner with the hot food was a welcome diversion, although stew and tinned peaches served in the same mess tin made for a novel cuisine.'[101]

One of the most intriguing and illustrative accounts depicting life in an echelon comes from the history of the 5th Royal Inniskilling Dragoon Guards, and recounts a story not of ammunition or fuel trucks being taken forward under fire – although such things did happen – but of a humble water bowser crew. The incident happened during the break-out and advance to the Seine, where 'these long daily moves now placed a severe strain upon our supply lines and the tired echelon drivers were having to cover at least four times the distance of our advance in a continuous forward and backward movement'. The NCO in charge of the 200-gallon squadron 'water-cart' was Corporal Cyril Blanchard, who takes up the story:

> Keeping a squadron of tanks and the echelon supplied with water was a difficult and continuous chore but a very necessary one. Initially each

water-cart operator found his own supply and moved up the line to join the main supplies at night. During the dry, dusty months of July and August 1944 the demand was constant. As the troops moved forward, the problem became more difficult until eventually the Royal Engineers set up water points and we were free to draw water that had been tested by experts. The golden rule was to always drag water from rivers and canals, [as] running water cleans itself to some degree, while wells and ponds are static and easily polluted.

We could never keep up with the troops. There was no radio fitted to a water-cart, so there was no choice but to follow the main [traffic] signs of our division until we found our brigade, and then the regiment, and squadron. Maps were in short supply … Our slow moves up the line were tedious [with frequent halts]. Unbeknown to Bill and me, the other drivers on the convoy were filching our water from the taps at the rear. Infantrymen too obviously thought this oasis too good to miss. We arrived at the tank harbour and the crews came down to fill their usual two jerrycans each only to find we were dry! The squadron leader was not amused … After driving for miles in search of a stream we decided to stop at the next village in the hope of finding a well – I had to take a chance. We persuaded an old man to show us the village well and pumped it dry. After treating the tank with the usual chlorine and taste tablets and waiting the requisite twenty minutes, I offered the old man a mugful of the water. He would have none of it, so I brandished my revolver in desperation, [which, with a bribe of chocolates and cigarettes] persuaded him to drink. We waited another half an hour to see what it would do to the poor chap. Ever after that incident, which cost us a night's sleep, we kept a good watch on our taps during moves.[102]

The LAD

The other group within the regiment that requires recognition was the Light Aid Detachment, or LAD. Comprising both REME personnel (from September 1942) and regimental fitters, and under the overall command of the Regimental (or Battalion) Technical Adjutant, the LAD was responsible for repairs, modifications and recovery. Captain Pat MacIver of the REME attached to the 24th Lancers described the LAD:

The LAD was a small, mobile workshop in support of the squadron fitters. … In the 24th Lancers, where pride and fellowship were strong, the system worked particularly well. The squadron fitters would maintain and repair anything they could with hand tools … this was like the mechanically minded owner of a good car doing his best not to let it out of his hands into

A LAD half-track parked up in the lee of a building. The Jeep in front has a wire-cutter fitted, to break any wires strung across a road at head height.

Probably the dirtiest job anywhere in the army, tank fitters repairing a gearbox; the censor has blotted out their cap badges in the name of security.

a garage. The 'garage' in this case was rather special, a mobile workshop which was proud to be part of the regiment and to go wherever they went. This LAD cared for instruments such as watches, compasses and gun-sighting equipment. It cared for the tank guns and machine guns, and for the rifles and pistols. And of course it cared for the AFVs and B vehicles … The LAD had a mobile workshops which included an instrument workshop, and a 15-cwt truck equipped for electric and gas welding. There was a binned stores lorry which carried spare parts, and a heavy recovery vehicle to pull vehicles out of ditches and to tow them back for repair. The couple of dozen REME tradesmen were almost as possessive of the regiment as were the squadron fitters.[103]

Not all repairs were within the capabilities of the LAD, and vehicles needing more extensive repairs were sent back to the Second and Third Line Workshops. Of all tanks reported as being knocked out, it was estimated that about 60 per cent could be subsequently repaired and put back into action; the main reason why the remainder could not, was that they were burned out.

The Padre and the Doc

Finally, let us not forget the critical role played by two other non-RAC members of the regiments: the Royal Army Chaplains' Department military chaplain and the Royal Army Medical Corps Regimental Medical Officer (RMO), universally known as the 'Padre' and 'Doc' respectively. Padres were in much demand, not only because of their ability to provide spiritual comfort – often regardless of denomination – but also because of their secondary role as the 'soldier's friend', and as such were often able to restore combat power by simply spending time with a tired, scared and lonely soldier or officer. They were also required to organize the burial of soldiers killed in action, and frequently took on much more than this. Legendary, but by no means unique, was Captain Leslie Skinner of the SRY, who:

> … took on [the gruesome job] of removing dead bodies from burnt-out tanks. He himself wrote that he had 'buried the three dead and tried to reach remaining dead in tanks still too hot and burning … Horrible mess. Fearful job picking up bits and pieces and re-assembling for identification and putting in blankets for burial. Squadron Leader offered to lend me some men to help. Refused. Less men who live and fight in tanks have to do with this side of things the better.[104]

Padres normally worked out of the Regimental Aid Post (RAP), the preserve of the Doc and his small team. Regimental Medical Officers as a breed won the respect and admiration of the men they supported, often going forward even as a battle was being fought in their lightly armoured scout cars to recover and treat the wounded, with many receiving gallantry awards as testament to their courage. Such men, although brave and experienced, were not indestructible, and during autumn 1944 3RTR lost both their Padre, Captain Taylor MC, killed and their long-standing RMO, Captain MacMillan MC, wounded and evacuated.

Normandy: Assessing the Bigger Picture

Can the Normandy campaign be considered as a success for the armoured units? Although the campaign was very much an all-arms affair, there were a number of times when the armoured formations and regiments found themselves at the forefront of planned offensive operations, and the performance of some, particularly the veterans of 7th Armoured Division, has attracted criticism. Some of this criticism is undoubtedly valid, particularly concerning the cocksure attitudes prevalent in some of the veteran units and formations shipped back to the UK specifically to 'strengthen' the inexperienced units. This manifested itself in two apparently contradictory ways. Firstly, the veteran soldiers and units were accused of being arrogant, resting on their laurels and boasting of their exploits 'up the blue', with their deep tans, Africa Star medal ribbons, and reluctance to adhere to regulations. They were also accused of being 'windy' in action, not showing the drive and aggression that they had been specifically brought back to demonstrate. The British army hates the labelling of units as 'elite', but that is what the Desert Rats were meant to be. This sort of generalization is of course unfair on the individuals and units who did perform well, and they were probably in the majority.

There seems to have been an expectation at the most senior levels that the mere presence of the 7th Armoured was a panacea for all tactical ills, and their deployment would inevitably lead to success. When this did not happen the disappointment was all the more difficult to explain, and the blame fell squarely on the shoulders of the likes of Erskine and Hinde, not without some justification, but there were other factors at play. For one thing, the nature of the campaign was very different to those fought in Libya, Tunisia, Sicily and Italy, and changing deeply ingrained habits and tactical drills was difficult. It was also the case that none the units were totally veteran: the proportion of Mediterranean veterans in the units was declining all the time, and it is probable that in some units the majority of troop leaders and tank crewmen were as inexperienced as the remainder of the invasion force. The real veterans were few; they were to be found as the squadron leaders and second in commands, the sergeant majors and troop sergeants, and a lot of them were now doing jobs in the echelons. It must also be noted that some of the units that had returned from overseas and placed into different formations performed well; this applied to 3RTR in 11th Armoured Division, the Greys in 4th Armoured Brigade and SRY in 8th Armoured Brigade, amongst others. And let us not forget the human factor: there is some justification in the complaints from those veterans that they had 'done their bit'. Such comments came, in numerous cases, from soldiers and officers who had been in more or less constant action for three years, had often had to bail out of burning vehicles more than once and who had seen their close friends burned alive. The observation that it should now be the turn of others had a lot of validity.

Organization and Tactics

Where there was clear failure was in the organization that the armoured formations went to Normandy with, and in the tactics used by the units. A comprehensive explanation of the development of British armoured doctrine and organization is yet to be completed, but what is clear is that the effects of the pre-war (predominantly RTC) systems and concepts still influenced the way that training was conducted prior to 6 June. Lessons from other theatres had been disseminated, but the RAC as a whole lacked the experience to be able to cherry-pick the pertinent and discard the remainder. At unit level, training in the UK was conducted to please the particular wishes of the formation commander, and tended to concentrate on the massed movement of armour – impressive when seen on Pathe or Movietone in the cinema but fatal in war. This was at the expense of troop and squadron fire and movement, and was particularly lacking in two areas: how to advance against an emplaced enemy with anti-tank guns and how best to provide close support to the infantry in the attack. In its place was a deal of confusion regarding doctrine, and the arrival of Montgomery served to muddy the waters in the critical few months before D-Day, as he forced his opinions of armoured warfare on 21st Army Group. Place noted that 'when the British army returned to France in 1944, there was no greater consensus over armour [doctrine] than there had been five years earlier'.[105] According to Michael Carver, the best way to organize the elements within the armoured division had been discussed before D-Day, but as it was assumed that the break-out from the bocage would be speedier than happened, nothing much was done, and the formations were left organized ready for an armoured thrust, not as a balanced all-arms grouping.

Although from autumn 1943 both infantry and tank brigades had been instructed to do some cross-training in each other's roles, the: 'scale of the training, even after Montgomery took over, was quite inadequate. The different attitudes that went with the different roles were too deeply ingrained for a few days here and there of alternative training to remove them'.[106] In any case, the most important element of Infantry tank co-operation, particularly in the light of doctrinal muddle and a lack of strong, centralized control, was to practise with the unit that was being supported prior to the battle. In general terms, those units that did this were able to evolve sensible procedures and were often successful, whereas those that did not were more likely to fail (and then blame the other).

In far too many cases, the armour was sent ahead of the infantry in the hope that they could use their inherent mobility to punch through the defences, and that their armour protection might be just sufficient to allow this to happen. Attempting to use armour en masse as a modern battering ram ran counter to doctrine and experience but was nevertheless tried a number of times during the Normandy campaign, with a notable lack of success. It might have worked against a weak, unprepared or less resolute enemy, in favourable terrain, but Normandy did not offer that. As Liddell Hart once said, 'No general is justified in launching his troops to a direct attack upon an enemy firmly in position.'[107] Too many times in Normandy senior generals, who should have known better, tried to use the armour – the arm of mobility and exploitation – as a blunt instrument, a battering ram.

It is necessary to return to the problems caused by insufficient – and just plain incorrect – training in the UK. Units preparing for a new campaign were, naturally, unaware of exactly what would face them. The veteran units returned from the Mediterranean sometimes fell into the trap of trying to 'shoehorn' the new situation into their current tactical understanding and procedures, whereas the totally inexperienced units could only rely on the mountain of (often contradictory) tactical publications. When exercising, the presence of umpires often actively handicapped development – one cannot help but think that if the umpires were of the highest quality, they would not be in that job, but would be the ones commanding the tanks. As but one example, on exercises umpires almost always penalized commanders who had their heads out of the turret, but this was doctrinal fascism and failed to recognise the need for commanders to take the risk when it was necessary – almost every account by a commander who fought in the campaign comments on the need to make their own mind up as to when to take the risk, as well as the blindness that resulted from being closed down in action.[108] Bill Bellamy, a Cromwell commander in 8KRIH, recorded that, 'I can't remember any operation during which I had my head inside the turret, it was always out and I kept my two turret [hatches] open, using one on either side to give me some protection.'[109]

Working with the Infantry

One of the criticisms raised time and again is the lack of understanding when working with the infantry. Boardman opined that, 'There is a sort of mutual respect between infantrymen and tank crews, neither liking each other's job. The tankmen see the PBI as having to depend upon rations brought forward for them, usually getting very wet, sleeping with one blanket, and having a thankless task.

The infantryman sees a tank as a fire trap, noisy and attracting fire, sometimes on themselves.'[110] For a view from the other side of the divide, Lieutenant Sydney Jary, an infantry platoon commander with 4th Bn Somerset LI, commented that in Normandy:

> Denied scope for manoeuvre, our tanks were reduced to the role of blind, slow and highly vulnerable infantry support guns. The German infantry had by far the most effective short-range anti-tank weapons ... we had to devise a means of identifying those cunningly concealed targets for the tank commander. We soon learned not to climb onto the tank and shout; due to engine noise he could seldom hear us, and it proved a lethal pastime. We tried firing Verey lights towards the target and also Bren bursts of all tracer rounds, but neither was satisfactory. The most successful arrangement was for the tank commander to throw out a head set, but even then, engine noise made if difficult.[111]

What became clear was that whilst doctrine and tactics could be amended – and frequently were, in the light of increased experience – the critical aspect was that two units must not simply be thrown together just before the start of an operation. What was needed was, at the very least, time to meet, talk and agree the basic procedures, including the means of communication. Wherever possible, a chance to rehearse the agreed procedures added even more to the chances of success. John French was clear that:

> Units that worked together on a regular basis could develop a close camaraderie. The 1st Gordon Highlanders of 51st Highland Division and a squadron of the Northants Yeomanry of 33rd Armoured Brigade co-operated so frequently between Normandy and the Rhine crossing that the latter look on themselves as being almost Gordon Highlanders.[112]

With the bond of shared experience and, in many cases, friendship it was much easier to work out how best to deal with specific tactical problems. Stuart Hills of SRY recalled how co-operation took place during Operation Bluecoat and in the bocage:

> In this sort of country, the infantry proceeded along the sides of the roads in advance of the tanks, as this lessened the chances of the tanks being hit by Panzerfausts. If Spandau [MG] fire opened up on the infantry, they immediately went to ground in adjoining ditches and it was then that the tanks had to move forward ... this might involve moving through gaps into the fields, but we were wary of getting too far ahead of our infantry and they liked us around to give them shelter and protection.[113]

This of course came about not because of the pre-invasion training, but due to intelligent and increasingly experienced officers experimenting until they came upon the best solution; the intensity of the campaign made it difficult to share thoughts between formations, which is why each of the armoured divisions ended up doing things differently. Tanks had originally been developed to support the infantry. Inter-war doctrine emphasized the need for intimate co-operation, but it was not until July 1944 that methods were devised to optimize such co-operation, and these served the army well for the remainder of the war. 'It was not until the middle of the Normandy campaign that the army finally abandoned the last remnants of its pre-war conviction that tanks and infantry within armoured divisions could and should operate separately.'[114]

The Effects of Terrain

The bocage country to the west of Caen was described in one French tourist information booklet as 'pleasantly shaded woodland'. It can be confidently stated that no one, whichever uniform they wore, found the countryside pleasant in summer 1944. The small fields, dating back to medieval times, were surrounded by high banks, hedges and trees. Driving down one of the many sunken lanes between the fields, a tank would be vulnerable to attack at short range, with only the commander able to see above the surrounding foliage. Driving into a field was possible, Churchills finding it particularly easy (although some Sherman and Cromwell tanks were fitted with an American-designed extemporized device to assist in cutting through the earth banks), but this exposed the under-armoured belly of the tank to anti-tank fire and *PanzerFauste*. Additionally, even without the bocage problem, Normandy offered some specific terrain challenges. The countryside was littered with small villages and farmyards, generally between 1 and 2 miles from their neighbour. These were strongly constructed from stone, often having cellars which gave soldiers using them protection from indirect fire, and were ideal for conversion into strongpoints, with the distance between them perfect for interlocking arcs of anti-tank and MG fire. A number of hills and high spots dominated surrounding areas, and a series of ridgelines around the east and south of Caen became vital ground, which offered a huge advantage to the defender in terms of both observation and fire. The Germans, as they invariably did, made the most of these terrain advantages, by deploying a thin and permeable forward 'outpost' screen designed to begin the engagement, slow the advance and inflict early casualties, and warn the main defensive line of the approach. The main defensive line was often up to 2km deep, which meant that whilst break-in might be achieved, this defence in depth made break-through and break-out very difficult.

Failing to develop tactics for, and then train for, the specific problems caused by the bocage must be held as a major error in the lead up to D-Day. Although the terrain had been studied in detail, it seemed to come as a shock to most of the units; one commentator has since suggested that the RAC and infantry units earmarked for Normandy should have been put through a battle school in Herefordshire, the English county most resembling the bocage.[115]

The German Defence

There is a military aphorism that states that no plan survives contact with the enemy, and another that says that however good the plan, the enemy will have a vote in its execution. By 1944 it was widely understood that the German soldier presented an exceptionally resolute, well-trained and quick-thinking enemy. Even very junior NCOs were expected to display initiative, and at all levels Kampfgruppe (battlegroups) could be formed almost instantly from whatever troops were at hand. The troops defending the invasion beaches were generally third-rate, but still put up a stout defence. The subsequent deployment of the elite Panzer Divisions, as well as some SS and Parachute formations, meant that the British army frequently found itself fighting against the cream of the Wehrmacht, and this compounded the problem.

One of the often under-reported factors about the campaign was the German insistence (verging on fanaticism) of not giving up ground, but instead hanging on desperately, often foolishly, to tactically unimportant terrain. What the Allies were slow to realize was that this German 'no-retreat' policy had been in operation for at least two years in Russia, and that it came straight from Hitler. It was now their turn to have to prise the Germans out of every last ridge, village and farmhouse and, once they had done so, to have to beat off the inevitable counter-attack. As we have already seen, over the course of the campaign this policy had its advantages, as it led to the constant erosion of German reserves, particularly armour, that could not be easily replaced and thus in overall campaign terms can be seen as a positive – even if such attacks created constant casualties when repelling them.

Britain and its Commonwealth allies also fought a much more armour-centric campaign in Normandy than the Americans to the west. This was because Montgomery had always stated that his intention was to draw the German armour to the eastern (British and Canadian) sector of the beachhead, in order to allow the US army in the west more opportunities to break out, by swinging south and west before moving east towards Germany, and using Caen as the pivot in the hinge. Whether or not that was sensible – and it is questionable bearing in mind Britain's precarious manpower situation – the effect was certainly achieved, as the table below demonstrates.

German Formations Deployed in Normandy

Date	Opposing British/Canadian Forces (Caumont to Caen)			Opposing US Forces (Caumont to Cotentin)		
	Panzer Divisions	Infantry Battalions	Tanks	Panzer Divisions	Infantry Battalions	Tanks
15 June	4	43	520	½	63	70
25 June	5	49	530	1	87	190
30 June	7½	64	725	½	63	140
5 July	7½	64	690	½	63	215
10 July	5½	65	560	2½	72	240
15 July	5½	68	580	2½	78	240
20 July	7	71	720	2	82	189
25 July	7	92	750	2	85	190

Source: G.S. Jackson, *Operations of Eighth Corps* (St Clement's Press, 1948), p. 113. (Tanks probably includes SPGs.)

Up against such a preponderance of Panzers, including the very latest models, insufficient firepower remained the major technical problem for the RAC. Although they did not realize it, the tank crews' strident demands for increased armour were unrealistic, particularly because of the short engagement ranges that were common, as well as the increasing German use of hand-held anti-tank weapons by their infantry. What was achievable was increasing the firepower available, thereby allowing the British tanks to duel with the Germans at combat ranges on equal terms. The introduction of the 17-pounder allowed this, but the delays in development, deployment and, not least, the struggle to mount the gun into a tank turret, meant that only one tank per troop was a Firefly at the beginning of the campaign, and the need to replace combat losses meant that the desire to add a second Firefly to each tank troop was delayed. And in any case, the Churchill-equipped tank brigades were not allocated Fireflies at all, having to rely on the support of American M10 'tank destroyers' from the RA anti-tank regiments.

Success?

In amongst the many failures there were also plenty of examples of success. The development of specialized armour played a critical part in getting the assault troops ashore and consolidated, and was used successfully thereafter; it can be argued that without the support of the specialist armour, it is likely that the D-Day forces would have been pushed back into the sea. Most units fought with grim determination, despite knowing that they lacked the firepower to really compete with the larger German tanks, and were determined to do what they could to support their friends in the PBI. It had become clear that the more units worked together, the better the co-operation between them. Morale remained remarkably high, often buoyed by that unusual combination of Tommy's black humour combined with understated British determination to triumph against the odds. There were plenty of examples of units adapting quickly to the dual challenges of difficult terrain and a professionally determined enemy, and the reconnaissance units invariably showed great drive and determination, despite having to ply their trade in lightly armoured cars.

What really made the difference was threefold: the reliability of the tanks; the effectiveness of the armour replacement organization; and the revision of doctrine and organization at the formation level, to allow more effective all-arms co-operation to be developed. All of these elements remained in play until the end of the war. Despite the difficulties – and the casualties – the Normandy campaign was a success. The German defences creaked for weeks and then finally broke under pressure, allowing the much-heralded break-out to happen and the advance eastward towards Germany to begin, always with the armour in the van. It is appropriate to give the final word on Normandy to one who was there. Major Creagh Gibson, the OC of A Squadron 5DG, wrote to his father in mid-August 1944, summarizing the war he found himself in:

There is no doubt that the Boche has made good use of the terrain. He has proven himself to be clever, subtle and crafty. A few determined men, well sited and camouflaged and manning an anti-tank gun, can give an armoured regiment a very bloody nose in a very short time. The first indication of their presence is when the leading tank is knocked out. Even when this happens, you cannot tell from whence the shot came ... They also employ many snipers who have very accurate rifles with telescopic sights. They play havoc with the crew commanders ... they also dig-in their tanks and these are a devil to deal with. They can only be dealt with by an armoured piercing shot ... Our casualties have really been light. Those we have suffered have nearly all been caused by mines, shelling or mortar fire ... sometimes you have to get out and it is then that chaps get caught.[116]

Chapter Eight

Endgame

Break-out: The Great Swan

Once the Falaise pocket had been closed, the Germans found themselves with no readily defensible obstacle to the west of the Seine River. The forces that had escaped the encirclement streamed eastwards in disarray, having had to abandon their heavier equipment and weapons. Where fuel allowed, vehicles were used to transport them, but many escaped on foot. Clearly, it was to the Allies' advantage to keep the pressure on, and to exploit the advantageous situation that they found themselves in. This was exactly what the proponents of armoured warfare had been waiting for; the opportunity to use the tanks in the spearhead of the advance, supported by increasingly mechanized infantry and the self-propelled guns of the RA. Unlike during the Normandy campaign, where tanks had been used as battering rams against strong defensive positions, there was little organized resistance until the Seine and even beyond, allowing powerful armoured thrusts to be undertaken by the armoured divisions across north-eastern France – and passing through battlefields that many soldiers realised that their fathers had fought over – and into Belgium.

The armoured crews referred to this period of the war, lasting for just over a fortnight, as The Great Swan. Swanning was a phrase that had come from the old desert hands, as it had been used in North Africa to describe seemingly aimless armoured movements across the desert trying to locate the enemy. Used to being penned in to the bocage, with set-piece advances measured in a few miles per day at best, the troops found themselves exhilarated to be making 30 or even more miles progress each day, often only pausing because they were running out of fuel, or so tired that they could not sensibly carry on. After a few hours of snatched sleep and a hasty refuel once the echelon caught up, the advance would begin again. This is not to imply that no casualties were taken: it was not in the German's psyche to allow the Allies to make progress against no resistance, and so small stay-behind parties and mines continued to cause deaths and injuries, but nothing like on the scale that they had become accustomed to. The armoured cars led the way, often with the Cromwells and Shermans hard on their heels, in a bold attempt not only to liberate land and capture port facilities, but also to 'win the war by Christmas', which in early September looked like a real possibility.

Cromwells each carrying a section of infantry forward, out of action. There were never enough transport lorries to go around, and for the footsore infantry, such a ride would be a real blessing. The formation of a close bond between the tank crews and 'their' infantry was a real force-multiplier.

It had become practice to try to avoid night operations other than on non-tactical route marches, the units preferring in any case to withdraw into a leaguer, preferably with friendly infantry all round to prevent enemy interference. In any case, as has been noted, the crews had to replenish and maintain the vehicles, as well as grab some sleep. Another technical reason for a reluctance to attempt night combat was that the HF radios were notoriously tricky to use reliably at night, due to atmospheric problems.[1] However, some night advances were attempted and could achieve spectacular results. During the break-out from Normandy and advance to 'bounce' the crossings over the Somme River in late August, General Brian Horrocks, commanding XXX Corps, recalled that:

> At 4:15pm I arrived at the HQ of 11th Armoured Division and ordered Pip Roberts, the divisional commander, to continue the advance throughout the night in order to capture the bridge at Amiens, some thirty miles away, by first light next day. This may seem a curious way to employ an armoured division, but I was a great believer in using tanks at night. I tried it on three occasions and was successful each time … This was asking a lot of the division. Driving a tank is a very tiring business, and the drivers had already been on the go for some thirty-six hours. But Roberts never hesitated. The

division halted so that all tanks and vehicles could refill with petrol, and then started off on what proved to be one of the most fantastic night drives of the war ... utterly exhausted, the drivers fell asleep at every halt, and very often German vehicles were intermingled in our columns ... Early next morning ... the leading elements of the division had captured the bridges intact ... this was a remarkable performance which could have only been achieved by a very highly trained division.[2]

In most cases, of course, the advance was conducted in daylight, and the units were delighted to discover that resistance has largely disappeared – for the time being, at least. This was not without risks; where opposition was encountered, the tanks would find themselves beyond the range of their artillery, the majority of which was still towed by wheeled vehicles, and their supporting infantry. However, the biggest hindrance to the advance into western Belgium came not from the enemy but from the Belgian citizens, who turned out in numbers in every village and town to welcome their liberators; often progress was slowed down to a crawl, and hospitality was the order of the day:

> That evening I went into the centre of Antwerp ... the atmosphere was terrific, everyone seemed to be enjoying the biggest party of their lives. All drinks were on the house ... I vaguely remember finishing up at the Century Hotel where a member of the Belgian resistance ... promised to collect me and take me back to the battalion ... where we arrived soon after reveille.[3]

As the advance continued German resistance began to stiffen, and the weather became autumnal, with a fair amount of rain that threatened to waterlog the fields; it was therefore imperative to keep to the roads as much as possible. Not all of the few defenders encountered seemed to have their heart in it: a troop of the Skins discovered eight German soldiers asleep in a barn, and this led to the usual quandary faced by troops mounded on AFVs: 'What to do with them? They ... found SQMS Nipper Daley there with his 15 cwt truck. He took the Germans over with reluctance and spent an uncomfortable two hours guarding them with an empty pistol and no ammunition.'[4]

In early September, 3RTR was still able to report that 'resistance was nil'; all the armoured units were being pushed by their headquarters to keep moving east as fast as possible, with Pip Roberts' 11th Armoured Division heading towards Antwerp, and the Guards Armoured Division on their way to Brussels.[5] This was the role that armoured divisions had been created for, to exploit success. Johnny Langdon:

> It was beginning to get dark when we finally called it a day and leaguered south of Alost. We were now only twelve miles north-west of Brussels which

the Guards Armoured Division had entered and taken during the afternoon. We had made a record run during the day, having covered approximately seventy-five miles. Although [this was] a considerable strain on the crew no-one appeared to be tired, and morale was at its highest. The night's rest was brief; reveille on the 4th being at 0530. At 0630 the battalion moved off continuing the advance towards Antwerp ... Orders were to reach and enter the city with all speed and proceed straight to the docks area with the object of preventing demolitions.[6]

Unfortunately, occupying the city proved to be a mistake; although preventing damage to the vital docks installations was necessary, there were other factors in play. A glance at a map will show that Antwerp is a major port city, but access to its docks could only be gained if the Scheldt estuary to the north was clear of enemy, and this was not the case. Not only were the Germans still in possession of the island of Walcheren (also known as the Beveland isthmus) which commanded the northern shore of the estuary, but tens of thousands of German soldiers from the Fifteenth Army which had been held in reserve by Hitler in order to defend expected landings in the Pas de Calais area were allowed to escape eastwards, and these would have to be defeated in the coming months. General Horrocks was extremely honest and self-critical when he admitted that:

It never entered my head that the Scheldt would be heavily mined, so that Antwerp could not be used as our forward base for some time ... or, worse still, that the Germans would succeed in ferrying across the estuary [about eight divisions] a total of 82,000 men [of the Fifteenth Army] plus 530 guns. If [only] I had ordered Roberts to bypass Antwerp and advance for only fifteen miles north-west to cut off the Beveland isthmus, the whole of this force, which played such a prominent part in the subsequent fighting, might have been destroyed or forced to surrender.[7]

Strategically, the Allies now had a number of problems: they had to keep up the pressure on the Germans to prevent strong defensive lines being constructed; they had to clear the Scheldt estuary to allow Antwerp to come into use, thus greatly shortening the logistic lines of communication that stretched all the way back to the one functioning Mulberry harbour in Normandy; and they had to look for other suitable ports that might be used. Included in this was the operation to capture the strongly fortified harbour of Le Havre on the Channel coast, which had been declared a *Festung*, or fortress, by Hitler, meaning that it was to be defended to the last man and not surrendered. Despite this, three days of set-piece attacks starting on 10 September managed to break into the town, with particularly valuable assistance once more from the Funnies, including AVREs from the RE, two squadrons of Crab flail tanks from the 22nd Dragoons and Crocodile flamethrowers from 141RAC, as well as infantry carried in Kangaroo APCs. Once again, the effort in developing specialized armour to support infantry assaults against fortifications paid dividends, by reducing casualties and preventing the battle turning into a siege. Even whilst this largely Canadian mission, known as Operation Astonia, was progressing, Second British Army, and XXX Corps in particular, had to focus on supporting a massive upcoming operation, known as Operation Market Garden – the attempt to capture a number of bridges to facilitate a bold move into Germany via the cities of Eindhoven, Nijmegen and Arnhem.

The story of this gallant but ultimately fruitless operation is well known, but less well understood is the part played by the Guards Armoured Division in trying to force a corridor open to reach the beleaguered paratroopers in Arnhem. The decision to drop strong parachute and glider forces in order to capture a series of bridges over major water obstacles, to allow the north-east of the Netherlands to be secured as a precursor to a drive into the heart of Germany, was a very imaginative but also hazardous operation. Had it succeeded, it would have been hailed as one of the most brilliant and innovative military operations of modern times, but in such risky adventures the margins are fine, and the gamble ultimately failed at the last hurdle. In large part this was due to the inability of the Guards Armoured Division to force its way along a single route

The ubiquitous AVRE, in Germany in early 1945. Allowing the sappers to keep up with the leading armoured troops was a great advantage, with the Petard able to deal with any strongly fortified positions.

to reach Arnhem in time to relieve the airborne soldiers there and take the 'bridge too far'. Horrocks, the corps commander, explained the plan in broad terms, as well as the single most important intelligence failure:

> Dempsey and I … were to plan the break-out from the Meuse–Escaut canal, and the subsequent advance of XXX Corps through the airborne carpet to the Arnhem bridgehead, from where we were to advance right up to the Zuider Zee, VIII Corps on the right and XII Corps on the left were to advance, clearing up my flanks … I had no idea whatever that the 9th and 10th SS Panzer Divisions were refitting just north-east of Arnhem.[8]

In fact the two German divisions were on the point of entraining away from the area, but we must accept Horrock's word that the ground forces started the advance not knowing that these two experienced armoured formations, depleted in strength though they might be, were going to contest the ground, particularly as the Guards closed in on the town of Arnhem. The major problem faced by the armoured soldiers was that there was simply no alternative to the line of advance used, no scope for manoeuvre. Once again, armoured forces would be in the role of battering ram, with senior commanders hoping that their mobility and armour would be sufficient to overcome resistance – despite the experience from Normandy showing that this approach was unlikely to succeed.

Initially led by the tanks of the Irish Guards, 20,000 vehicles would attempt to advance – and be supplied along – a single main road, with the surrounding countryside low-lying and waterlogged, making off-route deployment a very difficult proposition. In order to avoid alerting the defenders and preventing a possible false start, the armoured advance was not started until the airborne drops took place, which meant that quite a few hours were lost on the first day, 17 September. The advance was only started at 1435, led by Lieutenant Keith Heathcote of 3rd Squadron, 2nd Armoured Irish Guards. For a short while the advance was unopposed and the leading tanks crossed the border into the Netherlands less than half an hour after setting off, but then, in Horrocks' words, 'suddenly nine of the Irish Guards' tanks were knocked out almost all at once and a furious battle began in the woods in front of me'.[9] Progress then slowed dramatically, and rocket-firing 'cab rank' Typhoons had to be called in to assist in prising open strong pockets of resistance, often firing as close as 100yd from the lead tanks. By the end of the first day it was already becoming clear that the advance would struggle to reach Arnhem in time to relieve the paratroopers, and the advance had only reached Valkenswaard by last light, still short of the first big objective, Eindhoven. Progress over the next few days was simply not rapid enough, and Nijmegen was not reached until the 19th.

American paratroopers hitch a ride on a 4th Coldstream Guards Churchill. Note the additional 'protection' added in the form of track links – common practice, but of little actual use.

It was clear that the Germans had worked out what the strategic objective was, and realized that preventing the advance depended on their ability to block the solitary route. Close behind the lead tanks were the Royal Engineers, who had to build a number of Bailey bridges to keep 'Route Club', the XXX Corps axis, open.[10] On the 20th the Irish Guards tanks assisted the artillery from both nations in supporting assault boat crossings of the Waal by the US 82nd Airborne. Having established a precarious bridgehead on the north of the river, it was now vital to get armour across in order to support them, and the Grenadier Guards were given the task of crossing the 400yd-long bridge. Knowing that it was almost certainly rigged for demolition, No. 1 Troop of A Squadron commanded by Sergeant Robinson led the way, and after changing tanks when his was disabled, he and Lance Sergeant Pacey knocked out the offending enemy gun and proceeded to cross the bridge in their Shermans, under a hail of anti-tank rounds, *PanzerFauste* and sniper and MG fire. Miraculously reaching the far side, they managed to demolish a roadblock by skid–turning a Sherman broadside into it, allowing other troops to cross and enlarge the bridgehead.

By the 22nd, 2HCR armoured car patrols had got as far as the Lower Rhine, and one of them spotted a German steamboat towing four barges which they engaged, damaging the steamer and sinking three barges. Having reported the contact, they received the message: 'Congratulations on brilliant naval action. Splice the mainbrace.' Even in the middle of a desperate battle, a sense of humour could work wonders, but style and wit could not conceal the fact that progress was simply too slow. The only option was to evacuate the remnants of the exhausted 1st Airborne Division and the Polish Airborne Brigade, which was conducted on the night of 25/26 September.

Horrocks took the blame for the inability of his forces to get through to Arnhem in time. He later considered that he might have profited had he ordered the 43rd Infantry Division to cross the Waal River to the west of Nijmegen, which could have allowed a left hook to drive into Arnhem from the west. But this did not happen, and the best that could be done was to help to extract the remnants of the airborne forces. In Horrocks' summary, he concluded that all operations are beset by unpredictable elements, and that a big dose of good fortune can often play a part, but in Market Garden 'nothing seemed to go right'. Once again, the Germans fought with a dogged determination, aided by the knowledge that they were fighting a delaying battle and time and geography were both on their side. The failure of the attempt to capture the bridge too far meant that the hopes of finishing the war by Christmas were over, and the armies in the Netherlands were condemned to a winter of largely static warfare in some of the most dreadful weather for years that was just starting to make its presence felt.

Staghound armoured cars doing what such units do best – finding their way along tracks deep into enemy territory. The Staghound was generally thought to be too large for front-line recce work, but was ideally suited as an SHQ command vehicle.

Almost concurrently with the start of the airborne assault, the First Canadian Army began to clear the Scheldt estuary. At the northern end of the estuary lay South Beveland, and beyond that was Walcheren, a strongly held German defensive position. To the south was an area of flat land below sea level and enclosed by dikes, known as polder country. Directly supporting the Canadians were two specialist armoured regiments, 11RTR and 5th Assault Regiment RE, both now re-equipped with the Buffalo Mk IV armoured assault vehicle, and smaller M29 Weasel amphibians. The Buffalo had a rear loading ramp and could carry a platoon of infantry or a jeep, or a large amount of ammunition or stores. All were armed with Browning machine guns, and some carried an additional 20mm Polsten cannon. The Buffalo would prove to be invaluable in moving around the flooded polders in what would turn out to be a monotonous and dangerous campaign; from mid-October, following the failure to secure Arnhem, Montgomery made the clearance of the Scheldt the top priority, in order to assist the logistic efforts necessary to prepare for the push into Germany in the spring. After hard fighting in which the RAC regiments involved once again proved their flexibility, including the use of a squadron's worth of Sherman DD tanks operated by B Squadron Staffordshire Yeomanry, the area was finally secured in early November, although mine clearance and repair to the port facilities in Antwerp meant that the first Allied shipping could not use the port until the end of the month, and the winter weather was now closing in.

TWELFTH KNIGHT, an RHQ Sherman III of the 13th/18th Hussars, overlooks the Waal in the bitter winter of 1944. The name is a pun on both the Shakespeare play and the tank's call sign.

The Winter Campaign, 1944–5

The winter of 1944/45 was atrocious. As well as the ground conditions making vehicle movement difficult, the poor weather grounded the Allied air forces for much of the time, making the air support so essential to combined operations unavailable. Attempts to move armour around in the increasingly boggy conditions were doomed to failure; in one such attempt 8th Armoured Brigade reported losing twenty-three tanks to the conditions, and for a time the scarce ARVs became the most important vehicle type. Diaries from the period record just how bad the conditions were, including the reminiscences of Trooper John Howell of 1st Northants Yeomanry:

> Our next treat was the appearance of an army shower unit. A shower in a tent and a change of underwear, in a temperature of about thirty degrees below zero … the roads were under deep snow making it difficult to keep the tanks on the road, some tanks slid into a valley and we were unable to get out the other side, [so we] decided to leaguer in a field in about three feet of snow. We parked two tanks at right angles and built a four foot high snow wall on the other side and put a tank sheet over the top; I was the last one in and found myself up against the tracks and spent a very uncomfortable night in a temperature of minus thirty seven degrees centigrade … The

A white-washed LVT Buffalo makes its frozen way through the Low Countries. The amphibian was to prove its value time and again over the winter, from the Scheldt campaign to the crossing of the Rhine.

following day we continued, passing a dead German who was frozen still, standing upright in a field … we fired at some German tanks [but] after our first shot we were unable to fire again, as due to the cold, the firing pin had snapped.[11]

Some units were ordered to paint their tanks white to blend in with the snow, but a muddy brown would often have been more appropriate. The AFV crews were lucky to be issued the new winter tank suit just as the conditions worsened, which at least was a practical garment that kept the worst of the cold and wet out, but other than that, life was miserable. The front lines stagnated on the German/Dutch border, and little tactical movement was attempted, or even possible, until the new year, giving the German defenders some breathing space to prepare for the next onslaught. For a couple of months around Christmas low-level engagements were the order of the day, with tank crews being sent forward to offer what support they could to the infantry manning the front line; some unfortunates found themselves operating as infantry, or manning isolated positions with their dismounted machine guns. It was clear that not all of the armoured units now in North-West Europe would be needed all the time, and the opportunity was taken to repair and maintain equipment, and in some cases to receive brand-new vehicles – in December, the three regiments of 29th Armoured Brigade handed in their tired and almost obsolete Shermans, and started to train on the latest British-designed Cruiser tank, the excellent Comet. The by-now

Cromwells and a Challenger struggling in the mud of a terrible winter. Although the tank was well designed and had good mobility, there are still always limits to where tracked vehicles can operate.

veteran soldiers of the RAC did not always appreciate the efforts being made on their behalf to 'bring them up to date':

> A youngish sergeant from the permanent staff of the Gunnery School at Lulworth was sent out to talk to the Recce Squadron and was horrified to see that we had welded a case to hold the ammunition box directly onto our Brownings, and thought that someone would be in trouble! The poor, ill–informed NCO went on to explain that the school desperately wanted to get hold of a King Tiger intact and that if we saw one, we were not to shoot it up but capture it. The gathering fell about the floor laughing. The replies he received are unprintable.[12]

Elsewhere, units took what comforts they could. The Fifth Skins recorded that they:

> … withdrew to the area west of Echt, where there were plenty of extra houses and we were able to live warmly and in comfort for two weeks: trips to the mines for a bath, letter writing again, new clothing, maintenance galore, and even some sport. There was a move to Opoeteren near Bree, and there was more short leave to Brussels.[13]

Although the front had become largely static, opportunities for home leave were not available for the majority, and so a number of leave and rest centres were opened up, with Brussels and Antwerp being the most popular destinations. The 4th/7th Dragoon Guards noted that:

> For the first time since D–Day, parties of all ranks were given leave, indulging in the luxuries of real beds, hot baths and the gastronomic delights of hotels. On his 48 hour pass to Brussels, Major Jenkins made a diversion to visit the field of Waterloo, and noted that the area fought over by some 200,000 troops 'would now be a brigade position at most, or perhaps one squadron of tanks'.[14]

But even here, the war could not be completely left behind. On 16 December 1944 a V2 rocket landed on the packed Cine Rex in Antwerp, where a cowboy film was being shown, killing 557 people including nearly 300 Allied servicemen. But the Germans also had plans for more direct attacks, and on the same day, the Ardennes offensive was launched, later to become known as the Battle of the Bulge. Although the battle was being played out in the American sector to the south of 21st Army Group, the developing situation became serious enough for British troops to be rushed to the area; in 29th Armoured Brigade often hung-over crews from leave centres were hurriedly re–mounted on their old Shermans

Their once pale-cream 'Pixie' suits now stained and grimy, these crewman from either 1 or 5RTR would be grateful of the additional warmth these well-designed garments gave them.

on the 20th and rushed towards Givet, Dinant and Namur, there to await the German Panzers. Fortunately, the defensive line they held in the snow was to prove to be at the very limit of the German advance, and the fighting was less intense than the crews were used to. On Christmas morning, the tanks of 3RTR were ordered to advance to contact against German Mk IVs and Panthers, but to their annoyance received as much fire from American forces as from the Germans, including being strafed by American fighter bombers. On Boxing Day three British infantry divisions, assisted by the tanks of 33rd Armoured Brigade, arrived – shifting a complete infantry division operationally required masses of transport that was not available within the division, and was a major undertaking. By the 27th the US army had largely stabilized the front and the limits of German penetrations were reached, and by mid-January the last of the British tank crews were able to return to the Belgian coast and 29th Armoured Brigade was able to carry on the task of converting to their new tanks, ready for the final offensives.

The Rhine, Germany and Victory

With the arrival of 1945 both sides knew that the big push into Germany was inevitable as soon as the weather permitted. The Germans had not been idle, and in order to bolster their defences tens of thousands of *PanzerFauste* had been produced –these cheap and cheerful weapons would be responsible for the majority of tank casualties in the final months, and featured so prominently in crewmen's recollections:

> A figure came from the cowshed which I had already passed. He ran down the hedge and was only the width of a garden away when I saw that he was carrying a bazooka. He had not seen me because I had no turret, and he was obviously intent in trying to ambush Sergeant Strickland who was close behind me. At ten yards range, and without even bothering to sight my Browning, I gave him a long burst and he fell behind the hedge.[15]

Numbers of tanks, SPGs and anti-tank guns were still to be found, however, carefully and cleverly sited as always, and in addition there was also the ever present threat of snipers and, increasingly, mines. Mines were a problem throughout the war, partly because only limited armour protection was used on the vehicle floors, but to the crews they seemed to become more prevalent as the units forged deeper into Germany, in part this was because of the desperate defence by the Germans, fighting on their own soil, but also because of the critical lack of more sophisticated weapons as Germany's industry collapsed:

> The leading tank had hardly moved off when it struck a mine and slewed into the ditch ... Trooper Bill Whitcombe, the driver, was slumped in his seat and I could see that the tank's bottom plate had been blown upwards. When they started lifting Bill from his seat, I could see the heel of his boot protruding from underneath the vehicle. He was still conscious despite the loss of a foot. The other foot was so damaged as to be almost unrecognisable. Both his arms were broken ... we used bivouac poles to splint his arms and, as his foot was just hanging by skin, we had to cut it off. It was a gruesome business ... When the carrier arrived with a stretcher, Bill was placed carefully on the vehicle, which was turning when it struck yet another mine. This time Bill was killed instantly, and the crew of the carrier became casualties.[16]

Everyone realized that getting across the Rhine quickly and in strength was going to be crucial, but before that could be attempted there were still significant areas that had to be cleared of defenders. Included in these was the so–called Roermond triangle on the Dutch/German border, occupied by elements of the German 15th Army that had escaped across northern Holland. The operation to clear the area was codenamed Blackcock, and involved 7th Armoured Division supporting 43rd and 52nd Infantry Divisions. Starting on 13 January, the operation lasted a fortnight, and involved numerous small attacks to liberate well-defended villages in often terrible weather. Although casualties within the armoured units were relatively light, it was noted the German resistance was stiffening, and the defence of German – as opposed to Dutch – territory was particularly tenacious. Although the war was entering the closing months, no one was sure how long the final defeat might take, and horrors were still to be found on a daily basis. Syd Swift of B Squadron, the Fifth Skins remembered that, 'It was here that I saw a pig eating a dead German soldier by the roadside.'[17]

Crossing the Rhine could not be attempted until late March, and followed after another Canadian-led operation, Veritable. This was in effect the northern part of a pincer movement coordinated with American forces in the south, designed to clear the Reichswald area to the west of the Rhine, and involved heavy fighting for the towns of Kleve and Goch during February. Supporting the six infantry divisions involved were many armoured formations and units, including the 11th and Guards Armoured Divisions, 4th Armoured Brigade, 6th Guards Tank Brigade and 34th Tank Brigade.[18] The various specialist amphibious vehicles were again much in demand, as were the Crocodile flamethrowers of the Funnies.

Operation Plunder

On the night of 23 March 1945, the crossing of the Rhine began, known as Operation Plunder. Following hard on the heels of the night-time river assault was Operation Varsity, the airborne drops east of the river on the early morning of the 24th and which included eight Locust Light tanks from 6th Airborne Armoured Reconnaissance Regiment.[19] During the operation one of the large Hamilcar gliders carrying Sergeant Dawson's Locust disintegrated in mid-air, causing the tank to be ejected and the crew to fall to their deaths. Another tank crashed into a house on landing, damaging the main 37mm gun which burst when fired for the first time, although the tank continued in action using only its machine gun, and a third was knocked out almost immediately after landing by a German SPG. In the evening – and typical for the high attrition that accompanies airborne landings – only four of the eight tanks were available, and only two of these were fully fit. By the 26th the remnants of the force were handed over and exchanged for Cromwell tanks, allowing the complete regiment to become part of the order of battle of 21st Army Group, and fight in a more conventional manner, ending up near the Baltic coast before the regiment was returned to the UK by the end of May 1945, an unusually rapid repatriation, as will be explained in the third volume of this work.

Meanwhile, back on the Rhine, Operation Plunder was mounted to get the armies across the major river obstacle of the Rhine. In order to prepare the ground, literally, much construction was carried out on the western (home) bank, to allow the armoured divisions and brigades to advance to the river without turning the sodden ground into a quagmire. Making the initial assault

A Locust Light tank emerges from a Hamilcar; eight of these small tanks were used by the 6th Airborne Armoured Reconnaissance Regiment as part of the airborne assault east of the Rhine. The crew of one of them was tragically killed when the glider broke up in mid-air.

An M10 tank destroyer operated by the Royal Artillery, with some of the gliders from Operation Varsity behind. M10s were often allocated to Churchill units, which did not have their own 17-pounder armed tanks.

in the British sector between Emmerich and Wesel were XII and XXX Corps, supported by the Funnies of 79th Armoured Division, including Buffaloes and DD Shermans. The Rhine presented significant problems for the amphibious armour, including a fast-flowing current and steep and muddy banks on both sides. This required the training wings of the division to develop special techniques, including entering the river well upstream from the intended landing point, as well as using Buffaloes in a special reconnaissance role, in which they laid matting where they exited to allow subsequent vehicles an easier passage up and out of the river. The DD tanks of the Staffordshire Yeomanry led the advance of 8th Armoured Brigade across the river, followed by the 4th/7th Dragoon Guards, and then the 13th/18th Hussars, with the Sherwood Rangers Yeomanry in reserve. To their credit the Staffs only lost two tanks during the hazardous night crossing, and 44RTR, who had only had three weeks of conversion training on to DDs, followed the next morning in daylight.[20] Another unit hastily converted to a specialized role was 1st Northamptonshire Yeomanry, now manning Buffaloes. Trooper John Howell recalled:

> As I entered the water the troop leader asked if I had [uncaged the gyro] and I said yes, but I had been so consumed by the occasion [that I had not] … when I realised, I didn't tell the troop leader as I knew that there was an eight-knot current and I was confident that I knew where I was going.

A Buffalo carrying – just about – a Jeep and a 6-pounder anti-tank gun. The ability to get such loads across rivers and other water obstacles was key in maintaining pressure on the German defence.

I headed up the river and we crossed in exactly the right place. We landed in a sandy bay, there were a number of explosions, some under the track and others killing and wounding the infantry. The troop leader told me to reverse, which cheered me up no end. We carried on, taking across Bren gun carriers, 25 pounders, infantry and all manner of supplies. During this three or four days we had very little sleep and we were taking Benzedrine to stay awake.[21]

Overall though, and despite pockets of fanatical opposition, German resistance was not as fierce as had been expected, largely due to the much diminished combat power available to the Wehrmacht, now fighting a losing withdrawal-in-contact battle on multiple fronts. By the 27th the Allied bridgehead was over 30 miles wide and already 20 miles deep; with Russian forces advancing in the East, the end was now in sight.

The Final Push to the Baltic

Once the bridgehead had been established and enlarged, and the extremely long Bailey bridges built, it was time to push the armoured divisions and brigades deep into northern Germany, in their intended role as armoured punches, avoiding strongpoints wherever possible and thrusting deep into the heartland of the Reich, leaving the less-mobile infantry divisions to consolidate and clear up, assisted by the armoured brigades and, where required, by the Funnies.[22] In some ways this final phase of about five weeks resembled The Great Swan, as distances covered in a single day were sometimes measured in many miles, although the resistance was much stiffer and casualties continued to be taken right up to the end. Craters and felled trees were designed to impede the advance, and mines and *PanzerFaust* teams presented the greatest danger, and whilst becoming rarer, small-scale armoured actions to destroy the last German tanks and SPGs continued to the end.[23]

The armoured divisions were each given an axis on which to lead the multi-pronged advance. 7th Armoured, the famed Desert Rats, took the line Borken–Rheine–Ibbenburen–Diepholz–Hoya–Fallingbostel–Soltau–Harburg–Hamburg, and which included crossing the obstacles of the Weser-Ems Canal and the River Weser itself, as well as taking frequent risks with an open left flank up towards the North-Sea coast. At Ibbenburen the division's 22nd Armoured Brigade faced a particularly tough time, as the town was defended by the instructors and students from a nearby German officer-cadet and NCO school, including many battle-hardened veterans. During this period, the Skins recorded that they were often the object of accurate sniper fire directed against commanders; Lieutenant Fitzgerald was killed when a bullet penetrated his neck; he died from blood loss before he could be treated. Lieutenant Elkins was also shot, through the stomach,

The Intelligence Officer of 3RTR leads a Comet through Germany in the closing days of the war. By now the greatest threat came from PanzerFauste, *but mines, snipers and the occasional tank action still caused casualties.*

and later died. Sergeant Bob Price was luckier: 'We were mortared. I reached up to close my hatch and a bullet struck the upright hatch between my thumb and first finger. The bullet shattered and cut my hand, and a piece of it entered my mouth and broke two teeth without touching my lips.'[24] At Hamburg the British troops were amazed how orderly the city was, despite being largely destroyed by RAF bombs; the streets had been largely cleared of rubble and broken glass swept up. Lieutenant Colonel Wainman, the CO of the 11th Hussars who were in the vanguard as always, 'arrived in his Dingo dressed in an American combat jacket, a pair of corduroy trousers and an 11th Hussars cap. He produced a packet of army biscuits and proceeded to feed the pigeons' – before accepting the surrender of the city.[25]

11th Armoured moved towards Lübeck, from Xanten/Wesel–Schoppingen–Mesum–Eversheide–Diepenau–Nienburg–Winsen–Wietzendorf–Essdorf–Oldesloe. The 15th/19th Hussars, partially equipped with the new Comet tanks, encountered unexpectedly strong resistance from a German Marine Division in the area of Winsen, and recorded the action against them as the

145RAC captured a Panther which they renamed as DESERTER. The comparative size of the German tank is obvious.

Two Cromwells inside Germany. Most crews realized that the finish was in sight and there was a natural reluctance to take risks so close to the end.

hardest they fought in the entire war. Two days later, parts of the division were horrified to find themselves liberating the Belsen concentration camp, which came as a huge shock because to them, until this point, the place was 'just another name on the map'. The camp area housed over 13,000 unburied corpses, and typhus was rife amongst the pitiful survivors. The troops involved in the liberation of that terrible place saw sights that would stay with them for the rest of their lives, worse than any of the other horrors of war that they experienced on the battlefield. As the end neared, and not surprisingly, 'No-one wanted to take any risks any more. The men in lead tanks knew that they would be the first to get it if we bumped into a last-ditch battlegroup. People were reluctant to drive round corners. [Major Bill Close 3RTR] gave orders that no chances were to be taken with bazooka merchants'.[26] Orders like this were necessary but resulted in many buildings being destroyed just in case the enemy were using them. In the last few days of the campaign, Patrick Delaforce recalled that:

> Very few enemy tanks were now encountered. Very few minefields or Nebelwerfers, but the ubiquitous 88mm anti-tank guns turned up with discouraging frequency. The advance was now through rich Prussian cornland with large well-stocked farms ... It was difficult to predict which villages the Germans would defend wholeheartedly. ... [One] village that caused a great deal of trouble was Steimbke, defended by a company of Hitler Youth. The 23rd Hussars entered Steimbke, knocked out two towed 88mm guns and a 75mm gun, but lost a Comet to a bazooka ... a squadron of the Hussars surrounded the village on three sides and fired HE non-stop. The SS fought fanatically and each house had to be cleared individually.[27]

Comets of the 29th Armoured Brigade roar through a German village; although the white-flag-waving civilians look relaxed, the crews are still keeping low in the turret, so the enemy cannot be too far away.

The Guards Armoured followed the line Rees–Lichtenvoorde–Eibergen–Hengelo–Lingen–Nordhorn–Lengerich–Nienburg–Elsdorf–Rotenburg Bremervorde–Stade, which took them east and then north of the major port of Bremen, ending up on the estuary of the Elbe north-west of Hamburg. Typical of the sort of tragedies that could happen even at the very end of the war was the death of Captain Wheaton, an artillery FOO whose OP tank was destroyed on 4 May, being blown up by an emplaced sea mine, killing all the crew.

At the cessation of hostilities, ordered for 0800 on the morning of 5 May, there was a bewildering variety of emotions, from wild celebrations to quiet reflection. The pause was short, however, and almost immediately after the official Victory in Europe Day (8 May), all the troops found themselves involved in the first operation of the peace, Operation Eclipse. This required them to administer the newly defeated Germans, including guarding prisoners, hunting war criminals, and dealing with the business of feeding the populations, not just Germans but also thousands of Russian POWs and Displaced Persons from all over Europe. The RAC units were to find themselves posted into garrison towns, many of which were in places that they had fought through over the last few weeks, and in which the corps would remain for decades to come.

There was also another genuine fear. As the war concluded in Europe, there was a concern amongst the units stationed there that they would soon be packed off to the Far East: soldiers of the British Liberation Army, or BLA, joked that

The end. Displaying one of their souvenirs, these RTR crews of the Desert Rats must be relieved that the European war is over, but the threat of being sent out to the Far East was a lingering possibility.

the initials now stood for Burma Looms Ahead. They were not wrong. Plans were being made, under the title Force 143 (later renamed Operation Minerva), to send considerable armoured forces, including one armoured division, two tank brigades, one DD brigade as well as two armoured car and one flail regiment, to the Far East. Although some of these were already on the way, arriving in August 1945, the majority remained in the UK or Europe, and the end of the war against Japan brought great relief all round.

Summary of Key Dates in the North-West Europe Campaign

1944

June

6: D-Day (8th Armoured Brigade, 27th Armoured Brigade, 34th Armoured Brigade, elements of 79th Armoured Division).

7: 7th Armoured Division lands in Normandy.

10: Operation Perch (to 14th): 7th Armoured Division into action. 4th Armoured Brigade lands in Normandy.

13: Villers-Bocage (4CLY/7th Armoured Division). First V1 attacks on southern England. 33rd Armoured Brigade lands in Normandy.

Mid-June: 11th Armoured Division lands in Normandy.

19: 31st Tank Brigade lands in Normandy. Severe storm wrecks the American Mulberry 'A' harbour.

26–30: Operation Epsom: 11th Armoured Division into action.

30: the last of the four British corps, XII, becomes active in Normandy.

End of June: Guards Armoured Division, 34th Tank Brigade lands in Normandy.

July

Early July: 34th Tank Brigade lands in Normandy.

8–11: Operation Charnwood.

10–11: Operation Jupiter.

18–20: Operation Goodwood: all three Armoured Divisions in action.

20: 6th Guards Tank Brigade lands in Normandy.

21: Caen liberated.

23: First Canadian Army activated, including I (Br) Corps.

25: Operation Cobra (American break-out) and Operation Spring.

30: Operation Bluecoat (to 6 August).

August

1: 1st Polish Armoured Division lands in Normandy.

7–10: Operation Totalize.

14–21: Operation Tractable.

21: Falaise gap closed.
25: Paris liberated.

September
1: Dieppe liberated.
2: Allies enter Belgium.
3: Brussels liberated.
5: Antwerp liberated.
8: Ostend liberated.
12: Le Havre liberated.
17–25: Operation Market Garden.

October
18: *Volksturm* created.

November
1: Operation Infatuate.
28: First supply ship convoy arrives Antwerp.

December
16–26: Ardennes offensive.

1945

January
13–27: Operation Blackcock.

February
8: Operation Veritable (to 11 March).

March
23: Operation Plunder – crossing the Rhine.

April
15: Arnhem liberated. Belsen captured.
19: 2nd Army reaches the Elbe.
30: Hitler's suicide.

May
2: Fall of Berlin. Lübeck and Wismar captured.
3: Hamburg captured.
4: Surrender of German forces in north-west Germany, Netherlands and Denmark on Luneburg heath.
8: VE Day.

Armour in the Far East, 1942–5

Only a small percentage of RAC units served in the Far East theatre, and not all of them in an operational capacity. These were: 7th Armoured Brigade, Third Dragoon Guards (Carabiniers), B Squadron, 3rd Hussars, 7th Hussars, 25th Dragoons, 26th Hussars, 2RTR, and no less than eight RAC Regiments: 116, 146, 149, 150, 158, 159, 160 and 163. Some of these regiments found themselves serving under the command of, or alongside, the Indian Armoured Corps that was formed on 1 May 1941. Uniquely, at one point, an RAC formation was placed under Chinese command: General Bill Slim, commanding the 'forgotten' Fourteenth Army, recorded that he decided that the British should not be 'in support' of the Chinese, but under command of them, and he was pleased to record that the 'long-suffering Brigadier Anstice, commanding 7th Armoured Brigade, rose to the occasion'.[28]

The initial – and unsuccessful – attempts to employ tanks to fight the Japanese came in early 1942, using regiments hastily sent out from the Middle East; the majority of the available armour was retained in India in case the Japanese managed to penetrate through the north of Burma. A handful of Valentines belonging to 146 RAC were used in the Arakan campaign in early 1943, but the experiment failed with the small tank force being easily knocked out. However, as the Japanese threat to India diminished, from 1944 onwards the available tanks became used more frequently in support of the advancing infantry, recapturing territory as the Fourteenth Army advanced south to Rangoon.

The first and particularly tragic attempt to use armour in the region involved the total loss of B Squadron, 3rd Hussars. Serving in North Africa, the squadron, which had just seen service in Tobruk, was warned off for deployment to the Far East in late 1941, eventually departing on a ship from its regimental base on Cyprus in early January 1942. Equipped with twenty-five Light tanks Mk VIb, the squadron comprised about 170 officers and men (including a detachment of RAOC fitters) and landed in southern Sumatra in mid-February. Almost immediately, the squadron was ordered to redeploy to the neighbouring island of Java, where they would come under Dutch command. The Japanese invasion of the western part of the island began on 1 March, and the Hussars found the terrain to be totally unsuitable for the tanks which were unable to deploy off the few roads. Fighting numerous delaying actions in torrential rain, the task was beyond them and the surrender of the Dutch forces on 7 March led to orders being given the following day to destroy their remaining fifteen tanks, which was achieved by removing vital parts and pushing them down into a deep ravine. Of the troops taken prisoner, fifty-five were to die in captivity, including twenty-nine when the prison ship they were travelling on, the *Suez Maru*, was torpedoed in November 1943.[29]

The M3 Stuart-equipped 7th Armoured Brigade (7th Hussars, 2RTR) was also withdrawn from the fighting in the Western Desert in early 1942 in order to be sent to Malaya, but before they arrived, Singapore had already fallen to the Japanese and so they were diverted to Rangoon. The tanks of 2RTR were offloaded on 21 February 1942, and the crews, as so often, found their tanks in a terrible state after the voyage, having been poorly stored. Nonetheless, within three days B Squadron was in its first action with the Japanese, followed swiftly by the rest of the regiment as they withdrew in the face of Japanese pressure. In a by-now all-too-familiar tale, the tanks were sent too late, and became embroiled in a fighting withdrawal northward, towards India; in some instances, the Japanese infantry attacks were pressed so relentlessly against the tanks that the commanders had to resort to spraying them with Thompson sub-machine-gun fire from the turrets. The tanks performed marvellously, although there was little time or facilities for maintenance; in eleven weeks some of them covered 2,400 miles, with very few breakdowns until the end. On 9 May the remaining vehicles had to be destroyed and the crews took to their feet, arriving after three weeks in Ranchi where the regiment regrouped.

Concurrently with this, the 7th Hussars had formed a second defensive line through which 2RTR withdrew, although the extremely bad going made life very difficult for the crews. Lieutenant Palmer of B Squadron, 7th Hussars recorded his impressions of his first battle against this new enemy:

> By the time we were approaching Payagi there was a thick mist with visibility down to ten yards. I was stopped by a 2RTR patrol and told that the area was full of Japanese snipers ... The opportunity was taken to replenish the tanks, but no sooner had the petrol lorry arrived at my troop than a storm of small arms fire broke out all around the area. This was the first of many ambushes we were to be involved in during the next few months. However, this attack was quite harmless as they appeared to have no anti-tank weapons ... There was a slight diversion when one of our troop leaders reported on the air that he could see either tanks or elephants, but was not sure which.[30]

An early – and rare – tank-versus-tank engagement occurred at this point, when A Squadron encountered two Japanese Type 95s: 'They appeared very lonely and untrained, remaining stationary in the middle of a field. They were knocked out before they knew we were there.'[31] A less conventional engagement happened slightly after this:

> A senior Japanese officer on a white horse charged one of the Hussars' Stuarts and managed to scramble aboard, attacking the tank commander with his sword. The commander chose a more technical weapon, a hammer, with which to defend himself, and closed with the Jap before he could do any damage, striking him a severe blow on his head so that he tumbled down the front of the tank, which was moving, and which passed over both his legs.[32]

As this part of the campaign in Burma came to its conclusion, it was realized that there was no chance of recovering the remaining Stuarts from the area, and in the middle of May the remaining tanks in the Brigade were ordered to be destroyed. The 7th Hussars recorded the method of destruction:

> In the evening the final destruction of the tanks and remaining vehicles was carried out. Some were destroyed by draining the oil from the sumps and racing the engines until they seized up. One squadron lined up its tanks close together, packed the men's blankets, soaked with petrol, into the turrets, connecting each tank with its neighbour in a continuous chain; one match set light to the whole lot.[33]

This act allowed the crews to escape on foot – with the Hussars officers defiantly wearing their regimental cross belts as they withdrew.

Directly related to Japanese successes in the Far East was Operation Ironclad, undertaken in the Indian Ocean. Using the codename Operation Ironclad, Force 121 invaded Madagascar off the east coast of Africa in early May 1942, in order to take control of the Vichy-French island to deny its possible use by the Imperial Japanese Navy operating in the Indian Ocean. Comprising two infantry brigade groups, included in the invasion force were six Valentine and six Tetrarch tanks of B Special Service Squadron RAC, a light squadron formed mainly with personnel from 47RTR. Preceding Dieppe by three months, this was the first British amphibious landing since the Gallipoli campaign of 1915, and although little known, was the scene of some fierce fighting, the squadron losing most of the tanks to emplaced artillery by the end of the second day, but contributing meaningfully to the eventual success of the venture.

In the next attempt to use tanks in the Far East proper, eight Valentines of C Squadron 146 RAC under Captain da Costa were transported by sea and landed at the mouth of the Naf River in northern Burma in late January 1943 as part of the campaign that came to be known as the First Arakan. The purpose of their deployment was to support an attack by an Indian division at Donbaik on 1 February. Too few tanks were used – da Costa believed that the task required a complete regiment – and after some early success the tanks were disabled in anti-tank ditches and easily knocked out by Japanese artillery. At this point, it seemed that the many critics who claimed that tanks had no role in this type of terrain had been proved correct. This then had an unfortunate result as no attempt was made to integrate the tanks available with infantry formations, leading to an ignorance of the capabilities of the tanks that would not be remedied until well into 1944.

The development of tank tactics from this point was therefore not straightforward, as the earlier setbacks had made many infantry officers – and commanders – sceptical of their worth. In India, the 3rd Carabiniers, 25th Dragoons and three RAC regiments trained initially on Valentines, but were later mainly equipped with the M3 Lee, the American version of the British Grant that had so troubled the Germans in the deserts of North Africa.[34] Although outdated in Europe by this time, the M3 was found to be very useful in jungle fighting in 1944. The crews liked having the choice of two guns, and the 37mm was provided with canister shot which, despite its small size, was useful for breaking up massed attacks. The Lee's hill climbing proved to be much better than anyone expected, particularly with track grousers fitted, allowing support to be provided in unlikely places, and the accuracy of the 75mm gun meant it could be used for bunker-busting, where it was reckoned that the third shot was guaranteed to go straight through a weapon slit and explode within the bunker. Infantry became comfortable in manoeuvring only 20yd from AP impacts, and 50yd from HE. The replacement of some of the Lees by Shermans towards the end of the war was seen as a bonus, but there is no doubt that the crews generally liked the older tanks. As noted, there was little tank-versus-tank action; the biggest danger they faced was from artillery pieces and from improvised explosive devices; the Japanese would often rig two or more mines together to provide the detonation, and add a 150mm HE shell to increase the explosive power. Another problem was close-range assaults, verging on suicidal; single Japanese soldiers would charge the tanks armed with a magnetic 'sticky' bomb, and some even managed to clamber onto the tanks and had to be killed with pistols.

An M3 Lee of the 3rd Carabiniers. Although completely outdated in Europe by 1942, the Lee gave valuable service in Burma, where the 75mm gun was often used for bunker-busting.

Thus equipped, the 25th Dragoons found themselves involved in very heavy fighting in early 1944, including at the action known as the Admin Box, in which not only did the regiment provide intimate support for the infantry, it also briefly served as an infantry divisional HQ after the real headquarters was overrun, using its radio expertise – despite the difficulties of operating them in the terrible tropical conditions – to great effect to restore command and control. An additional task that the tanks found themselves conducting was acting as armoured supply carriers, taking ammunition and other essentials forward to infantry units under heavy enemy fire. The 3rd Carabiniers were also often used out of role, at one point acting as a reconnaissance force for Slim's offensive, and also used their mobility to move casualties across difficult terrain to the rear. At a battle conducted in hilly terrain at Nungshigum in mid-April 1944, all the Carbs officers in B Squadron were out of action killed or wounded, and Squadron Sergeant Major Craddock took over command, possibly a unique event in the history of the RAC, later receiving an exceptionally well-earned Distinguished Conduct Medal.[35] Later in the year the Carabiniers managed to get one of their Grant tanks onto the top of the nearly 9,000ft-high Kennedy Peak, claiming that it was the highest tank anywhere in the world. General Slim later commented on the successful use of tanks during his difficult campaigns. He recorded a rare event in March 1944, a genuine tank battle:

> On the 20th, one of the few tank versus tank actions of the campaign took place, between a troop of the 3rd Dragoon Guards and Japanese medium and Light tanks. The enemy armour was routed with the loss of four tanks destroyed and one captured, which, to the great satisfaction of the Dragoons, they were able to bring back.[36]

The following year, he was to record an even rarer event – a tank battle at night:

> During the night of 9th/10th April, three Japanese medium tanks were rash enough to approach ours. A brisk action ensued in the light of our searchlights, and all three enemy tanks were destroyed in the only night tank versus tank encounter of the campaign.[37]

During 1945 some squadrons found themselves involved in amphibious landing operations to capture island fortifications, but the main effort was still in supporting the infantry advancing on Mandalay, which fell on 21 March. At one point during the advance, a Japanese officer managed to climb onto a Carabiniers tank, killing the commander and 37mm gunner with his sword before being shot dead by the 75mm loader using his pistol. During this whole period the M3- and later M4-equipped units found themselves involved in lots of detached work, often working as squadrons, half-squadrons or even troops, in order to parcel

Track-bashing was necessary across the globe, and it must have been especially hard work in the heat and humidity of the Far East.

them out because demand always outstripped supply. As Macksey observed, 'for much of the time a single leading tank represented the full width of RAC frontage in action'.[38]

When Rangoon was retaken at the start of May, 150 RAC were in the van, but by the time of the dropping of the atomic bombs in August, only 116 RAC remained in action, the other units having been withdrawn to India for rest and refitting prior to the presumed invasion of Japan. The plans to bring out substantial armoured forces from Europe in preparation for the invasion were cancelled when the Japanese surrendered. Despite many detractors claiming that tanks could play no useful part in jungle campaigns, the crews involved proved them wrong. Bill Slim summed up their performance at the end of the Imphal campaign: 'The RAC and the Indian Armoured Corps had silenced all their critics, and had no greater admirers than the infantry who they had supported so staunchly, and with whom they had cooperated so closely and skilfully'.

Chapter Nine

Conclusion

In June 1945, the RAC Directorate assessed the total figures for AFVs held and lost over the course of the conflict. In terms of vehicle casualties, it was reckoned that the RAC had lost 15,844 tanks and 1,957 armoured cars, a total of nearly 18,000 AFVs, although whether these were just operational losses or included obsolete vehicles struck off strength and scrapped, or otherwise disposed of, is not clear. At the same time, RAC units worldwide were assessed as holding nearly 32,000 AFVs: 9,994 armoured cars, 5,443 Light tanks, 13,667 Cruisers and 2,823 Infantry tanks. It is clear from the proportions (31.3 per cent, 17 per cent, 42.8 per cent and 8.9 per cent respectively) that the days of the Infantry tank were coming to an end, although the amount of armoured cars and Light tanks held may come as something of a surprise, and the latter represents in large part the numbers of American Stuart tanks on strength in the role of reconnaissance vehicles.

During the course of the conflict, the turnover within all of the RAC units was huge. In May 1945 3RTR had only four of their original members from September 1939 still on strength: Captain (QM) Paddy Hehir, Staff Sergeant Major John Myers, Sergeant Steward and Corporal Mitchell. The reasons for the turnover were many, but of course casualties tended to be the ones mostly deeply felt and remembered. According to the official figures, nearly 11,000 RAC crewmen died during the war, with over 18,000 wounded. The figures are as follows:

RAC Casualties

	European Theatre		Far East Theatre		
	Officers	ORs	Officers	ORs	Total
Killed In Action	821	6,059	45	208	7,133
Died of Wounds	253	1,502	5	48	1,808
Died/Non Battle Deaths	192	1,516	25	204	1,937
Wounded	2,373	15,482	74	504	18,433
Missing	22	184	15	144	365

Source: Bovington Tank Museum Casualty File, AG Statistics Branch, 2 September 1953.

These statistics mask real human tragedy, including horrific deaths and disabling wounds. An investigation into tank crew casualties by R.M. Mayon-White estimated that of those classed as severely wounded, 90 per cent suffered tissue

Smartening up; peacetime standards were soon put back in place, and within a few months the scruffiness of wartime soldiering was a thing of the past.

damage and 25 per cent burns, meaning that some suffered both. Almost invariably, those burned were inside the tank, and gunners suffered more from burns than any other crew position, presumably because they generally did not have their own escape hatch and thus took longer to get out.[1] However, around half of all wounds were suffered when a crewman was outside the protection of the tank, either partially exposed (for example, a commander with head and shoulders, or even just a hand outside) or fully outside; this tended to affect commanders more than any other crew position, because of the need to observe or to leave the tank for orders. When the tank commander was inside, his protection was comparable with all other crew positions. When asked why they were outside the AFV when wounded, the most popular answer was to cook or make tea (22 per cent); 16 per cent said that they were wounded whilst they were baling out; and 13 per cent were in a harbour.[2]

A fascinating description of crews baling out revealed that it was unusual for crewmen to need assistance to leave the tank – even badly wounded soldiers often escaped unaided, only realizing the full extent of their wounds when cover was reached, and it was only then that the pain hit them. A near comical description of crewmen exiting the tank described how they would often leap straight off the top of the turret, with legs and arms flailing as if running, which was described in the report as 'resembling a Disney cartoon'. Other investigations into AFV casualties summarized that in all theatres, 65 per cent of hits occurred on the hull, the remainder on the turret. But of these, about 40 per cent hit the tank on the frontal aspect, so it was noted that statistically the best place to put any additional armour was on the front; if it was possible to make the front invulnerable, then 40 per cent of all shots hitting a vehicle would not penetrate.

Although the largest and most costly war ever fought by mankind would lead to huge losses on all sides, there is no doubt that better tanks and tactics could have reduced some of those figures within the RAC. The RAC in 1945 was very different from the very new and woefully ill-prepared organization that had started the war, and the arrival of peace simply presented the corps with a raft of new challenges; these will be examined in the next volume. But what were the main lessons learned during the war, regardless of operational theatre? As before, we can usefully group them as technical and tactical.

Lessons Learned?

Technical Aspects

Probably the main technical issue raised during the war was the ever increasing demand for more armour protection – the desire for invulnerability that was impossible to fulfil. Despite many pre-war experts decrying the prospect of tank-versus-tank combat, the gun-versus-armour race was the major technical feature of the war. With few exceptions, meaning the heaviest tanks, most nations started the conflict with mainly Light or Medium tanks, and with maximum armour thicknesses of only around 25mm. Within two years it had become clear that this was insufficient, and by 1943 at least 75mm of frontal armour was seen as the minimum, with some tanks carrying double that – and preferably using a sloped glacis plate like those on the T34 or Panther.[3] The reason for this was the increasing power of the anti-tank gun, whether it was carried on a tank, on a self-propelled carriage or on a wheeled carriage.[4] The increased power of the German guns over the course of the war almost invariably led the race; shortly after the fall of France, the Wehrmacht decided to make the 50mm gun their standard weapon, and this was followed by the 75mm being introduced in early 1942. And of course, even in 1940 the 88mm anti-aircraft gun was used against tanks, so that even the 150mm of frontal armour carried by the later marks of the Churchill did not – could not – provide the total immunity at battle ranges desired by the crews. What most crews did not realize was that it was impossible to make their mounts immune from all anti-tank weapons, even more so when the hand-held 'bazooka'-type infantry designs became available, using high-explosive anti-tank (HEAT) technology that, despite the small size, was capable of penetrating thick armour plate.

Another factor handicapping the British crews throughout the war was the tardy introduction of their own improved anti-tank weapons. The 6-pounder gun could have been brought into service in 1940 but was deliberately delayed for production reasons, and did not enter service until early 1942. The 17-pounder was likewise delayed, only entering service in small numbers at the very end of 1942, and only becoming available in very limited numbers as a tank gun in 1944, on the Sherman Firefly. Poor optics – certainly in comparison with the German equivalents – often meant that the best could not be got out of these weapons, but in one field British science was supreme, that of ammunition design. In particular, the introduction of armour piercing discarding sabot (APDS) ammunition in the late summer of 1944 was a game-changer, with even the 6-pounder APDS shot being capable of penetrating around 130mm of sloped armour at 1,000yd. Unfortunately, the continued use of the M4 Sherman series, which had been such a revelation at El Alamein, meant that most British tank crews ended the war still using the same 75mm medium velocity gun (and its similar British variant fitted to the Churchill and Cromwell) that had been just good enough, but no more than that, in autumn 1942. This gun had the advantage of being able to fire the well-liked M48 high-explosive shell, and this was important as it has since been estimated that around two-thirds of all main armament rounds fired by British crews during the Second World War were HE. But when it came down to tank-versus-tank combat, the 75mm gun could not cut it, and was unable to fire APDS ammunition. During the North-West Europe campaign there were demands from some tank officers to replace their 75mm guns with the 57mm 6-pounder, which with APDS was a really effective anti-tank weapon, but these calls were not heeded. Had better guns been fitted to British tanks earlier, the cries for more armour protection would have been reduced, as the effective battle range of British-operated tanks would have increased and the disparity between British and German tanks would have been much less apparent. The lesson was learned the hard way, and at the very end of the war the excellent Comet was in service with four regiments, and the first few examples of the Centurion were about to enter service.

Tank Design

On the automotive front, the terribly poor reliability of the early generation of British tanks was masked to a large degree by the mechanical competence provided by the pre-war tank crew training regime. When the amount of time available to train brand-new conscripts with no previous mechanical knowledge was reduced, the defects in every single one of the service tanks quickly became apparent. The lack of inherently reliable tanks, coupled with poor basic design and a lack of spares, handicapped British tank crews for the whole of the mid-war period, and only the supply of large numbers of American Medium tanks was able to make up for the qualitative difference. When the Meteor-engined

Cromwell (and its later derivative, the Comet) was introduced, the RAC finally had a British-designed and built tank with the desired reliability, surpassing even that of the Sherman series, and probably taking the prize for the most reliable tank of the war. The design of armoured cars, on the other hand, was less problematic. Although the cars that the RAC started the war with were either obsolete (Rolls-Royce) or modern but poorly designed (Morris CS9) types, industry managed to develop a number of workmanlike designs by the middle of the war, and by the end the excellent Daimler Armoured Car was in widespread use, armed with the same 2-pounder gun that had equipped the battle tanks of 1939/40. Backing this up were the nippy and reliable scout cars designs from Humber and Daimler, used in the reconnaissance and run-around roles.

Possibly the greatest doctrinal error committed can be tracked back to the early 1930s, when the decision was made to equip the armoured units with three different types of tanks: Light, Cruiser and Infantry. Although less capable than their larger cousins, the need for Light tanks was to some degree proven during the war, in order to equip the reconnaissance forces with something larger and heavier than armoured cars, as well as having a capability to operate in theatres that did not suit, or need, heavier and more powerful tanks. But the artificial distinction between Cruiser tanks (lightly armoured, fast, designed for exploitation) and Infantry tanks (heavily armoured, slow, designed for infantry support during set-piece attacks) led to two totally separate lines of development that hindered the armoured commanders by removing their flexibility. Having two very different types of tank also meant having two different types of tank unit, with different tactics, doctrine and training, and largely unable to carry out the other's role. At the heart of the problem was the fact that battlefields are always confused and random places, and that it was impossible to divide the tanks neatly into two different roles in reality – what was needed was a tank that was designed in such a way as to be able to undertake both roles when required: a well-armoured, fast and reliable tank that had sufficient firepower to both support the infantry (meaning the ability to fire HE and use MG fire) and to defeat enemy armour (meaning firing armour piercing shot).[5] Such a tank design would bring about another characteristic, one that was never mentioned at all in specification documents of the time – flexibility.[6]

Unfortunately, changing the in-place doctrine that had been agreed nearly a decade before the war started proved to be extremely difficult, with some senior RTR commanders such as Martel remaining completed wedded to the idea of two very different types of tank, and indeed of tank units.[7] Montgomery, who loved to try to 'tidy up' his battlefields, realized that the doctrinal distinction was wrong and was causing him and his subordinate commanders problems, and came down heavily in favour of a single Universal (or Capital) tank. His solution was to use the Sherman (and later the Cromwell) in this role, which was in itself an error, as both types were much too lightly armoured to be able to survive in the infantry support role. He also tried to remove Infantry tanks – meaning the Churchill – from the order of battle, as he perceived them as being too slow to be used in a break-out or exploitation role.[8] In fact, the slower top speed of the Churchill was not too much of a handicap, as the faster cruisers were only rarely able to take full advantage of their (on paper better) mobility, and on a typical unopposed day march during The Great Swan, for example, the Churchills could cover about the same distance as the Cromwells.

Montgomery was correct about the need for a single type of universal tank, but he was wrong in trying to shoehorn the Sherman into the role.[9] The British, had they made the decision to concentrate on such a tank before the war – the old 'Medium tank' role – could have built such a tank. It is salutary to note that, other than the development of APDS ammunition, there were no major technological leaps made during the war. All the technologies in use on Comet, Centurion and the later marks of 'heavy' Churchill already existed in 1939, including the welding of armour and the outstanding tank engine of the war: the Meteor, based on the Merlin aero-engine. What was needed was putting them together in the right balance, with at least 100mm of sloped and welded frontal armour, sufficient armour on the sides and underneath (to reduce the threat from mines), a genuine 'hole-puncher' anti-tank gun like the 17-pounder that was also capable of firing a large HE shell, good optics, a commander's all-round vision cupola, a radio system to allow commanders at all levels to communicate and control the force and, not least, excellent reliability. The RAC eventually got such a tank in mid-1945 in the shape of the Centurion, but only after inching its collective way towards the formula in painful increments, and always too slowly in respect of the more powerful tanks fielded by the Germans.[10]

The second production model of the A41 Centurion; the tank that arrived in Germany a few days too late to see active service, but which over the next twenty years was developed into a fine battle tank. At the very end of the war, Britain had finally produced a reliable and powerful balanced design, what Monty would have called a universal tank.

Because of the (generally fair) criticisms levelled at British tank designs up to about 1943, it is often easy to forget that the British were outstanding in one particular aspect of tank design – the development of specialist armoured vehicles. Britain led the way in using tank chassis in order to create vehicles for specific battlefields roles, including amphibians, bridge-layers, self-propelled guns, engineer assault vehicles, recovery vehicles, mine-clearers and flamethrowers. The development of these, and the grouping of many of them into the highly specialized 79th Armoured Division, gave Britain a real advantage in specific campaigns, not least of which was during the Normandy landings. Britain also generally trained its tank crewmen to an extremely high technical standard, although the same cannot always be said of its tactical training, especially concerning its armoured officers, both junior and senior, who mostly had to learn their trade on the job – see below. Other areas of AFV design in which Britain excelled included tank gun and ammunition development, the design of gearboxes and final drives, and the production and especially the operation of radios.

Tactical Aspects

Despite the widespread use of radio nets, with all AFVs in RAC units carrying at least one radio capable of transmitting and receiving, the command and control of armoured forces was not always done well. In particular, senior officers commanding formations frequently found themselves in a 'sink or swim' situation – often this was due to the very rapid promotion of pre-war regular officers. Herbert Lumsden, a Lieutenant Colonel commanding 12th Lancers in 1940, found himself four ranks higher as a temporary Lieutenant General commanding a Corps only two years later, where he was sacked after falling out with Montgomery. Others did better; Pip Roberts started the war as an RTR Captain and was extremely successful as both an armoured brigade and then division commander within a couple of years. The point here is that there was no system for selecting and then training the likely stars, and men of real quality, like Lumsden, could still find themselves overwhelmed by the demands on their mental agility required to command armoured forces in rapidly changing situations. A similar problem existed within the middle and lower officer ranks, where tactical training opportunities were at a premium, and the opinion of one's superior was often the key doctrinal influence.

When exercising command – at any level – there was a notable reluctance to assign tactical responsibility to the lowest levels. This came about because the British army was still trying to shake off the shackles of over prescriptive planning, which was particularly unsuitable for the demands of fast-paced armoured warfare.[11] Detailed planning was essential for set-piece battles. This was particularly important in the first stages of an attack, when the element of surprise and the initiative rested with the attacking forces, and the need for a safe but effective artillery fire plan was a key element, but as the battle developed and the overall plan went out of kilter – as it always did – the need for decision-making by commanders at all levels became apparent. The best units adopted simple, actionable plans and allowed greater freedom of action at the lower levels, and this paid dividends in developing thinking commanders who were able to anticipate the needs of their bosses. Unfortunately, too many units did not allow such freedom, and preferred the 'conform to me' type of command. It would not be until the post-war period that junior tank commanders, including the troop sergeants and troop corporals, were routinely expected to apply judgement, initiative and make tactical decisions.[12]

Co-operation with other arms remained a significant weakness throughout most of the war. On occasions it was done well, and these were almost invariably when the armour and infantry had time to plan and rehearse together, before conducting the operation. At least as advantageous was when the same units were 'paired', allowing a much deeper understanding to develop during operations, leading to the state whereby armoured units considered their unarmoured friends to be 'their' infantry. However, such intimacy was in the minority, and this was due in part to the pre-war Cruiser tank doctrine – and training – that emphasized independent operations. War diaries and campaign accounts are littered with examples of poor or no co-operation between the arms, particularly but not exclusively in the first half of the war. As experience was gained matters improved, and initiatives such as the formation of armoured assault regiments with Royal Engineers mounted in specialist AFVs and the provision of observation post tanks for the RA forward observation officers semi-permanently attached to RAC units all pointed to a resolution of the issue, which would receive much more emphasis in post-war training and doctrine.

At the lowest level, the manoeuvring of individual tanks was often suspect, and was similar to the experiences of early fighter pilots – the key was to survive for long enough to gain experience and then become effective. This was due to serious failings in one particular aspect of tank-crew training, that of the NCO tank commander and officer troop leader. Neither received sufficient tactical training in troop and squadron manoeuvre and had to learn their trade on the job; again, this would not be fully resolved until post-war. Had this been done correctly, low-level tactics capable of being adapted to match the terrain and the enemy could have been developed, and wherever possible these should have been turned into a drill. The purpose of such a drill would be to reduce the intellectual burden on every commander, allowing them to concentrate all their attention onto problem solving and effective decision-making. As it was, procedures such as 'snake patrol' had to be devised in action, which meant that it was difficult to identify the most effective unit tactics and spread the word, not only throughout a particular theatre but back to the UK in order to influence training.[13]

Let us finish on a positive note by mentioning another great strength of the RAC throughout the war. This is also the element that traditionally comes last, but which is critical to everything else: logistics. Within the armoured units this refers to the central importance of the well-devised echelon system, which produced without doubt many of the unsung heroes of the RAC, those unsupervised and unheralded individuals who drove ammunition and fuel lorries forward to the front lines, in order to feed the armoured machine as it ground its way towards victory.

Appendix A

Mechanization in Other Arms

The Further Mechanization of the Infantry

Despite the provision of a carrier platoon for most battalions by the late 1930s, the majority of infantry continued to be 'foot-sloggers' in the old tradition, as the carrier was not meant to be what would later become known as an armoured personnel carrier, or APC. This was for two reasons: firstly, the carrier itself was far too small to carry more than three or four men at most in the back, and secondly, because it was provided to add mobility to the heavier support weapons (medium machine guns, mortars, etc.) and their equally heavy and bulky ammunition, rather than to carry infantrymen.[1] After much experimentation, by mid-war some battalions within Armoured Divisions had been converted to become Motor Battalions, and these were provided with the best available APC, the open-topped American 'White' half-track. Each could easily carry one section with all of its equipment and, although nowhere near as mobile cross-country as a tank, could stay close enough to allow better cooperation. Unfortunately, radios were not provided in the half-tracks which would have allowed the tank crews and infantry commanders to stay in touch more easily in the heat of battle, and the vehicle crews were found from amongst the infantry battalion, and who were not trained how to move the vehicles tactically – once again, it was something that had to be learned 'on the job'.

In most cases, the remaining battalions in the infantry and armoured divisions were known as 'lorried infantry'. This did not mean that each battalion possessed sufficient lorries to transport itself, far from it. The lorries to move them around – non-tactically, it must be stressed – came from RASC companies provided for the purpose and held by the division. Lorried infantry could not be used in areas where the threat of direct or indirect fire was too high, meaning that the infantry had to dismount some miles from the front line and revert to the traditional, unprotected method of getting into battle – the wearying task of marching forward, carrying all the ammunition, weapons and kit required. However, even this system meant that although in tactical terms the British infantry of 1944 was not equipped for a fast-moving mobile battle, it did possess operational mobility that the Germans could only dream of. The creation of the Motor Battalion in each armoured division in 1942 was a step in the right direction, but was insufficient, as there were three armoured regiments in the division, or four once the so-called armoured reconnaissance regiment, also mounted in tanks, was included. Achieving balance was difficult therefore, as if they were parcelled out equally, each armoured regiment would receive only a single motorized rifle company, and which was *sans* support weapons in the shape of mortars and medium machine guns.

The carriage of infantry on tanks was a generally frowned upon idea. It was something that both the Germans and the Russians were frequently happy to do, with the Soviets being particularly sold on the idea of 'tank-riders', but it met with a great deal of opposition from within the British army. The RAC argued that it prevented the tank from doing its real job, and some of the infantry were concerned that whilst it certainly brought additional mobility, and saved the leg muscles of the PBI, the infantry remained terribly vulnerable to virtually every type of direct and indirect fire; additionally, if the tank needed to manoeuvre or traverse its turret suddenly in reaction to a threat, the infantry would be forgotten and thrown off or crushed. It could also lead to a lack of cohesion, as the infantry unit being carried could easily find itself dispersed across the battlefield, with no simple means of concentrating together, or indeed communicating with each other. But this is not to say that it did not happen. There were certainly instances of infantry being carried on the backs of Valentines during the latter stages of the North African campaign, and whilst the practice was never widespread, it sometimes happened in Europe too, particularly in the Infantry tank units. However, the need for a genuine APC was identified very quickly during the Normandy campaign; as early as 17 June Lieutenant Colonel Bowring, an official observer attached to XXX Corps, stated that: 'The tanks require a great deal more infantry with them than is provided by the Motor Battalion. [It is] only sufficient to clear a limited number of localities and [to] protect them at night.'[2]

Numbers aside, although given greater mobility through being carried in the (lightly armoured and open-topped) American half-tracks, these were still not genuine APC-borne infantry. Indeed, the perceived role of the Motor Battalions was to 'restore mobility to the armoured units when they met anti-tank defences that were beyond the ability of armour alone to handle. This meant not a combined attack in which the tanks supported the infantry, but a single-arm infantry attack by troops from the motor battalion.'[3] It was not until APCs were improvised in both North-West Europe and in Italy during the second half of 1944, allied to the willingness of (some) armoured formation commanders to re-organize their infantry and armour to achieve better balance and routine co-operation, that the best way forward was discovered. As the saying goes, success has many fathers but failure is an orphan. Who first had the idea to convert AFV hulls into APCs is open to debate, but there is no doubt that the Canadian General Guy Simonds was a key player in suggesting that this happened during the Normandy campaign. Surplus Priest 105mm SPGs were modified to become Kangaroos, the name chosen to reflect the animal that carries its young in a pouch.

Operation Totalize marked the very first use of Kangaroos on 8 August 1944; these were based on American Priest 105mm SPGs, now surplus as the British and Canadians had switched to the use of Sexton 25-pounder SPGs in order to standardize ammunition supply; see below. To create the APC the 105mm gun and ammunition stowage was removed, the gun aperture plated over, and bench seats fitted. Seventy-two examples were used during Totalize. Other versions used both Sherman and, most commonly, surplus Ram training tank hulls, with the latter having the advantage of a hull-mounted Browning .300 in MG turret which had a wider arc of fire than the ball-mounted hull MG in a Sherman.[4] Some tanks had additional MGs fitted to the turret ring, but this was unofficial practice. The two main disadvantages of the Kangaroo were the lack of overhead protection and the necessity to dismount – and remount – over the sides of the vehicle. However, the armour elsewhere was completely adequate, providing protection from small arms and even cannon fire, or from anything but a direct hit from artillery or mortars – they did of course have the same vulnerability to mines as the host vehicles. The Kangaroos had to be crewed by tank soldiers, as there was no mechanical expertise in the infantry. By December there were sufficient vehicles to equip two Kangaroo regiments, one British (49 RTR) and one Canadian, both with the Ram variant, and not surprisingly the units were controlled and administered by 79th Armoured Division, although on operations they were placed under command of armoured or infantry formations. Kangaroos remained in use throughout the remainder of the campaigns in North-West Europe and Italy, and stayed in service post-war with the RAC demonstration unit, only being replaced with bespoke wheeled then tracked APCs in the 1950s.[5]

Artillery Mechanization and the Self-Propelled Gun

Despite the use of gun carrier tanks in the First World War and the development of the Birch gun in the 1920s, Britain entered the war without any self-propelled guns, with all the field artillery being towed either by Dragon tracked vehicles or 'Quad' wheeled tractors; in short order the latter became the preferred method of towing the 25-pounder guns. However, this meant that the mobility of the increasingly tracked armoured divisions was much greater than the supporting field regiments, which was clearly a disadvantage when operating in the break-out and exploitation roles. Despite some opposition to the idea of an SPG – possibly rooted in the suspicion amongst the more senior RA officers that such weapons would be operated by the RAC – in June 1941 the Birmingham Railway Carriage and Wagon Company, a tank builder, was asked to design a mounting for a 25-pounder gun on the chassis of a Valentine tank. Within two months the prototype was ready and resulted in the Bishop SPG; 150 were constructed, and used in the Tunisian and Sicilian campaigns.

Concurrently, the RA was allocated some American made M7 105mm SPGs, built on the chassis of the M3 Lee tank, with ninety being received just in time to see service at El Alamein in October 1942. These quickly acquired the nickname of Priest, due to the MG mounting that resembled a pulpit, and this led to the convention of naming such guns using ecclesiastical terms, which ended post-war with the Abbot. Although the Priest was a successful design, for reasons of standardization a 25-pounder version was made in Canada, which was known as the Sexton; it was the introduction of this SPG in 1944 that rendered the Priests surplus – or should that be surplice? – and allowed them to be converted into Kangaroos, as detailed above.

In addition to the SPGs which solved the problem of how to keep the artillery support up with fast-moving armoured formations, there was a need to do the same with the RA Forward Observation Officers, or FOOs. In the first years of the war the FOOs were mounted in specially adapted carriers, but these had a number of problems. They were small and therefore cramped, needing to container the driver, FOO and his assistant or 'ack', as well as two radio sets and other specialist equipment. Carriers also found it difficult to match the mobility of tank units operating on some types of terrain, and the protection afforded by the carrier was very limited, including having no overhead cover. Therefore, putting the FOO and his equipment inside a modified tank solved the problem, and a number of different tank types were converted to become OP, or Observation Post, vehicles. Such OP tanks were usually fitted with a fixed turret and a dummy (wooden) gun. One of the advantages that the crews of OP Shermans had over the fighting versions was that the tank did not need to carry ammunition, meaning that it was less likely to catch fire if hit, giving the crews more time to bail out. The use of OP tanks allowed the best use to be made of the excellent British system of artillery fire control, and which was so hated by the Germans, who respected and feared British artillery techniques and weight of fire.

It should also be recorded that in addition to the field artillery, some RA anti-tank units also used types of self-propelled guns. Initially and in the Western Desert only, these came in the form of Portees, in which a 2-pounder gun was mounted on the back of a flatbed truck. The idea was to give the gun mobility, and although the weapon could be fired when mounted in an emergency, the intention was to offload the gun using ramps, and place it in a fire position on the ground. A later version called the AEC Gun Carrier or Deacon, again following the ecclesiastical naming theme, used a 6-pounder gun in a lorry featuring an armoured cab, but this was a halfway house and never really satisfactory.[6]

From 1944 some of the anti-tank regiments were equipped with the US M10 tank-destroyer, with over 1,600 being supplied through Lend-Lease. Although this resembled a Sherman tank and indeed shared a similar hull to the M4A2 version, the 3in gun-equipped M10 was thinly armoured with a maximum of only 57mm, and was again an attempt to improve mobility, not to turn the weapon into a tank. The American 3in gun was a better anti-tank weapon than the indifferent 75mm, but in order to increase its effectiveness even more, many were converted to carry the 17-pounder, making them a formidable defensive weapon and as such they were frequently sent to give additional firepower to Churchill regiments, as these were not equipped with Firefly tanks.

The Royal Engineers

As has been described in the main text, a number of operations pointed to the requirement to put sappers into armoured vehicles, to allow them to operate in the front line with a degree of protection, mobility and, not least, to carry and operate specialist RE weapons and equipment. This included the experience gained from the Dieppe raid and the campaigns in Tunisia, Sicily and Italy, all of which – fortunately – led to the development of a range of specialized armoured vehicles, used not only for amphibious landings, assault river crossings or the reduction of fortresses, but also for the day-to-day routine engineer tasks – clearing minefields and other types of obstacle, crossing gaps and demolitions.

This would include the development of roller, flail and plough mine-clearing tanks, scissors bridge-layers, ARK ramp carriers, box-girder bridges, carpet-layers, flamethrowers and amphibious vehicles. What is often forgotten is that these types were all crewed by RAC soldiers. It was only the development in 1942 of another vehicle designed specifically for the RE, the Armoured Vehicle Royal Engineers or AVRE, that was to lead to the sappers creating their own highly specialized armoured squadrons and regiments. It was not until well after the Second World War that almost all of the specialized types would be grouped together under RE rather than RAC command, and this will be described in the next volume.[7] The Churchill AVRE with its 290mm Spigot mortar (usually called the Petard or Flying Dustbin) was capable of demolishing concrete formations, although the limited range of the weapon meant that the crews had to close to 100yd or less from the target. The 40lb bomb could only be loaded from outside, meaning that the job of reloading the weapon in action was the least enviable of the whole crew, and fell to the man in the co-driver's position. AVREs could also carry fascines on the hull front and on the rear decks, as well as a range of other heavy and bulky stores, which included 'General Wade' and 'Beehive' explosive charges which had to be placed by hand, but which could be detonoted from within the tank. AVRE crews generally had an RAC driver, the remainder being RE sappers.

Appendix B

Armoured Formations

The Armoured Divisions

Ten armoured divisions were formed during the war from RAC units. In addition to these, the Guards Armoured Division was formed, equipped with tanks but independent of the RAC, and both the 4th and 5th Canadian Armoured Divisions and the Polish Armoured Division were trained and equipped on British lines.

The Armoured Divisions

Division	History and Operational Service	Main RAC Units (by Seniority)[1]
Mobile Division/ 1st Armoured Division	Formed 1938. Redesignated 1st Armd Sep. 39. France, North Africa, Italy. Ceased to be operational 28 Oct. 44. HQ disbanded 11 Jan. 45.	Bays, Royals, 9L, 10H, 12L, 2RTR, 3RTR, 5RTR, 6RTR, YD, 2RGH, 3CLY, 4CLY
2nd Armoured Division	Formed 15 Dec. 39. North Africa. Disbanded Egypt 10 May 41.	KDG, 3H, 4H, 3RTR, 5RTR, 6RTR, 2RGH, 3CLY, 4CLY
6th Armoured Division	Formed 12 Sep. 40. Tunisia, Italy.	16/5L, 17/21L, 2LBH, 1DY, 1RGH, 1NY, 2NY
Mobile Division Egypt/The Armoured Division/7th Armoured Division	Formed 28 Sep. 1938. Redesignated The Armd Div Sep. 39. Redesignated 7th Armd 16 Feb. 40. North Africa, Italy, NWE.	5DG, 3H, 7H, 8H, 11H, 1RTR, 2RTR, 4RTR, 5RTR, 6RTR, 7RTR, 8RTR, 44RTR, 2RGH, 3CLY, 4CLY, 3/4CLY
8th Armoured Division	Formed 4 Nov. 40. North Africa. Disbanded 1 Jan. 43.	40RTR, 41RTR, 45RTR, 46RTR, 47RTR, 50RTR, 2DY
9th Armoured Division	Formed 1 Dec. 40. UK only. Disbanded 31 Jul. 44.	4/7DG, 5DG, 13/18H, 15/19H, 1RGH, 1FFY, 1ERY, IOC
10th Armoured Division	Formed 1 Aug. 41 from 1st Cavalry Division, Palestine. North Africa. Disbanded 15 Jun. 44.	1HCR, Royals, Greys, 3H, 7H, 2RTR, 3RTR, 6RTR, 8RTR, 40RTR, 50RTR, RWY, WY, YH, SRY, SY, 2DY
11th Armoured Division	Formed 9 Mar. 41. NWE.	15/19H, 22D, 23H, 24L, 27L, 3RTR, 1LBY, 2FFY, WD, 2NY

Division	History and Operational Service	Main RAC Units (by Seniority)[1]
42nd Armoured Division	Formed 1 Nov. 41 from 42nd Inf Div. UK only. Disbanded 17 Oct. 43.	22D, 1LBY, WD, 1NY, 107RAC, 108RAC, 109RAC, 110RAC, 111RAC, 112RAC, 145RAC
79th Armoured Division	Formed 14 Aug. 42. Responsible for specialized armour from Apr. 43. NWE.	4/7DG, 13/18H, 22D, 4RTR, 7RTR, 11RTR, 42RTR, 49RTR, 49 APC Regt, 1FFY, 1LBY, WD, 2NY, ERY, 141RAC, 162RAC

The Armoured and Tank Brigades

Twenty-eight brigades – of various types and designations – were formed within the RAC during the war.[2] At the start of the war, there were two main types of brigade designations; the Armoured Brigades (which during 1939/40 were sometimes further classified as light or heavy) were those equipped with Cruiser tanks, whereas the Army Tank (later Tank) Brigades were those equipped with Infantry tanks. The first category were usually part of, and employed within, armoured divisions, and thus had less of a separate identity; they wore the divisional insignia on uniforms and vehicles, for example.[3] Tank brigades were independent formations, usually under control of a Corps HQ, and were parcelled out to support infantry divisions for specific operations; they wore their own insignia. The tank brigades only comprised units of the RTR and RAC regiments, the role never being fulfilled by cavalry or yeomanry units. By the last year of the war, with the rise of the Universal or Capital tank, the days of the tank brigade were over, and in the post-war period, all were termed armoured brigades, regardless of equipment.

By 1944 there was some confusion as to what an independent brigade was for. Of the seven brigades deployed to Normandy, three were labelled as Tank Brigades and equipped with the Churchill Infantry tank, whereas the other four were known as Armoured Brigades and used the Sherman. This came about because Montgomery – rightly – did not want to differentiate between tank and armoured brigades, and wanted there to be one type only, able to operate in both the infantry support and the exploitation roles. The problem was two-fold: the tank did not exist that could fulfil both roles, and doctrine continued to be unclear as to what was required of either. During January and February 1945, the remaining tank brigades were renamed as armoured brigades, although their role did not change. It was not until the post-war period that it became clear that tank units must be able to deliver in both roles, and the tank existed – the Centurion – that could do both.

There was a lot of movement between brigades over the course of the war, with very few units remaining in the same brigade for all (or at least the majority of) the war; the six lucky regiments who suffered less disruption caused by frequent brigade moves were: the Bays, 9L, 10H, 16/5L, 17/21L and 2LBH. On the other hand, 3RTR served in five different brigades and, remarkably, 4RTR in no less than six – despite not appearing in the order of battle for over two years during the middle of the war.

The Armoured Brigades

Brigade Designation(s)	History and Operational Service	RAC Units (by Seniority)[+]
1st Light Armd/1st Armd	Change of designation 14 Apr. 40. NA, Greece. Between Aug. and Oct. 42, it was used for tank delivery, and then disbanded.	KDG, 3H, 4H, 8H, 1RTR, 3RTR, 6RTR
1st Army Tank/1st Tank	Change of designation 14 Apr. 40. BEF, NA, NWE. Disbanded 21 Nov. 44.	4RTR, 7RTR, 8RTR, 11RTR, 42RTR, 44RTR, 49RTR
2nd Light Armd/2nd Armd	Change of designation 14 Apr. 40. BEF, NA, IT.	Bays, 9L, 10H
1st Heavy Armd/3rd Armd	Change of designation 14 Apr. 40. BEF, NA. Ceased to function after heavy losses, absorbed by 32nd Tank Bde Sep. 41. HQ officially disbanded 11 Jan. 43.	KDG, 3H, 1RTR, 2RTR, 3RTR, 5RTR, 7RTR
Heavy Armd Bde Egypt/4th Heavy Armd/4th Armd	Change of designation Feb. 40. Second change Apr. 40. NA, IT, NWE. Still in existence at end of war.	KDG, Royals, Greys, 7H, 8H, 11H, 12L, 1RTR, 2RTR, 3RTR, 4RTR, 5RTR, 6RTR, 7RTR, 42RTR, 44RTR, 46RTR, 50RTR, SY, 3CLY, 3/4CLY
Light Armd Bde Egypt/7th Light Armd/7th Armd	Change of designation Feb. 40. Second change Apr. 40. NA, FE, Palestine, Syria, Iraq, IT. Still in existence at end of war.	7H, 8H, 11H, 1RTR, 2RTR, 4RTR, 6RTR, 8RTR
8th Armd	Formed Jul. 41 from 6th Cavalry Brigade. Palestine, Syria, NA, NWE. Still in existence at end of war.	4/7DG, Greys, 13/18H, 24L, 3RTR, 3/5RTR, SRY, SY
9th Armd	Formed 4 Aug. 41 from 4th Cavalry Brigade. Iraq, Persia, NA, IT. Still in existence at end of war.	1HCR, 3H, 4H, 7H, RWY, WY, YH
10th Armd/Tank	Formed Nov. 41 from 125th Inf Bde. UK only. Disbanded 25 Nov. 43.	108RAC, 109RAC, 143RAC

Brigade Designation(s)	History and Operational Service	RAC Units (by Seniority)
11th Armd/Tank	Formed Nov. 41 from 126th Inf Bde. UK only. Disbanded 25 Nov. 43.	107RAC, 110RAC, 111RAC
20th Light Armd/ Armd	Change of designation Apr. 40. UK only. Disbanded Apr. 43.	1RGH, 1NY, 2NY
21st Army Tank/ Tank	Formed as 21st Army Tank Bde (Territorial). Designation change Jun. 42. IT. Still in existence at end of war.	12RTR, 42RTR, 43RTR, 44RTR, 48RTR, NIH, 145RAC
22nd Heavy Armd/ Armd	Formed Sep. 39. Change of designation Apr. 40. NA, IT, NWE. Still in existence at end of war.	5DG, 1RTR, 5RTR, 2RGH, 3CLY, 4CLY
23rd Army Tank/ Armd	Formed as 23rd Army Tank Bde (Territorial). Designation change Nov. 40. NA, IT, Palestine, Syria, Greece. Still in existence at end of war.	8RTR, 40RTR, 46RTR, 50RTR
24th Army Tank/ Armd	Formed as 24th Army Tank Bde (Territorial). Designation change Nov. 40. NA. Effectively disbanded Mar. 43, designation used for various dummy tank operations.	41RTR, 45RTR, 47RTR
25th Army Tank/2nd MMG/25th Army Tank/25th Tank/B Assault Bde RAC/ RE/25thArmd Engr RE	Formed as 25th Army Tank Bde (Territorial). 1st Designation change Jun. 40. 2nd Designation change Dec. 40. 3rd Designation change Jun. 42. NA, IT. 5 Jan. 45 became B Assault Bde RAC/RE (51RTR, 1st and 2nd Asslt Regts RE.) 6 Apr. 45 became 25th Armd Engr Bde RE.	11RTR, 12RTR, 43RTR, 49RTR, 51RTR, NIH, 142RAC, 1 Asslt Regt RE, 2 Asslt Regt RE
26th Armd	Formed Oct./Nov. 40 from 1st MMG Bde. NA, IT. Still in existence at end of war.	16/5L, 17/21L, 2LBH
27th Armd	Formed Nov. 40 from 1st Armd Recce Bde. The DD Brigade for D-Day. NWE. Disbanded 31 Aug. 44.	4/7DG, 13/18H, SY, ERY, 148RAC
28th Armd	Formed Nov. 40 from 3rd MMG Bde. UK only. Disbanded 9 Sep. 44.	5DG, 15/19H, 1FFY
29th Armd	Formed Dec. 40. NWE. Still in existence at end of war.	22D, 23H, 24L, 3RTR, 2FFY
30th Armd	Formed Dec. 40. NWE.	22D, 23H, 4RTR, 11RTR, 1LBY, WD, 141RAC

Brigade Designation(s)	History and Operational Service	RAC Units (by Seniority)
31st Army Tank/ Tank/Armd	Formed 15 Jan. 41. 1st Designation change May 42. 2nd Designation change 2 Feb. 45. NWE. Still in existence at end of war.	Greys, 4RTR, 7RTR, 9RTR, 10RTR, 11RTR, 49APC, 1FFY, 141RAC
32nd Army Tank	Formed Sep. 41 from remnants of 3rd Armd Bde for defence of Tobruk. NA. Ceased to exist when Tobruk captured 21 Jun. 42.	1RTR, 4RTR, 7RTR
33rd Army Tank/ Tank/Armd	Formed Aug. 41. 1st Designation change Jun. 42. 2nd Designation change Jan. 45.	4RTR, 11RTR, SY, 1NY, ERY, 43RTR, 144RAC, 148RAC
34th Army Tank/ Tank/Armd	Formed 1 Dec. 41 from 226th Independent Inf Bde. NWE from Jul. 44. Still in existence at end of war.	7RTR, 9RTR, NIH, 107RAC, 147RAC, 151RAC, 153RAC
35th Army Tank/ Tank	Formed 1 Dec. 41 from 225th Independent Inf Bde. Designation change Aug. 42. UK only. Still in existence at end of war.	RWY, WY, 49RTR, 151RAC, 152RAC, 155RAC
36th Army Tank/ Tank	Formed Dec. 41 from 205th Independent Inf Bde. Designation change Aug. 42. UK only. Disbanded Jul. 43.	154RAC, 156RAC, 157RAC
137th Armd	Formed Jul. 42 from 137th Inf Bde. UK only. Disbanded 23 Sep. 43.	113RAC, 114RAC, 115RAC

Appendix C

Gunnery

Shooting on the Move

A doctrinal problem that British tank crews suffered from throughout the first half of the war was derived from the pre-war RTC insistence on shooting on the move. This demanded high levels of training – not to mention training time, ranges and ammunition – and was conducted somewhat artificially in order to make firepower demonstrations more impressive. RTC gunners became so proficient at it that after their first few shooting practices at static range targets that was deemed too easy and so as much time as possible was spent firing from moving tanks. When training a huge conscript army with less facilities it became difficult to manage, although it was such an auto-da-fé, being inculcated into generations of gunnery instructors, that it was generally accepted without question. The insistence on it also affected tank design, as it required that the guns were mounted in 'free' elevation, and controlled up and down by the gunner using a shoulder piece attached to the gun mounting, which in itself was less accurate when precision shooting when static was called for.

It was not until complaints and comments from the Western Desert campaign started to filter through from 1941 that thought was given to changing the doctrine to concentrate on shooting accurately from well-chosen static fire positions, preferably from a hull-down position. Eventually this became officially the norm, shooting on the move being restricted to trying to keep an enemy's head down when surprised in the open. The change in doctrine led to a change in design, as tanks had to be fitted with a more precise form of gun elevation, in the shape of an elevation gearbox controlled through a gunner's elevation handwheel. By 1944 this arrangement was standard, and led to a better ability to hit targets when static.

Machine Guns

Another pre-war practice that was deeply indoctrinated was the use of machine guns as the prime 'killer' of infantry and 'soft' targets.[1] This led to flawed tank designs in which all-but-unworkable MG sub-turrets were shoehorned onto the front of tanks, in the process increasing the size of the crews to larger than really necessary: these included the A9 and Crusader cruisers. By mid-war this policy had been discarded, but even before them many Crusader crews in North Africa had removed the turrets, plated the aperture over and used the space for additional ammunition.

At the start of the war the British MG of choice was the water cooled Vickers medium machine gun, an extremely reliable .303in gun that took up a lot of space and did not work very well in the confines of a tank. By 1940 new designs were being fitted with the 7.92mm BESA MG, a Czech design that became the MG of choice in British AFVs for the majority of the war; despite the complications caused by the adoption of the unusual calibre, the weapon was simple and reliable and seems to have attracted few complaints. The other MGs used by those crews equipped with American tanks were the Browning MGs, the .30in and it's bigger brother, the .50in, which was intended for use as an anti-aircraft gun and, even then, often removed by the crews as unnecessary. The belt-fed .30in Browning became both familiar and popular in action, and when prototypes of the Centurion were revealed and trialled just as the war was ending, comments from the crews led to it being adopted as the co-axial and turret MG on the tank, although the BESA continued to soldier on in those earlier AFVs that continued in service after the war, including for example the Comet tank and the Daimler Armoured Car. As well as these MGs being used in coaxial and hull mountings, other types were used, notably the Bren LMG, often with a 100-round drum magazine for use in the AA role, and the twin air cooled Vickers guns used on some scout cars.

Ammunition Development

Hitting the target is one thing; having the desired effect upon it is another entirely, which is where ammunition comes in. The RA have a saying to the effect that the weapon is the shell, not the gun. Britain in the Second World War led the world in many respects in terms of ammunition design, which allowed the best to be got out of guns which, after 1940, in terms of calibre and performance, were generally at least a year behind where they needed to be. In broad terms three types of ammunition were used in the tank and armoured car guns: Armour Piercing (AP), High Explosive (HE) and smoke – training natures will be ignored here. To understand how ammunition impacted upon weapon performance and thus also on doctrine and tactics a basic understanding is required.

Armour Piercing (AP)

AP is used as a generic term for all anti-armour natures relying on kinetic energy for their effect, but when used more specifically it refers to simple solid-shot projectiles. The AP round is the oldest type of the anti-armour family and the simplest in operation to describe. A dense plug of ballistically shaped (pointed) metal is fired at high velocity. The combination of the mass of the projectile and the striking velocity causes the projectile to 'punch' through armour plate. The projectile therefore requires to be made of sufficiently dense material to prevent shattering on impact, and the tip is often heat treated to harden it. Typical metals used include steel, tungsten, tungsten–carbide, nickel–chromium–molybdenum and silicon–manganese–chromium. German face-hardened armour was designed specifically to try to break up AP shot on impact.

Armour Piercing Capped (APC)

APC was a development which saw the addition of a malleable (soft) steel or iron cap to the nose of an AP projectile in order to resist the tendency to shatter on impact. APC is simply a development of AP, and came into service when it was realized that AP rounds tended to shatter on striking German armour plate. The cap fitted to the tip of the AP projectile absorbs the initial impact of the projectile and makes it thus much less likely to break up on impact; a useful side effect was a reduction in likelihood of ricochet. The shape of the cap needs to be blunt to do this, and this makes it aerodynamically inefficient, hence the subsequent development of APCBC.

Armour Piercing Capped Ballistic Cap (APCBC)

The addition of a ballistically efficient ogive over the nose of an APC projectile improved its aerodynamic performance. With APCBC a hollow cap was fitted over the soft APC cap to maintain velocity and improve accuracy; APCBC projectiles are therefore noticeably more pointed than APC.

Armour Piercing Discarding Sabot (APDS)

The original concept was developed by the French Edgar Brandt company just before the war, and turned into a workable projectile by the practical improvements made by the British designers Mr L. Permutter and Mr S. Coppock (of the Armaments Design Department, Ministry of Supply) during the conflict. It first entered service in very limited numbers in mid-1944 and gave a step-change in penetrative performance. APDS consists of a small dense sub-projectile made up to the full calibre of the gun barrel by one or more lightweight supporting 'shoes' or 'sabots', usually made of Duralumin. These discard after leaving the muzzle due to rotational forces and air resistance, allowing the sub-projectile (the penetrator) to travel at greatly increased muzzle velocity and thus penetrative power. It also has a very flat trajectory, leading to increases in the chance of a hit due to range finding errors being less important. Technically, APDS was the most complex ammunition type to be developed, with such things as the muzzle brakes on tank guns complicating the design. Although there was no doubt about its effectiveness, there were two main problems with it: firstly, the scarcity of it during 1944 until production 'ramped up', and secondly, a lack of consistency which meant that it was more difficult to hit the target using APDS than with APCBC.[2]

High Explosive

HE ammunition consists of a steel or similar casing, an explosive filling (or bursting charge) and a fuse. HE can be set via a fuse to function before, on or after impact. Because HE is fired at a much lower velocity than AP types, it has a more curved trajectory and therefore is reliant on the range being established accurately, but on the other hand this means that if HE misses the target, the gunner can correct fire by making adjustments using his sight. The other key factor about the explosive impact of the shell, too small and it will be ineffective, so within reason, the bigger the gun the better.

High Explosive Anti-Tank (HEAT)

HEAT makes use of the 'Munroe effect', in which a cone-shaped explosive charge is initiated at a stand-off distance from the target. This is made more effective if lined with copper (the Neumann principle). These effects when combined produce a low-mass but very high-speed (*c.* 10km/s) 'jet' of near-molten copper which is focused on a very small area of the armour; if this penetrates, the jet and associated copper 'slugs' cause great damage within the target. It was this principle that was used with such effectiveness by the German *PanzerFaust* and *PanzerSchreck* crews. Unlike AP natures, the effectiveness of HEAT does not diminish with increased range, and on British tanks during the war this ammunition was mainly confined to use in the 95mm gun/howitzer.

Smoke

This is a projectile designed to emit clouds of dense smoke, in order to screen either the enemy from friendly forces, or friendly forces from the enemy. There is no doubt that Britain placed far too much emphasis on the role of Close Support tanks to provide local smoke screens, rather that HE effect, but the smoke shells developed were effective when used correctly.

The 2-Pounder Gun

The main gun that almost all British tanks were equipped with during the first three years of the Second World War was the 40mm 2-pounder. When introduced, the gun was the best anti-tank weapon in the world, and it remained so until the Germans introduced a 50mm gun during 1940. The General Staff requirement for a new tank gun had been placed in 1934, to replace the 47mm medium velocity 3-pounder used in the Medium tanks, and which was not effective as a modern anti-tank weapon. Subsequently, in January 1935 it was decided that the same 2-pounder weapon would be developed in a slightly modified form as a towed anti-tank gun mounted on wheels, and destined for employment within the newly created RA Anti-Tank Regiments.[3] Approved for service in January

1936, the 2-pounder became the main armament of all the next generation of British tanks: the A12 Matilda II, the A9 and A10 Cruisers, the A13 Cruiser, the early marks of the Churchill and the Valentine infantry tanks, and the Covenanter and Crusader tanks, as well as many different types of armoured car.

The reason for its selection as the tank gun of choice was made because of a sensible policy; to standardize ammunition, production and spare parts for the towed and vehicle-mounted versions. However, there was one great flaw in this: the calibre of the weapon was too small to allow the development of an effective High Explosive shell. One such shell was made, with a TNT fill and a No. 243 fuse, but it was too small to be of much use and there are no records of it being issued to RAC units. This led to the situation in the desert where the tank crews were unable to deal with small, dug-in anti-tank guns at range, as the solid AP shot was not effective unless it scored a direct hit on the gun, rather than just punching a hole through the gun shield. Replaced by the 6-pounder in 1942–3, the 2-pounder had an extension to its service life when the so-called Littlejohn adaptor was introduced in 1943; this was a squeeze-bore design, firing specially tapering ammunition.[4] This decreased the calibre towards the muzzle down to 33mm, and which thus increased the muzzle velocity. Unable to fire other types of ammunition, the Littlejohn was nevertheless fitted to later war armoured cars, such as the ubiquitous Daimler, in order to give it enhanced anti-tank performance.

The 6-Pounder and the British 75mm

The design of a replacement for the 2-pounder, capable of penetrating at least 60mm of armour, started in 1938; it was one of the great tragedies of the war that it was prevented from being introduced until at least a year after it might have been. Design approval following trials was given on 9 September 1940, and it should have gone into mass production immediately. However, the timing of the approval came during the start of the 'tank crisis' following Dunkirk, and it was thought by the Director of Munitions Production that for every 6-pounder made, six of the earlier guns could be produced. This was wildly incorrect, but the damage was done. As a result of the early battles in North Africa with the Germans, their Panzer III tanks sporting increased armour and 50mm guns, it was quickly recognized that more firepower was needed, which led – belatedly – to a cry within the Ministry of Supply for '6-pounders at all costs!', but production of guns, mountings and ammunition could not be switched overnight, and the first of the new guns were not fitted onto tanks until December 1941, with the first wheeled versions not arriving in North Africa until April 1942. Although it was issued with an HE shell, this had indifferent explosive performance, and the first type of armour piercing round issued was a plain AP which struggled to defeat the German face-hardened armour. The introduction of improved APC ammunition in October 1942 and then the even better APCBC in early 1943 reduced this advantage and allowed the 6-pounder to become a genuine tank-killer of all but the heaviest Panzers. The introduction of APDS ammunition in summer 1944 restored its capability and extended its service life even further, with the gun able to penetrate 131mm of German F-H armour at 500yd, a typical engagement range during the Normandy campaign and more than a match for the 100mm on the Tiger I glacis and 120mm on the turret front, or the 80mm on the Panther glacis; at that range, the gun/ammunition combination had similar penetrative performance to the much bigger 17-pounder firing APCBC. Some units in Normandy equipped with the British 75mm gun requested that they be issued a proportion of their tanks with the 6-pounder using APDS ammunition as tank-killers, a sort of mini-Firefly, but this was not authorized.

The introduction of the American M2 and M3 75mm guns in the Grant, Lee and Sherman during 1942 gave the RAC crews, for the first time, the HE shell that they needed to tackle anti-tank guns at range, and it was therefore decided to develop the 6-pounder into a 75mm version, initially referred to as the 8-pounder and subsequently the 12-pounder, but finally and officially designating it as the 75mm (as it used the same ammunition as the American guns) made sense. The modifications required were in fact quite simple: the barrel and liner were changed, the recoil system strengthened (including fitting a muzzle brake), and the extractors altered – the breech ring and mechanism were the same design as the 6-pounder. Another advantage was that very little crew retraining was necessary, and although tanks carrying the new gun needed revised ammunition stowage and sights, none of this was in any way difficult. The performance of the British 75mm was slightly less than that of the American gun as the barrel was shorter, so in anti-armour terms it was, for 1944, a very indifferent weapon, but remained in service in Churchills, Cromwells and Valentines until the end of the war. It was estimated that in terms of main armament rounds fired by tanks in Italy and later in Normandy, around 70–80 per cent were HE, which was why there was so much resistance to developing a purely armour-defeating main gun.

The 17-Pounder

The development of the 17-pounder as the 6-pounder replacement started as early as April 1941, although it was not ready for production until late 1942. The unusual size came about from a calculation, in which it was shown that to have the penetrative performance required from a gun firing an AP shot at 2,700 fps, a 3in (76.2mm) calibre gun was required, and this further showed that a 17-pound AP shot would be necessary, and the rest of the gun design stemmed from this. This meant that it was a large weapon, much bigger than its predecessor and thus difficult to fit into tanks, where a lot of room and a large turret ring diameter was required. Unfortunately, contemporary tank design had not been consulted about the need to fit the gun, and such tanks as the Churchill and Cromwell were designed around the 6-pounder/75mm, and could not accept the 17-pounder. Eventually it was crammed into the Sherman to produce the Firefly, and also on other less successful designs such as the A30 Challenger and, to a lesser extent, the Archer tracked anti-tank gun, in which it was mounted – facing rear – on a Valentine tank chassis.

In Normandy, the Sherman Firefly proved its worth, although attracting the unwelcome attentions of the German gunners in the process. The addition of APDS ammunition in late August 1944 to the already reasonably effective APCBC made its performance truly exceptional, on a par with the much-vaunted 88mm but at a fraction of the size.[5] There was some criticism of the early HE ammunition; as always, the comparisons were made with the well-liked American M48 75mm HE shell. As a result, a 'High Capacity' shell was introduced to improve performance, coupled with a smaller propellant charge in the cartridge case to reduce the velocity. It was the 17-pounder with APDS and HE-HC ammunition that gave British tank crews, for the first time in their history, a genuine dual-purpose weapon.

The 77mm

As a result of the inability to fit the 17-pounder into the new A34 Comet tank, a Vickers-designed private venture 75mm gun was redesigned and enlarged to be able to use the 17-pounder family of 76.2mm ammunition projectiles, coupled to a smaller cartridge case, necessary to make the whole thing fit together at the overall size required. This allowed it to be used in the new design of Comet turret, where it was inaccurately called the 77mm simply in order to distinguish the ammunition from that used on the 17-pounder. As a result of the reduced amount of propellant and a shorter barrel, the velocity imparted to the AP projectiles was slightly less that that achieved from the 17-pounder, meaning that its performance was slightly reduced, but it was found to be a remarkably accurate and consistent weapon system, particularly when firing the new and still temperamental APDS ammunition, available in limited quantities from spring 1945.

It is instructional to note how much of a step-change the introduction of the 17-pounder and the 77mm, particularly when firing APDS ammunition, was. Table 1 on p. 292 compares the performance of these two guns firing both APCBC and APDS with the two most-feared German guns: the long 75mm on the Panther and the 88mm as fitted to the Tiger and Jagdpanther; the results are ranked in order of performance. The target in all cases is RHA sloped at 30°, and penetration is shown in mm.

Table 1: Gun/Ammunition Penetration at Various Ranges

Weapon/Ammunition	600yd	1,000yd	1,600yd
17-pdr/APDS	183	172	155
88mm/APCBC	178	157	131
77mm/APDS	178	150	131
17-pdr/APCBC	127	124	112
75mm/APCBC	119	100	95
77mm/APCBC	110	105	91

Source: Mark Hayward, *Sherman Firefly* (Barbarossa Books, 2001), p. 37.

As well as outperforming the 88mm, the 17-pounder was a much easier gun – and ammunition – to produce in resource terms, and also had a faster speed of loading.

Close-Support Weapons

Doctrine pre-war had identified the requirement for a small number of tanks in each squadron to be able to 'fill in the gaps' when artillery fire from the RA was not available. It was decreed that two tanks (usually) per squadron headquarters should be equipped with tanks designed for the role, and known as Close Support or CS tanks. As has been noted, this might have proved to be a wiser decision had HE shells been plentiful, but the emphasis was on smoke, some CS tanks in the desert campaign being stowed only with smoke. (When CS tanks were sent to the USSR, the Russians could not believe the fallacy of the argument, and insisted on much more HE being shipped, which they got.)

Pre- and early war versions used were a 3.7in weapon incorrectly known for some reason as a mortar, as used on the Medium II, A9 and A10 CS tanks, and a 3in gun used on Matildas, Valentines, Crusaders and early Churchills. The definitive CS weapon did not arrive until 1943, and coupled a 25-pounder field gun breech to a cut-down 3.7in AA gun barrel. (Such is how – amazingly effective – weapon design was sometimes conducted during the Second World War.) The lesson of over reliance on smoke had been learned, and the HE shell was large enough to be effective; a HEAT round, designed for emergency self-protection against armour, was also devised. The 95mm proved to be very useful in the last years of the war, but what was really needed was a universal tank with a dual-purpose gun, and not tanks that only had narrow, limited roles on the battlefield.

Accuracy, Consistency and Penetration

This is a much-misunderstood area – many commentators talk about the accuracy of guns when they really mean consistency, so what follows is an explanation of the two terms when used in gunnery, and then penetration is briefly examined. The explanation here refers only to direct-fire weapons. Accuracy is essentially the ability to hit the target, or to put it another way, to make the point of aim and the point of impact the same. Consistency on the other hand is the ability to fire a group of shots (a minimum of three) under the same conditions and have them land as close as possible together. Accuracy in combat, as opposed to under test conditions on a range, usually depends on two main things: firstly, the correct alignment between the sighting instrument (telescope, periscope or similar) and the axis of the bore, and secondly, establishing the exact range to the target.

As the sight will always be offset away from the bore, the optical line of sight and the axis of the bore can only be aligned perfectly at one distance, often the usual battle range, for example, 500yd or 800yd.[6] The design of the sighting system can be built to take this into account, so that provided this alignment (sometimes known as the gun–sight relationship) is set up correctly, the pattern of aiming marks in the gunner's sight (graticule or reticule) will take the offset into account at all other ranges, from very close range all the way up to the limit of the range marked in the sight. This has to be regularly set up and if necessary adjusted; in British parlance this was known as T&A – Testing and Adjusting.

A common method of conducting T&A would be for the crew to affix crosshairs made of greased thread or cotton onto the muzzle of the gun (look closely and many muzzles have faint lines inscribed at the 12, 3, 6 and 9 o'clock positions). The gunner would then lay the appropriate mark in his gun sight onto a clearly defined object at the prescribed range; let us say the top right-hand corner of an ammunition box or a scout car positioned for the purpose at 500yd. Another crew member would open the breech (or, with the breech closed, remove the striker assembly to allow the firing pin aperture to be used as a peephole) and, looking down the bore of the gun, where possible using binoculars, give the gunner instructions to move his hand controls until the cross was laid exactly onto the aiming mark. With the gun – but not the sight – now pointing at the aiming mark at the exact desired range, the gunner would unlock the mountings that held the telescope in position and, without disturbing the lay of the gun, make adjustments until his 500yd aiming mark was also laid onto the target. He would then carefully lock up the telescope in this position, and the gun–sight relationship was thus 'established'. This could also be checked by 'shooting in', also known as 'zeroing', involving firing one or more shots to check that all was well, making further small adjustments if required.

The American system as used on the Sherman involved pointing the main armament barrel at a clearly defined object 1,000yd distant, and then adjusting the whole telescope in its mounting until the cross in the sight graticule that represented the zero range mark was also pointing at the same object. This method would be guaranteed to cause the first round fired to go well minus of the target as no elevation equivalent to the range had been added to the position of the barrel, unless the sights were then re-adjusted by shooting in! After reports from North Africa of British units noticing this problem and coming up with an adjustment to compensate and 'adding greatly to the accuracy of these weapons', British trials were conducted at Lulworth in June 1944 and as a result it was recommended applying a compensating downward adjustment of 1 Mil (the equivalent to 1m at 1,000m) to the graticule after T&A, in order to have the effect of raising the gun barrel in order to allow for the range. It was incredible that this situation took so long to be identified; in Egypt in October 1941 the inexperienced 7th Queen's Own Hussars quickly noted:

> During October training consisted mainly of range practices with the 2 Pounder. It had been noticed that on measured ranges, when the telescope sights had been tested as laid down in the tank gunnery textbook, an accurately laid shot fired at a target 1000 yards away fell 300 yards short, or 11 feet vertically below the point aimed at. If, therefore, the range to a precision target such as an enemy tank had been judged accurately the shot would miss ...[7]

As the Hussars had correctly realized, knowing the exact range to the target is critical. As long as the gun-sight relationship has been set up correctly, it might be thought that as long as the exact range to the target is known, the gunner will always hit it first time. However, other factors come into play, for example, the effect of crosswind or headwind, particularly as range increases. But range itself IS the most important simple factor; Allied crews in the Second World War did not have the range-finding devices that became common after the conflict – stereoscopic, coincidence, stadia metric, ranging guns, lasers, etc. The crew commander had to estimate the range (with an average error of at least 25 per cent) and the gunner would then fire the first shot, and, having (probably) missed, adjust fire until the target was hit. Firing AP natures made life easier, as the higher MV gave the projectile a flatter (although not flat) trajectory and thus range-finding errors were less critical.[8] Correcting fire with AP was however more difficult, as the faster shot was more difficult to see, even with tracer fitted.

Other factors conspired against the Allied crews: the Germans always benefited from their superior optical instruments, both in terms of quality and magnification; many Allied vehicles used very low powers of magnification, making aiming difficult. The 3.7in Mortar used the Sighting Telescope No. 22A, which had no magnification at all – the No. 24B telescope used on the 2–pounder A/T gun only used x 1.9. Even at the end of the war the Tortoise, with its long range and very accurate 32-pounder gun, was only provided with a x 3 sight for the gunner, despite a recommendation made in early 1943 to use x 5 magnification on future systems – from the 17-pounder on. Even the design of the aiming marks within the sight could make accurate aiming extremely difficult. In the 75mm

Sherman tank, for example, the M70F Telescope used vertical lines as aiming marks for firing the M61 APC ammunition. These were only clearly defined and marked every 400yd, so the gunner had to 'guestimate' where the intermediate markings were in order to hit his target. With the M4/M38 Periscopic sight on the Staghound armoured car, things were even worse for the gunner, with aiming marks only provided at 0, 300 and 1,000yd! With different natures of ammunition, where the graticule was only marked for one type, usually AP, the gunner had to learn various rules or formulae to be able to use the correct mark for the others. For example, with the 77mm on the Comet, where the markings were for APCBC, in order to fire APDS with its flatter trajectory the gunner used this table:

Table 2: Comet 77mm APCBC Range Table

Actual Range	Use APCBC mark
400	100
600	150
800	200
1,000	300
1,200	400

Source: G.M.O. Davy, *The Seventh and Three Enemies (7th Hussars)* (Naval & Military Press, 2014).

None of this made life easy for the crew, and of course added both time to the engagement and to the likelihood of a first-round miss. Some late-war sights did allow the gunner more of a chance of a hit: when the Littlejohn adaptor was mounted to 2-pounder armed vehicles, a new graticule pattern was used, which had scales for APCBC, APSV and also MG. With this system, the aiming mark used for APSV at 1,200yd was the same as that used for APCBC at 1,000yd, but both were clearly marked.

Penetrating the armour and destroying the target are, or course, different things. The most consistent and accurate gun/ammunition is worthless if they can hit the target every time but fail to have the desired effect upon the target – the terrible image of seeing one's shots bouncing off the enemy armour.[9] To quote the 7th Hussars again:

> The 2 Pounder was a very accurate weapon when fired from a stationary tank … but something more than accuracy was required for the task with which the 2 Pounder was soon to be faced. This was hitting power, and the 2 Pounder had not got it. The many dents in those enemy tanks which were left on the battlefield testify alike to its inadequacy in weight and to the excellence of the shooting.[10]

This is at the heart of the perennial battle between armour and gun: when the enemy produces armour which is capable of defeating your attempts to penetrate it, they have gained a temporary advantage. You must then quickly develop a better gun and/or ammunition to overmatch their protection. When you do, you have regained the advantage and the enemy will then set about trying to improve the armour once again on their vehicles. And, of course, you do not wait to lose the advantage, rather you must try to anticipate what the enemy is likely to do next, and try to pre-empt them in the design phase.

A term used to give an indication of the accuracy of a gun/ammunition combination at a set range is the Probability of a Hit, or PH.[11] The three tables below give examples of PH. Each defines the vehicle, the weapon and the types of ammunition fired at a number of ranges from short to long. The target in all cases is the same: a 5ft wide by 2ft deep canvas screen target that represents the approximate surface area of a German Panther tank turret. Table 3 below shows only the PH for a first-round hit, whereas the second shows the probability of any one of three rounds fired hitting the target. The third expands on the latter, and shows interesting comparisons between British and American systems – in short, the British could produce better hole-punching ammunition, whilst the Americans tended to put together more consistent weapon systems. The tables therefore cannot be compared like for like, but interesting lessons can be drawn from the statistics – as indeed they were by the wartime scientists advising on maximum range.

Table 3: PH With First Round – Sherman Firefly 17-Pounder v. 5ft x 2ft Target

Range (yd)	APC (%)	APDS (%)
400	91	57
600	73	34
800	57	22
1,000	45	15
1,500	25	7

Source: WO 291/1263.

Table 4: PH with Any One of Three Rounds Fired – Churchill 6-Pounder v. 5ft x 2ft Target

Range (yd)	APCBC (%)	APDS (%)
500	89	74
800	84	50
1,000	81	37
1,500	62	20

Source: WO 291/762.

Table 5: PH with Any Round Fire for Effect (i.e. at a Known Range) v. 5ft x 2ft Target

Range (yd)	Churchill III 6-Pdr	Churchill IV 6-Pdr	Sherman Firefly APC	Sherman Firefly – APDS	Comet – 77mm	Sherman 75mm – APC M61	Sherman 76mm – APC M62
500	74	74	88	42	98	100	100
800	73	50	66	21	86	96	100
1,000	62	37	52	14	76	90	99
1,500	42	20	32	7	53	73	92

Source: Bovington Tank Museum 17-pounder files.

As can be expected, in all cases the PH decreases as range increases. It is also clear that APDS, despite being a great 'hole puncher', was not as accurate as the natures that it was replacing – due to problems with achieving consistency. At 1,000m it was unlikely to hit the target. Based on the evidence shown in Table 3, the scientists recommended that the maximum range that Churchill firing 6-pounder APDS should start an engagement from was only 800yd; this was for reasons of accuracy, not penetration. And even then, there was only a fifty/fifty chance that any one of three rounds fired would hit! One has to question whether the crews would have been happy with this if they had been privy to these sorts of details. As can be realized from this, the first task of the weapon designers was to produce ammunition that would consistently hit the target. Having achieved that, penetration could be addressed. Therefore, it can be appreciated how accuracy, consistency, PH and penetration are all inter-related.

One of the other problems with which the British wrestled was that of the 'big hole' versus 'small hole' argument. In essence, full-calibre ammunition that was able to penetrate caused bigger holes and much greater damage, whereas the sub-projectiles of, in particular, APDS and HEAT, caused smaller holes and consequently much less damage on the target. The trouble was that small hole penetration was easier to achieve by modifying the ammunition, whereas improving big hole performance usually meant introducing a larger gun and often a larger tank – witness the British 32-pounder and the Tortoise.

What follows is my attempt to extrapolate usable figures from a number of sources which quote penetration figures. However, for such data to be meaningful and allow direct comparisons between different weapon systems (i.e. gun and ammunition combination) certain of the potential variables have to be fixed: the target type (armour material, angle of attack) and the meteorological conditions (preferably zero wind, and barometric pressure and air temperature within specified tolerances) are the most important. Unfortunately, many of the sources neglect to detail this information, and in some cases where they *are* noted, they cause a different problem with comparisons. For example, some of the figures were obtained by shooting against German face-hardened armour, which performs very differently to the standard target of rolled homogenous armour (RHA). Also, in many cases the exact gun and/or vehicle platform are not recorded, nor are the exact type/marks of ammunition. Another problem is that some British penetration tables originally used an 80 per cent likelihood of penetration as the benchmark, whilst others do not mention whether the figures quoted are for 80 per cent or 100 per cent! For example, it can be seen in Table 5 how different British natures were recorded in 1942 as performing against both RHA and face-hardened armour, but these figures use the 80 per cent figure, which has the effect of changing the apparent penetration when compared with other penetration data:

Table 6: 2-Pounder and 6-Pounder – 80 Per Cent Likelihood of a Penetration (mm) Against Homogenous and Face-Hardened Armour Sloped at 30°

Gun	Ammunition	RHA 500yd	RHA 1,000yd	F-H 500yd	F-H 1,000yd
2-pdr	AP	52	41	44	33
	APC	50	40	54	39
	APCBC	55	48	56	47
6-pdr	AP	73	63	64	51
	APC	68	57	80	64
	APCBC	74	66	81	71

Source: RAC half-yearly report No. 6.

Table 6 represents my best attempt at squaring the penetration circle, and gives performance figures for the main anti-armour rounds used by the UK, using both British guns and the ones found on American tanks and tank destroyers. Unless stated otherwise, the figures in Table 6 represent average penetration in millimetres achieved when firing the specified ammunition from the specified gun at a target of RHA angled at 30° to the vertical.

Table 7: UK and American Ammunition – Average Penetration (mm) Against Rolled Homogenous Armour Sloped at 30°

Weapon	Ammunition	500yd	1,000yd	Remarks
UK				
2-pdr	AP	54	42	
	APCBC	56	50	
	SV	88	72	
3-pdr	APHE	NK	25	

Weapon	Ammunition	500yd	1,000yd	Remarks
6–pdr	AP	75	70	
	APC	79	73	
	APCBC	98	75	Figures are for face-hardened armour, not RHA.
	APDS	131	128	
17–pdr	AP	NK	109	
	APC	NK	118	
	APCBC	140	128	Figures are for face-hardened armour, not RHA.
	APDS	190	186	231mm at 1,000yd at 0°.
77mm	APCBC	120	109	
	APDS	182	165	
95mm	HEAT	110 (all ranges)		
US				
75mm	APC/APCBC	69	61	From M3 gun: slightly better performance from APCBC than APC. Around 10mm less performance from early M2 gun (Grant, Lee). Slightly decreased performance when used in British 75mm gun.
76mm	APC	88	90	See text above.
	APCBC	96	89	
	HVAP	145	133	Limited use only from 1944.
	APCR	110	NK	
3in	AP	NK	NK	
	APC	99	89	

Source: John Salt, *World War Two Armour Penetration Statistics* (privately published, 1999).

Maintenance and Servicing

One of the tasks of the gunner, loader and – where appropriate – the hull gunner – was to ensure that the tank was fit to fight in all respects from a gunnery perspective. Whilst some of this could be done during the fighting day, the majority of maintenance and servicing had to be completed when in harbour or leaguer. Ken Tout described how this was done on Shermans in 1944 in his book *Tank!* as follows:

> The 75mm gun is a good friend but a hard master. In needs endless cleaning, servicing, checking, pampering. To clean the barrel there is a stiff brush with an extremely long handle, like those used by old-time chimney

sweeps ... Once the barrel has been thoroughly scoured and polished from without, the breech can be tackled from within ... We crouch around the gun in confined space and wrestle with the breech block, a heavy, uncooperative lump of polished steel ... the next chore is the cleaning and checking of the smaller guns, the Browning .300" machine guns – neat, squared, black; mass-produced but highly efficient American weapons. I [as gunner] extract and dismantle the turret Browning and then the other browning from the co-driver's compartment. Stan, Keith and I can all strip a Browning blind-folded, disconnecting it bit by bit down to is dozens of component parts ... My last task is to check the gun sights. Crawling under the gun and into the loader's perch, I [use] the breech lever and swing open the breech block. I can now peer up the brilliant, silver-blue steel barrel to the sky beyond. I crawl under the open gun, stretch up, and [drop down] onto the ground. I pull two hairs from the abundant growth on my head. The muzzle end of the big gun has tiny slits in cross shape, and, with a little grease, I fix the hairs to form a cross shape at the end of the orifice. Back up [into the turret], I jam my eye against the telescope fixed to the gun. Fine lines on the telescope indicate exactly where the gun is, or should be, pointing. I depress the gun until the distant cornfield comes into sight, then a lorry nearer at hand. The turret turns so that the gun sight comes to bear precisely on the top of the white identification star painted on the door of the lorry. Now all I have to do is check that the hair cross seen through the gun barrel is also dead-on the same spot. If not, I adjust the telescopic sight to correspond to the actual aim of the gun as indicated by my two surrendered hairs ...[12]

Appendix D

Wiggly Amps – AFV Communications

Second World War

A new design from the Pye company and the Signals Experimental Establishment was the No. 10, which eventually emerged in 1941 as the renowned No. 19 set, with which the RAC was to be equipped for the next fifteen or so years; although much smaller than its predecessors, it still weighed nearly a hundredweight complete. The No. 19 was a great improvement on anything that had gone before, using amplitude modulation and valve technology which assisted in keeping the set on frequency, and usefully was in fact two sets in one: the 'A' Set had a longer range (10 miles R/T, 15 miles W/T) whilst the 'B' Set was R/T only and used for troop communications with a range of less than a mile between two mobile stations. The 'A' set was an HF design, operating between 2 and 8 MHz, with the 'B' set using VHF between 229 and 241 MHz. The choice of HF made the A Set rather temperamental, as it was dependent on good operating drills and siting, but it could be – and frequently was – used to pick up the BBC on 6.2 MHz, a major bonus for AFV crews.

Additionally, a sophisticated radio 'harness' was used, providing each crewman with junction boxes to allow control of the radio and its inbuilt IC system, dependent on their role; their headsets and microphones plugged into these boxes.[1] War diaries and personal accounts are full of references to tank crews selecting the wrong set, and broadcasting their (often extremely colourful) instructions intended for the driver to the whole squadron or regiment! Towards the end of the war the small and short-range No. 38 infantry man-portable set was sometimes fitted into some tanks to allow direct communication with accompanying infantry (who were at last receiving their own versions of this man-portable radio); initially the infantry version was jerry-rigged into the tank and retained its own large dry cell battery, but then the WS 38 was developed from it specifically for use in AFVs, allowing the battery to be discarded. The No. 38 operated between 7.3 and 8.9 MHz, which, theoretically at least, could achieve a range of 2 miles with a 12ft rod antenna. Another set used in a similar way was the infantry No. 18 manpack; the SRY noted that each SHQ tank had a No. 18 fitted just before D-Day. The No. 18 operated between 6 and 9 MHz. Also, from about 1943 the harness system was adapted to allow Infantry tank telephone boxes to be fitted to the rear of tanks, for the same purpose of allowing Infantry tank communication but using the vehicle's IC system accessed via a handset rather than a radio.

One complaint that was frequently made by RAC signallers during the war was that their training concentrated far too much on Morse, which they hardly ever used, and they thought that much more time should have been spent on radio operation. Another huge failing was the lack of codes and security, which left the radio nets open to intercept; during Operation Battleaxe, Rommel's interception of a somewhat panicky message from a divisional to a corps commander gave him the incentive to continue his assault and turn a defensive battle into an offensive victory.[2] Such poor discipline was exploited ruthlessly by Rommel in the desert, who often had a clearer picture of British dispositions than HQ Eighth Army, but over the course of the war, the British made much more extensive, and better, use of radio than their opposition.

Introduced as one measure to add more security in speech was the system of Appointment Titles, with some surviving to this day. These included: Sunray = commander; Molar = HQ; Pronto = signaller; Shelldrake = RA; Holdfast = RE; Playtime = transport; Starlight = medics; Rickshaw = ordnance; and Bluebell = REME. The phonetic alphabet was different to the NATO standardized one used currently, and was as follows: Able, Baker, Charlie, Dog, Easy, Fox, George, How, Item, Jig, King, Love, Mike, Nan, Oboe, Peter, Queen, Roger, Sugar, Tare, Uncle, Victor, William, X-ray, Yoke and Zebra.

In addition to radios, other communication methods were employed. Flag pennants flown from radio antennae were extensively used to indicate squadron and troop leaders, particularly in the desert campaign. Such pennants were 9in high by 1ft long, in black. In an unnecessarily complicated system, two bands of a colour denoting the troop number were placed diagonally across the pennant, for example, red for the first troop and yellow for the second. It is doubtful that they could be made out much over 100yd, particularly when covered in dust. Other rectangular flags were also carried to be displayed in certain circumstances; these included flags denoting 'rally', 'come on' and 'out of action'. Although some specific flags were carried on the rear of DD tanks during the D-Day landings, their use was largely on the wane, and the identification of individual squadrons, troops and tanks in the last two years of the war was mostly denoted by a system of symbols and numbers, or just numbers, painted (usually) on the turret sides and rear. These derived from experiments carried out between the wars by the RTC, and eventually settled down into the system still used today, wherein geometric shapes denoted the squadron, with a diamond for RHQ and HQ squadron, a triangle for A, a square for B and a circle for C.

The policy of providing every tank and armoured car with a radio set, allowing the commander to both receive instructions and to send information, was a major benefit to efficient tactical handling, allowing rapid responses to changing circumstances and meaning that fleeting opportunities could now be seized. During the course of the war over 550,000 wireless sets were produced for the army, with the RAC and RA being the largest users of them, besides the Royal

Signals. (Many more could have been produced, giving the infantry reliable man-portable communications and allowing much better Infantry tank co-operation, but the RN and RAF had much greater priority over production.)[3] There is no doubt that the use of voice radio by the British armoured forces during the war acted as a major force-multiplier. It allowed reconnaissance units to report on enemy activity – and inactivity – in real time, contributing to the exploitation of opportunities. Control of armoured formations and units was exercised by such means, and those with good technical knowledge allied to slick communication procedures were able to make the most of the equipment provided.[4]

Unit Badges

The Life Guards.

The Royal Horse Guards.

The King's Dragoon Guards.

The Queen's Bays.

The 3rd Carabiniers.

The 4th/7th Royal Dragoon Guards.

The 5th Royal Inniskilling Dragoon Guards.

The Royal Dragoons.

The Royal Scots Greys.

The 3rd King's Own Hussars.

The 4th Queen's Own Hussars.

The 7th Queen's Own Hussars.

The 8th King's Royal Irish Hussars.

The 9th Queen's Royal Lancers.

The 10th Royal Hussars.

The 11th Hussars (Prince Albert's Own).

The 12th Royal Lancers (Prince of Wales's).

The 13th/18th Royal Hussars (Queen Mary's Own).

The 14th/20th King's Hussars.

The 15th/19th King's Royal Hussars.

The 16th/5th Queen's Royal Lancers.

The 17th/21st Lancers.

The 22nd Dragoons.

The 23rd Hussars.

The 24th Lancers.

The 25th Dragoons.

The 26th Hussars.

The 27th Lancers.

The Royal Tank Regiment.

The Royal Armoured Corps.

The Reconnaissance Corps.

Notes

Chapter 1

1. *In Harbour* (by unknown author), quoted in Kenneth Chadwick, *The Royal Tank Regiment* (Leo Cooper, 1970), p. 78.
2. The movement was, on the whole, extremely impressive. The first staff officers crossed the Channel on 4 September, stores and advance parties started to move on 10 September and the main fighting units on the 22nd. By 11 October 158,000 men and 25,000 vehicles had been shipped, including the 4 divisional cavalry regiments and 4RTR as the sole Infantry tank regiment; 7RTR followed in early May.
3. Divisional cavalry regiments were equipped with twenty-eight Light tanks and forty-four scout carriers, organized in three sabre squadrons. These units were not equipped to deal with the heavier German tanks, and even the Panzer II with its 20mm cannon was more than a match for the Light tanks.
4. In some cases, during the battle, half-charge Boys ammunition used in training was inadvertently issued, which was unable to penetrate any sort of armour. Gregory Blaxland, *Destination Dunkirk* (Pen & Sword, 2018), p. 116.
5. The severe winter, the worst for years, also forced Hitler to delay his intended offensive from November until the spring.
6. 1st Fife & Forfar Yeomanry, 1st Lothian & Border Yeomanry and 1st East Riding of Yorkshire Yeomanry. All three had been RTC armoured car companies during the inter-war period.
7. 1st ARB: ERY & 1FFY. 2nd ARB: 5DG & 15/19H.
8. To be fair to the French, the majority of senior German generals also thought it impossible. It took the persistence of General von Manstein, chief of staff of Army Group A, to convince firstly his boss Guderian and then Hitler to get the strike through the region added to the plan in late February 1940.
9. Blaxland, *Destination Dunkirk*, p. 57.
10. Blaxland, *Destination Dunkirk*, p. 75.
11. In a throw-back to the previous war, 12L also made use of pigeons, although how useful they really were is not recorded.

12. It must have been galling for the units, being forced to withdraw without having fought their battle and without having been defeated.

13. J.M. Brereton, *History of the 4th/7th Royal Dragoon Guards* (4/7DG, 1982), pp. 368–9. Smart was awarded a well-deserved MM.

14. According to Blaxland: 'The Lancers maintained wireless touch better than anyone'. Blaxland, *Destination Dunkirk*, p. 97.

15. Note: modern Belgian place names often differ from those used in 1940.

16. C Sqn had four troops, whilst A and B Sqns only had a single troop each. They started the campaign with eighteen troops.

17. The reason for the profusion of 37mm-sized guns lay in the 1868 St Petersburg Declaration, which had outlawed the use of explosive filling in shells weighing less than 400g, just under a pound, which in practice meant a maximum calibre of about 1½in or 37mm.

18. P.F. Stewart, *History of the XII Lancers* (OUP, 1950), p. 370.

19. German comments after the campaign spoke in glowing terms of the fortitude of the British soldiers, and included the Territorials in this assessment. Sheer guts could not overcome materiel and training deficiencies, however.

20. All six Light tanks were knocked out on 24 May, in an action in which Lieutenant Furness, commanding the Carrier platoon of 1st Bn Welsh Guards, won the VC using his vehicles' mobility to attach a defensive position.

21. At the end of the campaign the overall strength of the *Panzerwaffe* had decreased by 13 per cent – but Hitler clearly realized the advantages that the tanks had brought to the campaign. On 23 June he ordered that thirty-five infantry divisions were to be disbanded or placed into suspended animation, but that the number of tank and mechanized divisions was to be doubled.

22. Lieutenant Ussher, a troop leader with 5DG, recorded elsewhere how grateful he was to have his own Michelin touring maps; the issued maps, where they were available, were 'hopelessly out-of-date Great War editions', C.J. Boardman, *Tracks in Europe (5 DG)* (City Press, 1990), p. 39.

23. It was reported that Armit's Matilda was hit no less than thirty-six times. He later wrote that because of the damage it was decided that his tank should be replaced by one from the RAOC spare pool, but before this could happen, a road move over cobbles caused the turret to split down a line weakened by eight anti-tank gun hits! One observer thought that Armit should have received the VC for his conduct that day, but 'as so often, his action was not observed by anyone senior enough to recommend him'. Tim Strickland, *Strick: Tank Hero of Arras* (Casemate, 2021), p. 54.

24. Lieutenant Colonel Fitzmaurice of 4RTR was killed when his Light tank was hit by artillery, and Lieutenant Colonel Heyland of 7RTR died when trying to use hand signals to restore order to his tanks; he was shot dead when outside the cover of his tank.

25. Later, an unclear order told the regiment to destroy its tanks; it started to comply but was then ordered to stop after five had been set on fire, leaving only nine Cruisers intact.

26. The tanks could not even use their smoke dischargers to provide some cover, as no smoke ammunition for the weapons had been issued.

27. At one point all of 3rd Brigade's remaining tanks were *hors de combat*, in workshops undergoing essential repairs and maintenance.

28. Reported as being fourteen A13 Cruisers and twelve Light tanks.

29. Losses to June 1940 totalled 691: Mk VIb x 345, VIc x 62, A9 x 24, A10 x 31, A11 x 97, A12 x 29, A13 x 103. (This includes 3 Light tanks of C Sqn 3H sent to Norway in early May 1940, but which were sunk en route.)

30. David Fletcher summed up the situation thus: 'Without a captured German tank of their own to evaluate under controlled conditions, the British could only fall back on rumours, highly coloured opinions, and vivid imagination to explain their defeat. From this early debacle … can be traced the origins of the Panzer myth that soon permeated all allied armies to the end of the war and beyond. A formidable legend had been born.' It would be nearly a year before the 88mm gun was identified as the weapon which could overcome even the heavily armoured Matilda II.

31. Daniel Todman, *Britain's War: Into Battle 1937–1941* (Penguin, 2016), pp. 329–30.

32. Basil Collier, *The Defence of the United Kingdom* (IWM, 1957), p. 124.

33. David French, *Raising Churchill's Army* (OUP, 2000), p. 275.

34. Pope recommended appointing an 'armoured adviser' to formations. In this he was also wrong, what was needed was a generation of front-line generals who knew how to command armour themselves, and not have to rely upon an 'adviser'.

Chapter 2

1. Left behind were around 11,000 machine guns, 2,500 artillery pieces, 64,000 vehicles and nearly 700 tanks, plus 77,000 tons of ammunition and 165,000 tons of petrol. In May 1940 only 138 new tanks of all types were produced in the UK, and for the next 2 months the rate of production actually fell.

2. Between June and August 1940, over 320,000 men joined the army, with the majority going to the infantry. Todman, *Britain's War*, p. 598.

3. For example, the Armoured Replacement Groups, the Armoured Delivery Regiments and Squadrons, the Forward Delivery Squadrons, the Armoured Reinforcement Units, Tank Delivery Units etc. In addition, it should also be noted that small units were formed to provide tanks in such locations as Gibraltar, Cyprus and Malta, which, although classed as operational for defence purposes, were never put to the test.

4. For example, in the lead up to Second Alamein, a fictitious 74th Armoured Brigade was created, comprising the equally fictitious 39, 118 and 124RTR.

5. The lineage of the cavalry regiments is tortuous; at the peak of the Napoleonic Wars there had been thirty-three regiments of light cavalry, variously described as Light Dragoons, Hussars and Lancers. The 22nd, 24th and 25th regiments had last existed in 1819. The 23rd was disbanded in 1817 (having been renumbered from the 26th in 1803) and the 27th in 1803.

6. For example, the 23rd Hussars became the senior regiment within 29th Armoured Brigade in 1944/45, despite 3RTR being a regular army battalion.

7. There is no doubt that some of the war raised cavalry, yeomanry and RAC regiments were disbanded not because of any failing on their part, but because the War Office would not contemplate retaining them whilst simultaneously disbanding regular regiments. For example, the amalgamation of the 3rd and 4th CLY was in part brought about by the need to get 5DG into action in Normandy, and 2NY were replaced by 15/19H within 11th Armoured Division in August 1944.

8. The Battalion Technical Adjutant was the specialist equipment manager. This was not a job for the faint-hearted, as the equipment availability of the unit was on his shoulders. The BTA course was eight weeks long, with four weeks spent on D&M engineering, and another four weeks learning the procedural side. In modern parlance, the BTA was a cross between the OC LAD and the QM(T).

9. Unfortunately, in the time-honoured tradition of the army, many of these volunteers proved to be the 'problem children' from the infantry units, and although some became good tank soldiers, the majority needed to be replaced with new recruits from the UK before the regiment could become effective.

10. At the time, the Royal Tank Regiment battalions were generally abbreviated as 'RTanks', but for consistency with the modern use of 'RTR' post-war, the latter is used in this work.

11. Eight of these had existed as Armoured Car Companies of the RTC between the wars, giving them a head start when the time for true mechanization eventually came.

12. This had happened in the First World War, with the 2nd or duplicate unit intended to remain in UK and act as the home base for recruiting, training etc. In the Second World War this distinction was abandoned, and all units were made operational and liable for overseas service.

13. When the six wartime cavalry regiments were subsequently raised between December 1940 and February 1941, they took precedence after the 17/21L and before the NIH.

14. The TA did not have units in Northern Ireland until 1947. The equivalent units in Ulster were known as Special Reserve, renamed as Militia from 1 October 1921.

15. Some units referred to themselves as being disbanded, others as being ordered to disperse or placed into suspended animation prior to disbandment – the effect was the same: the unit ran down its personnel and equipment until it ceased to exist. Some units still existed de facto but not de jure for a few weeks or days after the official day of extinction.

16. The official RAC record lists the date of formation as 13 July, but this probably reflects the date when the decision to amalgamate was made.

17. In the odd case some battalions were reconverted even before any meaningful training had been undertaken, which must have bewildered the soldiers involved.

18. Part of the defending force at Habbaniya was two RAF armoured car squadrons, still equipped with the First World War-era Rolls-Royce armoured cars.

19. The Syria campaign was strategically important, and conducted with minimum resources. In 1941 the 4th Cavalry Brigade (still horsed) became the basis of Habforce in Iraq, with the two remaining horsed cavalry brigades garrisoning Syria. Habforce comprised 1HCR, RWY and WY. In August 1941, the cavalry division was disbanded, with its units mechanized and becoming the 10th Armoured Division.

20. According to the regimental histories, in October 1941 there was some high-level talk of forming a second Guards Armoured Division, but nothing came of it.

21. The 6th Brigade began life as an armoured brigade, changing its designation to become a tank brigade in January 1943 and then back to armoured in February 1945.

22. In 1935 the course had lasted thirty-five weeks, so no doubt many RTC soldiers saw the reduction in training time in 1938 as destroying standards.

23. When the Recce Corps passed to the RAC, both of its training centres were closed, and a combined centre opened in their place in Catterick.

24. Barnard Castle was a large centre of training activity, with five training regiments there; some accounts link the place to Catterick, as that garrison was quite close.

25. Kenneth Macksey, *A History of the Royal Armoured Corps 1914–1975* (Newtown, 1983), p. 141 and George Forty, *Bovington Tanks* (Wincanton Press, 1988), pp. 63–70.

26. Today usually known as Basic or Phase One Training.

27. Norman Smith, *Tank Soldier* (The Book Guild, 1989), pp. 25–6.

28. This system lasted until 1948, when the Primary Training Wings and Centres were closed down, and all basic military training was once more conducted within the corps' training regiments.

29. Smith, *Tank Soldier*, p. 29.

30. RAC six-monthly report No. 9.

31. Smith, *Tank Soldier*, p. 38. Smith noted that his choice was 'based on nothing more substantial than the glamorous sounding name of the regiment'. (The 5th Royal Inniskilling Dragoon Guards.) See also Edward Wilson, *Press On Regardless (5RTR)* (Spellmount, 2003), p. 307. Most recruits had no knowledge of any of the regiments, so they often selected them on the basis of staying with their mates or because they liked the look of the cap badge!

32. Peter Beale, *Tank Tracks (9RTR)* (Budding, 1995), pp. 3–4.

33. Each regiment required four officer and seventeen NCO instructors in D&M, the same numbers for gunnery, and four officers and twelve NCO instructors in wireless. From this it can be seen that every troop was meant to have an NCO instructor in both D&M and gunnery, and the majority of troops would also have a wireless instructor. The officer instructors were meant to oversee their discipline at the squadron level.

34. Wilson, *Press On Regardless*, p. 189.

35. Wilson, *Press On Regardless*, p. 347.

36. Abbassia was also the barracks from whence a young Winston Churchill set out for the Battle of Omdurman in 1898! During the Second World War it became the location of the Middle East RAC School and Base Depot.

37. Fred Thompson, 'India: The RAC Depot Poona September 1943', *Tank Magazine*, Vol. 86, No. 767.

38. '*Selection of Potential Officers*', 1941.

39. Todman, *Britain's War*, p. 267.

40. '*Selection of Potential Officers*', 1941.

41. When the Oriel College site was closed down in 1944, there was an outcry, and a new RAC Tactical School (with reduced capacity) was opened up in Lulworth, where it remained into the post-war period.

42. Cavalry units still horsed (Royals and Greys) sent their cadets to 3rd Cavalry Regt OCTU in Edinburgh.

43. The NCOs from the IoC were used as assistant instructors, and in due course the majority of them were commissioned without having to undergo the training themselves.

44. On 20 January 1943, the name changed again to 100 (Sandhurst) OCTU RAC.

45. Lieutenant John Langdon was in the 1st Reinforcement Unit (RAC) in Olivetti, outside Tripoli in July 1943 when he applied to join 3RTR based on a recommendation from an infantry major; he was lucky enough to be granted his wish. On the other hand, Lieutenant Eric Stevenson was commissioned at Sandhurst in May 1944, and initially sent to the 'infamous and enormous' RAC Holding unit at Catterick, where he expected to remain for some time. However, within 30 minutes of his arrival, he found himself put on a train bound for an unknown destination. On arrival he had to ask his new CO which regiment he had just joined, and was told it was 5RTR. Wilson, *Press On Regardless*, pp. 306–7.

46. These figures are for British cadets only. About 600 more were commissioned into other Allied armoured forces, the majority being Canadian.

47. The Guards Division always operated their own PO system in the form of the notorious 'Brigade Squad', at the Guards Depot.

Chapter 3

1. Also in the division was the so-called Pivot Group (later renamed the Support Group), containing the Royal Artillery and infantry. Divisional troops included the RE, RASC, RAOC and RAMC.

2. Michael Carver, *Dilemmas of the Desert War* (Batsford, 1986), p. 13.

3. In May 1943, the KDG war diary recorded that the journey from Cairo to Tunis took seven days.

4. Navigation was greatly aided by the invention of the sun compass.

5. Hobart's dismissal is a tale in itself, and reflected badly on those who conspired to have him removed. He was undoubtedly a prickly character, and was too fond of the 'all tank' idea, but the course of the early desert war might well have been different had he remained in command; we shall never know. Robin Neillands summed him up nicely: 'He was not the most tactful of men, and the combination of being both right and successful was bound to make him enemies.', Robin Neillands, *Eighth Army* (John Murray, 2004), p. 11.

6. Italian Libya consisted of three provinces, the two coastal ones, Cyrenaica (east) and Tripolitania (west), were the sites of most of the battles. The term Libya is used here for convenience.

7. Richard Brett-Smith, *The 11th Hussars* (Leo Cooper, 1969), p. 227.

8. WDF, later to become the Eighth Army. The Western Desert was the British term for northern Egypt and Libya, whereas the Eastern Desert referred to Sinai, the River Nile being the dividing line between the two.

9. Over 130,000 prisoners were captured during Compass.

10. French, *Raising Churchill's Army*, p. 214.
11. The battleground was famously referred to by the captured German von Ravenstein of 21st Panzer Division in November 1941 as 'the tactician's paradise, but the quartermaster's hell'.
12. *RAC Journal*, April 1952, pp. 93–4.
13. The Italian Ariete armoured division was also despatched at about this time.
14. In a later book on the desert war, he even referred to 'some A9s dragged out of various war museums and exhibitions', a blatant exaggeration but reflecting the contempt in which he held the pre-war designs, Bob Crisp, *Brazen Chariots (3 RTR)* (Norton, 1959), p. 15.
15. John Grehan and Martin Mace, *Operations in North Africa and the Middle East 1939–1942* (Pen & Sword, 2015), p. 42. It must be noted that the vehicles arrived in no condition to fight. A problem that persisted for much of the war was the terrible way in which tanks were loaded for shipping, often being damaged in transit, batteries drained and tools and equipment stolen. On arrival, each tank needed many days of work to make the necessary modifications for desert warfare, as well as repairs caused by the voyage.
16. Just before the Germans struck, even this formation was severely understrength. 5RTR had only twenty-three cruisers out of fifty-two available, and 3H twenty-nine Light tanks instead of thirty-six – B Sqn was in Crete. 6RTR, with their diesel-powered Italian tanks, had only managed to form one squadron.
17. 'Rommel' is used as shorthand for the combined Italian and German forces from this point on, although this fails to portray the complicated command relationship within the Axis forces, in which Rommel was nominally under Italian command.
18. Grehan and Mace, *Operations in North Africa and the Middle East 1939– 1942*, p. 42.
19. The first German tank losses took place in an engagement with 5RTR which was attempting to block the German advance. Two Panzer IIIs and one Panzer IV of the 2nd Abteilung of Panzer Regiment 5 were knocked out, their fuel tanks being hit and the tanks burned out. For the loss of the three tanks the British lost five, which may have seemed a favourable rate of attrition at the time, but over the coming months would increasingly be seen by the Germans as unsustainable in view of the overwhelming materiel superiority of the British.
20. Until September 1941 the unfortunate 3rd Armoured Brigade was the controlling armour HQ in Tobruk. Following heavy loses, it was disbanded, and the remnants absorbed by the newly created 32nd Tank Brigade.
21. 6RTR, freshly equipped with the new Crusader, had just nine still running. 2RTR was still using the older Cruiser models.

22. All three armoured brigades were within XXX Corps, whilst XIII Corps had only the 1st Tank Brigade.

23. Part of the plan was to use 70th Infantry Division, part of the Tobruk garrison, to break out and act as a cut-off to retreating Axis forces. Tobruk therefore remained a magnet to the British commanders, drawing troops towards it.

24. The desert, more rock than sand, required blasting before troops could dig in, and therefore fire trenches and weapon pits were generally shallow, exposing the occupants to direct and indirect fire, as well as air attack.

25. At the start of Gazala, it is estimated that Rommel had about 240 Panzer III, 30 Panzer IV and nearly 300 lighter Panzer II and Italian tanks of various types. His armoured cars were generally better armed than the Allied counterparts but were no match for tanks of any type. The Allies possessed around 800 tanks, including 167 Grants, but many units still had to use the outclassed 2-pounder Crusaders and 37mm Stuarts, and the tank brigades still had the slow and obsolescent Matildas and Valentines, again armed with the 2-pounder.

26. As happened later in Italy and again North-West Europe, the 88mm usually took the credit/blame, whereas in most cases it was the smaller and more easily concealed 50mm and 75mm guns, as well as captured Russian 76.2mm guns used as self-propelled artillery, that did the majority of the damage.

27. Sir Baker Creed Russell KCMG CB, https://www.1879zuluwar.com.

28. French, *Raising Churchill's Army*, p. 223.

29. Lumsden, a hero of the BEF as a lieutenant colonel in 1940, found himself promoted to acting lieutenant general and commander of XXX Corps in 1942. He clashed with Montgomery and was sacked after Second Alamein and, bizarrely, was killed on the bridge of the USS *New Mexico* in January 1945 by a kamikaze attack.

30. Brian Horrocks, *A Full Life* (Collins, 1960), p. 138. The lesson had to be learned by other regiments: 16/5L conducted a charge 'in the old cavalry style' at Bordj in Tunisia on 11 April 1943. In the light of confusion over tactics, and a lack of realization of the importance of fire and movement, the practice also could be seen in the UK. Timothy Place recounts how the Guards Armoured Division in particular seemed to place great emphasis on charges during training in summer 1942, and that 20th Armoured Brigade did likewise – as a complete brigade – in July. Timothy Harrison Place, *Military Training in the British Army 1940–1944* (Frank Cass, 2000), p. 108.

31. Carver, *Dilemmas*, p. 131.

32. This was the sixth VC won by members of the RTR and its predecessors since 1917, and each of them had one factor in common: all the officers had

spent a significant amount of time outside their tanks, on foot. Whereas many awards have been made to officers of the RN and RAF when commanding ships, submarines and aircraft, there seems to be a systemic reluctance to award the VC to soldiers mounted in AFVs.

33. The crisis caused the three Valentine regiments in 23rd Armoured Brigade, which arrived at Suez on the 6th, to be hurriedly thrown into the offensive on the 17th, with entirely predictable results.

34. A possibly apocryphal story about Monty sums this up. He was being driven in his staff car past a column of lorries and noticed a driver who was stark naked apart from a top hat and his boots. Feeling that for once he had to issue an order on the subject of dress, the order simply stated that, 'Top hats are not to be worn in Eighth Army'!

35. It is this author's contention that this lesson has been entirely forgotten over the decades. Although the modern army espouses a philosophy of Mission Command, emphasizing devolved action at the lowest levels, it is not practised because of the dictatorship of modern technology. The staff work able to be generated by an inflated headquarters in which every staff officer sits at a PC and produces reams of paperwork, results in operations orders which take hours or even days to compose, are inches thick, full of unnecessary detail and entirely useless to the fighting soldier. This will be the undoing of the field army against an agile enemy.

36. Six examples of the Churchill Mk III Infantry tank also took part in the battle, as 'Kingforce', under the command of Major Norris King MC, RGH; unfamiliarity with the design led to some of them being hit by friendly fire during the battle.

37. Neillands, *Eighth Army*, p. 181.

38. By this time Rommel had lost his invaluable radio–intercept company, and British voice procedure had become somewhat more secure, adding greater security to the operation.

39. Carver, *Dilemmas*, p. 143.

40. P.W. Pitt, *Royal Wilts 1920–1945 (RWY)* (NMP, n.d.), pp. 136–43. The RWilts were organized with A Sqn in Shermans and C Sqn in Grants as the two 'heavy' squadrons, and B, the 'light' squadron, in Crusaders.

41. An order given to the CO 3H who protested about the plan.

42. Rommel had been at home on sick leave when Second Alamein was started, but hurried back to take command.

43. Armoured formations, notably 1st and 7th Armoured Divisions, were transferred from 8th to 1st Army during the campaign, an unwelcome move for the seasoned desert warriors.

44. The Infantry tank Mk IV Churchill came close to being scrapped when it was first introduced (in haste) in 1941, being notoriously unreliable as only British tanks could. However, it was extensively reworked, and the reliability

problems solved, becoming well-loved by its crews for its protection and spaciousness. It was used as the basis for many of 79th Armoured Division's 'Funnies', which cemented its place in history.

45. Strickland, *Strick*, p. 129.
46. Peter Gudgin, *With Churchills to War (48RTR)* (Sutton Publishing, 1996), p. 101.
47. On average, when a tank (of any type) was hit, one crewman would be killed or injured.
48. Crisp, *Brazen Chariots*, pp. 46–7, 92–3, 113.
49. Horrocks, *A Full Life*, pp. 115–16.
50. Lieutenant Colonel Martin, '42RTR History 1938–1944' (privately published, n.d.).
51. One area where the Germans enjoyed a marked superiority over the British for the whole of the war was in the production of optics, particularly those used for the gunner's sights. Famous German optical firms such as Zeiss and Leica made the sighting telescopes for German tanks, with two major advantages over the British equivalents. Firstly, the quality of the optical glass was maintained at an excellent standard, and, secondly, they tended to employ much higher powers of magnification than the British equivalents. The gunner's Leica-made TZF5 telescope on the Panzer III used a magnification of x 2.5, on the Panther the TFZ12 had selectable magnification of x 2.5 or x 5, whereas the British tanks for much of the war used only x 1 (no magnification), or a maximum of x 1.9, only moving to a standard of x 3 in late 1944. Additionally, British crews complained that the aiming markings inscribed within their sights were too thick, so that at 1,000yd the intended target was completely obscured by the marks, making precise aiming impossible. As late as 1944 British tank crews were still investigating knocked-out German tanks and marvelling at the quality of their optics.
52. Crisp, *Brazen Chariots*, p. 21.
53. The Grant was the British 'export' version of the M3 Lee, with a different turret that allowed the radio to be carried inside, in accordance with British doctrine.
54. Horrocks, *A Full Life*, p. 132.
55. B.H. Liddell Hart, *The Rommel Papers* (Da Capo Press, 1953), Ch. XI.
56. For example, most infantry divisions lacked anything like sufficient transport, meaning that they became immobile. And such lorries as were owned could not be kept within the defensive boxes, as they were far too vulnerable to artillery fire, meaning that they had to be kept well to the rear, exacerbating the problem and preventing rapid moves.
57. Niall Barr, *Pendulum of War: The Three Battles of Alamein* (Overlook, 2005), p. 411.

Chapter 4

1. The glacis of the early marks was 102mm, 4in, which matched the Tiger 1. The later Mk VII and VIII had 150mm.
2. The crews preferred the smaller Dingo, for its better armour and ability to reverse quickly.
3. Legend has it that this was because when the first one was taken for a 'spin' after arriving in Egypt, the driver climbed out and stated, 'She's a honey!'
4. At the very end of the war a few recce troops in armoured regiments received US M24 Chaffee Light tanks, fast and armed with a 75mm gun. The Skins noted, 'If only we had had them for the Normandy campaign. I had no training on these vehicles and spent much time reading the instruction book.' Boardman, *Tracks*, p. 245.
5. The first examples of the M3 arrived in Egypt in November 1941, but as a completely new type required extensive training delivered by US army instructors before they could be used early the following year. The RAC also operated a smaller number of Lees alongside the more numerous Grants, both in North Africa and in the Far East.
6. The MG itself wasn't useless, but the mounting made it difficult to use by an overworked commander.
7. Leading it to be allegedly known as the 'Ronson' by the Allies (after the popular cigarette lighter advertised as 'lights first every time'), it was apparently called the 'Tommy Cooker' by the Germans. The fault, thought to be due to its fuel, was in fact much more related to poor protection of ammunition.
8. It is difficult to make direct comparisons, but REME figures for The Great Swan of autumn 1944 seem to indicate that the Cromwell was half as likely to breakdown as the Sherman. During the same period, Sherman breakdowns in the brigades within the armoured divisions and independent armoured brigades requiring workshop attention were as follows: Guards AD 59, 11th AD 44, 1st Polish AD 50, 8th AB 57, 4th Canadian AB 57, an average of 53. For 7th Armoured Division, the only formation operating Cromwells, the figure was 38. One report stated that the Fireflies in Cromwell units were unable to keep up with the British Cruisers.
9. For more details of ammunition development, see Appendix C.
10. 9L recorded being issued the first twelve 76mm Shermans, along with six 105mm Shermans, in August 1944 in Italy.
11. After the war, for a period in the late 1940s and early 1950s, some RAC regiments were equipped with M10s in what were known as Divisional Armoured Regiments, supporting infantry divisions.

Chapter 5

1. The remainder of 46RTR was still converting to Shermans and arrived on the 22nd.
2. The armoured brigade HQs did not arrive until later in the campaign.
3. The *PanzerFaust* was improved throughout the war, but its range remained limited to about 30m or less; it could penetrate around 200mm of armour. The *PanzerSchreck* had a similar penetration but a greater range of up to 150m; it did, however, create a distinctive back-blast.
4. The Desert Rats would only be in Italy for two months, and the division was withdrawn on 19 November in order to be sent back to the UK.
5. The Apennines are not central but are closer to the Adriatic, meaning that the coastal plain on the western (US) side is about twice as wide as that on the eastern, British side.
6. Neillands, *Eighth Army*, p. 342.
7. As an illustration of just how steep and inaccessible the terrain was – and thus impassable for tanks – was the fact that, increasingly, mule trains had to be employed as the only method of getting supplies to the forward troops, a process of reverse-mechanization.
8. Neillands, *Eighth Army*, p. 303.
9. The 16th/5th Lancers reported that of their seventeen months in Italy, '[for not more] than five were we employed in conditions that an armoured regiment enjoys'.
10. Joan Bright, *The 9th Queens Royal Lancers 1936–1945* (Naval & Military Press, n.d.), p. 169.
11. Gudgin, *With Churchills to War*, p. 126.
12. The lessons of Anzio were not lost on those preparing Operation Overlord. Montgomery, on first seeing the plan for the Normandy invasion, realized that much more combat power was required and increased the number of landing areas to five, spread over a larger area and thus making it impossible for the Germans to counter-attack with sufficient strength simultaneously.
13. Morale took a dip when the troops in Italy were outrageously accused of being 'D-Day Dodgers, always drinking vino, always on the spree.' It did become clear to them that they were no longer on the main effort.
14. This was a great improvement in firepower, as well as simplifying ammunition supply. The officer who suggested the conversion, Captain Morrell REME, was only allowed to carry out the project on the understanding that if it failed, his career would be over! It worked, he was promoted to major and awarded the MBE. David Fletcher, *Mr Churchill's Tank* (Schiffer, 1999), pp. 157–9.
15. Neillands, *Eighth Army*, pp. 345–6.
16. Neillands, *Eighth Army*, p. 374.

17. At the end of October 1944, the 10th Hussars was delighted to receive its first Sherman Firefly tanks equipped with the excellent 17-pounder gun, which until then had been prioritized for NWE.

18. Anon., *1st Derbyshire Yeomanry Scrapbook 1939–1947* (Bemrose, 1947), p. 105. The crews did return, complete with twenty-three German parachutists as prisoners.

19. This was common practice. The Fifth Skins in NWE called theirs 'sawn-off', and fitted two .30in Browning MGs to them.

20. Anon., *The 10th Royal Hussars in the Second World War* (Gale & Polden, 1948), pp. 160–1.

21. G.M.O. Davy, *The Seventh and Three Enemies (7th Hussars)* (Naval & Military Press, 2014), p. 336.

22. Only 46RTR went to Greece with their Shermans, including one squadron of armoured cars. The other two units, 40 and 50 RTR, were reorganized as infantry battalions.

Chapter 6

1. The Cromwell had a 57in diameter ring, the Sherman had 69in and the German Mk IV 64in.

2. Sealing a rivetted hull could be achieved with Bostik sealant but was a laborious process. It was much easier using a welded hull, which in mid–war were entering production and made the waterproofing task very much easier.

3. The D-Day RAC units operating DD Shermans (two squadrons each) were 4/7DG, 13/18H and SRY.

4. In some armies, command tanks had their main armament removed and replaced with a dummy barrel to allow more space in the turret. British practice was to retain the gun to allow the tank to fight if necessary, resulting in a compromise between the space inside needed for the gun, ammunition and the communications equipment.

5. At the start of its life, it was sometimes referred to as an *Assault* Vehicle Royal Engineers.

6. During the war some RA anti-aircraft searchlight batteries were employed to reflect their light off the underside of low clouds, in order to increase the ambient light, and were sometimes known as 'Monty's Moonlight'. In the late 1950s Centurion tanks were modified to mount 22in searchlights on the gun mantlet, which could operate either as 'white light' or with an infrared filter; this was to allow shooting at night, rather than as a dazzle device. Chieftain had a similar 19in Light Projector fitted as standard within a lightly armoured box on the turret side, and both Chieftain (as an upgrade) and Challenger tanks were fitted with the TOGS thermal imaging night-fighting system. This will be discussed in more detail in Volume 3.

7. Once made reliable, the large, well-armoured and spacious Churchill became the preferred basis for many of the Funnies.

8. Later, C Sqn 7RTR deployed with Crocodiles to Korea in 1950.

9. The Germans operated a huge and bewildering fleet of vehicles, wheeled and tracked, many of which were based on captured types: British, French, Russian, Czech etc. They did develop some ingenious devices, including the Goliath remote-control unmanned demolition vehicle, as well as some flamethrowing and deep-wading tanks, but nothing on the scale of the British effort.

10. In early 1945 it had under command 5 brigades (17 regiments), 21,430 men and 1,566 tracked AFVs.

11. The Linney Head (Castlemartin) complex became the range of choice and was unable to satisfy the demand. After investigating Anglesey, eventually Minehead was chosen as the site for a new range complex and opened in August 1942. Both Castlemartin and Minehead were then handed over for sole use by the US army in 1943. Lulworth (Bindon) range became unsuitable as it could not be used for engagements over 2,000yd, leading to the acquisition of the Heath ranges area in late 1943, more than quadrupling its size and allowing shoots of up to 4,500yd. The evacuation of Tyneham village to allow this was not necessary, as a lack of manpower meant that the additional ranges did not come into use before the end of the war, so the profit was only realized later.

12. Notwithstanding this, many of these officers chose to go into action in a tank as the ninth crewman, crammed in behind the commander, and General Elles of course spent the first part of the Battle of Cambrai within Hilda of H Battalion.

13. During the Second World War, the sabre squadron SSMs and the RSM in RHQ were all mounted in tanks.

14. In October 1938, in an attempt to compensate for a shortfall in junior officers, the rank of WOIII was created to allow experienced SNCOs to take the appointment of TSM: Troop Sergeant Major, and thus officially command a troop. The influx of wartime commissions removed the requirement for these, and the remaining WOIIIs were allowed to 'waste out' after 1940. Another 'funny' was the rank of lance sergeant; this was used to promote corporals to become sergeants but without pay.

15. Under armour all crew positions were roughly as dangerous when hit, with only slight variations due to different vehicle types. Commanders were the one crew position that had to spend more time out of the tank, either partially or fully, when in action, hence the higher casualty rate.

16. The first official crew commander courses were not started until November 1943, and there is little record of them, thus not allowing a detailed look at the syllabus.

17. During the Second World War, a total of 15,225 MMs were awarded, with 177 bars, denoting a second award. Fred Kite, recommended for a DCM, had it downgraded by Montgomery to a third MM, a unique achievement.
18. Alan Brooke, *War Diaries* (Phoenix, 2001), pp. 186–90.
19. They would come to change their minds regarding the Cromwell, but that was in the future.
20. G.L. Verney, *The Desert Rats* (Hutchinson, 1954) , p. 180.
21. Patrick Delaforce, *Battles with Panzers (1 & 2RTR)* (Sutton Publishing, 2003), p. 92.
22. William Moore, *Panzer Bait (3RTR)* (Leo Cooper, 1991), p. 124. Geordie Reay was badly burned when his tank was hit by a German SPG during Operation Epsom, in part because he remained on the burning tank to pull his gunner, Trooper Eatock, out of the turret.

Chapter 7

1. This book is about the British experience, but it would be churlish to not at least record the presence in Normandy, using British organization and tactics, of the Canadian armour: the 4th Canadian Armoured Division and the 2nd Canadian Armoured Brigade, as well as Polish and Czech formations. Within the Sherman-equipped armoured divisions, the armoured recce regiment was equipped with Cromwells and, in the Cromwell-equipped 7th Armoured Division, the extra punch of the 17-pounder gun could only be included by equipping them with a Sherman Firefly per troop. The attempt to up-gun the Cromwell by designing the A30 Challenger was not a great success.
2. The lack of DD tanks precluded all three squadrons being equipped with DDs, although this had the advantage that the third squadron, landed conventionally, could include Fireflies.
3. All timings are in the time used for the operation, British Double Summer Time.
4. The third regiment in 8th Armoured Brigade, the 24th Lancers, landed conventionally on D-Day and D+1.
5. As part of the pre-landing procedures, each tank operator had to 'tune and net' the No. 19 radio, which cannot have been easy in a pitching LCT, controlled by cold and clammy fingers.
6. Stephen Napier, *The Armoured Campaign in Normandy* (Spellmount, 2015), pp. 18–26.
7. By 22 June 2nd Army had managed to land 326,5000 men, over 57,000 vehicles and 133,000 tons of stores. By the end of July over 150,000 vehicles had been landed, along with nearly 700,000 personnel.
8. The Corps' armoured car units in June 1944 were as follows: I Corps: Inns of Court Yeomanry; VIII Corps: 2HCR; XII Corps: The Royals; XXX Corps: 11th Hussars.

9. Historians argue over the final date of the Normandy campaign, as clearing up operations continued beyond this date.

10. The whole issue of 'battle-hardened and experienced' regiments is a tricky one to quantify. Reinforcements and replacements were a matter of life, particularly after action, and so the personnel element of a regiment was constantly changing. The key was to retain sufficient personnel in senior and command positions to be able to distil the experience into the new personnel, particularly the replacement officers.

11. The wooden gun barrels were used for deception, as the 75mm guns were removed to give much more space for radios and signallers needed for the OP task. If there was one consolation it was that the OP Shermans did not catch fire as easily as the gun tanks, as they did not carry ammunition.

12. Importantly, he failed to destroy his own tank as orders specified, presumably because he had confidence that the British would be thrown out of the town, and it could then be repaired.

13. Napier, *The Armoured Campaign in Normandy*, pp. 127–8.

14. Although the various reports are confused and often contradictory, it seems that Wittmann's Tiger was hit six times by 75mm fire before being disabled by either a 6-pounder or the Firefly. According to an official vulnerability chart issued to crews, the Tiger was only vulnerable to 75mm M61 APCBC at two spots in the rear hull, the tank being invulnerable elsewhere. What was required was – easy to say – to either use AP to disable the tracks or suspension, or to use HE in order to damage sights etc.

15. Napier, *The Armoured Campaign in Normandy*, p. 131.

16. This was Richard O'Connor, who had been captured in North Africa in 1941; he escaped from captivity in Italy in late 1943.

17. Starting with four Panzer Divisions in France, the Germans had already been forced to move two more, 9th and 10th SS Panzer, from Russia to France. Montgomery was aware of this, and was keen to get Epsom moving before they arrived.

18. The Czech Independent Armoured Brigade Group, trained and equipped with two regiments of Cromwells, arrived in August.

19. 3rd and 4th CLY were merged on Carpiquet airfield at the end of July, and fought for the rest of the war as 3/4CLY in 4th Armoured Brigade.

20. Cecil Blacker and Henry Woods, *5th Royal Inniskilling Dragoon Guards: Change & Challenge* (William Clowes, 1978), pp. 46–7.

21. The development of artillery fire control by the British in the Second World War is well worth studying. By 1944, the tactical control of artillery was almost perfect, and for large assaults such as Charnwood, all the guns in range, regardless of who they normally 'belonged' to, could be quickly brought to fire onto a single target.

22. Michael Carver, *Out of Step* (Hutchinson, 1989), pp. 193–4.

23. The best estimate is: 109 Panzer IV; 46 Panther; 35 Stug III; 43 Tiger I; 12 Tiger II; and 30 75mm SPG.

24. G.S. Jackson, *Operations of Eighth Corps* (St Clement's Press, 1948), pp. 76–7.

25. Other RAC units directly involved in Goodwood included 2NY, the Inns of Court, 22D and 2HCR, as well as 22nd Armoured Brigade.

26. Another impact of this lack of space was that the RA field guns would quickly find themselves unable to support the lead elements, until they could be allowed to cross the river and find new gun positions in range. The Luftwaffe made a (fortunately belated) appearance during the night of the 18th/19th, attacking the bridgehead area and causing casualties amongst the replacement tank crews being assembled there.

27. An Ultra intercept from only 36 hours before the operation made it clear that a major attack was expected.

28. The extremely narrow frontage was caused by the terrain, with the city of Caen to the west and a large, wooded area to the east.

29. Subsidiary diversionary attacks named Operations Greenline (15–17 July) and Pomegranate (16–17 July) were launched west of Caen to make the defenders think that the plan was to encircle Caen in a pincer movement. 27th Armoured Brigade plus 144RAC were used to support 3rd and 51st Infantry Divisions in a flank screening operation to the east of Goodwood.

30. 3RTR had G Coy and H Bty; 2FFY F Coy and I Bty; and 23H H Coy and G Bty.

31. French, *Raising Churchill's Army*, p. 245.

32. This had effects in other theatres: in Italy, infantry battalions were reduced from four to three rifle companies in an effort to divert sufficient trained infantrymen to Normandy. Some artillerymen, and anti-aircraft gunners in particular, suddenly found themselves in the infantry battalions. 59th Infantry Division was broken up in late August.

33. For example, in late 1942 the intakes into the various RAC Training Regiments were 2,100 men each month; by 1944 this had dropped to only 900. By the end of 1944 only one RAC formation, 35th Armoured Brigade, remained in the UK.

34. Napier chose to describe it as a 'gentle trot', as it was not conducted at full speed, Napier, *The Armoured Campaign in Normandy*.

35. On 11 July, 3rd Company had ambushed 148RAC in the Colombelles area of Caen, knocking out nine Shermans without loss.

36. John Langdon, *The Sharp End (3RTR)* (privately published, 2003), pp. 44–6. The following day, in a replacement tank with an inexperienced new crew, Langdon was knocked out again, very close to the position where he had been hit the previous day. With no tanks available, he and his crew made their way back to the echelon.

37. Famously, Lieutenant Gorman of the Irish Guards spotted a Tiger II and with a jammed 75mm in his Sherman, rammed it at full speed and then he and his crew bailed out. The Grenadier Guards eventually cleared Cagny by 1930.

38. As soon as the Germans discovered the capability of the Firefly, they made it a priority to try to knock them out first, making the role of a Firefly crew somewhat more hazardous than normal. Attempts were made to conceal their identity, including barrel camouflage and even traversing the turret rear, laying the 17-pounder barrel over the back decks, and fitting a false 75mm gun to the rear of the turret to try to make it look like a standard Sherman. For the Firefly crews in Cromwell regiments, they were even more conspicuous.

39. Jackson, *Operations of Eighth Corps*, p. 100.

40. Strenuous efforts were made overnight to bring the regiments back up to strength with replacement tanks and crews, and by the following day 3RTR had received ten new tanks and was able to create two understrength squadrons, each of ten Shermans, with two in RHQ.

41. These thirty-seven tanks of 2NY were lost over the two days. Where the Allies retained possession of the battlefield, many of the tanks 'knocked out' could be recovered and repaired, with around two-thirds usually able to be put back into action.

42. John Buckley, *British Armour in the Normandy Campaign* (Frank Cass, 2004), p. 36.

43. Over the three days VIII Corps recorded losses of 314 tanks, of which 140 were destroyed. German losses according to Napier were eighty-three tanks and SPGs, roughly equivalent to the strength of a fully equipped panzer division, Napier, *The Armoured Campaign in Normandy*.

44. After the war, O'Connor claimed that he had suggested that some form of Armoured Personnel Carrier, better than the half-track, was needed for the infantry, but was turned down by Dempsey – although it was about to appear, as we shall see. Buckley, *British Armour*, p. 35 and endnote.

45. The GOC, Erskine, and 22nd Armoured Brigade commander, Hinde, were both sacked by Montgomery in early August, along with the XXX Corps commander, Bucknall.

46. The 11th Armoured was only used in Bluecoat as there was no infantry division available for the task. Napier, *The Armoured Campaign in Normandy*, p. 273.

47. French, *Raising Churchill's Army*, p. 272–3.

48. The 11th Armoured had to move 25 miles across the British front, and the Guards no less than 45 miles.

49. Napier, *The Armoured Campaign in Normandy*, p. 272.

50. On the first morning No. 3 Squadron 2nd Gren Gds lost their OC and another tank commander to sniper fire.

51. The expression originates in the First World War, and literally meant being made a civilian. It was still in use in a less literal sense in the Second World War to mean being fired. When Montgomery sacked Lumsden in North Africa, the latter explained it away in his club in London by saying that, 'I've just been sacked because there isn't room in the desert for two cads like Monty and me'.

52. Napier, *The Armoured Campaign in Normandy*, p. 279.

53. Langdon commented that, 'It was the best way we could think of for advancing relatively safely', intimating that it was a locally devised tactic which had not been taught or practised in the UK, John Buckley, *Monty's Men* (Yale University Press, 2013), p. 154.

54. Given the German lack of mobile combat power, what was probably more dangerous were the many small pockets of German infantry armed with anti-tank weapons that had been bypassed during the advance but remained extremely dangerous.

55. Napier, *The Armoured Campaign in Normandy*, p. 277. One of the Germans had in fact suffered track damage which led to it being abandoned about a mile away, after being set afire by the crew.

56. Napier, *The Armoured Campaign in Normandy*, pp. 280–1.

57. Moore, *Panzer Bait*, pp. 163–4.

58. Before the infantry arrived, the commander of the half-squadron, Captain Denny, reported on the radio that the Hussars were finding things 'rather lonely' on the summit! Brian Horrocks, *Corps Commander* (Sidgwick & Jackson, 1977), pp. 34–5.

59. French, *Raising Churchill's Army*, pp. 262–3.

60. Ian Daglish, *Operation Bluecoat* (Leo Cooper, 2003), p. 74.

61. The 5RTR War Diary was nothing if not honest, recording on 17 August, 'Forty fresh reinforcements arrive to replace personnel unsuitable in the unit.'

62. Napier, *The Armoured Campaign in Normandy*, p. 304. Dempsey stated that Bucknall was 'not fit to command a corps in mobile operation'. This is key: many experienced and extremely competent commanders were found to be wanting in the rapidly changing context of armoured warfare, which placed enormous stresses on the commanders and their staff – only the very best would thrive in such an environment.

63. 5RTR took great pride in their nickname of 'The Shitty Fifth', exhibiting a complete and deliberate disregard of dress regulations. Bill Jackson was posted from the 24th Lancers to the Fifth as a reinforcement, and noted that, 'It was quite a shock to someone who'd been expected to always be properly dressed to see this rag-time outfit ... The first man I saw when I reached 9 Troop was wearing a top hat and a monocle on a piece of string. He turned out to be the Troop Corporal.' Another, Trooper Glynn,

habitually went into battle wearing carpet slippers. Wilson, *Press On Regardless*, pp. 373–6.

64. The Battle of Amiens started on 8 August 1918, the so-called 'black day of the German army'.

65. Over the course of the next eight months, 34th Brigade served in both 2nd British and 1st Canadian Armies, and came under the command of no less than nine divisions.

66. In Totalize, the newly landed 1st Polish Armoured Division (Shermans) was used for the first time.

67. The loss of Worthington Force was in some ways the Canadian equivalent of Villers-Bocage, caused by the force getting lost in the dark and attacking the wrong high feature.

68. During the attack, Major David Currie of the South Alberta Regiment was awarded the VC for stubbornly holding onto to an exposed position; once again, the award was linked to him spending much of the time on foot, again showing how reluctant the authorities were to award the VC to mounted soldiers.

69. John Fisher, *Sharpshooter Snapshots (4CLY)* (privately published, 1996), p. 75.

70. Boardman, *Tracks*, p. 132.

71. Boardman, *Tracks*, p. 133.

72. Buckley, *Monty's Men*, p. 166.

73. Wilson, *Press On Regardless*, p. 355.

74. Boardman, *Tracks*, p. 136.

75. French, *Raising Churchill's Army*, p. 241.

76. Vehicle casualties were classed as X, meaning repairable within the unit; Y, meaning work required in the second-line workshops; and Z, or write-off. Gudgin, *With Churchills to War*, pp. 94–5.

77. Langdon, *Sharp End*, p. 33. One of the great advantages of the five-man tank was that the maintenance load was shared out. In particular, the co-driver helped the driver in leaguers and could also take turns at driving, particularly on route marches and when out of action.

78. Boardman, *Tracks*, pp. 156–7.

79. Wilson, *Press On Regardless*, p. 327.

80. Langdon, *Sharp End*, p. 44.

81. Langdon, *Sharp End*, p. 40.

82. Fisher, *Sharpshooter Snapshots*, p. 115.

83. The danger from airburst was increased because of the tendency to conceal armoured formations from aerial reconnaissance by leaguering up in woods. It has been estimated that as many casualties were caused by wood splinters when trees were hit, as from metal shell fragments.

84. Bill Close, *Tank Commander (3 RTR)* (Pen & Sword, 2002), p. 116.

85. Langdon, *Sharp End*, p. 42.
86. Bill Bellamy, *Troop Leader (8KRIH)* (Sutton Publishing, 2005), p. 62.
87. Boardman, *Tracks*, pp. 225–6.
88. Boardman, *Tracks*, pp. 198–9.
89. Fisher, *Sharpshooter Snapshots*, p. 49.
90. Langdon, *Sharp End*, p. 49.
91. Boardman, *Tracks*, pp. 134–5. Sergeant Archie Carr went on to win a DCM in September.
92. Bellamy, *Troop Leader*, pp. 100–1. A three-colour camouflage version was also made, but was extremely rare.
93. Boardman, *Tracks*, pp. 163–5.
94. Boardman, *Tracks*, pp. 159–60.
95. Boardman, *Tracks*, pp. 238–9.
96. This occurred on 9 August 1944. Boardman, *Tracks*, p. 136.
97. Boardman, *Tracks*, pp. 203–4.
98. Boardman, *Tracks*, pp. 137–8.
99. Langdon, *Sharp End*, pp. 29–30.
100. Langdon, *Sharp End*, p. 48. Due to the lack of tanks the regiment was reorganized into two squadrons, A and B, with C Squadron's personnel and vehicles divided up between them. None of Langdon's new crew had been in action before. In extreme cases two regiments would be temporarily merged together.
101. Beale, *Tank Tracks*, p. 47.
102. Boardman, *Tracks*, pp. 141–4.
103. Leonard Willis, *None Had Lances (24L)* (24L OCA, 1986), pp. 51–2.
104. Stuart Hills, *By Tank Into Normandy (SRY)* (Cassell, 2002), p. 90.
105. Place, *Military Training*, p. 81.
106. Place, *Military Training*, p. 92.
107. Sir Basil Liddell Hart, 'Strategy of the Indirect Approach', *The Royal United Service Institution Journal*, June 1970, p. 38.
108. The problems were well known, and a lot of effort was expended in developing the all-round vision cupola, which was retro-fitted to tanks during the campaign, and which improved things greatly.
109. Bellamy, *Troop Leader*, p. 63.
110. Boardman, *Tracks*, p. 151.
111. Sydney Jary, *18 Platoon* (Jary Publishers, 1994), pp. 20–1.
112. French, *Raising Churchill's Army*, p. 265.
113. Hills, *By Tank Into Normandy*, p. 119.
114. French, *Raising Churchill's Army*, p. 269.
115. Training conducted in the UK in the lead-up to D-Day did not always prove to be suitable for what followed, and there are indications that the D-Day assault troops, particularly the DD tank units, had to spend far

too much time training in the technically complex task of swimming their tanks, as opposed to how to fight in them once ashore. See, for example, David Render, *Tank Action (SRY)* (Orion, 2016), p. 75.

116. Boardman, *Tracks*, pp. 148–9.

Chapter 8

1. Although night moves were frequent, night combat was unusual, in all theatres, throughout the war. Whilst the advantages that darkness could confer were recognized, these were more than countered by the disadvantages, particularly when the Germans developed short-range anti-tank weapons. It was not until May 1943 that orders were given, via an Army Training Memorandum, for units to practise night operations during training, beyond just the usual policy of sending out foot patrols to dominate ground and gain intelligence. Although night-vision devices were in the future, it was becoming obvious that fighting was frequently taking place at night, and whilst often confusing and hard to control, the side that was best prepared held the advantage. Such actions presented great difficulties for the tank crews, as the noise and size of the vehicle made surprise difficult to achieve, and shooting accurately was impossible.

2. Horrocks, *A Full Life*, pp. 197–8.

3. Langdon, *Sharp End*, p. 79.

4. Boardman, *Tracks*, p. 167.

5. Brussels was taken on the 3rd, Antwerp on the 5th.

6. Langdon, *Sharp End*, p. 77. The commander of the garrison, General von Stolberg-Stolberg, was captured along with many others; the problem of holding them was solved by the simple expedient of utilizing the cages in the zoo, which was empty of animals.

7. Horrocks, *Corps Commander*, p. 81.

8. Horrocks, *Corps Commander*, pp. 92–3. In his orders, Horrocks noted that despite the intention for the other two corps to advance either side, initially at least, the lack of resources caused by the extended advance – now 300 miles from the Mulberry harbours – meant that XXX Corps would be out on their own, 'possibly for quite a long period'.

9. Horrocks, *Corps Commander*, pp. 102–3.

10. The route remained under near constant German artillery fire throughout the operation, and just like the tank crews in the van, the echelon drivers had no option but to follow the narrow route and hope for the best.

11. John Howell, 'My War Story (1NY)' (unpublished, 2020).

12. Boardman, *Tracks*, p. 217.

13. Boardman, *Tracks*, p. 217.

14. Brereton, *History of the 4th/7th Dragoon Guards*, p. 403.
15. Boardman, *Tracks*, p. 228. This may have been a *PanzerSchreck*, but the American slang term bazooka came into use to describe hand-held anti-tank weapons. The British PIAT, pronounced Pee-At, was not included, probably because the name was already short enough.
16. Boardman, *Tracks*, p. 230.
17. Boardman, *Tracks*, p. 224.
18. During February 1945 and for the final time, the designation of the Tank Brigades was changed, so that now all armoured brigades, regardless of role or equipment type, were known as Armoured Brigades.
19. 6th AARR was formed on 1 April 1944 from the Airborne Armoured Reconnaissance Regiment RAC, itself formed on 14 January 1944.
20. The final use of DD tanks in NWE came when the Staffs Yeo swam an enlarged squadron across the Elbe on 29 April.
21. Howell, 'My War Story'.
22. Ten Bailey bridges were built across the Rhine in the area of Plunder, including six Class 40 bridges capable of taking tanks. The longest of these, Blackfriars, was completed mid-morning on the 26th and was nearly 600yd long.
23. Post-war estimates reckoned that around 20 per cent of tank casualties were caused by mines. In NWE, as the campaign progressed deeper into Germany, the estimate of casualties caused by hollow charge weapons rose from 10 per cent in Normandy to nearly one-third in Germany.
24. Boardman, *Tracks*, pp. 235–6.
25. Patrick Delaforce, *Churchill's Desert Rats*, 2 vols (Chancellor 1994, new edn Sutton Publishing, 2002), p. 183.
26. Patrick Delaforce, *The Black Bull (11th Armoured Division)* (Sutton Publishing, 2002), p. 254.
27. Delaforce, *The Black Bull*, p. 255.
28. William Slim, *Defeat into Victory* (Pan, 2009), p. 76.
29. Brian Williams, *The Forgotten Squadron (B Sqn 3KOH)* (Greyhound, 2017).
30. Bryan Perrett, *Tank Tracks to Rangoon – British Armour in Burma* (Hale, 1992), p. 35.
31. Perret, *Tank Tracks*, p. 36.
32. Perrett, *Tank Tracks*, pp. 39–40.
33. Davy, *The Seventh and Three Enemies*, p. 299.
34. Grants were also used in the theatre.
35. Macksey, *History of the Royal Armoured Corps*, pp. 185–7.
36. Slim, *Defeat into Victory*, p. 350.
37. Slim, *Defeat into Victory*, p. 567.
38. Macksey, *History of the Royal Armoured Corps*, p. 188.

Chapter 9

1. It was noted that many burns could be prevented by wearing any form of clothing, so that soldiers in the desert often suffered burns on their exposed arms and legs. Many phosphorous burns were reported to be caused when the 2in smoke bombs in the turret were ignited by a penetration.
2. R.M. Mayon-White, 'Tank Crew Casualties', PhD thesis, December 1948.
3. This simple innovation was not achieved during the war. A careful study conducted during the war by Major J.M. Whittaker RTR concluded that the optimum slope for a frontal plate was 57°. The advantages were known, but not applied until the Centurion was designed.
4. Most nations realized the advantages in production, training and ammunition standardization of using the same basic gun type for all applications. In Britain, this was the case with the 2-pounder, 6-pounder and 17-pounder guns.
5. This was to be recognized post-war when the two roles of a tank were described in the *Armour* doctrine pamphlet as: 1 The destruction of enemy armour, and 2 The close-support of our own infantry, ending decades of debate as to what the tank was there to do.
6. Another error was that the two Close Support tanks in each squadron were used mainly to fire smoke ammunition, whereas using them in the HE direct-fire role would have allowed the neutralizing or destruction of many German anti-tank guns.
7. Martel remained convinced of the need for the distinction, even after the experiences of the war, and post-war continued to write articles calling for the two types to be used.
8. He was partly successful, which is why the Infantry tank units were slow in being deployed into Normandy, and why there were always fewer of them compared with the number of armoured brigades.
9. Doctrine must never be purely theoretical but must match the technical capabilities of the force, so the army must either match its doctrine to the resources available, or develop the resources – here meaning vehicles, training systems and support systems – that can apply the doctrine.
10. In part as a result of the experience in using the new American Sherman Medium tank, in late 1942 the RAC six-monthly progress report noted that, 'The General Staff have definitely stated that their main requirement is for a standard "all-purpose" medium tank … utilised as the equipment of the armoured divisions and armoured brigades … thus the conception of the heavy, slow, powerful infantry or assault tank had definitely receded'. Unfortunately, that did not lead to the adoption of, or even much energy expended in the search for, such a tank. Even the Centurion, the tank that came to fill the role, started life as a heavy Cruiser.

11. Trying to use such plans in circumstances other than set-piece attacks generally led to failure, and took up too much time in any case. However, as tactical training at the various schools emphasized this approach, it was very difficult to change whilst in action.

12. This will be covered in more detail in Volume 3, but it is interesting to note how the development of this approach was almost entirely reliant on the German model.

13. This is not to say that a lessons identified process did not exist. It did, and if anything produced far too much material, much of it confusing or contradictory. How was an inexperienced junior commander expected to be able to sift through the mountains of reports and advice in order to work out which lessons identified in e.g. Tunisia or Italy might be pertinent to the upcoming invasion of Normandy?

Appendix A

1. Later, by 1944, carriers were also used to tow the 6-pounder guns of each battalion's anti-tank platoon.

2. Place, *Military Training*, p. 155.

3. Place, *Military Training*, p. 101.

4. The first use of the Ram version was Operation Astonia, the assault on Le Havre in September 1944. Some reports from Italy, where the Kangaroo system was also adopted, indicated that the RAC units using the vehicles thought that the versions based on the Priest were superior to the Ram, possibly because of the additional side and front armour plating.

5. In Italy both 4th Hussars and 14/20th Hussars were converted to become Kangaroo regiments, a fact conveniently overlooked post-war when the cavalry units successfully argued that they should only operate Cruiser tanks or armoured cars, and that the RTR should be solely responsible for all specialized armour.

6. The Deacon was not a portee, as the gun had a wrap-around armoured shield and could not be easily dismounted.

7. Armoured Recovery Vehicles (ARV) were also created, and operated by both regimental tradesmen and REME crews.

Appendix B

1. The units shown, in order of RAC seniority, are those which officially served within the formation for a reasonable length of time at any point during its existence, and do not represent the chronology of the formation.

2. This excludes the armoured recce brigades, the temporary and short-lived formations set up in 1940 and 1941 for home defence, or the two Guards armoured/tank brigades.

3. In many cases armoured brigades led a more independent life; at various times, the following brigades were all used independently: 1st, 2nd, 4th, 7th, 8th, 9th, 20th, 21st, 22nd, 23rd, 24th, 27th, 29th, 30th, 34th, 35th, 137th.
4. The units shown, in order of RAC seniority, are those which officially served within the formation for a reasonable length of time at any point during its existence, and do not represent the chronology of the formation.

Appendix C

1. The 'Open Range Practices' pamphlet of 1942 specified that all non-tank targets, including anti-tank guns, were to be engaged with MG fire, completely missing the mismatch between the effective ranges of the two weapons.
2. Making APDS truly consistent was not achieved until after the war, with the 20-pounder and 105mm tank guns on Centurion.
3. The infantry at this stage and until about 1941/42 relied on the .55in Boys rifle for their A/T defence.
4. APCNR, or Armour Piercing Cap Non-Rigid, sometimes called Armour Piercing Super Velocity (APSV).
5. If there was criticism of the APDS ammunition it was three-fold: it was less accurate/consistent than APCBC; it was impossible to observe the fall of shot due to muzzle flash and blast; and when it did penetrate, being a smaller calibre, it did less damage than APCBC.
6. In British use the 'battle range' represented the average (most common) range that an engagement was expected to take place at, and therefore coincidence between the axis of the bore and the sight axis at this range would maximize the chance of a first-round hit.
7. Davy, *The Seventh and Three Enemies*, p. 132.
8. A flatter trajectory was due mainly to air resistance combined with the effects of gravity, although other much less important factors also came into play, including skin friction, the curvature and rotation of the earth, etc.
9. When crews witnessed this, what they mostly were seeing was the tracer element in the base of the AP shot flying through the air, as the AP round itself did some damage to the surface of the armour but not enough to penetrate.
10. Davy, *The Seventh and Three Enemies*, p. 133.
11. PH does NOT consider the chance of a penetration or indeed a kill; these can also be expressed mathematically and will always be less than the PH.
12. Ken Tout, *Tank!* (Hale, 1994), pp. 26–8.

Appendix D

1. Earlier systems used loudspeakers in place of headsets for some crew members, and also used buzzers to alert the commander.
2. Some ex-Indian army officers resorted to speaking Hindustani to each other.
3. French, *Raising Churchill's Army*, p. 254.
4. For example, 3RTR used an 'all-stations' regimental radio net, in which all tanks and fighting vehicles operated on a single common frequency. This required excellent discipline but allowed the whole unit to understand, and contribute to, the battle picture.

Bibliography and Sources

General

Anglesey, Lord, *A History of the British Cavalry Volume 8*, Leo Cooper, 2012

Anon., *His Majesty's Regiments of the British Army*, Metro-Provincial, 1949

Baker, Anthony, *The Genealogy of the Regiments of the British Army: The Yeomanry*, BMH, 1999

Baker, Anthony, *Battle Honours of the British & Commonwealth Armies*, Ian Allan, 1986

Barker, Dennis, *Soldiering On*, Deutsch, 1981

Barr, Niall, *Pendulum of War: The Three Battles of Alamein*, Overlook, 2005

Blaxland, Gregory, *Destination Dunkirk*, Pen & Sword, 2018

Blumenson, Martin, *Sicily: Whose Victory?*, IWM, 1968

Brett-Smith, Richard, *Berlin 1945*, Macmillan proof copy, 1966

Brooke, Alan, *War Diaries*, Phoenix, 2001

Buckley, John, *Monty's Men*, Yale University Press, 2013

Buckley, John, *British Armour in the Normandy Campaign*, Frank Cass, 2004

Carr, John, *The Defence and Fall of Greece*, Pen & Sword, 2013

Carver, Michael, *Out of Step*, Hutchinson, 1989

Carver, Michael, *Dilemmas of the Desert War*, Batsford, 1986

Clayton, Anthony, *The British Officer*, Routledge, 2013

Collier, Basil, *The Defence of the United Kingdom*, IWM, 1957

Crow, Duncan (ed.), *Armoured Fighting Vehicles 1919/40*, Profile, 1970

Daglish, Ian, *Operation Bluecoat*, Leo Cooper, 2003

Dawson, Malcolm, *Uniforms of the RAC*, Almark, 1974

Delaforce, Patrick, *Battles with Panzers (1 & 2RTR)*, Sutton Publishing, 2003

Delaforce, Patrick, *The Black Bull (11th Armoured Division)*, Sutton Publishing, 2002

Delaforce, Patrick, *Churchill's Desert Rats*, 2 vols, Chancellor 1994, new edn Sutton Publishing, 2002

Delaforce, Patrick, *Taming the Panzers (3RTR)*, Sutton Publishing, 2000

Doherty, Richard, *British Armoured Divisions and their Commanders 1939–1945*, Pen & Sword, 2013

Ellis, Chris and Peter Chamberlain (eds), *Handbook on the British Army 1943*, Arms & Armour Press, 1976

Fletcher, David, *The Rolls-Royce Armoured Car*, New Vanguard, 2012

Fletcher, David, *Mr Churchill's Tank*, Schiffer, 1999

Fletcher, David, *British Military Transport 1929–1956*, The Stationery Office, 1998

Forty, George, *Bovington Tanks*, Wincanton Press, 1988

Forty, George, *Armoured Cars in Two World Wars*, Blandford Press, 1984

Fraser, David, *And We Shall Shock Them*, Cassell, 1983

French, David, *Raising Churchill's Army*, OUP, 2000

Gibbs, N.H., *History of the Second World War, Vol. 1, Grand Strategy*, HMSO, 1976

Gorman, J.T., *The British Army*, Collins, 1940

Grehan, John and Martin Mace, *Operations in North Africa and the Middle East 1939–1942*, Pen & Sword, 2015

Grehan, John and Martin Mace, *Operations in North Africa and the Middle East 1942–1944*, Pen & Sword, 2015

Grehan, John and Martin Mace, *The BEF 1939–1940*, Pen & Sword, 2014

Griffith, Paddy, *WW2 Desert Tactics*, Osprey, 2008

Guderian, Heinz, *Achtung, Panzer!*, Cassell, 1999

Hallows, Ian, *Regiments & Corps of the British Army*, Arms & Armour, 1991

Halstead, Ivor, *The Truth about our Tanks*, Lindsay Drummond, 1942

Hayward, Mark, *Sherman Firefly*, Barbarossa Books, 2001

Holmes, Richard, *Soldiers*, Harper, 2011

Horrocks, Brian, *Corps Commander*, Sidgwick & Jackson, 1977

Jackson, Robert, *Dunkirk*, Cassell, 2002

Jary, Sydney, *18 Platoon*, Jary Publishers, 1994

Kipling, Arthur and Hugh King, *Head-Dress Badges of the British Army, Vol. 2*, MBW, 1979

Kite, Ben, *Stout Hearts: The British & Canadians in Normandy 1944*, Helion, 2014

Levin, Eliot (ed.), *The Rolls-Royce Armoured Car*, Rolls-Royce Enthusiasts Club, 2016

Lester, J.R., *Tank Warfare*, George Allen, 1943

Liddell Hart, B.H., *The Rommel Papers*, Da Capo Press, 1953

Mayon-White, R.M., 'Tank Crew Casualties', PhD thesis, December 1948

Murphy, Gerry, *Where did that Regiment Go?*, Spellmount, 2016

Napier, Stephen, *The Armoured Campaign in Normandy*, Spellmount, 2015

Neillands, Robin, *Eighth Army*, John Murray, 2004

Pallud, Jean Paul, *The Desert War Then and Now*, After The Battle, 2012

Perrett, Bryan, *Tank Tracks to Rangoon – British Armour in Burma*, Hale, 1992

Place, Timothy Harrison, *Military Training in the British Army 1940–1944*, Frank Cass, 2000

Pugh, Roger, *The Most Secret Place on Earth*, Larks Press, 2014

Russell, John, *Theirs the Strife*, Helion, 2020

Slim, William, *Defeat into Victory*, Pan, 2009

Smith, John A., *British Armoured Formations 1939–1945, A Bibliography, Supplement 1*, Tank Factory, 2017

Smith, John A., *British Armoured Formations 1939–1945, A Bibliography*, Tank Factory, 2014

Smith, Norman, *Tank Soldier*, The Book Guild, 1989

Taylor, Dick, *The Second World War Tank Crisis*, Pen & Sword, 2021

Taylor, Dick, *Firing Now!*, MMP, 2016

Taylor, Dick, *The Men Inside the Metal, Vols 1 and 2*, MMP, 2014

Thompson, Fred, 'India: The RAC Depot Poona September 1943', *Tank Magazine*, Vol. 86, No. 767.

Thompson, Graham N. and Teddy Nevill, *The Territorial Army*, Ian Allan, 1989

Todman, Daniel, *Britain's War: Into Battle 1937–1941*, Penguin, 2016

Tout, Ken, *Tank!*, Hale, 1994

Ventham, Philip and David Fletcher, *Moving the Guns*, HMSO, 1990

Verney, G.L., *The Desert Rats*, Hutchinson, 1954

White, Arthur, *A Bibliography of Regimental Histories of the British Army*, NMP, 1992

Corps and Regimental Histories

Anon., *The 10th Royal Hussars in the Second World War*, Gale & Polden, 1948

Anon., *A Short History of The Royal Tank Corps*, 5th edn, Gale & Polden, 1938

Anon., *A Short History of 7th Armoured Division June 43–July 45*, n.p., 1945

Anon., *The 1st & 2nd Northamptonshire Yeomanry*, repr., Naval & Military Press, 1946

Anon., *Short History of the Royal Dragoons*, Gale & Polden, n.d.

Anon., *Historical Record of the 9th Queen's Royal Lancers 1945–1960*, 9L, 1993

Anon., *The Queen's Own Hussars*, Roundwood, 1985

Anon., *Regimental History 3rd Carabiniers*, n.p., 1957

Anon., *The Story of 79th Armoured Division*, repr., Naval & Military Press, n.d.

Anon., *The Story of the 23rd Hussars*, repr., Naval & Military Press, n.d.

Anon., *The Story of 34th Armoured Brigade*, repr., Naval & Military Press, n.d.

Anon., *49th Unparalleled (49 RTR)*, Parchment, n.d.

Anon., *1st The Queen's Dragoon Guards*, Gale & Polden, n.d.

Anon., *A Short History of the 9th Queen's Royal Lancers 1715–1949*, Gale & Polden, 1949

Anon., *A Short History of the 12th Royal Lancers*, Gale & Polden, *c.* 1952

Anon., *Short History of the 4th, 7th and 4th/7th Royal Dragoon Guards*, Gale & Polden, 1943

Anon., *Year of the Yeomanry*, Ogilby Trust, 1994

Anon., *A Short History of the Household Cavalry*, Household Cavalry Museum, *c.* 1986

Addyman, Ronald, *The 45th Royal Tank Regiment in the Second World War*, n.p., 2011

Bastin, Jeremy, *The History of the 15th/19th The King's Royal Hussars 1945–1980*, Keats House, 1981

Blacker, Cecil and Henry Woods, *5th Royal Inniskilling Dragoon Guards: Change & Challenge*, William Clowes, 1978

Blacklock, Michael, *The Royal Scots Greys*, Leo Cooper, 1971

Boardman, C.J., *Tracks in Europe (5 DG)*, City Press, 1990

Bolitho, Hector, *The Galloping Third (3rd Hussars)*, Murray, 1963

Brace, Basher, *1st The Queen's Dragoon Guards: A Pictorial History 1959–2009*, QDG, 2009

Braddon, Russell, *All the Queen's Men (Household Cavalry)*, Hamish Hamilton, 1977

Brereton, J.M., *History of the 4th/7th Royal Dragoon Guards*, 4/7DG, 1982

Brereton, J.M., *The 7th Queen's Own Hussars*, Leo Cooper, 1975

Brett-Smith, Richard, *The 11th Hussars*, Leo Cooper, 1969

Bright, Joan, *The 9th Queens Royal Lancers 1936–1945*, Naval & Military Press, n.d.

Brockbank, Robin, *A Short History of the 9th/12th Lancers 1960–1985*, 9/12L, n.d.

Brockbank, R. and R.M. Collins, *A Short History of the XII Royal Lancers 1945–1960*, 9/12 Royal Lancers, n.d.

Chadwick, Kenneth, *The Royal Tank Regiment*, Leo Cooper, 1970

Davy, G.M.O., *The Seventh and Three Enemies (7th Hussars)*, Naval & Military Press, 2014

Doherty, Richard, *Only the Enemy in Front (Reconnaissance Corps)*, BCA, 1994

Flint, Keith, *Airborne Armour*, Helion, 2010

Forbes, Patrick, *6th Guards Tank Brigade*, Naval & Military Press, n.d.

ffrench Blake, R.L.V., *A History of the 17th/21st Lancers*, Macmillan, 1968

ffrench Blake, R.L.V., *The 17th/21st Lancers*, Hamish Hamilton, 1968

Gill, Ronald and John Groves, *Club Route in Europe (XXX Corps)*, repr., NMP, 1945

Graves, Charles, *The Black Beret (RAC)*, Hutchinson, 1943

Hills, R.J.T, *The Royal Dragoons*, Leo Cooper, 1972

Hills, R.J.T, *The Life Guards*, Leo Cooper, 1971

Hills, R.J.T, *The Royal Horse Guards*, Leo Cooper, 1970

Hunt, Eric, *History of the 13th/18th Royal Hussars*, Light Dragoons CT, 1996

Hunt, Jonathan, *Hard Fighting (SRY)*, Pen & Sword, 2016

Jackson, G.S., *Operations of Eighth Corps*, St Clement's Press, 1948

Kemp, P.K., *The Staffordshire Yeomanry*, Gale & Polden, 1950

Keown-Boyd, Henry, *Remember with Advantages (10H, 11H, RH)*, Pen & Sword, 1994

Liddell Hart, B.H., *The Tanks Volume 1 (MGC, TC, RTC, RTR)*, Cassell, 1959

Liddell Hart, B.H., *The Tanks Volume 2 (RTR)*, Cassell, 1959

Loyd, William, *Challengers and Chargers (LG)*, Leo Cooper, 1992

Lunt, James, *The Scarlet Lancers (16/5L)*, Leo Cooper, 1993

Lunt, James, *16th/5th Queen's Royal Lancers*, Leo Cooper, 1973

Lunt, James, 'Shotgun Wedding (amalgamation of 16/5L)', *The Scarlet & Green Journal*, 1958

Mace, Paul, *Forrard (ERY)*, Leo Cooper, 2001

Macksey, Kenneth, *A History of the Royal Armoured Corps 1914–1975*, Newtown, 1983

Macksey, Kenneth, *The Tanks Volume 3 (RTR)*, Arms & Armour Press, 1979

Mallinson, Allan, *Light Dragoons*, Pen & Sword, 2012

Mann, Michael, *The Regimental History of the 1st The Queen's Dragoon Guards*, QDG, 1993

Manser, Roy, *The Household Cavalry Regiment*, Almark, 1975

Martin, Lieutenant Colonel, '42RTR History 1938–1944', privately published, n.d.

Mileham, Patrick, *The Yeomanry Regiments*, Spellmount, 2003

Mollo, Boris, *The Sharpshooters*, KCLY, 1970

Moore, William, *Panzer Bait (3RTR)*, Leo Cooper, 1991

Murland, J.R.W., *The Royal Armoured Corps*, Methuen, 1943

Murray, Major J.S.F., *A Short History of the 15th/19th The Kings Royal Hussars*, The Forces Press, 1954

Owen, Frank and H.W. Atkins, *The Royal Armoured Corps*, HMSO, 1945

Parkyn, H.G., *A Short History of the 16th/5th Lancers*, Gale & Polden, 1934

Pitt, P.W., *Royal Wilts 1920–1945 (RWY)*, NMP, n.d.

Pitt-Rivers, J.A., *The Story of the Royal Dragoons 1938–1945*, Royal Dragoons/William Clowes, n.d.

Rhoderick-Jones, Robin, *In Peace & War (QRH)*, Pen & Sword, 2018

Rosse, Captain and Colonel Hill, *The Story of the Guards Armoured Division*, Pen & Sword, 2017

Seaman, Peter, *For Hostilities Only (The War-raised Cavalry)*, York Publishing, 2009

Stewart, P.F., *History of the XII Lancers*, OUP, 1950

Strawson, J.M. et al., *Irish Hussar (QRIH)*, QRIHA, 1986

Thompson, Ralph, *The 15th/19th The King's Royal Hussars: A Pictorial History*, Quoin, 1989

Watson, J.N.P., *Through Fifteen Reigns (Household Cavalry)*, Spellmount, 1997

William-Ellis, Clough and A. William-Ellis, *The Tank Corps*, NMP, n.d.

Willis, Leonard, *None Had Lances (24L)*, 24L OCA , 1986

Wood, Stephen, *In the Finest Tradition (Scots DG)*, Mainstream, 1988

Personal Diaries, Photo Histories and Biographies

Anon., *1st Derbyshire Yeomanry Scrapbook 1939–1947*, Bemrose, 1947

Anon., *D-Day Remembered (WD)*, WDA, n.d.

Anon., *First In Last Out (5DG)*, W.H. Evans, 1986

Beale, Peter, *Tank Tracks (9RTR)*, Budding, 1995

Bellamy, Bill, *Troop Leader (8KRIH)*, Sutton Publishing, 2005

Close, Bill, *Tank Commander (3 RTR)*, Pen & Sword, 2002

Crichton, Peter, *To War with a 4th Hussar*, Pen & Sword, 2019

Crisp, Bob, *The Gods were Neutral (3 RTR)*, Ballantyne, 1960

Crisp, Bob, *Brazen Chariots (3 RTR)*, Norton, 1959

Crocker, Vincent, *There's a Soldier at the Gate (10H)*, Trafford, 2005

Fisher, John, *Sharpshooter Snapshots (4CLY)*, privately published, 1996

Foley, John, *Mailed Fist (RTR)*, Panther, 1966

Gudgin, Peter, *With Churchills to War (48RTR)*, Sutton Publishing, 1996

Hills, Stuart, *By Tank Into Normandy (SRY)*, Cassell, 2002

Horrocks, Brian, *A Full Life*, Collins, 1960

Howell, John, 'My War Story (1NY)', privately published, 2020

Langdon, John, *The Sharp End (3RTR)*, privately published, 2003

Lewin, Ronald, *Man of Armour (Lt Gen Vyvyan Pope)*, Leo Cooper, 1976

Mabyn Ross, Peter, *All Valiant Dust (3 RTR)*, Lilliput, 1992

Mabyn Ross, Peter, *To the Stars (RAC OCTU)*, RAC, 1946

Macksey, Kenneth, *Armoured Crusader (Maj Gen Sir Percy Hobart)*, Grub Street, 2004

Merewood, Jack, *To War with the Bays*, QDG, 1996

More, Charles, *From Arromanches to the Elbe (144 RAC)*, Frontline, 2019

Pile, Frederick, *Better than Riches (6, 1 RTR)*, Pentland, 1992

Render, David, *Tank Action (SRY)*, Orion, 2016

Robinson, M.P. and R. Griffin, *The RAC in the Cold War 1946–1990*, Pen & Sword, 2016

Strickland, Tim, *Strick: Tank Hero of Arras*, Casemate, 2021

Sumner, Ian and Roy Wilson, *Yeomanry of the East Riding (ERY)*, Hutton, 1993

Tout, Ken, *By Tank: D to VE Days (1NY)*, Robert Hale, 2007

Williams, Brian, *The Forgotten Squadron (B Sqn 3KOH)*, Greyhound, 2017

Wilson, Edward, *Press On Regardless (5RTR)*, Spellmount, 2003

Journals

The 4th/7th Royal Dragoon Guards Regimental Magazine

The 5th Royal Inniskilling Dragoon Guards Journal

The X Royal Hussars Gazette

The XI Hussar Journal

The Acorn (LG)
Armour (RAC)
The Army Quarterly
The Blue and Royal
British Army Journal
British Army Review
The Cavalry Journal
The Chapka (RL)
Combat (RAC, Infantry)
Conqueror (JLR RAC)
The Crossbelts (KRIH)
The Crossbelts (QRH)
The Crossbelts (QRIH)
The Delhi Spearman (9L, 9/12L)
The DRAC Newsletter
The Eagle (Royals)
The Eagle and Carbine (Scots DG)
The Feather and Carbine (3rd Carbs)
The Hawk (14/20H)
The Household Cavalry Journal
The Journal of the 4th Queen's Own Hussars
The Journal of the 13th/18th Royal Hussars
The Journal of the Queen's Own Hussars
The Journal of the Royal Dragoons
The Light Dragoon
The RAC Centre Bulletin
The RAC Journal
The Reconnaissance Journal
The Red Lanyard (1RTR)
The Regiment Magazine
The Regimental Journal of the 3rd The King's Own Hussars
The Regimental Journal of the King's Dragoon Guards
The Regimental Journal of the Queen's Bays
The Rhino (1st Armoured Division)
The Royal Hussar Journal
The Royal United Service Institution Journal
The Scarlet & Green Journal(16/5L)
The Scots Grey Journal
Sharpshooters Gazette (3/4 CLY)
Soldier Magazine
The Tank/Tank Journal/Tank Magazine (TC/RTC/RTR)
The Twelfth Royal Lancers Journal

Vanguard (Inns of Court Yeo)
The Vedette (QRL)
The White Lancer & The Vedette (17/21L)
The Wolf (SNIY)

Official Publications

HMSO, *Field Service Pocket Book, Pam 1*, War Office, 1939

HMSO , *Field Service Regulations, Vol. II Operations – General*, War Office, 1935

HMSO, *Dress Regulations for the Army*, War Office, 1934

HMSO, *Field Service Regulations, Vol. II Operations*, War Office, 1924

Mackintosh, Colonel H.W.B., *The Tank Factory: Seventy Years of Government Tank Design*, MVEE, 1984

Official, *Ballistics & Technical Aspects of Tank Gunnery*, RAC Gunnery School, 1996

Official, *RAC Trg Pam 40, General Principles of Shooting from AFVs*, MOD, 1981

Official, *Royal Armoured Corps*, MOD, 1970

Official, *Selection of POs, their Preliminary Training & Commissioning*, War Office, 1941

Official, *MTP No. 41, The Armoured Regiment*, War Office, 1940

Official, *MTP 4 Notes on Mechanized Cavalry Units*, War Office, 1938

Official, *Tank Training, Vol. II, Part I, Pam No. 1 Tank Gunnery*, HMSO, 1938

Official, *Standing Orders of the 5th Battalion Royal Tank Corps*, Gale & Polden, 1928

Regimental Museums

9th/12th Royal Lancers, Derby Museum & Art Gallery, The Strand, Derby, DE11BS

Household Cavalry, The Household Cavalry Museum, Horse Guards, Whitehall, London SW1A2AX, museum@householdcavalry.co.uk

King's Royal Hussars, Horsepower, Peninsula Barracks, Romsey Road, Winchester, SO238TS, assistant@horsepowermuneum.co.uk

Light Dragoons, Discovery Museum, Blandford Square, Newcastle upon Tyne, NE14JA

Queen's Dragoon Guards, Firing Line, Cardiff Castle, CF102RB

Queen's Royal Hussars, 1 Trinity Mews, Priory Road, Warwick, CV344NA, info@qrhmuseum.uk

Royal Dragoon Guards, 3A Tower Street, York, YO19SB, hhq@rdgmuseum.org.uk

Royal Lancers & Notts Yeomanry, RLNY Museum, Thorseby Park, Notts, NG229EP

Royal Scots Dragoon Guards, New Barracks, Edinburgh Castle, EH12YT, info@scotsdgmuseum.com

Royal Tank Regiment/RAC, The Bovington Tank Museum, Dorset, BH206JG, info@tankmuseum.org

Index

Tanks